Creating Alternative Realities at Work

Ballinger Series
on
INNOVATION AND ORGANIZATIONAL CHANGE

Michael Tushman and Andrew Van de Ven
Series Editors

Creating Alternative Realities at Work:

The Quality of Work Life Experiment at FoodCom

Michael K. Moch
Jean M. Bartunek

HARPER BUSINESS
A Division of Harper & Row, Publishers, New York

Grand Rapids, Philadelphia, St. Louis, San Francisco
London, Singapore, Sydney, Tokyo, Toronto

International Standard Book Number: 0–88730–225–4

Library of Congress Catalog Card Number: 90-31176

Printed in the United States of America

Library of Congress Cataloging-in-Publication Data

Moch, Michael K., 1944–
Creating alternative realities at work : the quality of work life experiment at FoodCom / Michael K. Moch, Jean M. Bartunek.
p. cm. – (Ballinger series on innovation and organizational change)
Includes bibliographical references.
ISBN 0–88730–225–4
1. Organizational change. I. Bartunek, Jean. II. Title.
III. Series
HD58.8.M58 1990 90-31176
658.4′063–dc20 CIP

90 91 92 93 HC 9 8 7 6 5 4 3 2 1

To the memory of Louis R. Pondy
1938–1987

Contents

List of Figures

List of Exhibits

Preface

We started this project in 1976 while both of us were associated with the Organizational Behavior Group at the University of Illinois at Urbana-Champaign. Michael Moch was a newly hired assistant professor. Soon after he arrived, he negotiated a contract with the Institute for Social Research at the University of Michigan to evaluate a quality of working life program that was to take place at the company we call FoodCom. Jean Bartunek was a newly hired visiting assistant professor. Her primary interest was in organization development. Moch invited Bartunek to join him in evaluating FoodCom's QWL intervention. Off and on, individually and jointly, in Urbana, Boston, Dallas, and East Lansing, we have been working since then conducting the evaluation and trying to understand the underlying dynamics of the intervention.

While we were at Illinois, we were both privileged to be able to work with Lou Pondy. Lou had a huge impact on both our professional and our personal lives. He introduced us to new ways of conducting research and taught us about appreciating underlying phenomena and about the excitement that can come from approaching a topic from various and even contradictory perspectives. Lou also helped us to avoid taking our world as a given and helped us to begin to appreciate our own responsibility for creating, maintaining, and changing appearances we had previously taken for granted. We have been trying to carry out this responsibility by learning how reality is socially constructed, maintained, and changed.

This book represents a large step in our learning process. We have attempted to bring a variety of perspectives to bear on the intervention in order to provide readers with a rich description and a deep theoretical understanding. We employ a social cognitive approach to describe a large-scale organizational change project in what we believe to be a distinctive fashion. By so doing, we hope to stimulate new ways of thinking about planned organizational change and about ways intervenors might act to develop the capacities and, eventually, the cognitive liberation of participants in planned social change interventions. We do not complete the task in this book. However, we hope we have begun it in a way that will enable us and others to make more rapid progress in the future.

We have had a great deal of help from several different people in addition to Lou Pondy. Corty Cammann, Ed Lawler, and Stan Seashore, then at the Institute for Social Research at the University of Michigan, gave us the initial opportunity to participate in the evaluation. Meryl Louis and Marshall Sashkin offered us intelligent advice and support at various stages of the project. Paul Rubin generously provided invaluable technical assistance and advice.

John Feather, then a graduate student at the University of Michigan, and Illinois graduate students Lee Bomblatus and Dale Fitzgibbons played crucial data-gathering roles. Cal Fields, Debra Legee, and Kareen Tidball, former graduate students at the University of Texas at Dallas, provided intellectual and personal support when it seemed that adequate theoretical understanding was beyond our grasp. Graduate students Parshotam Dass, Beth Ellis, Rich Gooding, and Dolly Malik at Michigan State encouraged us to believe that by studying cognitive change in a dynamic setting we could contribute substantially to the current body of knowledge. Graduate students Robin Reid and Kristi Schulze at Boston College provided research assistance and helpful comments on many chapters of the book.

We also are grateful to the secretarial staff in the management department at Michigan State, especially to Sue Polhamus, Pam Hake, Connie Williams, and Kathy Waldie, for helping with copies, mailing, computer accounts, and a myriad of similar activities without which we could not have completed our task. At Boston College, John Burke, Dan Henderson, and Karen Kiladis converted our files back and forth between IBM WordPerfect and Microsoft Word, and Clare White-Sullivan and Sharon Winans consistently provided helpful and efficient word processing and copying assistance. We also thank Boston College for its financial support for some of Jean Bartunek's travel expenses.

We are deeply grateful to Leslie and Sarah Moch; they patiently waited for the completion of what seemed to be a never-ending task. Their active support was critical for the success of the project. We are grateful to members of the Religious of the Sacred Heart living in Boston for their support and encouragement during the years we have been working on this project and to the Religious of the Sacred Heart living in the city where our plant was located. In particular, we thank Mary Burns, Jan Dunn, Betsy Hartson, and Lucy Lamy, who were there the entire time we were visiting the plant. They created a home away from home for both of us.

We are indebted to Marjorie Richman, formerly with Ballinger Publishing Company. Marjorie initially solicited our manuscript and encouraged us to submit it in book form for the Ballinger series on innovation and organizational change. Her successor, Virginia Smith, continued to provide support and encouragement. We are particularly grateful for her patience.

Even with all the help we received from colleagues, students, and staff, we are most indebted to the employees at FoodCom—labor and management—who struggled so intently trying to grasp and employ a new way of understanding events. With the exception of Ted Mills, who publicly initiated the project, we have given these individuals pseudonyms. However, they are real people, and the events we describe actually occurred. We report activities that, had the volume been published earlier, might have affected the careers or personal relationships of those involved. We trust that after nearly a decade, the dust has settled and that no one will be adversely affected by the publication of this book. Our purpose is not to provide information for those who desire to praise or blame particular participants. We seek solely to contribute to the body of knowledge on organizational change so that those facing a similar situation in the future can build on FoodCom's experience.

We are also grateful to the individual we call Tim Deigh. Tim had oversight responsibility for the QWL project at FoodCom. However, he assumed this responsibility only after the project had started. He was confronted with the difficulties associated not only with project implementation and management but also with our asessment team. Throughout the experiment Tim managed this difficult relationship with considerable grace. He paid a price for our presence and often for our mistakes. We sincerely hope that, although he will doubtless disagree with some of our positions, both he and the QWL movement to which he is so dedicated will benefit from this publication.

Directory

List of Names and Positions of Participants in the QWL Intervention

Name	**Position**
ACQWL	American Center for the Quality of Work Life (initially called NQWC)
Ashley, Ben	Foreperson in packaging department
Atteberry, Josh	Alternate FWIU representative on second EJEC
Bailey, Barbara	FWIU representative on second EJEC; packaging department
Baker, Fred	Management representative on second EJEC; superintendent in baking department
Barrett, Joel	Management representative on second EJEC; superintendent in packaging department
Campbell, Tony	Head of training and development for FoodCom (Seldon's subordinate)
Charlton, Greg	Plant director of personnel at Reginal
Clayton, Bobby	FWIU representative on first EJEC; warehouse department
COD	Center for Organizational Design
Coy, William	FoodCom executive responsible for manufacturing at Gorland
Dalton, Mark	Environmental services department superintendent in Reginal
Daly, Nancy	FWIU representative on first EJEC; packaging department
Deigh, Tim	Associate director of the NQWC and "quality control" manager for the FoodCom intervention
DeLeo, Wally	Head of maintenance department
Drew, Eric	COD president and consulting team member
Drinan, Neal	Chief steward of IEU local
Drisko, Russ	Warehouse supervisor
Duffield, Leonard	Head of the Packing Department in Reginal
EJEC	Employee Joint Enrichment Committee managing the intervention at Reginal

Name	Position
Farr, Miles	FoodCom executive responsible for manufacturing at Reginal
Ferrer, Teresa	COD consulting team member
Franks, Joan	Alternate EJEC member for Jack Resler
FWIU	Food Workers' International Union (local number 50)
Gib, Tom	FoodCom corporate director of training and development
Gleason, Andy	IMU chief steward in Reginal
Griffith, Dennis	Head of packing in Reginal
Gromanger, Joe	First site coordinator in Reginal
Hendy, Emil	Edward Scigliano's replacement as FWIU executive vice-president and JQWLAC member
Hoban, Rich	IMU business agent in Reginal
Hughes, Bernard	FWIU representative on first EJEC; chief steward
Hurley, Brian	Management representative on first EJEC; mixer
IDU	International Distribution Union
IEU	International Electricians' Union
IMU	International Machinists' Union
ISR	Institute for Social Research
Jones, Irene	Supervisor in packaging department
Josephson, Chuck	Management representative on first EJEC; superintendent in maintenance department
JQWLAC	Joint Quality of Work Life Advisory Committee overseeing intervention in Reginal
Keeley, Vincent	Head of assembly and baking in Reginal
Kochems, Jim	Head of industrial engineering for FoodCom
Lewis, David	IMU steward in Reginal
Linz, Martha	FWIU staff communication specialist
Lowery, Scott	IEU representative on EJEC
Martin, Judy	FWIU Representative on second EJEC; packaging department
Martinez, Jose	Alternate FWIU representative on second EJEC
Matson, Roger	Plant manager in Reginal
McCarthy, Marie	FWIU representative on first EJEC; packaging department
McCue, Kevin	FWIU local president in Reginal
Mills, Ted	Head of NQWC
Morse, Paul	Management representative on first EJEC
NCOP	National Commission on Productivity

Name	**Position**
Newman, George	FWIU business agent for the Reginal plant
NQWC	National Quality of Work Center (later called ACQWL)
O'Neil, Cy	Plant manager in Gorland
Orlandon, Leo	Assistant (second shift) plant manager in Reginal
Pacheco, Keith	Head of maintenance department in Reginal
Papp, John	FWIU research director, JQWLAC member
Pepin, Johnny	Management representative on first EJEC; general foreperson in packaging department
Pond, Dalmar	Head of manufacturing in the bakery division of FoodCom, JQWLAC member
Premater, Donald	FWIU vice-president and JQWLAC member
Pula, Sam	Chemist at Reginal
Quane, Alan	FWIU representative on first EJEC
Quin, Steve	Comptroller in the bakery division of FoodCom
Resler, Jack	FWIU representative on first EJEC; environmental services department
Roper, Patricia	Management representative on first EJEC; packaging supervisor
Sanchez, Leticia	FWIU representative on first EJEC; packaging department
Schwab, Carl	Office manager in Reginal
Scigliano, Edward	FWIU executive vice-president/ JQWLAC member
Seldon, Horace	Head of labor relations for FoodCom, JQWLAC member
Shapiro, Gene	Alternate EJEC representative from baking department
Sheffer, Susan	Management representative on first EJEC; packaging supervisor
Sholl, Wayne	COD consulting team member
Struthers, Frank	President of FoodCom's bakery division
Summers, Max	Former training officer for another company; hired by COD to conduct survey feedback sessions
Talbot, Curtis	FWIU representative on second EJEC; baking department
Thayer, Alfred	Candidate for second site coordinator position in Reginal
Tippett, Margaret	Second site coordinator in Reginal

Name	Position
Touchette, Marjorie	FWIU representative on second EJEC; packaging department
Wilhelm, Warren	Management representative on second EJEC; superintendent in environmental services
Young, Louis	FWIU representative on first EJEC; baking department
Youngman, Billy	Assistant (first shift) plant manager in Reginal

1

Introduction

In 1971, a task force reporting to the United States Department of Health, Education, and Welfare submitted a report on the quality of work in the United States (*Work in America* 1973). The task force described a number of serious problems. For example, it stated that significant numbers of American workers were dissatisfied with the quality of their working lives, in part because the type of work they were doing was intrinsically boring. Work modeled on assembly line patterns had been appropriate in the past for a comparatively uneducated population, but it had not changed in response to changing worker skills, attitudes, aspirations, and values. One of the effects of the design of assembly line work was that blue collar workers were experiencing the "blues" and white collar workers were disgruntled.

This report generated considerable public attention and stimulated several conferences aimed at developing new designs for work. One outcome of the conferences was that beginning in the middle 1970s, a group of agencies—the National Commission on Productivity (through its Quality of Working Life program), the Ford Foundation, and the U.S. Department of Commerce—sponsored several demonstration experiments called Quality of Working Life, or QWL, experiments in labor-management cooperation (Seashore, Lawler, Mirvis, and Cammann 1983; Cammann, Lawler, Ledford, and Seashore 1984). The experiments introduced new methods for labor-management cooperation in unionized settings through the implementation of joint union-management committees. These committees would work together outside the framework of the collective bargaining agreement to solve problems experienced commonly by labor and management. Thus the committees would modify the nature of labor-management relationships. The experiments were to be assessed by research teams under the auspices of the Institute for Social Research (ISR) at the University of Michigan.

Several of these experiments have been described in book form. These include the interventions in the Rushton coal-mining facility (Goodman 1979), in a pharmaceutical company (Perkins, Nieva, and Lawler 1983), at the Tennessee Valley Authority (Nurick 1985), and at Parkside Hospital (Hanlon, Nadler, and Gladstein 1985). A summary of the experiments has been presented by Cammann and colleagues (1984).

We were the primary assessors for the QWL experiment that took place at a food-processing facility called FoodCom. The intervention and our assessment of it, although similar in some ways to many of the other QWL experiments, differed from them in significant ways that we will detail later. In this book we describe the events that occurred during the intervention we assessed. We also explain these events from the perspective that evolved for us as we tried to make sense of them.

The perspective that came to take on the most meaning for us is one of multiple, or alternative, "realities." Briefly, these realities represent the various events and interpretations of events experienced by different actors in the situation. Our notion of multiple realities is not original; it has been developed in considerable detail in the cognitive sciences and elsewhere (e.g.,Brown and Covey 1987; Gergen 1982; Giddens 1979; Markus and Zajonc 1985; Martin and Meyerson 1988; Meyerson and Martin 1987; Sims and Gioia 1986; Smith 1982; Strasser and Bateman 1983). However, it has rarely been applied to help understand large-scale organizational change (for partial exceptions see Brown and Covey 1987; Ramirez and Bartunek 1989).

In this book we examine several issues associated with the interaction among the multiple realities operating during the

FoodCom QWL experiment. We describe the perspectives held by different actors such as consultants, company and international union officials, plant managers and supervisors, and members of the different unions in the plant; the effects of these perspectives on varying responses to apparently identical stimuli; the methods used to change people's perspectives; and participants' responses to attempts to change their perspectives. We address several of the dilemmas that result when multiple realities are present during an intervention designed to create an alternative reality for the participants.

We spent several years assessing the events at FoodCom and more time since then trying to understand the events that occurred. Consequently, we have our own perspective on the events that took place. It is likely that our perspective differs not only from the perspectives of those directly involved in the intervention, but also from the reader's. Many communication problems at the plant seemed to arise because people who understood events from one perspective were often unaware that other people viewed events from different perspectives. This experience taught us that conveying a particular understanding of an event is likely to be much more difficult than it would appear at first glance.

How do we present the perspective of multiple realities in a way that conveys our meaning adequately and makes readers more conscious of their own perspectives? How do we avoid some of the pitfalls that members of FoodCom encountered simply because they were not aware of the different realities experienced by the various actors there? How do we avoid being interpreted solely in terms of the reader's perspective if the reader does not initially share our view that perspectives are variables rather than unchangeable assumptions about how organizations function?

Although we may not be able to avoid these pitfalls entirely, we may convey our perspective as clearly as possible by linking it closely with the events we observed. In the remaining pages of this introduction we describe our approach in more detail. In subsequent chapters we intersperse the story of the intervention with descriptions of the differences in perspective and understanding that were present throughout the intervention. At various points we graphically depict the perspectives employed by various participants. We have tried to distinguish between description and interpretation by presenting interpretations in distinct blocks throughout the text. The one exception, Chapter 7, is entirely interpretive. It is never possible to keep facts (the story of the intervention) and their meanings (interpretations based on perspectives) entirely separate. By distinguishing between them in our mode of presentation, however, we attempt to illustrate a central thesis of this book: that events and the understanding of them interact and affect each other over time. People can gain a measure of control over the effects of their interpretations, therefore, by becoming aware of them and of the ways they influence their experience of ongoing events.

In most of the published accounts of the QWL experiments, the description of the assessment of the intervention has been presented separately from the description of the intervention itself (e.g., Goodman 1979; Nurick 1985; Perkins, Nieva, and Lawler 1983). In the intervention we evaluated, however, the assessment processes were not external to the intervention; data collection and feedback were affected by and had an impact on the intervention process. The assessment process contributed its own reality to the ongoing process of the intervention. Consequently, in this book we do not separate the quantitative data collection from the description of the intervention. Rather, we integrate it into our overall discussion.

A Brief Introduction to Multiple Realities

The cognitive sciences suggest that the world as we experience it consists of few events that are meaningful in themselves. Rather, ways of understanding events are guided by organizing frameworks, or "schemata," which we referred to earlier as perspectives. People use different schemata to make sense of their experiences, causing the reality experienced by one person to differ dramatically from the reality experienced by another. People therefore interpret situations differently even when the objective circumstances are identical. In organizational settings, for example, people in different groups (Meyerson and Martin 1987), functional areas (Strasser and Bateman 1983) or hierarchical or status levels (Smith 1982) often see what is apparently the same event very differently. This basic notion underlies the phenomenon of multiple realities.

Schemata serve several important functions. They enable individuals to identify what they are experiencing and how they can make the experiences relevant to their purposes. Schemata are also the means by which experiences are integrated into a coherent, purposive whole (e.g., de Mey 1982; Neisser 1976; Taylor and Crocker 1981). Unmediated by schemata, experience would be overwhelming. There would be no way to decide what one was experiencing or which stimuli to attend to and which to ignore. Schemata therefore function as implicit (unconscious but not necesssarily unintentional) data reduction devices and enable individuals to grasp what would otherwise be an overwhelming flow of sensations. As data reduction devices, schemata guide people to attend to aspects of their experiences that are relevant to their purposes and to ignore the irrelevent aspects.

Schemata do not necessarily predispose individuals to particular courses of action. However, they do guide and give meaning to behavior: They suggest implications of particular actions, make events meaningful in terms of what participants seek and seek to avoid, and enable people to act intentionally—to identify goals and behave in ways consistent with goal achievement. Because people use various schemata to make sense of their experiences, they identify their experiences differently, see them as uniquely meaningful, and act in differing ways, even in apparently similar situations. Thus people operate, as well as perceive, out of multiple realities.

Changes in Schemata

Schemata, once established, tend to endure. In fact, several studies have suggested that individuals often act according to already established schemata long after these frameworks are clearly dysfunctional (e.g., Nystrom and Starbuck 1984; Staw 1976). However, it is sometimes possible for schemata to change if the impetus is sufficiently strong. Graham (1986), for example, describes a process through which individual employees who later become whistle-blowers come to change their schemata in response to their organizations' reactions to wrongdoing. For Graham, whistle-blowers are employees who observe activities they believe are improper and take their complaint to outside authorities rather than to their organizational superior. She suggests that employees typically begin with an assumption that their superior, once made aware of some instance of wrongdoing, will deal adequately with the problem. Consequently, if an employee observes something questionable, he or she tells the supervisor. When an adequate response on the part of the superior doesn't occur and the supervisor appears to ignore the wrongdoing, the eventual whistle-blower undergoes what Graham calls a "transformation," or consciousness-raising experience, about the supervisor or the nature of the organization itself. (This contrasts with the experience of non–whistle-blowers, who do not change their schema for understanding the organization's response.) Whistle-blowers' previous assumptions of good faith are called into question, and they often experience disillusionment or cynicism. This change in schema leads whistle-blowers to change assumptions and, consequently, strategies: They abandon normal reporting channels and take their concerns outside previously defined boundaries.

This example illustrates aspects of the relationship between schemata and actions as well as changes in schemata. It suggests that schemata guide individuals' initial actions (reports to supervisors based on assumptions of good faith), and that events that do not turn out as expected may lead to changes in schemata (loss of faith when the supervisor doesn't respond as expected). These changes in schemata will then affect subsequent actions (a change in strategies for reporting wrongdoing).

The understandings and actions illustrated in the example can be depicted in a more abstract way that enables greater breadth of application in a model of the process of human problem solving adapted from Newell and Simon (1972). This model is presented in Figure 1-1. As the model suggests, people develop an understanding of particular situations on the basis of their schemata. Their understanding generates notions of desirable conditions and these inform the means available for implementing these conditions. Based on the available means, they decide upon and take a course of action. The action generates outcomes that are expected to realize these desirable conditions. When these types of outcomes do not oc-

Figure 1-1 Illustration of a Simplified Model of Problem Solving

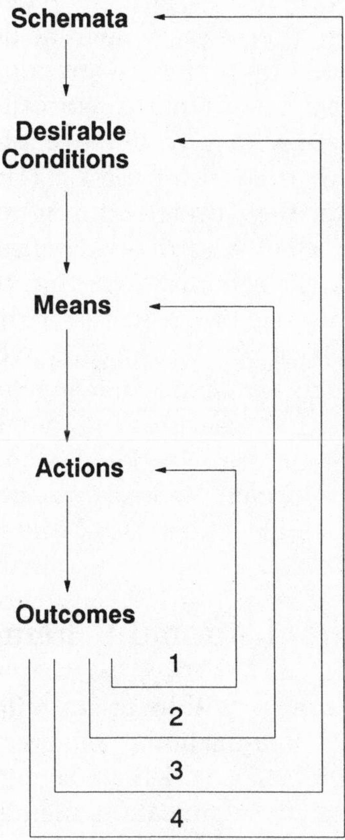

cur, participants can alter their actions (arrow 1), their means (arrow 2), their understanding of what constitutes desirable conditions (arrow 3), or their underlying schemata (arrow 4). This latter type of shift is referred to as a change in schema: All the other actions represented in the model illustrate occasions in which the original interpretation of the situation is not challenged.

In the preceding whistle-blowing example from Graham, organization members are likely to be operating out of a schema of good faith in the organization, which includes the absence of organizational wrongdoing as a desirable condition. When wrongdoing first occurs, these organization members are likely to take an action from their already developed repertoire, such as informing their supervisor (arrow 1). If this action is not successful in changing the practice, they are likely to try to find some other means, such as informing an upper level superior (arrow 2). If this means also fails, they might change their assessment of what constitutes wrongdoing: Perhaps the behavior they saw really was acceptable (arrow 3). Finally, if they have tried all of these alternatives unsuccessfully, they may alter their understanding of the nature of the organization itself. They may reject their assumption of good faith and change their schema regarding the entire situation (arrow 4). This may lead them to see other conditions, such as public awareness of the wrongdoing, as desirable and to use new means, such as whistle-blowing, to achieve this condition.

Schemata exist on an organizational level as well as an individual level. It is to organizational level phenomena that we now turn.

Organizational Schemata

Organizations or groups within organizations frequently negotiate specifically organizational or group level schemata (Bartunek and Moch 1987), which are schemata shared among significant numbers of organization members. For example, most organizations or organizational groups have schemata that specify appropriate relationships among managers and employees. Many organizations' schemata employ family imagery, in which managers act as and are treated as parents and employees act as and are treated as children (Bern-stein 1985). Some organizations and groups operate out of a managerial control schema that conveys the assumption that management must remain in control of events at all costs (e.g., Feldman 1986; Hanlon, Nadler, and Gladstein 1985).

As is the case with individual schemata, organizational schemata tend to be implicit. That is, organizations and subgroups within them are typically unaware that some particular perspective is guiding their understanding and action. Recently the popularity of the concept of corporate culture (e.g., Kennedy and Deal 1982) has raised organization members' awareness that organizations have an underlying self-understanding. However, the particular schemata that guide the everyday activities of organization members typically remain inaccessible to the participants' conscious awareness.

Shared schemata allow participants to have a common orientation towards events. Thus organizational schemata, which are sometimes referred to as the organization's culture (cf. Goodenough 1981), generate shared meanings for the organization as a whole or for subgroups within it (e.g., Bartunek 1984; Gray, Bougon and Donnellon 1985; Louis 1985; Martin and Meyerson 1988; Meyerson and Martin 1987; Ouchi and Wilkins 1985; Smircich 1983; Shrivastva and Schneider 1984). The development of organizational and group level schemata is a function of individual and group choices motivated by individual and collective interests (Showers and Cantor 1985).

Although largely implicit, organizational schemata are often evoked, sustained, and communicated through organizational myths, stories, and dominant metaphors (Martin 1982; Martin, Feldman, Hatch, and Simkin 1983). Schemata have pervasive effects. They guide members of an organization or group in their interpretation of the environment, their selection of desirable conditions, and the means and actions they take for realizing these conditions. Like individual schemata, organizational schemata tend to endure. Most organizational problem solving revolves around potential changes in actions, available means, and, occasionally, desirable conditions. However, some forces, such as the fact that organizational schemata serve different members' interests differently, have the potential to initiate changes in an organization's shared understandings (e.g., Bartunek 1984, 1988; Giddens 1979; Gray, Bougon, and Donnellon 1985).

Changing Organizational Schemata

How do organizational schemata affect organization members' actions, particularly their problem solving activities? How and when do organizational schemata change?

Figure 1-1 may be taken as a simplified model not only of ways individuals solve problems, but also of many organizational problem solving or change attempts. In fact, parts of it bear considerable similarity to the model of action research that has guided organization development practice for years. We will use an action research model to illustrate Figure 1-1 on an organizational level.

As it is typically described, action research involves (1) systematically collecting research data about an ongoing system relative to some objective, need, or goal of the system, (2) feeding these data back to the system and conducting a collaborative diagnosis of the data, (3) planning and then taking action based on the diagnosis, and (4) evaluating the results of the action (e.g., French and Bell 1984; Pasmore and Friedlander 1982; Peters and Robinson 1984; Shani and Pasmore 1985; Sommer 1987). The results of the action are expected to be fed back into the system, possibly initiating another round of action research.

Many of the characteristics of action research are thus implicit in the first three arrows of Figure 1-1. One of the first questions addressed by action researchers (cf. Harrison 1987) is the adequacy of the current organizational outcomes: Do they correspond with the conditions desired? Problems are indicated by a lack of correspondence between outcomes and desirable conditions. On the basis of shared diagnoses of the problems identified, organization members may plan changes in specific actions (arrow 1), in the means through which they attempt to realize desirable conditions (arrow 2), or in the desirable conditions themselves (arrow 3). Then they take actions based on the plans they developed.

For example, in one recent action research intervention, top level managers at a health center were concerned that second level managers weren't acting in a way that facilitated the health center's goals. As a result of joint diagnosis by the top and second level managers, the top level managers realized that the main reason for the second level managers' lack of goal achievement was a lack of clarity of the goals themselves: The desirable condition of goal clarity wasn't present. The diagnostic and planning work based on this realization led the top and second level managers to reformulate and clarify the goals together to achieve this desirable condition. It also led them to develop new means, such as workshops and management training, to assist the second level managers in achieving the newly clarified goals (Ramirez and Bartunek 1989).

Action Research typically concerns itself only with actions, means, and desired conditions, the first three arrows of Figure 1-1. Although the issues addressed in these first three arrows are important, the change in the underlying schema suggested by arrow 4 may be crucial. As several authors have noted (e.g., Dunphy and Stace 1988; Kilmann and Covin 1987; Quinn and Cameron 1988; Tichy and Devanna 1986; Torbert 1987), in order to function in today's rapidly changing environment, an organization often has to change its understanding of fundamental aspects of its identity and mission as well as its view of particular conditions, means, and actions. But, as is the case with individuals, this type of change in understanding is very difficult to achieve (Nystrom and Starbuck 1984; Starbuck 1982, 1983). To address such situations, organizational change agents must possess a more sophisticated and encompassing understanding of various types of change. Specifically, they need to understand the desired outcomes and develop strategies and tactics for affecting the relationship between outcomes and schemata (arrow 4).

Problems associated with the relationship between outcomes and schemata have been recognized to some extent in the organizational change literature, although they have not always been identified in these terms (e.g., Argyris 1985; 1988; Argyris and Schon 1978). For example, several attempts have recently been made to grasp conceptually the transformation process by which a system moves from one way of understanding significant aspects of itself to another (e.g., Bartunek 1988; Dunphy and Stace 1988; Kimberly and Quinn 1984; Quinn and Cameron 1988). In addition, although many organization development (OD) practitioners do not use the terms schema and schemata, they frequently try to achieve schematic, or "gamma," changes in client systems (cf. Golembiewski, Billingsley, and Yeager 1976). The stated goals of the QWL experiments, for example, implied a desire for a change in the schemata that govern labor-management relationships: away from a schema that focuses exclusively on adversarial, bargaining relationships and towards a schema in which cooperation predominates (cf. Mohrman and Lawler 1985).

However, although OD practitioners are frequently concerned about issues that imply schematic change, OD literature and cognitive change literature have remained largely separate (Bartunek and Moch 1987). Consequently, in their interventions, change agents make comparatively little use of contemporary knowledge of cognitive social change. In this book we link OD and cognitive science closely. We discuss an intervention whose course was strongly affected by the various schemata, or multiple realities, the participants brought to it. We describe in detail the attempts some participants made to change the ways other participants understood their situation. In so doing, we address questions such as the following: What are the processes through which organizational schemata change or resist change? How do change agents' own schemata affect the strategies they use to achieve changes in perspectives (cf. Tichy 1974, 1975)? What happens when change agents' understanding of concepts relevant to the change is very different from organization members' understanding of these concepts? What happens when management and union members have different understandings but remain unaware of these differences? How can change agents design interventions that result in desired changes in understanding—cognitive changes—when participants respond to their efforts solely in terms of the dysfunctional perspectives the agents are trying to change? How can change agents use contemporary models of cognitive change to design intervention strategies and tactics that will improve their chances for success and will conform to generally accepted ethical principles?

These questions guide our attempt to understand, explain, and learn from the intervention we assessed. They keep surfacing as we reflect on the intervention and its outcomes and try to make sense of the experience in a way that will prove useful to practitioners and researchers alike.

2

Multiple Realities in the Workplace

During the 1975 contract negotiations between the Food Workers' International Union (FWIU) and FoodCom, both parties pledged to create a "job enrichment program" that would increase productivity and better the quality of work life throughout FoodCom's Bakery Division. Representatives from both the union and the company subsequently contacted Ted Mills, a highly visible proponent of such programs. Mills, who had previously directed the Quality of Working Life Program for the National Commission on Productivity (NCOP) and then ran the National Quality of Work Center (NQWC), proposed that NQWC design a program for FoodCom and the FWIU.

The program designed for FoodCom would be similar in both philosophy and structure to other experiments the NQWC had run earlier in the 1970s. Mills described the philosophy of these programs in a 1975 article published in the *Harvard Business Review.** In this article he argued that significant gains in productivity could be realized by changing the traditional pattern of corporate governance. Citing innovative programs initiated by such companies as AT&T, General Motors, Cummins Engine, Mead, Cutter Labs, and General Foods, he advocated increased use of joint labor-management

* Mills, Ted. 1975. "Human Resources—Why the New Concern?" *Harvard Business Review* 53: 120–134.

committees. By increasing communication and using mutual problem solving, these committees would reconcile corporate productivity needs with employees' needs for challenging and satisfying work.

The experiments designed and managed by NQWC were conducted only in unionized companies. With some company-to-company variations, each program usually called for the establishment of a labor-management committee composed of equal numbers of union and supervisory personnel (Drexler and Lawler 1977; Hanlon, Nadler, and Gladstein 1985; Nadler 1978; Nurick 1985; Perkins, Nieva, and Lawler 1983). These committees were given discretion to consider any work-related issues not explicitly addressed by the collective bargaining process. And, though they were generally advised by outside process consultants, committees were encouraged to find new solutions to productivity and quality of work life issues free from union, company, or other outside interference. A graphic representation of the NQWC model adapted from Nadler (1978) is presented in Figure 2-1.

After considerable communication among representatives of FoodCom, the FWIU, and NQWC, Mills met with FoodCom officials on February 5, 1976. The meeting was held at the company's international headquarters. Before the meeting, Mills,

Figure 2-1 The NQWC's Labor-Management Committee Structure

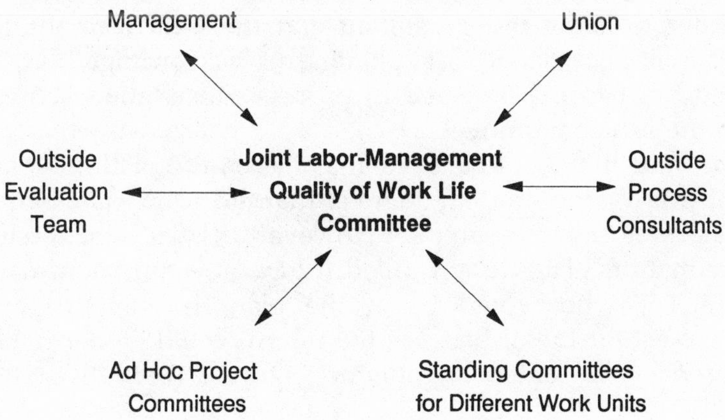

the FWIU people, and FoodCom's labor-relations and industrial engineering staffs had chosen FoodCom's plant in Gorland (a large city in the south) as the preferred site for the program. They had also negotiated a set of roles and responsibilities for each participant and had established a timetable. The staff people viewed the meeting as a ceremonial handing over of the project to "line ownership and control." The Bakery Division President, Frank Struthers, gave oversight responsibility for the program to William Coy, one of two line managers reporting to the division's chief of manufacturing for the Gorland region.

Mills wanted line management to be committed to the project, "to feel it was their own." Consequently, before the meeting began, he huddled with the FoodCom staff members who had handled the preliminary negotiations: Horace Seldon, head of labor relations; Jim Kochems, head of industrial engineering; and Tony Campbell, who ran the training and development programs and was Seldon's subordinate. Mills wanted to be sure they would present a united front in their discussions with line management.

Mills reviewed the consultant role with the staff people, reminding them that the selected consultant was to consider the joint labor-management committee to be his or her client. The consultant would not work for either the company or the union. The NQWC would supervise the program and manage the implementation process. It would assume the role of negotiator and arbitrator between the union and the company in order to allow the consultant and the local committee to focus their energies on local plant issues. Accordingly, NQWC would not become involved in process consultation activities with the local committee.

The staff members believed that the choice of the Gorland plant was a good one, and agreed that the plant manager, Cy O'Neil, was "above average." However, they did not agree on other matters. The design called for an assistant coordinator, an intern, who would be at the plant full-time to manage project business. Because the intern would gather data to be used by the outside evaluator (Figure 2-1), Mills thought that his or her salary should be paid from the evaluator's budget. Kochems believed that these funds should come from the NQWC's budget. The intern would be primarily engaged in managing the day-to-day activities, he pointed out, and this was NQWC's responsibility.

Mills then argued that the overall project was underfunded. He wanted more money than FoodCom had budgeted, and he wanted the funds disbursed before expenses were incurred. Kochems argued that funds were adequate and should be disbursed on a vouchered per-diem basis. Mills believed this would result in "nickle-and-dime haggling" unbecoming in such a large and profitable company.

The meeting with line personnel was conducted over lunch and was presided over by Division President Struthers. In his notes, Mills described Struthers as "42–45, slick, Ivy League, and 110 percent committed to the worker-involvement notion." Ed Coy, the line officer responsible for the program, was unable to attend, but Dalmar Pond, Coy's superior, and Steve Quin, the division comptroller, were present. Mills reviewed the agreements that had been reached by that time. He emphasized that the local labor-management committee should be given maximum autonomy and proposed that an oversight committee be established. This committee, composed of national-level union and company personnel, would review—but not direct—program activities and act as a vehicle for disseminating program information throughout the division. Initially referring to such a group as a "steering" committee, Mills later called it "the core group." This shift underscored an important point: The core group should in no way direct the local committee.

Those present at the luncheon agreed that the core group should include Seldon, Coy, and Pond. Mills urged Struthers to become a member, but Struthers was concerned that his membership might compromise the company's adversarial stance with the union on other matters. Because no FWIU representative was present, those attending the meeting could not officially recommend union members for the core group. However, the FoodCom people agreed that one union vice-president, Donald Premater, should not serve. Company officials believed Premater had "never grown up from being a steward." Mills pointed out that union representatives could appoint anyone they wanted. Faced with the prospect of Premater serving on the committee, one of the managers expressed the hope that by so doing the vice president would "learn about quality of work life cooperative thinking."

After lunch, Mills, Seldon, and Kochems met again with Struthers. Mills was concerned that Struthers might be promoted out of the division, leaving the QWL project without a powerful sponsor. Struthers discounted this possibility. He explained that even though he himself might be promoted out of the division, other officers were aware of the program and were very supportive. Mills asked that Struthers continue to act as a liaison to his FoodCom superiors and suggested that the existence of a QWL program at FoodCom be announced immediately.

At the end of the day, Mills met again with Seldon and Kochems. He urged them to contact the external evaluators and invite them to visit the Gorland site. The NQWC had received Labor Department funds to establish projects such as the one at FoodCom, and these funds were contingent upon securing competent outside evaluation. As in most of the other NQWC projects, the independent assessors for this project were to be researchers associated with the Institute for Social Research (ISR) at the University of Michigan.

Seldon, Kochems, and Campbell had already contacted ISR as part of their preliminary project planning. They had visited Ann Arbor, where ISR staff had described their program evaluation procedures. During this visit, ISR evaluators presented several assessment packages ranging from minimal to elaborate. At Kochems's urging, the FoodCom group chose an evaluation package on the basis of cost, noting, in Kochems's terms, that the evaluation should be "bare-bones, bare-bones all the way." Kochems also said he wanted FoodCom to retain control over the dissemination of information gathered during the evaluation process. ISR representatives explained that because ISR was a university-based research organization, it had to retain the freedom to publish whatever its assessors found during their evaluation activities. Kochems could not agree to this, so the matter was left to be settled at a future date.

After meeting with the FoodCom staff, Mills felt satisfied with the day's accomplishments. He recorded in his notes, however, that much had yet to be done. He had reached an agreement with the FWIU regarding its financial contribution to the program, but the FWIU still had to select its own members for the core group. Mills also needed to start thinking about when to call the core group's first meeting, which he thought should be on neutral turf. In any case, he thought the day had been a success. Mills concluded his notes with the exclamation, "Here goes [the project]!"

Were There Multiple Perspectives on QWL?

The preceding description of the early stages of the FoodCom project introduces some of the questions and issues we wish to address in this book. We start with the assumption that different individuals and groups of individuals in any social system operate according to different perspectives or interpretive schemata. One way we can interpret Mills's behavior is to call it an orchestration designed to communicate his perspective on labor-management cooperation and to persuade management to accept this perspective. Believing that the cooperation of line managers was an essential ingredient for success, Mills sought to convince them to adopt his vision of the QWL program as their own.

QWL ideas are frequently initiated by personnel departments or other staff offices (e.g., Krim and Arthur 1989). If properly implemented, however, these ideas affect line functions and redefine relationships among line personnel. The support and commitment of line management is therefore essential. Yet, as most management texts point out, line and staff officers frequently have very different points of view. For example, line managers are likely to be more conscious of operational issues and to approach subordinates less as persons and more as instruments for getting the job done than staff people from a human resources or personnel department. Alternatively, industrial engineers often see their primary function as finding ways to reduce costs. A "cost first" perspective, however, may clash with that of a line manager who is seeking ways to become more effective as well as more efficient.

Similarly, it is likely that Mills's perspective on QWL differed from that of FoodCom's management. However, if Mills was aware of any divergence between his vision of QWL and the view held by Coy, Pond, or Struthers, it was not apparent at the first meeting. The fact that Mills did not detail his understanding for FoodCom personnel suggests that he believed that FoodCom managers' assumptions about QWL and joint labor-management decision making were either (1) similar to his own or (2) different from his own in ways that might have derailed the program had they been allowed to surface at that time.

Mills might have been concerned primarily with completing the contract and thereby acquiring needed support funds for NQWC. This theory explains his effort to have the salary of the assistant coordinator paid from the assessor's budget rather than from NQWC funds and to have FoodCom funds paid in advance. Alternatively, Mills might have believed that line managers would understand QWL ideas only after they had seen them in operation and that they would wholeheartedly support the program once they had seen its impact on productivity. The form would therefore come first, and the substance or understanding would follow.

The First Meeting of the Core Group

Mills met with the FWIU representatives on February 11. One of the representatives, FWIU Executive Vice-President Edward Scigliano, had been involved with the QWL negotiations from the beginning. He believed that John Papp, the union's research director, and Donald Premater, a union vice president, should sit with him as members of the core group. Mills, recalling comments made about Premater at his earlier meeting with company management, argued unsuccessfully that Premater not be included. He successfully requested, however, that Scigliano provide 5 percent of the costs of the project from union funds, so long as FoodCom provided 95 percent.

While FoodCom, the FWIU, and the evaluators prepared to initiate the program, Mills began preparations for the first meeting of the core group. This group, it will be recalled, was intended to facilitate the activity of the local labor-management committee (Figure 2-1). It was not to interfere with local initiatives. Now, however, Mills reverted to calling it the "steering committee," which seemed to imply that it would direct QWL activities in Gorland. He drafted an agenda that called for a meeting on February 24. His proposed agenda for this meeting is presented as Exhibit 2-1.

At the meeting on February 24, Scigliano, Papp, and Premater represented the FWIU, and Coy, Pond, and Seldon represented FoodCom. Mills set the tone of the meeting by stressing that the FWIU-FoodCom project would be jointly owned by labor and management. He emphasized that the program was companywide and would not be limited to the experimental plant. Mills distributed copies of a report outlining the NQWC's first eighteen months. In this report, he described the underlying assumption guiding NQWC projects: "When employees in any kind of organization, public or private, are provided an expertly structured opportunity to contribute to designing and implementing activities for organizational change, the organization will become measurably more effective, and the quality of working life for all employees will improve."

The report reviewed previous NQWC projects, including the Rushton coal mine in Pennsylvania, an auto parts plant in Tennessee, the Tennessee Valley Authority, and a hospital in New York City. It also described the pending FoodCom project, despite the fact that neither the FWIU nor FoodCom had formally announced it to their own constituencies.

Mills stressed that the FoodCom project would have the same characteristics as the other projects initiated by NQWC and that this intervention would not undermine the traditional collective bargaining process. The local QWL commit-

EXHIBIT 2-1 Proposed Agenda for the First Meeting of The National-Level Quality of Work Core Group

. . . The following is a proposed agenda for the first official joint meeting of the committee, on February 24, 1976.

Present for FoodCom will be Messrs. Coy, Pond, and Seldon; and for the FWIU, Messrs. Scigliano, Premater, and Papp. NQWC will preside until duly selected and/ or elected officers are designated (see #7).

The proposed agenda, in the following proposed order and subject to any proposed revision, is as follows:

1. Examination of the long-range companywide and unionwide objectives of the Joint Quality of Work Project
2. Project Funding—
   - FoodCom contribution as grant: amount, terms
   - FWIU contribution as grant: amount, terms
   - Cancellation terms
3. Examination of the functions and values of this Committee in achieving those project objectives, including:
   - companywide focus
   - Gorland as first project only
   - experimental throughout
   - 18 months/ 36 months
   - other
4. Official, permanent name of this Committee:
   - Steering Committee?
   - Joint Steering Committee?
   - Joint Core Committee?
   - Headquarters Joint Committee?
   - Joint Labor-Management Headquarters Committee?
   - Senior Quality of Work Life Committee?
   - Senior Joint Quality of Work Life Committee?
   - Other
5. Parliamentary structure of now-named Committee:
   - consensus decisions?
   - majority decisions?

- two-thirds decisions?
- five-sixths decisions?
- other?

6. Terms of office of now-named Committee:
   - permanent?
   - annual renewal of participation?
   - other?
   - what if a member can't attend?
     a) send deputy who can vote?
     b) forfeit vote?
     c) other?
   - what if member must resign?
     a) who appoints successor?
     b) what if objection to successor?
7. Officers of now-named Committee:
   - who will chair?
     a) revolving chairmen?
     b) term of office? annual? 90 days? semi-annual?
   - who will establish meeting dates and places?
   - who will keep minutes?
     a) appoint a secretary? If yes, who, for how long?
     b) NQWC provide minutes?
   - who (union, FoodCom) signs NQWC agreement? When?
8. Frequency of meetings:
   - called by chairman?
   - regularly? If so,
     a) monthly?
     b) quarterly?
     c) semiannually?
     d) other?
9. Establishment of Gorland Project
   - who announces to O'Neil? To . . . . ?
   - name of Gorland committee?
     a) let Gorland decide?

b) Joint Quality of Work Committee?
c) Joint Working Committee?
d) Joint Labor-Management Committee?
e) Joint Plant-Wide Working Committee?

- inclusion of Distribution Group
  a) let Gorland decide?
  b) if decision here, does this mean another FoodCom manager involved?
- inclusion of IMU, IDU
  a) let Gorland decide?
  b) if decision here, who approaches IMU, IDU?
- timetable/schedule for Gorland establishment

10. Relationship of now-named Committee to Gorland committee
    - review only?
    - authority over Gorland decisions?
      a) matters involving cost?
      b) matters involving social structure?
      c) matters involving capital?
      d) matters involving contract/collective bargaining?
      e) matters involving technology?
      f) matters involving job security?
11. Who handles Project grant, payments, etc.?
    - if Gorland, what controls in now-named Committee?
    - if now-named Committee,
      a) delegate responsibility to non-Committee FoodCom representative?
      b) who likewise union representative? How integrate?
      c) NQWC is disburser of funds granted
      d) accountability of funds granted
    - NQWC?
    - now-named Committee
    - Gorland Committee
    - Other?

12. Consultant selection
    - rundown of current applicants
    - function of now-named Committee in selection
        a) approve on paper, send to Gorland?
        b) interview all? some? how select?
        c) individual union (this level) interview?
        d) individual management (this level) interview?
    - schedule of consultant selection (this Committee)
    - review of consultant costs: Gorland, this level?
13. Summary of decisions made
14. Next meeting, when, where, called by whom?

tee would not address issues typically handled through collective bargaining; moreover, should labor or management wish to do so, either party could terminate the project within twenty-four hours. Mills emphasized that the local committee would be given full freedom to identify and evaluate issues. If gains in productivity were realized, the local committee would decide how to share them. Members of the local committee would have the right to select the outside process consultant, who would work for them rather than for the union or the company. Finally, in response to Scigliano's concern that his union should not have gotten involved if the project were concerned only with Gorland, Mills again explained that the program would be companywide, not limited to the Gorland plant. Management representatives responded that the QWL program would be diffused throughout the division "if it's a success."

After considerable discussion, the core group decided to name itself the Joint Quality of Work Life Advisory Committee (JQWLAC). "Joint" highlighted the equal status of labor and management. Management and labor would each be free to appoint their own replacements. No limits were placed on the length of committee membership, and although NQWC would organize and chair future meetings, it would do so only as a "service." The JQWLAC was to be a full-fledged labor-management committee, not just an executive arm for NQWC.

The term "Advisory" in the committee's name was included to emphasize that the JQWLAC would not initiate activities, but that it would advise and support initiatives taken by the local committee.

All present agreed on the Gorland plant as the preferred site. Scigliano consented to inform the president of the local union, and Coy agreed to inform O'Neil, the Gorland plant manager. Mills stressed, however, that neither of these local officials should feel pressured to participate.

After choosing Gorland and deciding that the local officials should feel a sense of participation, the Committee also made the following decisions about the project:

- It would be the responsibility of the local committee to select its own name.
- The local union would decide whether its committee representatives would be elected or appointed.
- Union representatives on the local committee would include people from all shifts, both sexes, and all races. Employees in the distribution area of the plant would be included in the project, even though they belonged to a different union (International Distribution Union [IDU]) and the area reported to officials in another division of the company.
- The Gorland committee would have seven representatives from labor and seven from management.
- The Gorland committee would decide whether to include other unions in the project. (The International Electricians' Union [IEU], the International Machinists' Union [IMU], and the International Distribution Union [IDU] all had members working in the Gorland plant.)
- The employees in Gorland would select their own representatives to the local quality of work committee.

The participants agreed that the Gorland committee should have as much freedom as possible and should be allowed to make any recommendation "subject to the endorsement of the JQWLAC." The JQWLAC would suggest consultants, but the local committee would have the final choice of which recommended individual or group would be the outside process consultant. Mills provided a list of eight preferred consultants. Three of these were seen as unacceptable, and the JQWLAC decided to interview five.

In closing that first core group meeting, the JQWLAC advised Mills to draft a letter of agreement that would identify their QWL program policies and mutual expectations. This letter was subsequently posted in the Gorland plant. It is shown in Exhibit 2-2.

EXHIBIT 2-2 Letter of Agreement Defining the Mutual Expectations of Labor and Management

The undersigned have independently discussed with the National Quality of Work Center of Washington, D.C., the feasibility of establishing an experimental joint labor-management Quality of Work demonstration Project at FoodCom and by this letter agree to jointly pursue its initial establishment and initial implementation at the Gorland plant of the company.

It is understood and agreed by the undersigned that the Project or the participation therein of either party may be terminated within twenty-four hours of notice by either of the undersigned to the other that the party giving notice desires to terminate. Such notice may be given at any time during the Project's existence. Commitment by each of the undersigned to the continuance of the Project is predicated upon this irrevocable and continuing right to terminate.

If this right to cancellation is not exercised by either of the undersigned, it is understood and agreed that the proposed joint Project will continue in its experimental status for a period of approximately eighteen months, during which period a jointly-composed (three company, three union) steering (or other named) committee will be formed to direct the companywide activity of the Project, and to form, or cause to be formed, labor-management committees of a size to be determined with equal representation of company and union, at Gorland and/or other FoodCom sites, for the duration of the "experimental" period. It is further understood and agreed by both parties that such joint labor-management committees shall be considered the sole "client" of NQWC, and any consultant or assessment representatives NQWC shall furnish when so requested by the committees. It is understood and agreed that meetings of all such committees shall be conducted on company time, and that no member of any such committee shall lose pay or benefit from attendance at such meetings.

It is further understood and agreed by the undersigned that no employees in the work area(s) which may be included in the Project, whether union or management members, will suffer loss of or reduction in pay, loss of or reduction in benefits, or will be suspended from employment or terminated as a result of activities stemming from the Project. Change in employee status for reasons in no way related to the proposed experimental Project, such as decline in sales due to economic or other conditions, shall not be precluded by this agreement.

It is further understood and agreed by the undersigned that no activities implemented as a result of the experimental Project shall contravene, change, or otherwise affect any provisions of collective bargaining agreements in effect between any of the undersigned without prior approval of each of the undersigned.

It is further understood and agreed by the undersigned that the funds for the experimental Project will be furnished by the company and union in a ratio of contribution decided between them, and that such jointly-contributed funds will be furnished in the form of a charitable contribution to NQWC, a tax-exempt organization within the provisions of Section 501-c-3 of the Internal Revenue Code. NQWC shall thereafter manage disbursement of such funds.

So long as the Project is in effect experimentally, it is understood and agreed that the services of a team of expert consultants to be selected by the joint committees in the manner to be prescribed by them will be furnished to the Project, and that NQWC shall be the contractor for such services throughout the experimental period. It is further understood and agreed that the services of the Institute for Social Research of the University of Michigan for Project assessment will be provided. It is further understood and agreed that all additional Project costs, such as those arising from employee meetings on company time, provisions of relevant company operating data, and/or new training programs, if such activities are requested by the labor-management Project participants, shall be borne by the company.

Finally, it is understood and agreed by the undersigned that the Project will be the subject of various descriptive documents which will be disseminated and that the participants and/or Project location may remain anonymous at the request of either of the undersigned.

This letter of agreement shall be known as the Basic Experimental Agreement, which may from time to time be amended in any particular by mutual agreement of the undersigned.

Frank Struthers,
President,
Bakery Division
FoodCom

Edward Scigliano,
Executive Vice President,
Food Workers' International
Union

Was the Proposed Process of the QWL Program Consistent with the Process Used to Gain Its Acceptance?

The labor-management committee structure Mills proposed has the potential to alter the decision making process in the workplace significantly. It reflects a substantial divergence from traditional labor-management relations, emphasizing cooperation over competition, trust over suspicion, and the well-being of the company over the narrower interests of labor, management, or other stakeholders (e.g., Drexler and Lawler 1977; Hanlon, Nadler, and Gladstein 1985; Nurick 1985; Trist 1986). This structure implies that differing management and labor perspectives on particular events will be introduced and addressed in ways that enable their joint incorporation in problem solving and decision making.

No one would claim that it is easy to establish cooperative relationships, build trust, and stimulate a desire to transcend sectarian interests. There are bound to be different points of view that must be reconciled, differences that reflect varying underlying assumptions about the nature of social and economic life. Establishing joint cooperative relationships is even more complex when a national group does the initial planning for a program designed to be locally implemented by a group expected to have considerable autonomy. The initial implementation of the FoodCom project suggests two intertwined dilemmas involving QWL programs: (1) the development of appropriate ways to acknowledge union-management disagreements or other differences across groups, and (2) the determination of the way in which one (e.g., national) group can take initiative in a manner that enables another (e.g., local) group to maintain its autonomy.

The evidence was already present that the FoodCom experiment was not immune from these dilemmas, yet these problems were not the subject of discussion. The JQWLAC members were operating from different perspectives, but they never openly addressed them. For example, by choosing Premater (whom management distrusted) to serve on the JQWLAC, the union signaled that it might have a different view of "quality of work life cooperative thinking" from that of management. Yet the tension was never brought into the open. Underlying conflicts in perspective were avoided, rather than addressed.

In addition, JQWLAC rejected three of the process consultants proposed by Mills. Some of the management representatives held strong negative opinions about certain consultants, but never made their opinions explicit. With Premater's appointment and the consultant choices, the implicit norm seemed to be to allow labor and management representatives maximum discretion in their own areas of concern. This rule was made explicit in the case of choosing JQWLAC replacements: Each side would be free to choose its own current and future representatives.

The implicit decision not to surface and address contentious issues seems also to have guided the discussion of the respective roles of JQWLAC and the local committee. Despite Mills's advocacy of local autonomy, JQWLAC rejected several of the proposed consultants, specified the demographic composition and size of the local committee, determined that employees in the distribution area would be included in the program, and picked the site. Other controversial issues were also sidestepped. Profit sharing, or gain sharing, was only briefly addressed. No effort was made to determine what would constitute success (e.g., the relative weights for productivity and improvements in the quality of work life for employees) and thereby qualify the program for diffusion to other plants.

The dilemma posed when national-level groups plan programs that are expected to run locally was evident in the peculiar form used in the joint agreement (Exhibit 2-2). This agreement described the program primarily by listing what was not going to happen. Given the expectations for local autonomy, this may have been inevitable. Consistent with the JQWLAC acronym, labor and management representatives of the JQWLAC were "jointly" to make decisions that would "advise." The joint agreement reserved the right to specify program content for the local committee. Neither the JQWLAC nor the NQWC were supposed to initiate suggestions, even suggestions for the name of the local committee.

Perhaps a process that avoided confronting differences at the level of the JQWLAC might encourage a "bottom-up" approach to integrating management and union perspectives. A QWL program at the local level might provide suggestions and the momentum for addressing companywide differences. This strategy, however (if indeed it was a strategy), was compromised by JQWLAC's clear involvement in specifying the content of the local program, despite its stated preference to the contrary. A great many critical issues were considered out of bounds. Obviously, wage and salary issues could not be dealt with at the local level. By precluding consideration of all issues addressed through collective bargaining, however, the program excluded other topics as well, including the timing and length of breaks, the policy for handling absences, overtime regulations, and job and shift assignments.

The national level of FoodCom-FWIU not only excluded topics but also specified the participants in the program. Project participants at the Gorland site were told to include the IDU members working in the Distribution Center, and three consultant teams were removed from the proposed list almost immediately after Mills had stated that the local committee should be free to choose from the entire list. One consequence of JQWLAC's involvement in planning local program content was that a program intended to increase employee participation was designed without much employee involvement. The plant manager in Gorland and the local union president were *informed* that the program would take place under their jurisdiction: Plant managers and local presidents did not convene to identify the site, nor were line employees directly involved.

Managing the Assessment Activities

On February 26, representatives from ISR visited division headquarters to meet with line and staff personnel. Dalmar Pond, the manufacturing officer to whom Coy reported, expressed skepticism that the evaluators could assess the QWL program properly. He questioned the assessors' ability to measure all the factors that contribute to or detract from operating efficiency when this was a challenge for his own highly competent staff. He noted, for example, that the Gorland plant produced products of various densities and that different mixes of products were produced at separate times. This made it very difficult for FoodCom staff to assess operating efficiency using some overall statistic such as pounds produced per labor hour. How could the assessors solve this type of problem quickly when FoodCom's own people had worked on it unsuccessfully for years?

Kochems was angry that Mills had announced the FWIU-FoodCom project before either the union or the company had had an opportunity to do so. He also continued to insist that FoodCom retain the right to prevent publication of what he felt would be proprietary data. If the assessors were to publish information showing the company's operating costs, for example, competitors could benefit substantially. Finally, he urged the assessors to develop an evaluation system that could not be manipulated by plant managers trying "to make themselves look good."

Steve Quin, the company controller, clearly delineated what he believed was the ultimate criterion that would determine the success or failure of the QWL program. "Productivity is the name of the game," he advised. If the QWL program were to succeed, it must positively affect the "bottom line." Coy's more immediate concern was that the assessors would move too quickly and visit the Gorland plant before the program had been formally accepted by the union. Thinking that he would have enough trouble controlling the project without allowing NQWC or ISR staff to make contacts on their own, he insisted that any contact with the Gorland plant go through him.

After meeting with Pond, Kochems, Quin, and Coy, ISR staff met with Struthers to resolve Kochems's concern about release of proprietary information. The group agreed that no information would be made public during the experimental phase of the project. Moreover, any data gathered for assessment purposes would be made available to program participants, union, and management personnel only in raw, uninterpreted, and unanalyzed form. ISR also agreed to draft a disclosure agreement that would consider the needs of both parties. This document was completed on March 11. In it, ISR gave FoodCom the right to review and approve publication of proprietary information that had previously been confidential. However, the assessors were free to publish their interpretations of any data they gathered, subject to company review for factual accuracy. Finally, ISR agreed that it would not provide assessment data simply to serve the publicity needs of NQWC.

Introducing the Program in Gorland

On March 12 Mills went to Gorland to meet with local labor and management representatives, and on March 20 he returned to Gorland with an employee who had been involved in the Rushton quality of work experiment (Goodman 1979). That day the local union representing workers at the Gorland plant met to consider the FWIU's QWL proposal. Neither Mills nor the employee was given an opportunity to speak at this meeting. They were hooted from the speaker's platform. A vote on whether to participate in the program was overwhelmingly negative.

Numerous explanations were given for the vote. Kochems reported that some employees believed that the idea had been sprung on the local people too abruptly and that it had not been introduced properly. Some thought that members of the local may have resented the union and the company presenting the program as locally controlled when the local people had been given no part in it up to this point. Others believed that the resistance was racially motivated. The plant had been the site of racially related union unrest in 1969, and some union members believed the QWL program was a device to change racial attitudes and perceptions. Others believed the problem arose from internal local union politics.

The plant manager in Gorland, Cy O'Neil, was surprised by the outcome of the vote and tried to find out what had happened. He heard that some employees thought the program was a company trick. They had heard that NQWC had received funds from the Ford Foundation, which indicated to them that the program had the support of big business. Other employees had heard that the experiment would require that they work in teams and that they would therefore be pressured to "rat" on their fellow workers.

Resistance apparently wasn't restricted to union members. Some supervisors believed that the selection of the Gorland plant reflected badly on them. They assumed that if top management had selected Gorland for a labor-management relations improvement project, they were seen as having poor relations with their workers. Whatever the real cause, O'Neil concluded, the vote could have gone the other way had there been more "preselling" to both supervisors and union stewards. He believed that a major share of the blame therefore rested with the union: "This just points up how ineffective a union business manager can be . . . (It) happens all the time around here."

JQWLAC members speculated about whether the program could still be "sold" to the employees in Gorland, but generally agreed that such an attempt was likely to be counterproductive. They therefore decided to let the dust settle and to bide their time before looking for another site.

Different Perspectives Create Misunderstanding

When they discussed the proposed QWL program, the senior FoodCom line executives were almost exclusively concerned with control issues. Kochems tended to emphasize these concerns, but others shared similar views. Coy was worried that the program would escape his control. Pond speculated that the assessment methodology would be insufficiently rigorous and poorly informed. How could he determine whether the program had been a success unless program activities could be tightly linked to productivity increases in the form of indicators like pounds produced per labor hour? In general, the focus of top management seemed to rest upon what could go wrong rather than what could go right. They treated the program as a threat rather than an opportunity (Dutton and Jackson 1987; Frederickson 1985; Gooding 1989; Jackson and Dutton 1988).

Since the evaluation team was not allowed to visit the Gorland plant before the critical meeting, the perspectives of employees in the Gorland plant are difficult to document. According to the reports, however, there were many different points of view. Some employees seemed to view the program as a threat, and others thought the Gorland plant had been selected because of its weaknesses rather than its strengths. Still others felt the program was a trick. Whatever the perspective, however, employees responded negatively to the QWL program proposal.

There is little evidence that JQWLAC members felt tension between their planning activities and the voluntary nature of the QWL program. Like the staff members handing over the program to line personnel, they did not see any contradiction in designing a voluntary program for others to "own." The solution, therefore, seemed to lie in establishing better communication so that employees would be able to see what the program was really all about. JQWLAC members appeared to assume implicitly that everything would work out all right if employees viewed their work and the workplace in the same way JQWLAC did and that grassroots education would harmonize the different perspectives by introducing employees to the "right" viewpoint.

Applying the Generic Model of Problem Solving

The general model of problem solving presented in the previous chapter (Figure 1-1) might help illumine the basic issues. The specific application of this model is presented in Figure 2-2. The proposed QWL Program openly advocated greater labor-management cooperation as the desirable condition. Increased productivity and a higher quality of work life were the expected outcomes of this condition. The proposed program also clearly specified the local joint labor-management committee as the means for realizing labor-management cooperation. The committee was to make choices and take actions that would achieve

Figure 2-2 Application of the Problem-Solving Model to Explain the Failure in Gorland

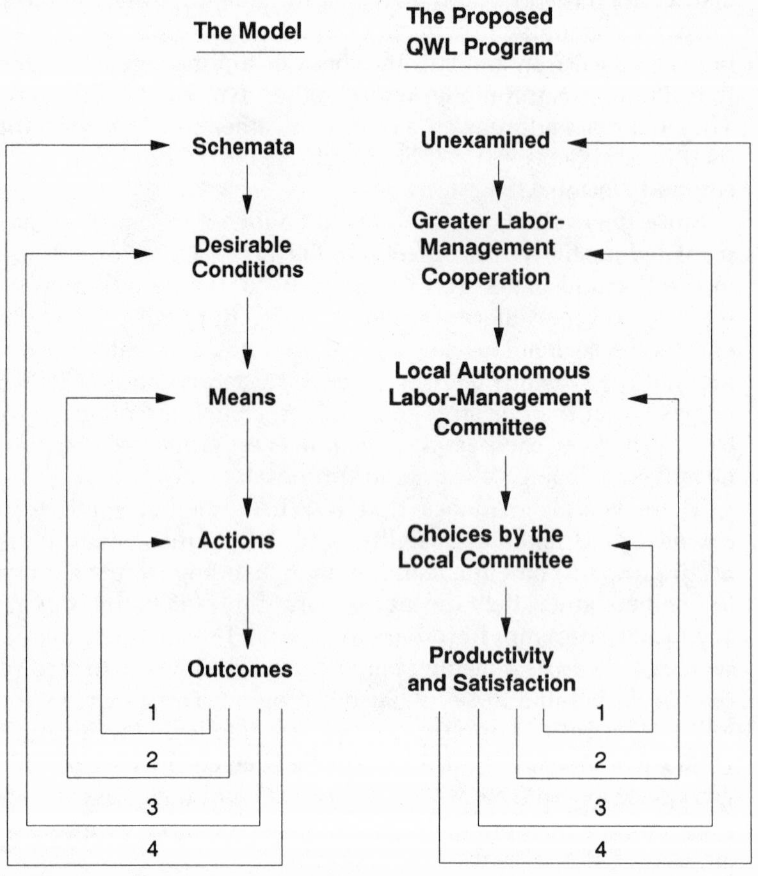

both increased productivity and an improved quality of life at work.

Information provided to workers at the Gorland plant, however, was incomplete. The local committee should have had discretion to change program activities on the basis of committee members' evaluation of the effectiveness of earlier actions (arrow 1). However, there was no provision for the Gorland Plant employees to change the local committee as a means (arrow 2) or labor-management cooperation as the desired condition (arrow 3). The proposed program implicitly assumed that greater cooperation was desirable and that a local joint labor-management committee operating on the basis of JQWLAC specifications was the best way to facilitate this cooperation. It is not surprising, therefore, that the proposal was understood by at least some participants as having been imposed from above, despite the clearly expressed intention that the local committee would have discretion to take whatever actions it deemed appropriate.

The greatest uncertainty, however, seemed to lie at the schematic level. Many employees in Gorland interpreted the program in ways JQWLAC members had not imagined. Employees whose perspectives highlighted racial issues were wary of a program that advocated greater cooperation. Likewise, those who viewed the proposal as a plan advocated by big business assumed that there was a hidden agenda and that cooperation would somehow be inconsistent with their own interests. For them the program was a company trick. Moreover, there was no provision for changing the means or the desired ends, once what they saw as the real purpose became clear. All the participants could do was stop the program entirely once it had begun. After the dust from Gorland had settled, JQWLAC members decided that their actions had to change and that they would have to do more selling if they wanted the program to be accepted. However, there was no reassessment of the means or desired conditions. There was also no indication that JQWLAC members were even aware of schematic differences between themselves and the employees in Gorland, as well as differences among themselves.

Disagreement over the appointment of Premater to the core group was symptomatic of opposing labor and management perspectives within the JQWLAC. The management representatives also seemed to be divided among themselves. Seldon appreciated the potential for greater labor-management cooperation, and Kochems saw the possibility for greater control. Quin was concerned exclusively about the impact of the program on productivity; he gave no consideration to employee satisfaction and the quality of working life in the plant. Division President Struthers saw an inconsistency between participation in the program and the traditional adversarial approach to labor-management relations. When forced to choose between the two, he opted for the traditional approach by deciding not to participate as a member of JQWLAC. Even Mills appeared to waver between two visions of the role of the core group with respect to the local committee. He openly advocated autonomy for the local committee, but alternated between calling JQWLAC a core group and a steering committee. He also did not confront JQWLAC members when they made important decisions that they had relegated to the local committee to decide.

These schemata held by the JQWLAC members generated widely differing interpretations of the program, some of which appeared incompatible with one another and even with the program itself. Introducing the project into a new plant, therefore, might raise many of the same problems and issues encountered in Gorland. New actions would be taken: Specifically, JQWLAC members and local participants would do a better selling job. However, the proposed program and the underlying differences in interpretation would remain the same.

At this point, it is not possible to determine whether the JQWLAC should have exhibited greater insight and flexibility. Achieving the capacity to question basic assumptions or perspectives is a very difficult and time-consuming task. In the early stages of project development, it was still possible for the program (once accepted at a site) to generate experiences that could help participants learn to reevaluate their assumptions. Whether or not this would occur, however, remained to be seen, because the program was rejected at Gorland.

3

Orchestrating Agreement

After the debacle in Gorland, Mills took less direct responsibility for the project. His role fell to Tim Deigh, a human resources consultant who joined NQWC as an associate director. Deigh's first assignment was to pick up the pieces of the FoodCom project. Scigliano began to informally assess the receptivity of union locals at different plant sites. In July, he told Deigh that employees in the Reginal plant were likely to favor the project but that initial contacts with the Reginal local should go through the international union. He advised Deigh not to speak directly with the people in Reginal.

Designing an Effective Strategy for Entry

On August 17, 1976, Deigh met with FoodCom officials at their corporate headquarters. All agreed that the program should be restarted. Deigh sought to expand the role of the NQWC to include process consultation with the local committee. Seldon was supportive, but Coy insisted that the NQWC maintain its quality control role. He wanted Deigh to monitor the process consultation activities, not to engage in them directly.

Deigh called for a JQWLAC meeting on September 27. By then the members generally assumed that the QWL program would be restarted in Reginal. During the meeting, the committee acquiesced to Coy's wishes by agreeing that the NQWC would not involve itself with process consultation at the new site. Deigh then suggested five consulting firms that NQWC thought could be effective. Two of these were rejected outright, but Deigh agreed to schedule presentations from the other three for the next meeting.

The JQWLAC members then turned their attention to developing an effective entry strategy. Timing would be important. First they would send letters to all the workers in the Reginal plant. The letters would be mailed November 2 and arrive November 4. Also on November 4, Deigh and the FWIU representatives to JQWLAC would meet with the local union membership. At the same time, the management representatives would meet with all plant supervisors. Both meetings would be billed purely as efforts to communicate. No decisions would be made. Deigh and the FWIU officers would meet with local union officers and stewards on November 5 and the FoodCom representatives would concurrently meet with the plant manager and department superintendents. Again, however, no decisions would be made. The meetings were intended to describe the nature and purpose of the proposed QWL program.

Introducing the Proposed Program in Reginal

Events followed the proposed script, more or less. Scigliano drafted a letter to local union members, which he sent to JQWLAC members for their comments and to George Newman, the local FWIU business agent in Reginal. It was subsequently revised and then sent out with Newman's signature (Exhibit 3-1).

Deigh arrived in Reginal the evening of Thursday, November 3. He huddled immediately with Seldon and Miles Farr, Coy's counterpart who had regional jurisdiction over the Reginal plant. Although Farr was not a member of JQWLAC, he had been the plant manager in Reginal before his promotion to regional manager and was generally reputed to have good relationships with plant personnel. Farr brought Roger Matson, the plant manager in Reginal.

EXHIBIT 3-1 Revised Letter to Union Members Concerning the QWL Program Proposed for the Reginal Plant

TO: All Members of Local No. 50 Employed at FOODCOM:

During contract negotiations between FoodCom and the Food Workers' International Union, AFL-CIO, in August and September of 1975, the FWIU proposed the idea of a job enrichment program. During the course of those negotiations the Company and the Union agreed to establish a joint committee to discuss job enrichment.

Based on this agreement, the National Quality of Work Center was contacted for assistance in developing such a project.

The National Quality of Work Center (NQWC) is a non-profit, non-governmental organization based in Washington, D.C., whose primary purpose is the development of joint labor-management efforts to improve the quality of life at work for all employees—supervisors, managers, union stewards, and employees alike and, thereby, improve the effectiveness and satisfaction of all involved in an organization.

With the assistance of the NQWC, top FWIU officials and top FoodCom management officials have established a Joint Quality of Work Life Advisory Committee (JQWLAC) composed of Executive Vice President Edward Scigliano, Vice President Donald Premater and Research Director John Papp from the FWIU and Dalmar Pond, Horace Seldon, and William Coy from FoodCom.

The purpose of the JQWLAC is to provide advice, assistance, and endorsement where needed for the activities of quality of work life improvement efforts—efforts that may occur within the Bakery Division of FoodCom.

The JQWLAC has already agreed in writing to the following guarantees if such a project is conducted:

- no employee (including supervisors and managers) will lose his or her job, status or pay as a result of any quality of work life improvement effort;
- the Union or the Company may stop the project at any time with a 24-hour notice;
- any and all actions that may result from a project would absolutely have to be approved by the Union and the Company before it is implemented;

- nothing arising out of the kind of activity being considered would in any way detract from the collective bargaining agreement between the Company and the Union.
- no one would be forced to accept or agree with any aspect of the project that is under consideration.

The important thing to be remembered is that the kinds of activities that are being considered can only be successful if those involved consider the effort to be worthwhile and understand that no one loses in the process.

We feel that this project under consideration can result in improvements that benefit everyone. However, no action can, or will, be initiated in the Reginal plant without the full understanding and acceptance of the members of Local No. 50.

To enable all of us to gain a complete understanding of what is being considered and provide ample opportunity for exposure to this program, our International Committee, along with your local officers, will meet with the shop stewards on Friday, November 5. Mr. Tim Deigh from the national Quality of Work Center will also be present at this meeting. Mr. Deigh will then be visiting in the plant the following two or three weeks to answer any questions the membership may have.

Before we embark on this program, we will schedule a membership meeting to decide whether we wish to participate.

I trust this letter outlines the procedure we will follow and with kindest regards, I am,

Fraternally and sincerely yours,

George Newman,
Business Agent

Deigh argued that Matson should play a central role in presenting the program to supervision so that the project would appear as locally motivated as possible. Because he had a strong local identity, Farr would also be valuable. Coy and Seldon, on the other hand, were seen only as national-level figures. During the presentations the next day, therefore, they would make a few introductory comments and then "take a walk," as Deigh put it, in order to "maintain the aura of a Reginal bakery-owned project as opposed to a corporate-imposed project." Although Coy did not arrive until later that night, he was informed of these tactical arrangements during a breakfast meeting.

After breakfast, Deigh and the FoodCom executives met with Reginal management. These local managers included Matson; Billy Youngman, the assistant manager; Greg Charlton, the personnel director; Carl Schwab, the office manager; and four of the five department superintendents. These four were Keith Pacheco, head of the maintenance department; Vince Keeley, superintendent of the assembly and baking department; Leonard Duffield, head of the packing department; and Russ Drisko, superintendent of the warehouse. Mark Dalton, the sanitation superintendent, was on vacation. Matson introduced Miles Farr, who provided a brief history of the QWL program and acted as moderator. He explained that the proposed project was part of a companywide movement toward more participative management. He then introduced Seldon, who offered to answer questions in the labor-relations area. Coy then described his role as liaison between the QWL project and national-level officers.

Deigh provided the Reginal management with a more detailed history of the project, including the problems encountered in Gorland. He described the proposed local labor-management committee, the role of the on-site intern, and the proposed assessment activities. He then offered the Reginal representatives a chance to ask questions. Youngman said he believed that by selecting the Reginal plant, JQWLAC was hinting that the plant was somehow in trouble and needed help. Farr countered with the explanation that the Reginal plant had been selected precisely because it was not in trouble. Participative management, he argued, was not a method for solving difficult labor-relations problems, but for preventing such problems from arising in the first place. Local management was also concerned that the proposal lacked content and didn't give them anything concrete. Deigh responded that specific QWL activities would be identified as the program went along.

Later that afternoon, Deigh met with George Newman, the local union business agent, and Kevin McCue, the local union president. Scigliano and Papp, who had not yet come to Reginal, did not attend (Premater did not come at all at this time). Newman and McCue immediately asked whether members of other unions could participate in the proposed program. Newman was particularly concerned that employees in the maintenance department be involved. The machinists in that department were represented by the International Machinists' Union, and the electricians were members of the International Electricians' Union. Deigh called Matson and asked him to arrange a meeting with officers of the IMU and IEU locals for the following week.

Deigh then told Newman that the members of the International Distribution Union (IDU) in the distribution center at the Reginal plant would not be asked to participate. Distribution was physically separated from the rest of the activities in Reginal, and more importantly, the relationship between the company and the IDU was not stable enough to support QWL activities at that time. Six months previously, for example, an IDU union steward had shot both the manager and a foreman of the distribution center. Deigh suggested that QWL activities be proposed for the distribution center at a later, more appropriate time.

Deigh was assuming that the QWL proposal would be put to the union membership for a vote and that union representatives to the committee would be elected. Newman and McCue argued that, as officers of the local union, they should decide whether the union would participate in the program. They also thought they were in the best position to select union representatives to the committee because they knew who would make the most constructive contributions. Rather than confront Newman and McCue at this time Deigh decided it would be best to postpone the issue. Scigliano and the other union officers were not there to support his case, and he did not believe he was in a position to press for his ideas over Newman's and McCue's opposition.

Deigh met with sixteen line supervisors at 7:30 Friday morning. Half of them were arriving for the morning shift, and the other half had just completed night duty. At 12:30 he met with twelve first-shift supervisors, and at 2:00 he displace to work. He wanted to convince the stewards that the program would make their jobs easier. He insisted that they, the local employees, were the experts, and he argued that program staff members would simply be resources the employees could call upon for assistance. The program would neither usurp their prerogatives nor provide line employees with an alternative to the standard grievance procedure.

The stewards were not yet convinced. Several stewards asked who would pay the union members for the time they would spend representing workers on the local committee. Deigh responded that the union representatives would be paid by the international union, not from local union dues. Some suspected that the twenty-four hour cancellation clause gave the company an easy way to stop the program, but their colleagues pointed out that the union would get the same right. Still others believed that the JQWLAC would act as a restraining force for both sides, precluding premature cancellation of the project.

His meetings concluded, Deigh returned to his office in Washington. Although he had not yet met directly with regular line employees or with representatives from the machinists' and electricians' unions, he was satisfied that he had done all he could to educate Reginal management and local FWIU officials. He scheduled a JQWLAC meeting for the next Thursday, November 11, and hoped to present an optimistic report.

Deigh returned to Reginal on Monday, November 8, and spent time between 11:00 A.M. that day and the swing shift Wednesday talking directly with regular line employees. Not wishing to appear aligned with management, he asked to be introduced to workers by FWIU stewards. Many workers had not received the letters that had been mailed the week before, and quite a few of those who had were suspicious. For example, some feared that the program was intended to overcome employee resistance to a line speed-up. Employees also voiced several complaints about the company and about their local union officers, especially about Newman. Deigh speculated that a new business agent might not be as resistant as Newman to electing, rather than appointing, QWL committee members.

cussed the QWL project with fourteen second-shift superviso who had come to work early for the meeting. Roger Matsc started each meeting by noting that the proposed program wa consistent with his personal philosophy. He stressed that th more participative approach had the support of both manag ment and the union. Miles Farr spoke next. He outlined th history of the project and introduced Seldon and Coy, wh told the supervisors that, should they decide to participate i the program, they would have upper-management support As planned, Seldon and Coy then left the meeting as Far introduced Deigh.

Several of the supervisors wondered why the program hac been proposed for Reginal, claiming "we're a well-run bakery now." Deigh, like Farr before him, stressed that the QWL program was designed to prevent problems from occurring, not to address problems after they had surfaced. When some supervisors wanted to know how representatives to the QWL committee would be selected, Deigh emphasized that this decision would be left to them.

Later that morning, George Newman introduced Deigh to the union stewards and members of the local's executive board. Thirty-three of a possible thirty-five stewards and board members attended, along with Scigliano and Papp. Newman opened the meeting by telling the stewards that the proposed program was designed by FoodCom and the FWIU in response to suggestions made by their own local during previous contract negotiations. Next, Scigliano provided a brief history of the project and introduced Papp, who made supportive remarks and introduced Deigh.

After a brief presentation in which he outlined the roles of the proposed committee and the outside consultants, Deigh asked if his audience had any questions. The stewards echoed many of the concerns raised by supervisors the day before. "Why pick on us?" someone asked. Hadn't they been doing an adequate job representing the membership and adjudicating grievances? What had they been doing wrong? Deigh again explained that they were doing an excellent job and that the program had been designed to make FoodCom an even better

Deigh returned to Washington Wednesday evening. He had not yet spent time with maintenance personnel. His discussions, however, had led him to appreciate the central role of the maintenance department. The plant was highly mechanized, and the machinists and electricians were the only ones who could keep the machinery operating. If the QWL program initiated activities involving any of the mechanical apparatus in the plant, they would need the machinists' and the electricians' cooperation.

The Vote

JQWLAC members, with the exception of Papp (who had a prior commitment), met in the FWIU offices in Washington on November 11. The assessment coordinator, Michael Moch, was present to discuss evaluation procedures. With Deigh's recommendation, those present tentatively decided to call for a plant-wide vote on QWL program participation on Saturday, December 4. They also interviewed representatives from two firms that were candidates for the consulting contract and received documentation on a third consulting company.

JQWLAC members worried that they could not afford another rejection of the QWL proposal. It was essential that there be no surprises when the vote came. Accordingly, Deigh returned to Reginal on Tuesday, November 16, and made himself available to employees through Thursday, November 18. Although his discussions in Reginal reassured him that the proposed program would be accepted, he was troubled by what seemed to be unrealistic employee attitudes. Several employees came to see him with the apparent expectation that he would resolve a variety of long-standing disputes and grievances, including pension management issues, line speeds, the lack of job rotation, and supervisor favoritism. He was even asked to make changes in the required uniforms. Deigh tried to explain that he could not resolve these issues: Some of them would be the job of the QWL committee, but others could only be handled through the established collective bargaining process.

Employees' suspicion that the program was a cover for a management-directed line speed-up persisted, and several workers expressed distrust of their local union officers. Such comments reinforced Deigh's commitment to provide direct elections for union representatives to the local committee. Newman continued to resist this, arguing that the committee had to be workable. It could not be composed entirely of "radicals." When Deigh told him that a vote had been scheduled for December 4, Newman began to support the idea of elections if they involved stratification by department or shift or both. These divisions would ensure that the committee would reflect what he considered to be balanced viewpoints.

Deigh scheduled a meeting with Rich Hoban, the IMU business agent, for Wednesday. Hoban could not show up, so he sent David Lewis, an IMU steward. Deigh described the proposed program, but Lewis saw absolutely no need for maintenance employees to participate. The next day Deigh tracked down Andy Gleason, the IMU's chief steward. Gleason told him he had heard that the program had been designed to provide management with a way to communicate directly with workers without going through the union officers. Deigh tried to convince him that participation would enhance, rather than undermine, the position of IMU stewards. Gleason was also concerned lest he find himself outvoted in a forum intended to allocate jobs to members of different unions. He did not want the FWIU to absorb IMU functions in the plant. Although the meeting was cordial, Deigh made no progress in gaining IMU participation in the QWL program.

When he returned to Washington, Deigh reported to Food-Com management that there was a high probability that the FWIU employees in Reginal would agree to participate. However, there was some resistance among lower-level supervisors. In addition, the "prima donna" attitude of the craftsmen would probably keep them out of the program. He recommended that a meeting be called with the lower-level supervisors on December 3, the day before the proposed FWIU vote, to address their concerns. In addition, to be absolutely certain that the vote would be positive, Deigh would attend the FWIU meeting and put the vote to the members only "if the mood of the meeting seems to indicate high likelihood of success."

Deigh flew to Reginal on Thursday, December 2. Because he anticipated a positive vote, he first went to a local university to interview candidates for the assistant coordinator position. He then went to the plant, where he spent the next several hours talking with line employees in the plant cafeteria and on the shop floor.

Early the next morning, Matson introduced Deigh to fourteen first- and third-shift supervisors who told Deigh that the success of the program would depend upon the support of the craft unions. Deigh said that the craft unions might be more inclined to participate after they had seen the program in action. The discussion then focused on how supervisory representatives to the QWL committee should be selected. One supervisor suggested representatives be selected by lot from a list of volunteers. Ten of the fourteen supervisors present volunteered, and all expressed their support for the program. Matson recorded the names of the volunteers.

Next, Matson convened a meeting of the top management personnel in the plant. Initially, several managers complained to Deigh that the program seemed "a one-way street" designed to help lower-level employees without doing anything for management. One participant said he believed that the program could help but that he was having difficulty convincing his foremen. Several thought the local committee could become a forum for grievances. For this reason, the management group suggested that union stewards and employees in the personnel department, including Greg Charlton, be barred from serving as QWL committee representatives. Finally, they emphasized their belief that the craft unions should be represented on the plant committee. Eventually, all those present expressed their support for the proposed program, and Matson took the names of those willing to serve on the local committee.

Deigh then met with additional groups of supervisors and discussed the same issues. Supervisors at a 12:30 meeting suggested that, if the craft unions refused to participate as full-fledged committee members, perhaps they would accept observer status. Almost all of those who attended these meetings expressed support for the program. Matson took the names of those willing to serve on the QWL committee. Altogether, the opinions of forty-five members of supervision were solicited. Of these, twenty-seven were willing to serve on the committee.

After all the planning that had gone into it, the FWIU meeting was a bit of an anticlimax. Only five percent of the union members attended. Newman pointed out, however, that this was twice the attendance of a normal meeting. Eighty-five percent of those attending voted to participate in the QWL program. Within two weeks, an unsigned notice was posted in the plant describing how union representatives were to be selected. This notice is presented as Exhibit 3-2. It was still undecided how management representatives would be chosen.

EXHIBIT 3-2 Procedures for Selecting Union Members for the Local QWL Project Committee

At the specially called meeting of Local No. 50 on Saturday, December 4, the majority of those members present voted to begin the quality of working life (job-enrichment) program as soon as possible. The next step in getting the program started is the election of union representatives to serve on the joint labor-management committee.

A total of seven (7) union representatives will be elected—three from the Packaging Department (one from each shift); two from the Bake Shop (one from first shift and one from the second and third shift together); one from the Environmental Services Department; and one from the Warehouse and Shipping Department.

An election will be held next week on company time in the bakery by departments and shifts. Representatives from the union for the joint labor-management committee do not have to be Stewards or Union officers.

Forms have been posted below to request the names of both volunteers to serve on this joint committee and the names of employees that you might like to nominate to serve on the committee. These forms will be removed from the bulletin board on December 17. Each person who is nominated will be contacted to see whether or not he/she would be willing to serve on the committee if elected.

The names of those nominated (volunteers and nominees willing to serve) will be typed into a slate for each department/shift for the election next week. When the election is held, the person receiving the most votes from that department/shift will be that department's/shift's representative with the person receiving the next most votes serving as the alternate representative for the department/ shift.

The names of those representatives/alternates elected will be posted by December 20 so that the entire membership can be made aware of the newly elected union committee members. The first joint committee meeting will be held in early January.

Imposing A Voluntary Program:
A Real Dilemma or Poor Practice?

In the previous chapter we discussed the different perspectives of the JQWLAC and NQWC staff members. Even more numerous differences were present at the local level. With the possible exception of Matson, local management saw little need for the program. In fact, they seemed offended by the implication that they could be doing a better job. Although most supervisors said they supported the program at the public discussions, their support may have been more superficial than real. Matson, the plant manager, was a vocal proponent of the program and was present at the meetings.

Local union personnel also had a mixed response. The local FWIU president and business agent clearly perceived a threat to their positions. They believed themselves to be pressured by radical elements who were only too happy to use the program as a forum from which to criticize union leadership. Officers of the IMU local saw the program as an unwelcome alternative to the traditional advocacy relationship mediated by union stewards and were concerned that the program might dilute their influence over job allocation to different departments. The rank and file FWIU members seemed more positively disposed, but appeared to view the program as a means for redressing past and current grievances. These views offered a stark contrast to national management's exclusive concern with the bottom line and with local management's and stewards' contentions that labor relations in the plant could be effectively handled without resorting to a QWL program.

As the preceding material suggests, each of the different groups at Reginal appeared to be operating on the basis of its own differing schema. Schematic differences generated different interpretations of the desirable conditions, the means, and the outcomes expected from the program. They also generated differing expectations of the relationship between particular means and outcomes. In addition, none of these diverse perspectives seemed completely consistent with the QWL program as Deigh understood it.

In Chapter Two we introduced the problem solving model that guided the QWL interventions. As our descriptions in this chapter of the various schemata held by different groups indicate, the model we presented is only one of several such models (or, more properly, "cognitive maps," of QWL interventions, cf. Bougon, Weick, and Binkhorst 1977; Weick and Bougon 1986) that could be constructed. Many of the groups at the Reginal bakery seemed to have their own cognitive maps of the intervention—their own perspectives on its conditions, means, actions, and the relationships among these factors.

In this chapter and in Chapter Four we will compare the QWL designers' map of such interventions with the alternative maps apparently held by different participants in the FoodCom QWL experiment. We begin the process in this chapter by contrasting the perspectives of some of the management members of JQWLAC with that held by Deigh. These proposed models are presented in Figure 3-1.

Both models appear to posit that increased cooperation between labor and management is a desirable condition (a). They agree that a means for realizing such cooperation is a functioning labor-management committee that will make choices and take actions (b) to improve employee productivity (c) and satisfaction (d). The models also agree that more satisfied employees are likely to be more productive (e). Both models also appear to assume that labor-management committee choices that increase productivity will positively reinforce or legitimize the local committee's activities (f) and the local committee itself (g), and facilitate labor-management cooperation (h).

Figure 3-1 Alternative Conceptions of How the QWL Program at FoodCom Would Work

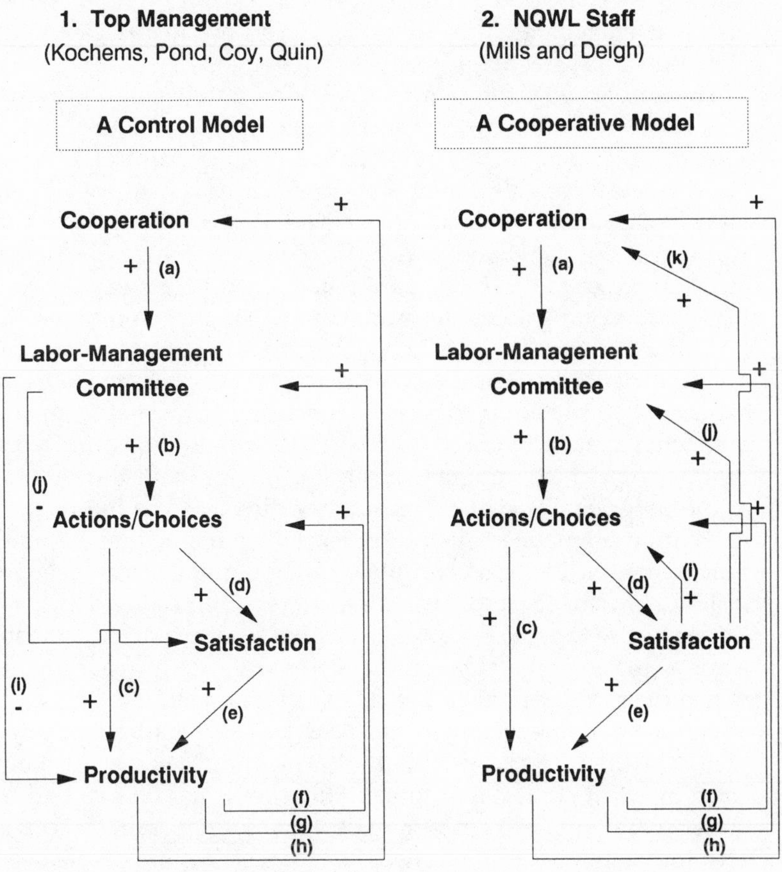

In at least two respects, however, the two models in Figure 3-1 are different. The NQWC cooperative model assumes that both productivity and employee satisfaction are valuable outcomes and will reinforce labor management cooperation (k), the labor-management committee (j), and the actions the committee takes (i). It specifies, in other words, that satisfaction is a separate and distinct outcome of the QWL program and that the program should be assessed, in part, on the basis of its contribution to the quality of work life of the company's employees. There are no such feedback loops in the top management control model.

Quin explicitly stated that productivity was the only criterion upon which the QWL program should be evaluated. We might infer that satisfaction is a desired outcome; however, from the perspective of top management, this would be true only to the extent that increases in satisfaction lead to productivity gains.

The second way the two models differ is reflected in the negative arrows (i) and (j) in the top management control model. Coy insisted that NQWC maintain its quality control function. He restricted Deigh's initial site access in order to avoid what he thought might be negative consequences. Kochems, Coy, and Pond insisted that FoodCom be given control over the release of QWL program information. Kochems had earlier expressed an interest in gaining access to productivity data that would be invulnerable to tampering by plant management. Top company management had been entrusted with the QWL program and were expected to bring it to a successful conclusion. This meant insuring that actions taken by the local committee would lead to increased productivity. If the program got out of control and the presence of the program decreased productivity directly (i) or indirectly by decreasing employee satisfaction (j), either the actions (f) or the functioning of the local committee (g) would have to be changed. Failing either of these alternatives, decreasing productivity might lead to reassessment of the desirability of labor-management cooperation (h), and create a negative cycle that would make matters worse than they had been before the program started.

Perhaps the management believed that this had already happened in the Gorland plant, thus explaining top management's concern about control in Reginal. However, this concern had few outlets within the QWL program as it had been initially conceived. The intervention design called for the establishment of a local committee that was independent of outside labor or management control. Top managers had been given the responsibility by their superiors for making the QWL program succeed. However, they were officially prevented from exercising control over the activities of the local committee, and, should they attempt to do so, could be held responsible for any program failures.

Some of the dominant themes of other participants' models of how the QWL program might work were becoming visible in Deigh's initial interviews. Some supervisors and stewards appeared to view the program as a threat rather than as an opportunity. In addition, IMU and possibly IEU union officers seemed to feel that cooperation itself could have negative consequences, at least for them.

A Strategy for Achieving Program Acceptance

Deigh faced a challenging task. His strategy seemed to be to get the program underway and then to negotiate a consistent set of perspectives as part of the intervention process. In the absence of a clear consensus, he orchestrated the agreement to start the process by using several tools to challenge problematic alternative conceptions of how the proposed program would operate. These tools included linguistic framing, timing, the manipulation of symbols, and coercion (e.g., Allen and Porter 1983; Moch and Fields 1985; Pondy et al. 1983). Following Farr's lead, Deigh tried to reframe the program by arguing that, far from being an implicit reprimand, the program was a compliment to the quality of Reginal's labor relations. In his conversation with Gleason, he did not deny that the QWL program would facilitate direct labor-management contact. He redirected the conversation, however, by emphasizing that the program would enhance rather than undermine union influence.

Timing was also important. Because Scigliano and Papp had not yet arrived when the meeting with Newman and McCue took place, Deigh did not initially press the issue of whether the union representatives should be elected or appointed. He successfully postponed consideration of this matter until he could be sure it would be resolved to his satisfaction. Confronting those who were concerned about the lack of program content, he argued that the content would become clear after the program began. He used the same argument to allay fears that the QWL committee would help lower-level personnel but not address top management problems. Top managers, he argued, would see things differently after the program got underway. Finally, he was prepared to postpone voting on the program if it appeared the vote might not go his way.

By placing Farr, Matson, and Newman in central positions in local meetings for their respective constituencies, Deigh symbolically communicated that the QWL program was driven by local initiative. The orchestrated exits of Coy and Seldon were designed to further this impression, with the additional benefit that Farr replaced the less enthusiastic Coy as the local employees' link to national level management. Similarly, the letter to union members, drafted by Scigliano, was sent out over Newman's signature. The vote itself had considerable symbolic significance, signaling local control even though only five percent of the FWIU members were present. The vote was communicated in percentage terms (eighty-five percent) rather than in absolute numbers.

Finally, the evidence suggests that some of Deigh's activities were coercive. Having secured Scigliano's support, he simply told Newman that there would be a vote on whether to proceed with the program. He used the authority of JQWLAC to announce that the IDU members would not participate in the program, despite a commitment to allow the local committee to make such decisions. Finally, we suspect that Deigh drafted the document specifying how union members were to be elected to the QWL committee. This presented Newman and McCue, who opposed any form of elections, with a fait accompli.

We concluded the previous chapter by claiming that, despite the events in Gorland, NQWC and JQWLAC members were still prepared to impose what they were labeling as a voluntary program. Although they were prepared to grant local people autonomy with respect to specific actions, their proposal did not allow employees at the site to alter the program's means (the local committee structure) or desired conditions (greater labor-management cooperation). In Reginal, without changing their problem solving model (Figure 2-2), JQWLAC members demonstrated much more sophisticated planning and execution. Largely due to Deigh's initiative in meeting with large numbers of personnel, they succeeded in enacting local support and, through the voting procedure, the perception of local ownership of a program designed elsewhere. In the process, the concerns of those who thought the local committee was an inappropriate means or that greater labor-management cooperation was not needed either went unheeded or were postponed.

THE DILEMMA OF ACHIEVING ACCEPTANCE OF PROGRAMS NOT INITIALLY UNDERSTOOD

Unlike many organizational changes that essentially focus on more effective actions toward achieving already agreed-upon goals, QWL programs are expected to lead participants to operate out of a new perspective. These programs introduce a qualitatively new way of understanding labor-management relationships (cf. Mohrman and Lawler 1985). Thus, such programs are not likely to be understood by potential participants who simply do not have the experience required to grasp the proposed alternative. Were program leaders to attempt direct communication at this point, as they did at Gorland, participants would view the intervention in terms of the multiple and perhaps conflicting perspectives the programs are designed to change or transcend.

Given the differing perspectives of program designers and potential participants, how should QWL programs (or similar programs) be introduced? Deigh's implicit strategy was apparently based on the following assumptions: (1) In order for initial acceptance to occur, QWL programs may have to be initially "sold" to differing subgroups of participants using linguistic and political strategies that take cognizance of the critical differences among the contracting parties (cf. Brown and Covey 1987); (2) QWL programs may have to be implemented before local participants can fully appreciate the program's true nature and function.

The need to deal with multiple perspectives has rarely been discussed in the OD literature. Instead, OD practitioners have typically used a collegial/consensus model that ignores differing subgroup interests in organizations (cf. Brown and Covey 1987; Greiner and Schein 1988) and implicitly assumes agreement (and, thus, shared schemata) between consultants and clients regarding the overall outcomes to be achieved by the intervention. This assumption of overall goal congruence enables consensus-oriented participation in decision making to be the major tool for OD consultants (cf. French and Bell 1984; Vroom and Jago 1988).

The existence of multiple perspectives, all of which differ from the QWL perspective, places change agents in a serious dilemma. If agents restrict their interventions to programs desired and understood by powerful local participants, they are likely to make the dominant subgroup perspectives even more entrenched (Ross 1971; Morgan 1984). This will increase alienation in other groups and foster attempts to undermine the intervention (Brown and Covey 1987). If the change agents attempt to help local participants change their operating assumptions, they must take some initiative in introducing other assumptions. But how can they do this and remain participative at the same time?

Deigh was moderately successful at addressing the multiple perspectives in the plant by obtaining support for the program from most of the subgroups. He achieved this by conducting separate meetings with the different groups and by emphasizing how the program would meet (or at least not interfere with) their own concerns. The major drawbacks of this strategy were (1) that participants were left with several different images of the program and (2) that everyone was presented with essentially positive feedback about current labor-management relations in the plant. This clearly contrasts both the model presented in Figure 1-1, which specifies that change is driven by negative feedback, and the usual assumption in OD/QWL that successful change requires initial "unfreezing."

The existence of differing perspectives between plant participants and program designers represented a more difficult dilemma in the FoodCom project. It appears that in dealing with these different perspectives, Deigh and the JQWLAC members may have been caught in a double bind (Watzlawik, Weakland, and Fisch 1974). Their desire to alter the nature of labor-management relations at FoodCom significantly was inconsistent with a common OD/QWL perspective that asserts that change should result from program participation rather than from imposition. Had they been operating out of a different, more adversarial perspective about the nature of change, they might have generated and implemented an alternative image of labor relations themselves and would have had no hesitation in imposing such an image. However, they wanted to change the traditional patterns and they believed that the alternative had to come from the subordinate system itself. They therefore ended up imposing a process for voluntarily changing the plant's rules of conduct.

We do not claim that the participants clearly understood the nature of this dilemma. Our own understanding has taken years to develop even though we were connected with the program as the assessors. Yet the participants clearly felt the tension, and much of the rest of the FoodCom-FWIU story revolves around how that tension was (and was not) managed. The dilemma is stated here in generic terms because it is not a phenomenon unique to FoodCom or the FWIU.

4

One Big Family

The Social and Technical Systems at Reginal

When it was built in 1949, the two-story Reginal bakery was state of the art. During the QWL intervention, however, it was still using essentially the same assembly-line production methods it had used when it opened. Production schedules detailing the amounts and types of products to be produced guided Carl Schwab's office staff as they ordered flour, sugar, salt, and other necessary ingredients. The materials arrived in Russ Drisko's warehouse department on the ground floor either at the truck dock or by rail.

Ingredients were vacuumed out of railroad cars that backed into the warehouse area on a dedicated siding. Pneumatic tubes then transported flour and other materials to humidity-controlled storage tanks located at one end of the plant. From there, the materials were put together in the assembly area. Most of the ingredients were mixed in large rotating mixers and vats using large auger-like devices. Specialty ingredients were added by hand in carefully measured amounts.

After water was added, the mixtures were poured into storage tubs that were then wheeled into a large enclosed room to allow the mixtures to rise. After rising, the material (now dough ready for baking) was rolled into a freight elevator for transport to the second floor. Here the dough was poured into large funnels that carried it back through the second floor into the tops of rolling and dough-cutting machines called laminators. Employees referred to these machines as " 'liminators," because they had replaced several manual jobs when they were introduced. The laminators were on the first floor and anchored one end of the ovens that stretched 300 feet before them. There were seven such ovens in the plant. The laminators placed pressed and cut dough onto conveyors that carried the products through each of a variety of baking, cooling, and drying processes. These activities were controlled by experienced bakers using a series of dials and manual controls located at various points along each oven's length.

Variations in the water content of the mixtures, plant humidity, oven temperature, and other factors could cause unacceptable variations in the baked goods. It was not unusual to have underdone or overdone material emerge from the oven. Such material had to be removed at that point as waste. Sam Pula's quality control staff therefore played an important role by testing mixture samples and reporting unacceptable variances to Vince Keeley, the baking department superintendent. Pula, a chemist, and Keeley, who had recently come to Reginal from the corporate research group, were trained technicians. Neither had had much experience in production or production management.

Once properly baked dough emerged from the ovens, the conveyors carried it through a thick insulating wall into Leonard Duffield's packaging area. Because the baked goods were perishable, packaging was an important function. The product had to be sealed as well as put into attractive protective boxes for shipping and display. Conveyors transported the baked goods to different packaging areas, depending upon the type of product. Some products were packed by hand by employees sitting on stools on either side of the conveyor. Other products were sealed into boxes by machines after other machines had lined the boxes with waxed paper.

The packaging machinery was unwieldy and often broke down. Employees seeking to fix it could be hurt: One employee was injured severely when her machine was restarted while she was attempting to realign the waxed paper being fed into it. The millwrights and electricians in the maintenance department therefore played a critical role by keeping the machinery in proper working order. They were also responsible for adjusting the machinery to produce and package different products. Because the bakery made more than thirty products and had only seven assembly, baking, and packaging lines, these adjustments occurred frequently. Keith Pacheco, the maintenance department superintendent, was having trouble getting the millwrights to respond to production requirements. Soon after the QWL program began, he was replaced in his position by Wally DeLeo. The plant could not afford the mechanical breakdowns or long down-times associated with unhappy mechanics.

Lines were also occasionally shut down for cleaning and health inspections conducted by workers from Mark Dalton's sanitation department. Dalton, like Leonard Duffield, assistant manager Youngman, and Matson, had spent his life in plant settings. These four were experienced production people.

The Social Organization of the Reginal Plant

With the exception of some affirmative action pressures, the plant seemed relatively unmoved by outside trends toward greater racial and sex equality. Blacks, replaced as bakers by white employees when the conveyor system made the baker's job attractive, seemed overrepresented in the sanitation department. Almost all of the nonsupervisory personnel in the packaging department were black or white women. Most of the bakers and assemblers and almost all of the electricians and machinists were white men.

Interaction patterns among the FoodCom employees reflected sex, race, level in the organization, and department affiliation. This was evident in the cafeteria during each of the plant's three shifts. Black, white, and Hispanic women sat on one side of the rectangular room near vending machines and a bank of pay telephones. Men from the baking department sat next to them but were located more toward the center of the room. White male machinists and electricians took up positions along the only wall that had windows, which was positioned at a right angle to the wall along which the vending machines and telephones were located.

The kitchen and serving line were across the room from the windows. Plant management, department heads, and an occasional white male foreperson or supervisor ate at tables closest to the kitchen area. Between them and the mechanics on the other side of the room, next to baking department personnel, sat blacks of all levels and both sexes. Although black women frequently ate with white and Hispanic women, the assessors saw only two white employees, both women, eating in the black area during the two-year period they observed the plant.

Seating patterns seemed to correspond to employees' feelings toward those of different sex and race. The machinists were frequently disdainful of female employees. When packaging equipment broke down, the women who were operating the machines would not call a male machinist for help, even if he were nearby or observing the breakdown. Machinists could be offended when asked to do something by a woman. If a woman were to initiate interaction with a machinist, therefore, it could forestall rather than hasten repair and hurt the packager's productivity in the process. Accordingly, the packaging employee would report any equipment malfunction to her supervisor who would ensure that a repair order would go through the proper channels. Eventually, the order would appear on a machinist's work schedule and the machinery would be repaired.

Maintenance workers told stories of how female employees in packaging would mishandle equipment and cause unnecessary breakdowns. They seemed to take particular delight in repairs that they could have completed quickly or ones that could have been accomplished by the packager herself if she had "had any sense at all." In these cases, delays caused by the scheduling process were attributed to packagers' ignorance or stupidity rather than to the machinists' reluctance to provide immediate assistance even if their assistance had been possible and practical at the time.

One frequently enacted ritual called for one machinist to tell another that he owned his own work tools. He then would ask how much the other machinist thought these tools were worth. After several low estimates, the first machinist would proclaim that his work tools were worth several thousand dollars. The machinists would then change roles, the second asking the first how much his tools were worth. After the second machinist proclaimed the true value of his tools, the first machinist would ask the second, "And what do the silly bitches carry in their purses?" Together the two participants would call out "Kotex!" Those listening, usually the employees sitting under the windows in the cafeteria, would smile and nod approval.

Bake shop personnel did not insist on as much deference from the packagers as those in the maintenance department did. Machinists criticized them for this, saying that the men in the bake shop were losing their manhood along with their superior income. Over two decades earlier, the machinists had been in the FWIU along with the bakers and packagers. At negotiation time, however, the women, who outnumbered the men, would vote for bargaining positions that favored absolute, rather than percentage, raises. Over time, the machinists could see that the substantial difference between their wages and the female packagers' wages would deteriorate. This was one reason that they subsequently left the FWIU to join the IMU. Their male counterparts in the bake shop showed no such concern. Consequently, they were nearing pay equity with women, a condition that was intolerable for the machinists.

Male employees in the bake shop, however, were not insensitive to the status difference that distinguished them from the female packagers. Packagers depended upon the bakers to provide packageable products. Because of the wall separating the baking and packaging departments, baking problems, such as burned or underdone products, would often be visible to packagers before the bakers knew anything was wrong. To alleviate this problem, each oven and associated packaging line was equipped with a telephone line that linked the bakers working the laminators with packagers at the far end of the packaging lines. However, female packagers seldom used these lines to inform laminators that they were producing bad products. They claimed that doing so would only make matters worse. The men receiving complaints would be offended at the indignity of taking orders from women. Consequently, packagers would either pack what they believed was a bad product or complain to their supervisor who would report to her supervisor until an appropriate male supervisor was found. This person then would contact his counterpart in the bake shop and attempt to rectify the situation.

Despite problems between bakers and packagers, relationships between FWIU members (bakers and packagers) on one hand and IMU machinists and IEU electricians on the other hand caused the most trouble. These problems were illustrated when FWIU personnel lobbied for a contract variance. They wanted to move the celebration of a local holiday from a Thursday to a Friday in order to have a three-day weekend. With official union support, they approached management. Because it was expensive to fire up ovens for only one day of operation, management quickly supported the idea. The FWIU and management then went together to the machinists.

The machinists, however, objected, saying they had not been consulted early enough in the process. If the FWIU and management could get together and successfully confront the machinists on this issue, what might happen when a more serious problem occurred? They were concerned that the FWIU, with management support, might force a plantwide vote that would change their union representation. They feared the FWIU would try to "recapture" them. They therefore felt compelled to reject any FWIU-management overture, including the request for a holiday change. Because many of their members really wanted a three-day holiday, the chief steward for the IMU local, Andy Gleason, chastised management and the FWIU for not allowing the machinists to initiate the idea.

Tensions among departments, races, sexes, and levels ran like fault lines through the plant's social fabric. In addition, the interests of senior workers frequently clashed with those of relative newcomers. George Newman, the FWIU business agent, lamented the loss of what he termed a "family atmosphere" in the plant. He had been with FoodCom twenty-four years. The first plant manager he knew had "operated the plant like it was his home . . . very firm . . . very fair." Over the last several years, however, affirmative action pressure had generated tensions between union officers and senior union members. In the FoodCom plant, in which sixty percent of the employees had more than fifteen years seniority, the effects were particularly severe.

In order to distribute jobs more equitably by sex and race, the union and company had confronted the seniority system. In the 1950s, seniority had been organized by department. At that time an employee in the disproportionately black sanitation department was not likely to bid for a more desirable job in the bake shop—even if he or she had been with the company for many years—because seniority was only allocated within departments. Likewise, a female packager was unlikely to apply for a job in the bake shop because changing departments meant losing seniority.

Within the packaging department, seniority had been based upon line assignment. In order to be reassigned to another line within the packaging department, an employee would have to start at the bottom of the seniority system on the new line. Consequently, it was very difficult to get women or blacks to apply for reassignments that required changes in departments or changes in line assignment within the packaging department. The introduction of plantwide seniority in the 1960s had helped resolve some of these issues and thus reduced sexual and racial inequality. However, as George Newman said, those employees who worked in a job for ten to twenty years tended to think they owned it. They did not give their jobs up easily when others with even more seniority bid on them. So although plantwide seniority helped resolve the structural problem, it left animosity and bitterness that undermined worker cohesiveness and mutual support.

Young workers were particularly demoralized. Not only were they the first to be laid off and the last to be rehired, but they were expected to wait ten to twenty years before they could bid on the best jobs. These workers therefore favored some form of job rotation. Older workers argued that they had put in their time and were entitled to the job preference they enjoyed, but Newman supported job rotation. He had also denied some senior employees the jobs they had bid for, claiming that they were trying to "bump" younger people simply to demonstrate their power and superiority. "I don't think seniority means you can have your cake and eat it too," he said.

Although Newman believed that the familial social climate in the plant had declined over the years, he nevertheless thought that the plant and the QWL program should be managed the same way parents should manage their children. He advised, "It's gotta be done on a gradual, firm, constructive approach. And I'm saying it should be done just like you would raise your child. I'm not saying they're children; I'm saying, you know, that sometimes you gotta police it like they were children." Newman also believed that the QWL program would help the company by reducing employee resistance to change, particularly to the changes in production technology that were required if FoodCom was to remain competitive: "You gotta insert this into 'em . . . . We've just gotta install into 'em that changes are really for the best."

Should OD/QWL Programs Address Labor-Labor Problems in Addition to Labor-Management Problems?

It is not unusual to find considerable status grading in the workplace; nor is it unusual to find tension between the technical and the social organization at work. Whyte (1948), for example, pointed out that the workflow in restaurants can force lower status waiters and waitresses to initiate interaction with higher status cooks. Cooks who feel offended because they have to take orders from their inferiors can delay filling orders just as the bakers and machinists delayed responding to so-called aggressive packagers. Subsequently, Trist and Bamforth (1951) documented how tasks designed to minimize movements and maximize efficiency can be rendered ineffective if they require behaviors incompatible with the workers' social organization. Many other studies have documented the necessity to find a fit between the social system and the technical system (e.g., Pava 1986; Trist 1981). Yet, with the exception of descriptions of structural interventions such as task forces, matrix structures, and presentations of intergroup imaging exercises (e.g., Huse and Cummings 1985) comparatively little is said about this problem in the OD/ QWL literature, to the detriment of some QWL interventions. For example, Hanlon, Nadler, and Gladstein (1985) report that differences between nurses and doctors at Parkside Hospital were not addressed and that this had a negative impact on the intervention there.

As in many QWL programs, the program in Reginal was created to address labor-management issues and job enrichment. However, as time went on, the program was forced to deal with several social fissures separating groups of workers. In the process of negotiating common assumptions for labor and management, it also had to consider tensions between workers differing in sex, race, and seniority in the FWIU and between the FWIU members and the IMU and IEU locals. Interunion tensions were made more difficult because the IMU and IEU employees were in powerful positions in the workflow and had to date refused to participate in the QWL project. Like mechanics in the tobacco factory studied by Crozier (1964), machinists and electricians in the bakery capitalized on the fact that they had a monopoly on critically needed knowledge and skills. They could even override the wishes of plant management, as they did in the case of rescheduling a holiday.

Despite the fact that these problems have been slighted in theoretical treatments of QWL, there is considerable evidence that differences among groups are often an important factor determining the success or failure of attempts to change an organization (e.g., Alinsky 1969; Blake and Mouton 1985; Brown and Covey 1987; Hanlon, Nadler, and Gladstein, 1985; Smith 1982). As we continue our explication of the FoodCom case, therefore, we will note ways that the absence of shared assumptions among union members and between members of different unions became a significant factor in the QWL program in Reginal.

The Reginal QWL Committee

Elections for the Reginal QWL committee were held as scheduled (see Exhibit 3-2), and the new QWL committee met for the first time on January 11, 1977. Eight representatives from the FWIU and, because of the presence of a management representative from the maintenance department, nine representatives from management attended. They took opposite sides of a large table in the center of the meeting room.

The FWIU representatives were Bernard Hughes, Nancy Daly, Jack Resler, Louis Young, Alan Quane, Marie McCarthy, Leticia Sanchez, and Bobby Clayton. Hughes, a white man, was the chief FWIU steward. He was George Newman's alternate and was present because George was unable to attend. Hughes was extremely easygoing and soft-spoken. Like many FoodCom employees, he was a long-time Reginal resident. His family had become wealthy by selling land that appreciated in value as the city grew. He worked in the plant, he said, because he didn't want to live off his principal. Besides, he liked to work. For health reasons, employees were required to cover their heads, and Hughes could be identified even at a distance by his ever-present white sailor cap.

Nancy Daly was anything but easygoing. A black woman of about thirty-five years of age, she was an outspoken advocate for the workers she believed were too afraid to speak up for themselves. She had volunteered for the QWL committee to make sure that something would be done about how people, especially women and blacks, were being treated. On a few occasions, George Newman had identified Daly as one of the radicals. She worked in the packaging department.

Jack Resler had been elected to the QWL committee from the sanitation department. He was a quiet white man, and if he had initial opinions about the QWL program, he kept them to himself. His primary interest outside the plant was a barbershop he owned. His required cap was a tall, striped railroad engineer's cap. It added a full six inches to his otherwise short stature and seemed to give him an added measure of distinction.

Louis Young, also a white male, was even quieter than Resler. He was a baker, relatively short and extremely thin. His clear brown eyes were set deeply into a well-lined face. Young was a long-time veteran at the Reginal plant, and he projected an "I've seen it before" attitude.

Alan Quane, another white man, was always ready with a

smile and a suggestion. He worked in the assembly and mixing area.

Marie McCarthy, a white woman, was elected to the committee from the packaging department. She worked the night shift. Initially skeptical of the program, she said she wanted to give it every chance for success. McCarthy was an independent thinker and a strong-willed individual. Perhaps she had to be: Her husband, a millwright and an IMU steward, was one of the most vocal critics of the QWL program. Though expressing disdain for women in general, he acknowledged that his wife was "an exception."

Leticia Sanchez, a Mexican-American woman, was another outspoken representative from the packaging department. She had once served as an officer in the FWIU local. Her primary interest in the QWL program lay in "getting people together," particularly supervisors and line employees. She could get very emotional and vocal over this issue, a fact that made George Newman glad she no longer held an official union position.

Bobby Clayton, a black male representative from the warehouse department, seemed to be the elder statesman for the labor representatives. He was extremely well-liked, perhaps the most popular employee in the plant among labor and management alike. He was also committed to the union. He had attended union meetings at the national level but had declined opportunities to become a union officer. He also had decided not to accept an offer to join management. Clayton stressed cooperation and compromise rather than confrontation and opposition. Though he was a grandfather, only a few gray hairs betrayed an otherwise youthful appearance. He projected an image of wisdom coupled with youthful enthusiasm.

The nine management representatives, in addition to Roger Matson, were Chuck Josephson, Mark Dalton, Paul Morse, Johnny Pepin, Patricia Roper, Brian Hurley, Susan Sheffer, and Vince Keeley. These representatives had been chosen by Matson to represent the different departments and constituencies. They were not elected by their peers. All but Josephson were to be voting members.

Chuck Josephson, a white man, was a foreman in the

maintenance department. Because there were no labor representatives on the committee from this department, Matson declared that Josephson would serve but not vote, a fact that Josephson did not appreciate. His presence, however, would not go unnoticed. He was stocky, strong-willed, and outspoken. He believed that he could repair just about anything and took pride in the fact that he drove 100 miles to and from work each day. He was especially proud that he sometimes would work straight through two shifts.

Roger Matson, a white man, was a relative newcomer to Reginal. He had served for twenty years as assistant manager at FoodCom's largest bakery in Monroe City but had been passed over for promotion in that plant and had been given the top job in Reginal instead. It seemed that this would be as far as he would go with the company. A short, portly, balding man, Matson wore distinctive clothes, including a bright yellow three-piece polyester suit that he would complement with a pair of white shoes. His outside interests revolved around church activities. He said he had started several churches and believed he knew how to keep parishioner interest at peak levels. The worst thing that could happen to a church, he said, was that it would pay off its mortgage. At this point, member interest and involvement would fall and the church would go into decline. He believed that the best strategy for maintaining member involvement was to keep a church deeply in debt.

Mark Dalton, the white, male superintendent of the sanitation department, was soft-spoken and kindly. He had been with the company for many years and was looking forward to retirement. His primary interest outside of work was his family, and he particularly reveled in telling stories about family camping trips.

Paul Morse, a supervisor in the warehouse, projected a more aggressive posture. He was one of two black men to represent management on the committee. His primary interest outside of work was preaching, and he had his own church. When asked what the major problem in the plant was, his answer was unambiguous: the low level of supervisor salaries.

Johnny Pepin was the number two person in the packaging department behind Leonard Duffield. Pepin was a wiry, active white man in his mid-thirties. He was highly regarded throughout the plant, but had a reputation for being a bit too free with his opinions. Other than his family, he did not appear to have significant outside interests. He put much of his considerable energy into his work and seemed destined for a higher position in the company. He signaled his primary interest through his choice of head covering: a baseball cap with the company logo prominently displayed on the front.

Patricia Roper, a white woman, stood about five feet eight inches tall and was heavy for her height. She converted her obvious presence into considerable influence throughout the plant and was highly regarded as competent and fair. She helped counsel subordinates when they had personal problems and also helped them at work. She was the only female supervisor in the packing department who would confront the bakers directly when they sent bad products through the wall into her area. In these instances she would not use the telephone line. She would get onto one of the electric scooters in the plant and take it the entire length of the bake shop to confront the offending laminator operator or baker face-to-face.

The laminator operators or bakers could see Roper coming from 100 yards away as she moved full speed through the swinging doors that marked the end of the baking area and the beginning of the packaging department, so they had plenty of time to consider a defense. Defenses quickly broke down, however, as Roper approached and dismounted. Towering over smaller men who were officially her subordinates in the plant, she would conduct an intense interrogation. "Do you have any idea what sort of product you're sending through the wall?" she would roar over the clamor of the machinery. A "yes" answer was clearly unacceptable, and a "no" would bring a colorful description of overdone, underdone, or otherwise unpackageable products and a clear implication of operator incompetence.

A laminator operator once tried a novel strategy when confronted by Roper's imposing figure: He did not respond at all. This simply led him to a sustained interrogation and, to him, extended abuse at the hands of someone he believed was his social inferior. After the ordeal, however, his only alternative was to complain bitterly to unsympathetic coworkers and to correct the problem. His fellow workers seemed to enjoy their colleague's predicament and ridiculed him after Roper left for letting himself be "chewed out" by a woman.

Brian Hurley, a white man, was responsible for much of the mixing activities in the bakery. He was alert, attentive, and punctual. His wife was the plant nurse.

Susan Sheffer, a black packaging supervisor, shared Leticia Sanchez's concern about improving the quality of interpersonal relations between labor and management employees in the plant. She had recently been promoted from the line into supervision and thought that her former union friends were treating her as if she had joined the enemy.

The final management representative on the QWL committee was Vince Keeley, a white, male bake shop superintendent who had recently moved to Reginal from corporate headquarters. Before taking up duties in the plant, he had worked in the company's research division. He had no production experience and had assumed the department head's position over more experienced candidates. He was extremely personable and responsive and appeared to have no negative history or interpersonal problems.

Early Meetings of the Committee

As the new committee members filed into the meeting room for the first meeting, Tim Deigh noticed they had assumed traditional adversarial positions on opposite sides of the table, so he turned his own chair around and sat facing away from them. As the resulting silence became heavy, the representatives, sensing the problem, redistributed themselves and took positions in which labor and management representatives alternated. Deigh then turned his chair back around and commenced the meeting. He first engaged the committee in a "Lost On the Moon" exercise (Johnson and Johnson 1975), which is designed to illustrate the advantages of consensus decision making and equal treatment of all group members.

The committee then got down to business. They decided to call themselves the Employee Joint Enrichment Committee (EJEC). The minutes of the meeting noted that

> Every effort would be made to arrive at a consensus decision on issues, suggestions, etc. If a consensus cannot be reached, a vote would be held on the matter. A two-thirds majority of the total committee (11 votes out of the total 16 committee members) would be required to pass or enact a suggestion.

and that

> The present committee representatives will serve for a period of 12 months. During the second week in January, 1978, one-half of the union representatives and one-half of the management representatives would stand for re-election by department using a method of voting similar to that used for the original election. Each six months thereafter one-half of both the union and management representatives would stand for re-election. Those elected would then serve for a period of 12 months with one-half of the total committee standing for re-election each six months.

Bobby Clayton and Vince Keeley were elected co-chairpersons. The chairpersonship was to rotate monthly. Clayton would assume the position first. Louis Young was elected as Clayton's alternate and Johnny Pepin was chosen as Keeley's alternate. Susan Sheffer was elected secretary. The committee then identified three topics for consideration. First, a way to keep the various constituencies at the bakery informed of committee activities had to be found. Second, regular meeting times had to be scheduled. Third, the committee had to find a way to identify the interests and concerns of all Reginal employees so that programs could be generated to address them. The representatives decided to place these considerations on the agenda for the next meeting.

The EJEC held meetings on January 18, 24, and 31. It began issuing monthly reports of its meetings and identified bulletin board spaces in the plant on which it could post minutes and progress reports. Deigh arranged for the assessment team to make a presentation to the committee on February 7 and planned to introduce the assistant coordinator on February 14. Candidates for the consulting role were scheduled to appear on February 21 and 22.

QWL committee members were not convinced they needed help from outsiders and asked Deigh to explain why consultants were being called in. His explanation, in the form of a memorandum, referred to the assessors, the assistant coordinator, and the proposed consulting team as external resources. This document is shown in Exhibit 4-1.

EXHIBIT 4-1 Deigh's Memo to EJEC

TO: Employee Joint Enrichment Committee
FROM: Tim Deigh, NQWC
SUBJECT: Explanation of need for external resources in project
DATE: February 7, 1977

During your last EJEC meeting on January 31, 1977, you requested that I jot down some explanations for the need for external resources in your project that might help you in explaining this need to the management and union employees in the bakery. First of all, the talent and skill to identify, diagnose, develop and implement plans to address those problem areas within the Regional bakery are already within the bakery in the form of all the employees there. However, a great deal of effort is required to ensure that the real problem causes are identified and that solutions that are developed are done so in a way that ensures impartiality and benefit to all, and the entire project must be accomplished in a fair and meaningful manner.

There are a number of specific skills and knowledge required to carry out a project of this type in a way that is fair, impartial and beneficial to all—the employees, the union and the company. The assistant coordinator will be working with you full time for the next eighteen months. This person, whom you will select, will be available on all shifts to assist in any way that he/ she might be needed. In addition, this person will work with the committee by assisting the Secretary in taking minutes, following up on action that has been or is to be taken, ensuring that information needed in making decisions by the committee is available, etc. This person will also assist you in communicating with the entire bakery operation by helping you develop and publish monthly progress reports and other communications that might be needed.

ISR resources will work with the EJEC to develop, with your advice and input, a questionnaire and other measurement methods so that you can determine the inputs of all employees as to what the problems are, what alternate solutions might be considered, and the relative importance of the problem areas so that you will know where to start and on what topics to work first. This second questionnaire will be conducted 18 months after the first one and then again in 36 months. In this way the EJEC can determine the effectiveness of the programs that are implemented and, if necessary, alter its direction if the results are not up to the standards that you have established as representatives of all employees.

The fact that ISR conducts these surveys and data gathering activities for the EJEC guarantees the confidentiality of all employees who respond in a way that no one within either the company or the union or the EJEC knows or can identify any one employee. This insurance of confidentiality should encourage employees to very open and honest in their inputs.

The Specialist Resource Team which you will select from four groups previously screened and okayed by the JQWLAC are experienced in assisting joint labor and management committees in analyzing the information from the questionnaires, your inputs and all other available sources. They are also experienced in working with joint committees in developing lists of alternative solutions to the problems that you identify and in assisting you in selecting the solution(s) that best suit your situation. In addition, they will be assisting the entire bakery to learn how to carry on with this kind of joint activity without the assistance of any external resources. In this way the efforts to make the quality of life at work for employees in the Reginal bakery can continue indefinitely as needed.

Throughout this entire project, I will act somewhat like a "quality control checker" to ensure that everyone benefits and that the actions taken are carried out in an impartial and fair manner.

I hope that these thoughts are helpful in your understanding of the purpose and need for the external resources that will be assisting you in the early stages of your effort. Please let me know if you have any questions that I can answer or if there is any other information that I can get for you.

Thank you,

Tim Deigh

Meanwhile, the JQWLAC met on January 31. Its members interviewed two more candidates for the consulting role and approved both. They also discussed how to manage public disclosure of information concerning the program. They concluded that any outside request for information would be referred to the EJEC for consideration, but that the EJEC's decision would subsequently be reviewed by JQWLAC before any disclosure was made. Seldon and Scigliano agreed to draft a standard response memorandum to outsider requests and to serve as contact persons between the JQWLAC and the EJEC on these matters. The standard response memorandum is presented in Exhibit 4-2.

EXHIBIT 4-2 JQWLAC's Memo to EJEC

MEMO TO: Reginal Employee Joint Enrichment Committee (EJEC)
FROM: Joint Quality of Working Life Advisory Committee (JQWLAC)
SUBJECT: Procedure for Responding to "Outside" Inquiries Regarding the EJEC Project
DATE: February 1, 1977

The JQWLAC suggests the following procedure:

All inquiries, requests for information, interviews, etc. made to the EJEC, individual members thereof, FWIU Local No. 50, the Food Workers' International Union and its representatives, Reginal Management, FoodCom, Inc. and its employees will be directed to the EJEC for response. The EJEC will prepare a response and forward it to the JQWLAC for endorsement. The response will then be returned to the EJEC for release.

The JQWLAC anticipates numerous inquiries of a general or simple nature such as "we heard there is a union/ management project underway at Reginal; tell us about it." To avoid repeated and/ or frequent communication back and forth between EJEC and JQWLAC, we suggest the following standardized response:

"FoodCom and the Food Workers' International Union are jointly sponsoring an experimental quality of work life project at FoodCom's Reginal bakery. Production workers at this bakery are represented by FWIU, Local No. 50.

The project, launched in January of 1977, is progressing to the satisfaction of all involved. At this point in time specific details or results are not available for release or publication."

The above is intended to facilitate your response to general inquiries. More complex requests should be handled in the manner outlined above.

If you have any comments, please advise.

(Signed) Horace Seldon

The assessment team (Michael Moch, Jean Bartunek, John Feather, and Dale Fitzgibbons) met with the EJEC on February 7. Before the team members could be introduced, however, Marie McCarthy and Patricia Roper took the floor to complain that despite the fact that the committee had been meeting for almost a month, nothing had been accomplished to deal with the problems in the plant. McCarthy and Roper were getting an earful from their respective labor and management constituents. Supervisors in the packaging department believed they had to cover for Roper while she was attending EJEC meetings, yet they were getting nothing in return. Line employees complained to McCarthy that their dues were covering her pay while she worked with the EJEC, but that they weren't getting their money's worth.

The presence of the QWL program had raised old gripes. For example, as noted earlier, there had previously been line-by-line seniority in the packaging department. Several years before, a line had been eliminated, and those who remained with the company had to restart their seniority on a new line. One woman was particularly bitter and had to be reassigned to a repackaging room off to the side of the main packaging area, so she would not bother other workers. The presence of the QWL program had given her new hope of recapturing her lost seniority. There were others in the same situation, and they all had become more vocal. The program, according to Pepin, had therefore "already hurt the relationships it had been designed to help."

The committee had started its second month of operation, so Vince Keeley had assumed the chairmanship. Acknowledging the seniority problem, he noted that the committee should do all it could to speed up its efforts to improve workers' situations. The assessment team would help the committee identify problem areas using its survey technique, and the committee could then develop programs designed to address these problems. The assessment team made a brief presentation and Keeley appointed a subcommittee to help the team develop a questionnaire. This group was carefully chosen to include labor and management representatives and members from each department. It consisted of Mark Dalton, Patricia Roper, Alan Quane, and Bobby Clayton. Clayton was appointed subcommittee chairman.

When the subcommittee subsequently convened, its members decided to develop a list of problem areas to guide questionnaire construction. They also agreed to recommend that the assessment team be allowed to conduct open-ended interviews with line employees. With the exception of Clayton, the subcommittee members believed that they should be responsible for drafting and approving the questionnaire. Clayton was concerned that this would take too much authority from the full EJEC. However, he acquiesced to the wishes of the other subcommittee members.

On February 14 the full EJEC met to consider its subcommittee's proposals and to meet the new assistant coordinator. Members agreed to help develop a list of problem areas and to recommend open-ended interviews by the assessment team. They would consult with their constituencies about problems in the plant and meet again in two days to put a complete list of problem areas together. The EJEC declined, however, to give the subcommittee the authority to compile a draft questionnaire based on this list. Like Clayton, EJEC members felt this should be a job for the entire committee.

The new assistant coordinator, Joe Gromanger, was then introduced. Gromanger, a graduate student in Organizational Behavior at a local university, was a soft-spoken white man of about twenty-five years of age. He had applied for the position, he said, because "the program reflected strongly my career objectives and would enable me to put to use much of my formal educational experience." Gromanger had received a B.A. in Psychology and Sociology from a small private college and had then taken a position with a manufacturer of refrigerators. In this job he had joined a union and had become involved in a wildcat strike when the company reduced work time because of a slowdown in business and a model changeover. He later received a Masters degree in Labor and Industrial Relations and had helped to establish a chapter of the American Society for Personnel Administration at the university where he received this degree. He therefore had both labor and management credentials. The committee members clearly liked Gromanger and readily concurred in his appointment.

Two days later, after conducting informal interviews with several plant employees, the EJEC assembled to compile its list of problem areas. This list is reproduced in Exhibit 4-3.

EXHIBIT 4-3 Problems and Questions Raised by Employees during Initial Interviews with EJEC Members

PROBLEMS, QUESTIONS, ETC.

1. Communication between shift foremen.
2. Communication between all departments.
3. Company and Union fail to notify individuals properly.
4. Better relationship and consideration of outside suppliers and receiving clerk by supervision.
5. Supervision and labor on job.
6. Poor and improper instruction by supervision.
7. Policy and rules of health and safety not posted and not adhered to and not followed.
8. Improve education of supervision in guides and rules of disciplining employees.
9. Improve employee education of government regulations.
10. All employees feel they are being discriminated [against] by some member of supervision and other employees.
11. Better security on parking lot.
12. Improper parking and littering.
13. Better cooperation between maintenance people and other employees.
14. Limitation of maintenance department supervision, due to agreement which limits their capability and authority.

15. Poor attitude and indifference cause other employees to react accordingly.
16. Poor morale of some employees.
17. Lack of recognition of work accomplished or a job well done.
18. Clothes: not enough, uncomfortable, indecent.
19. An upgrade person on sick leave has not been replaced by another person.
20. Proper areas for equipment to be cleaned in steam room.
21. Who contacts mechanics?
22. Baking sections of Bake Shop not represented on committee.
23. Rotation of job assignments.
24. Control on speed of cookies.
25. Why are some people on relief assignment yearly.
26. Staying over on relief.
27. Following classification.
28. Pay rate differences between different classifications are not high enough.
29. New refreshment area in lower Packing area.
30. Non-smoking area.
31. Classification consideration.
32. More systematic operation.
33. Consideration for Company property.
34. Rest rooms made more comfortable.
35. Get credit for every day and overtime work prior to retirement.
36. To place people on jobs strictly by seniority.
37. Ink on end seals causes rashes.
38. Training employees on assigned lines they have never worked before.
39. Each shift clean up their own mess left on production lines.
40. Incentive program to reduce absenteeism.
41. Improve communication for problem solving.
42. We permit employees a choice of higher classification on shift basis.
43. We permit employees the choice of a day off or a higher

classification without regard to working in the classification on a full time basis.

44. Company and Union fail to make decisions promptly involving employees' problems.
45. Union fails to get majority opinion of employees before entering into agreement with Company.
46. Company and Union fail to clarify standards of job opening.
47. Inability or non-concern of supervision to perform their duties.
48. Rotation of supervision by shift regardless of capability and endeavor to perform job.
49. Pressures on supervision and employees to perform impossible tasks.
50. Improve food services.
51. Attitude of some employees that Company is a big company that can afford their wishes and desires.
52. The realization that the Company must make a profit to stay in business.
53. Distrust.
54. Working together and helping one another.
55. Four-day, 10-hour work week to conserve gas.
56. Modification of machinery.
57. Better maintenance of equipment.
58. Why isn't efficiency established on total production by shifts.
59. No standard of capability for job classification.
60. Supervision does not give full explanation to all employees.
61. Lab personnel, when needing spot checks, should get their own.

Joan Franks, the alternate for regular committee member Jack Resler, proposed that the list be given to the assessment team so it could provide the basis for questionnaire development. Bernard Hughes seconded the motion, but the motion failed. Other committee members argued successfully that it was the committee's job to develop the questionnaire. The role of the assessment team was purely advisory.

At 5 A.M. the next morning four members of the assessment

team began to conduct open-ended interviews. After working for about two hours, the assessment coordinator was called to the telephone in the nearby warehouse department. It was Deigh calling from the NQWC. Why, he wanted to know, were the male members of the assessment team dirty and unshaven? The assessment coordinator explained that the four assessors had dressed casually in order to help respondents feel at ease. They were clean, however, and the two bearded members of the team had trimmed their beards before leaving their hotel for the plant. Deigh expressed frustration and advised the coordinator to stay by the telephone.

Within a few minutes Horace Seldon called from Food-Com International headquarters. Like Deigh had just done, he asked why the male members of the assessment team were dirty and unshaven. The team coordinator again explained that the assessors had dressed casually but that they were clean and the two bearded members had trimmed their beards. "Shit!" Seldon exclaimed. "I can't handle this from here! Go talk to the plant manager!"

The assessment team coordinator went to Matson's office on the second floor. Walking past the secretary, he could see the top of Matson's head as he was bent over his desk at the far side of a long rectangular office. It was the only carpeted room in the plant and had fine wood paneling. Matson's desk was large and imposing. With some trepidation, the assessment coordinator walked in unannounced, and standing directly in front of Matson's desk, said, "I hear you wanted to see me."

Matson looked up as though he had been accosted by an intruder. Pointing to a chair off to his right, he demanded that the assessor sit in it, and the assessor did. Matson then returned to his work, leaving the assessor to await his next move. After what seemed to the assessor to be a very long time, although it was probably no more than a minute, Matson rolled his chair back a couple of feet and swiveled it so he could look directly at the assessor. Leaning back, he took off his tie and threw it on the floor. He was not wearing a jacket. He then unbuttoned and untucked his shirt. Underneath he wore a sleeveless undershirt. Matson then turned up his shirt collar, messed up what little hair he had so that much of it stood straight up or stuck out at various unseemly angles, and slouched in his chair. In a demanding tone, he asked, "Do you respect me?"

The assessor, now somewhat shaken, responded by saying something to the effect that well-dressed people are often accorded respect. Pointing directly at the assessor, Matson literally shouted, "Exactly! From now on you and your people will wear ties in my plant!" The assessor said he would bring up the issue with his colleagues, but the frown on Matson's face indicated that this was not an adequate response. After attempting some conciliatory remarks, the assessor left the room.

The Role of Language and Ritual in Organizations

The bulk of the literature on OD has focused on organization members' behavior (e.g., Porras and Hoffer 1986), yet the ways organizational members understand and interpret events affect their behavior and their responses to proposed changes (e.g., Frost et al. 1985). Relatively little attention has been given to the ways OD interventions affect and are affected by the interpretive—essentially cultural—lenses that give meaning and coherence to organizational events. Even less attention has been paid to the ways members of organizations evoke, maintain, and change lenses. Yet as we suggested in Chapter One, OD/ QWL interventions are frequently designed to effect such cognitive—rather than just behavioral—changes (Bartunek and Moch 1987). As the QWL program in Reginal developed, language and ritual emerged as important factors guiding the change process.

Many authors have argued that different groups, organizations, and societies develop distinctive languages. When spoken or written, these languages direct individuals' attention to certain aspects of their experience and away from others. Lakoff and Johnson (1980), for example, illustrate how the words we use even condition our experience of time. When we say that time passes us by or marches on, we implicitly envision time in terms of linear space. Similarly, by labeling an individual as a delinquent or predelinquent, we can affect peoples' images of themselves in ways that can be self-fulfilling (Edelman 1964, 1967). Linguistic skill can therefore be an important component of social competence as participants vie for influence by linguistically evoking images that direct attention in ways consistent with their interests (Kipnis, Schmidt, and Wilkenson 1980; Moch and Huff 1983; Pocock 1973).

Deigh showed considerable linguistic competence in his February 7 memorandum dealing with external resources. EJEC members had thought that the presence of outsiders either reflected badly on them or reduced their control over the QWL program. Yet the outside consultants, the assessors, the assistant coordinator, and Deigh himself were required components of the program. Deigh had accepted the responsibility of monitoring the program and was therefore, to some extent, an agent of the JQWLAC. The assessors worked for ISR, and ISR had responsibilities that extended beyond the Reginal site. (For example, assessment instruments had to be standardized across all QWL sites and had to conform to established psychometric standards.) Deigh also felt pressure to conform to standard QWL practice. To act otherwise could jeopardize the standardized nature of the interventions across QWL experiments. Deigh therefore had little choice but to sell Reginal employees the whole prepackaged intervention. This was required by its experimental nature. For Deigh to make this explicit, however, would have raised the specter of an imposed program. It would have clarified the fact that the QWL model had been, to an extent, imposed on him as well.

Deigh chose to frame the role of outsiders in terms that might be acceptable to the local site. Outsiders were to be external resources whose apparent sole purpose was to assist EJEC members. Deigh's memo explicitly addressed EJEC members' concerns that they were not up to the task of managing the QWL program, noting that all the talent and skill required were available within the bakery. It then described how the outside resources would help ensure that everything was done in a fair and meaningful manner. Nowhere was it mentioned that the outside resources were mandated by the program in which the local employees had chosen to participate. Similarly, Deigh never explained why the local talent was insufficient to ensure fairness and meaningfulness. The February 7 memo appears explicitly to deny the negative inference drawn by employees that they were not up to the task. It then continues as though this inference were true.

As we noted previously, the role of the JQWLAC seemed embedded in a similar contradiction. On many occasions JQWLAC explicitly stated that the program would be run by the EJEC, yet the JQWLAC screened consultant groups, identified participants, and made many other decisions about how the program would be structured. The JQWLAC memo to EJEC regarding external inquiries built upon this precedent. The only communication EJEC would be allowed to issue on its own was a preapproved formal statement. Any more than that required JQWLAC approval. Consistent with Kochems's insistence on corporate control of public announcements, JQWLAC insisted on having the right to approve the language that would guide outsiders' interpretation of QWL events in the Reginal bakery. The appearance of local control could therefore be maintained, though in reality, the locus of control was at best ambiguous.

Linguistic skill was supplemented with considerable ritual in Reginal. Matson's explicit statements were compatible with QWL prescriptions concerning worker participation, yet, like Deigh's memo (Exhibit 4-1) and the JQWLAC's tendency to advocate EJEC control while simultaneously restricting their discretionary power, Matson's behavior frequently seemed to contradict his explicit pronouncements. The issue of the assessors' neckties is a case in point. Matson's linguistic and ritualistic enactment of power, or what Gephart (1978) has called status degradation, was repeated many times throughout the course of the QWL program. Several of these episodes have been analyzed more extensively elsewhere (Moch and Huff 1983).

The neckties issue illustrates several characteristics of the linguistic enactment of power. First, power can be enacted not only by raising the status of the speaker but also by degrading others. Second, ritualistic behaviors can accompany language in order to convey meanings that are intended but are inconsistent with the speaker's explicit public statements. By unbuttoning and untucking his shirt, messing up his hair, and slouching, Matson communicated how he and (by implication) other FoodCom managers would view the assessors were they to continue to work in the plant without wearing ties. By selectively ignoring the assessment coordinator and using intonations that conveyed anger when ordering the assessor to sit down, Matson enacted his own right to direct the assessors' behavior.

Finally, by evoking a locally recognized symbol, the necktie, Matson may have been trying to avoid a more general challenge to the established set of status and power relationships in the plant. The outside resource people were highly respected: They had university degrees and represented high-status organizations. Employee status in the plant was indicated by the different uniforms worn by the various types of workers. Ties distinguished management from supervision and line personnel. By not wearing ties, therefore, the high-status outsiders might undermine an important status indicator and undercut a source of power available to management. Matson did not have the formal authority to order the assessors to wear ties. He also could not justify such an order without explicitly contradicting his public statements supporting a more egalitarian, participatory style. Perhaps his only option was to enact management privilege through language and ritual and then leave his target audience to find an acceptable response to the apparent contradiction.

Interviewing Employees

The assessment team conducted unstructured, open-ended interviews with 163 of the more than 700 employees in the plant. Despite the fact that the interviewers were careful to initiate the interviews using neutral language, the vast majority of responses involved complaints. Interviews with several young women in the bake shop provide an example. When there were too many packagers in the packaging department, young women with the least seniority were sometimes sent to help clean the bake shop. A bake shop supervisor responsible for one of these clean-up crews claimed that crew members stole cleaning equipment. He also complained about having women on a clean-up crew in the first place. "Most of the women on my clean-up crew can't move the 300 pound cutters, so I have to ask one of the men to do something he's not supposed to do," he said.

Several of these women took the interviewer aside to complain of their plight. Because they were young, they were the first to be let go when orders fell off. Yet, they said, they would be laid off when others in the plant were getting overtime. In addition, they were not treated like adults. There were too many "write-ups," formal notices of improper employee behavior. There also was inadequate employee training and too much supervision.

A young male laminator operator had a similar complaint.

When there was not enough work, he would be laid off while workers in other departments, particularly sanitation, got overtime. He was also dissatisfied with management. "We never see 'em. We never sit down and say 'let's solve some problems here.'" The company, he said, listens to the older folks, so things don't change. A supervisor in the bake shop talked about the lack of proper training: "We need to train our people better. They don't know how to do their job, and they don't know what's happening in other parts of the plant."

Another laminator operator was upset because his representative on the EJEC was a mixer and so, according to the operator, was not really in the baking department. He also complained about the amount of flour dust in the air and about the lack of training on the best machines. Only older employees get to work these machines, he said. Finally, he claimed that "the administration is playing parent. They tell supervisors what they want supervisors to make us do, 'cause we're always wrong. Well, that game comes back on top, because we want to play parent and make them kids!"

An older employee in the mixing area thought that he shouldn't have to wait until age sixty-five to retire with full benefits. He also said that mixers should get more pay than bakers. After all, he said, "We're the engine that pulls the train." A middle-aged mixer was angry at "goldbrickers" who didn't return favors. He was willing to help others, but when he asked for help in return, the employees he had helped would say, "It's not my job."

Two young black supervisors in the baking department complained that "packing people call up (machine) operators and tell them how to do their jobs. They don't know what they're talking about, so the operator who could fix it doesn't, just 'cause he's pissed off." They acknowledged that "there are groups that don't like each other" in the plant.

A forklift operator in the warehouse complained that his supervisor frequently asked him to work outside of his classification. An employee in the sanitation department thought that mechanics were too stubborn or too busy to respond quickly when she needed a machine closed for fumigation. Bake shop workers weren't much better, she said.

Before moving to the sanitation department, she had worked in packaging. This department, she said, was a "little kid's playground" because of jealousy that "comes with women, not with men." Other employees in the bake shop, warehouse, and sanitation departments expressed similar sentiments and added others.

Warehouse worker: When the company got government contracts, things changed. Years ago, blacks were only in the warehouse and in sanitation. Many EEOC [Equal Employment Opportunity Commission] charges were filed against the plant and then jobs opened up. There's no problem now. . . . The committee should allow more decision making by people who aren't supervisors.

Second warehouse worker: Foremen and the supervisor don't communicate or coordinate. . . . There's no training anymore. When old-timers leave, no one will be left. . . . There's massive thievery. It's in the maintenance department and includes supervisors. But one can't tell, 'cause then we get in trouble.

Bake shop worker who mended conveyor belts: Sometimes the company expects menders to do more than they can do. Last night on number 3 we had problems and the foreman started cussin' and like that. People don't like to work in this situation.

Employee in the mixing area: They have a funny system of supervision here. They get on a guy who'll work and they ride him like mad. They get somebody who doesn't work and they leave him alone.

Supervisor in the bake shop: I don't have problems! I have 112 people, and they have problems! They're trained and they know what they're doing, but they're chiselers. It's their nature. I don't expect to be loved, but we've got to have production and efficiency! . . . They don't allow money to motivate people. We can't reward a person for working well; we can only give them a tiny bit bigger raise. So, good people say "what's the use?"

Sanitation department worker: We have a problem, because only a few people go to the union meeting and vote. Then the rest of us have to deal with their decisions.

Bake shop worker: The willing worker gets shit on.

Second bake shop worker: At times, it seems as if this is more of a prison or paramilitary kind of organization in the attitude of some supervisors toward employees. Supervisors behave as if they know it all. There is no interchange of information. . . . This company offers no enrichment in the goals of all human beings in terms of Maslow's hierarchy, other than job securing and even that's not guaranteed.

Interviews held in the packaging department, which various employees called the "playground," the "playpen," or the "sandbox," generated a similar but not completely overlapping set of complaints. For example, a general foreman thought that employees had little trust in management or the local union. He blamed the EEOC for forcing changes in the union contract that put "men in women's jobs." Female employees who had worked for years to gain seniority would find younger male employees being assigned to more desirable jobs.

Three white women worked in the repacking room where products were taken after packages had broken. They were bitter about being assigned to the repacking room and would not have selected that assignment if they had had more seniority. They believed that jobs should rotate to avoid boredom and that management should stop "working a good mule to death." In addition, they thought that black employees were allowed to "get away with murder," that it was either too hot or too cold on the floor, and that relationships among employees were "dog-eat-dog."

The three were particularly angry with their union. One woman said, "This union isn't us. I've been a steward. The company's bought the union." One of the repackers claimed that union representatives were making changes in the contract without informing union members. She described her position as follows:

> Instant classification! The union's letting 'em. My name's mud and I'm wrong regardless! Trust! They make up the rules. . . . Greg Charlton [the plant director of personnel] runs the plant. . . . Don't trust the union or management! George [Newman] hasn't given me a copy of the rules. I want some representation!

One packaging department supervisor seemed to think that the only way he could get his subordinates to work was to be harsh with them:

> The company wants us to be easy with employees. We're under pressure to be easy, but you just can't be nice to some people and expect anything. . . . People are just getting more and more sarcastic. Some people just haven't made their day 'til they've said something sarcastic. . . . Like the Bible says, people are becoming more animal every day.

These comments were more blatant and aggressive than most. However, the interviewers were treated to a veritable avalanche of negative statements, such as the following:

- "We don't have a lot of cooperation from the other shifts—there's stacks and stacks of work left from other shifts."
- "This isn't a work uniform. This is a play uniform!"
- "They should rotate the jobs around. Some girls sit down the whole time. Others stand all the time.
- "Our damn union don't represent us. They just stand still."
- "They don't relieve you for a water break. Even cattle can't go without water."
- "If supervision would work together. . . . You tell and they pass the buck to someone else."
- "Have one time on the clock instead of every clock with a different time."
- "Slow the lines down. They've got us working like machines here. . . . The union doesn't do anything about it."

- "The superintendent and assistant superintendent don't stick to what they say. They tell you one thing and behind your back they tell you something else."
- "[Supervisors] talk to you like you're a criminal. Then the next day they want you to speak to them."
- "George [Newman] will only fight for people he really likes. For most, he wouldn't get on the phone."
- "The union and the company make side agreements."
- "Blacks can get away with not working as hard as whites. A lot of people are afraid to mention the idea of discrimination."
- "Stewards do the best they can, but we don't have any leadership in our union."
- "We need a better relationship with Leonard Duffield. You don't appreciate being talked to like a child."
- "We need a better relationship with mechanics."
- "[They] push things over on black people. You get blamed when you're not involved."
- "People get along pretty good. Blacks and whites get along excellent. We're all treated equal. It would be good to have a black shop steward."
- "Mechanics here. You call one and he won't know what to do. Only one does all the work. They all get paid for it. They should teach all the mechanics what they're supposed to know."
- "We don't get along well with Spanish and colored."
- "Do something with Maintenance to keep these machines in order so they'll run."
- "The bake shop doesn't cooperate with packing."
- "Machinery trouble. A lot of problems stem from equipment and the attitude of the mechanics."

- "Some people stay on one machine for years. Others move around. All should rotate."
- "Some supervisors aren't qualified to be supervisors. They won't stop conversations to come help. Quite a few of them aren't very nice when they do come to help."
- "About three supervisors here are terrible. You can't relate to them. They talk to you like you're dirt under their feet. . . . They use people like guinea pigs. They give you an inferiority complex."
- "They don't hire any Mexicans in maintenance."
- "Foremen and supervisors are really good."
- "People at this plant are segregated, especially in the cafeteria. . . . [I] would like to have this eliminated."
- "Between first and second shift there's a generation gap. The older people (first shift) are attached to their jobs. Second shift is better than the day shift, but they change figures to make the day shift look good."
- "They don't treat you like an adult."
- "Blacks are discriminated against every day."
- "In some cases, people are too lenient on the black people and too strict on the white. It's a downfall in supervision."
- "Rather cut the pay and reduce the work than have them work us like slaves."
- "Discrimination against women. Men don't have to do the same things on the job, especially dirty work type things."
- "Fix all the clocks together."
- "Unions protect lazy employees. They think that the purpose of the union is to allow them to screw off and be protected by it."
- "Supervisors aren't backed up by management."
- "No cooperation from maintenance. [They're] lazy and powerful."

Metaphors as Interpreters of Experience

Many of the issues identified by the respondents in Reginal identified concrete, verifiable problems. The bake shop supervisor, for example, noted that some employees were physically incapable of doing their jobs. The older employee in the mixing area complained about the minimum age at which employees could retire with full benefits. The worker in the sanitation department was concerned about low attendance at union meetings. More than one respondent was upset that different clocks showed different times, which made it very difficult for workers to know when to go on or return from break. Job rotation was also a clear source of tension. Jobs were allocated on the basis of seniority, so younger workers advocated job rotation and older employees preferred to retain the more desirable (usually easier) jobs.

Most of the problems mentioned during the interviews, however, were not concrete and verifiable. They were interpretations, implicit or explicit assumptions, undocumentable statements of "fact," and ambiguous implications. Complaints about the lack of training, for example, masked assumptions that employees lacked adequate knowledge or skill. The mender who felt overworked assumed that management had clear expectations about how much he could do during a single shift. The bake shop supervisor who wanted more influence in decisions about pay raises assumed that financial incentives would increase employee responsiveness and productivity. The woman in the repacking room believed her union was colluding with management. The interpretations that management treated blacks more leniently (or more stringently) than whites may or may not have been correct, but for practical purposes they were undocumentable.

The interpretive nature of the comments seemed most evident in the frequent use of metaphors. As we noted earlier, metaphors are an important means through which individual, group, and organizational schemata are expressed. They describe employees' circumstances and, through frequent usage, create shared employee understandings of their world. Ortony (1979), for example, has argued that metaphors are more than just colorful elaborations guided by objective perception and analysis. Rather, they guide the interpretive process and create as well as reflect perceptions and analyses.

A belief that the company had "bought" the union, for example, generates more meaning than a description of specific activities does. The supervisor who believed his subordinates were becoming "more animal every day" might be able to link this view to specific events; however, it seems likely that once in place, this belief would guide his interpretation of subsequent experience. The same might be said of line workers who thought employees were being treated worse than cattle or worked like slaves or guinea pigs.

Because metaphors both reflect and create meaning, it may be instructive to study some of the metaphors noted in the preceding text literally and to use them to see the Reginal plant through the eyes of those who worked there. More than one respondent, for example, characterized some activities as thievery. Reflecting the feelings of someone suspected of stealing, perhaps, one employee claimed that she was being treated as a criminal. One man felt like he was in prison. Another employee said she was treated like dirt.

By giving events meaning, metaphors also have implications for behavior. An employee who thinks he or she is being "shit on" is likely to respond defensively. Workers who claim that supervisors "get on" employees and "ride" them are not likely to be responsive, and like abused animals, they are not likely to take initiative. A supervisor who classifies subordinates as chiselers is likely to behave in ways that can be interpreted as abusive and that encourage subordinates in turn to see supervisors as sadists and as bossy persons.

If any metaphor cut across departments, races, ages, and sexes, it was the image of a family. George Newman used the concept of a family as an ideal to recapture, but for others the family was not so positive an image. Employees in the packaging department frequently complained that they were not being treated as adults. They claimed that they worked in a sandbox and had to wear play uniforms rather than work uniforms. The uniforms were in fact pastel orange culottes. Supervisors in the packaging department, including female supervisors, wore white or tan pants.

It is dangerous to assume that one image, in this case the image of a large family, was the only guide for participants' understanding and interpretation of events. There were clearly multiple—and sometimes inconsistent—interpretive metaphors operating in the Reginal plant. However, family imagery was used frequently and seemed to provide a perspective in which all the contending factions had a role: Packagers (young female children), bake shop employees (dutiful elder brothers), maintenance personnel (delinquent juveniles), and supervisors (parents) did not get along with each other, like members of a contentious family. Even the resistance to playing a child's role could be interpreted using familial imagery. Such resistance occurs in all families as children grow and mature, and when the resistance is expressed, it is a tacit acknowledgement that the complainers are being given a subordinate role in the social system.

Awareness of the importance and underlying meaning of the various articulations of the family imagery in the plant might have helped Deigh and the others who carried responsibility for the QWL project in Reginal. To someone unfamiliar with its nuances and subtleties, the Reginal plant seemed characterized primarily by tension, animosity, and intergroup conflict. There was little evidence of the integrating devices and mutual support that are characteristic of an ideal family system. However, families that are racked by internal tension can exhibit fierce loyalty when threatened by outsiders. Similarly, members of the EJEC were wary of the external resources provided by the QWL program. The members asked Deigh to justify the presence of outsiders and insisted on retaining control of the questionnaire construction process. The specific ways the organization, or family, understands itself can therefore substantially affect its dealings with outside change agents (e.g., Hoffman 1981).

The assessment team concluded its interviews on February 18 and met with the EJEC questionnaire subcommittee to begin identifying relevant categories of questions. This meeting had just begun when Matson burst in, red-faced and visibly angry. He had just received a copy of the EJEC's list, "Problems, Questions, etc." (Exhibit 4-3).

Matson complained bitterly in strident tones that he had not been given his right to view all documents before they were publicly distributed. Looking at Patricia Roper, Bobby Clayton, Johnny Pepin, Mark Dalton, and Alan Quane, Matson yelled, "I pay your salary here and don't you forget it! I will sign and approve any communications, and I'll be the first to see them!" He then stormed out of the room. Dalton's face turned red and his hands began shaking. Roper became very angry, saying that even a plant manager had no right to treat people in such a manner. Clayton somewhat reluctantly agreed that Matson had been unjust. Quane, however, had a large grin. He seemed to have been working hard just to keep from laughing.

Matson later complained to the assessment coordinator that the EJEC had done nothing but resurface old issues that had been settled long ago through the grievance procedure. He complained that during the two months the program had been operating, almost as many grievances had been filed as had been filed during the entire previous year. Twenty-one grievances had been filed. Several of them involved previously settled changes in overtime and job classification rules, but many were based on current problems.

Matson held Deigh personally responsible. "They feel that now that we have quality of work, they'll get what they want. . . . These things have been brought up before," he complained. "They think Tim Deigh's going to get them back their [lost] seniority." Matson also criticized the union for failing to inform its members properly. Contract changes negotiated between Greg Charlton and George Newman were announced at union meetings, but because very few members attended these meetings, most employees remained uninformed.

Matson complained that some employees had been chastised for not wearing goggles and had taken offense, claiming they had not been told to wear them in the first place. Yet there were no fewer than six posted announcements of a new safety policy requiring employees to wear goggles. The company had started a newsletter, but employees didn't read it so it had been discontinued. Even his own supervisors were partly to blame. They weren't telling subordinates all they needed to know to understand why things were as they were. If the workers were only more aware, Matson said, they would understand and wouldn't grieve and complain so much. The QWL program, however, had created unrealistic expectations according to Matson. Thereby, far from facilitating good labor-management relations, it had only made matters worse. Matson was not alone in his views. Horace Seldon confirmed that the "loose-as-a-goose" approach that characterized the QWL program (demonstrated by such factors as the assessors' casual dress) could "open up things we don't want to handle."

Later, Deigh attempted to put the emerging complaints in a more positive light. Some complaints, he said, were good for the plant. They surfaced issues that could be resolved for everyone's benefit. He publicly argued that the grievances submitted during the early stages of the QWL project might be usefully seen as grumbles. Moreover, Deigh argued, there were different types of grumbles. These ranged from low-level grumbles that were not constructive suggestions for change to "metagrumbles" that could be used to further individual and organizational goals. Rather than reducing the number of grumbles, therefore, he advised the QWL program to try raising the frequency of metagrumbles. Evaluating and correcting metagrumbles would benefit everyone.

Meanwhile, the EJEC proceeded with its planned activities. The Questionnaire subcommittee continued its work, and the EJEC representatives selected an outside consulting team. In announcing their choice, committee members noted that they had evaluated four groups on the basis of eight criteria: (1) experience in job enrichment, (2) ability to communicate with members of the EJEC, (3) the EJEC's perception of the group's compatibility, (4) accomplishments, (5) back-up resources, (6) the availability of the members of the group for the project in Reginal, (7) the labor and management balance of the group members' backgrounds, and (8) ability to work with both sexes in a multiracial environment. A group from the Center for Organization Design (COD) was chosen over the three other contenders. The team consisted of Eric Drew, COD's president; Teresa Ferrer, an experienced specialist with joint job enrichment committees; and Wayne Sholl, a labor-management arbitration specialist. The fact that Wayne Sholl had had considerable experience with unions was a plus, as was the fact that Teresa Ferrer was a black woman.

Choice Models Reflecting the Variety of Schemata Held by Plant Employees

Differences in the schematic understanding of the QWL program held by top FoodCom management and by Mills and Deigh were outlined at the end of the previous chapter. Like most QWL advocates, Mills and Deigh believed that a labor-management committee would take actions that would lead to greater employee satisfaction and productivity. Increases in satisfaction and productivity would lead to increased cooperation that would in turn facilitate the functioning of the labor-management committee (Figure 3-1). Getting the committee in place, therefore, was the first step in initiating a self-amplifying process that would lead to positive outcomes for all participants.

Top FoodCom management was not so positive. Though they accepted the basic model advocated by NQWC staff, Kochems, Coy, and Pond seemed to think that the program might cause more harm than good. Unless adequate controls were in place, the presence of a joint local committee might actually hurt satisfaction and productivity. If this happened, cooperation and the ability of the local committee to function would be hindered (Figure 3-1). These three men therefore wanted NQWC staff to perform a quality control function and viewed JQWLAC and local plant management as critical components guiding the activities of the local committee. Perhaps to maintain his ability to control events, the plant manager, Matson, vigorously opposed any dilution of his prerogatives, including his right to be the first to see QWL program documents. He insisted on maintaining the plant's status system and even ordered the QWL program assessment team to wear ties to signal their management-level status.

Models illustrating perspectives held by plant management and other groups in the plant are presented in Figure 4-1. The cooperative model representing Mills and Deigh's perspective that was presented in the previous chapter [Figure 3-1] is reproduced here (model 1) to facilitate comparisons.

The Paternalistic Model

A model depicting the orientation of local plant and union management is presented in part 2 of Figure 4-1. We have termed this model "paternalistic." Matson, Newman, and McCue did not challenge many of the QWL assumptions. They seemed to agree that labor-management cooperation was desirable, that a local committee (a) was an appropriate response to increased cooperation, and that the local committee would initiate actions (b) that would increase employee productivity (c) and satisfaction (d). Moreover, they seemed to place more emphasis on employee satisfaction than representatives of top management did (see Figure 3-1).

Matson appeared to have a sincere desire for improvements in the quality of employees' working lives. As a working hypothesis, therefore, we might posit that he expected the local committee to initiate activities that would improve employee satisfaction and that he was prepared to support such activities to the extent that they accomplished this goal (k). He seemed to agree that increases in satisfaction would strengthen the local committee (l) and reinforce labor-management cooperation (m). Increased satisfaction would also stimulate greater worker productivity (e). Newman and McCue appeared to share these beliefs.

Matson and Newman both believed, however, that a local committee might hinder as well as help employee satisfaction. Newman and McCue were concerned lest FWIU radicals gain control of the committee (j), and Matson believed the QWL program could raise the visibility of long-standing problems and complaints. By doing so, it could actually decrease employee satisfaction (j) and thereby hinder both the functioning of the local committee (l) and the overall level of labor-management cooperation in the plant (m).

Local company and union officials were also concerned about the effect of the QWL program on productivity. They were familiar with top management's "bottom line" orientation. Committee work represented a drain on plant resources (i). Time spent doing QWL work might not be spent efficiently or effectively. The net result might be a net negative effect on productivity and declining company support for the program regardless of any positive effects the program might have on employee satisfaction. Consequently, committee activities designed to increase satisfaction would also have to generate productivity gains if QWL activities were to continue (f) and if both the committee and labor-management cooperation in general were to receive long-term company support [(g) and (h)]. Increases in employee satisfaction, therefore, were not sufficient. They must

Figure 4-1 Additional Alternative Conceptions of How the QWL Program at FoodCom Would Work: 1) QWL Staff; 2) Plant-Level Management; 3) Senior FWIU Employees; 4) Junior FWIU Employees; 5) Stewards and Supervisors; 6) Maintenance Department Union Officers and IMU/ IEU Employees

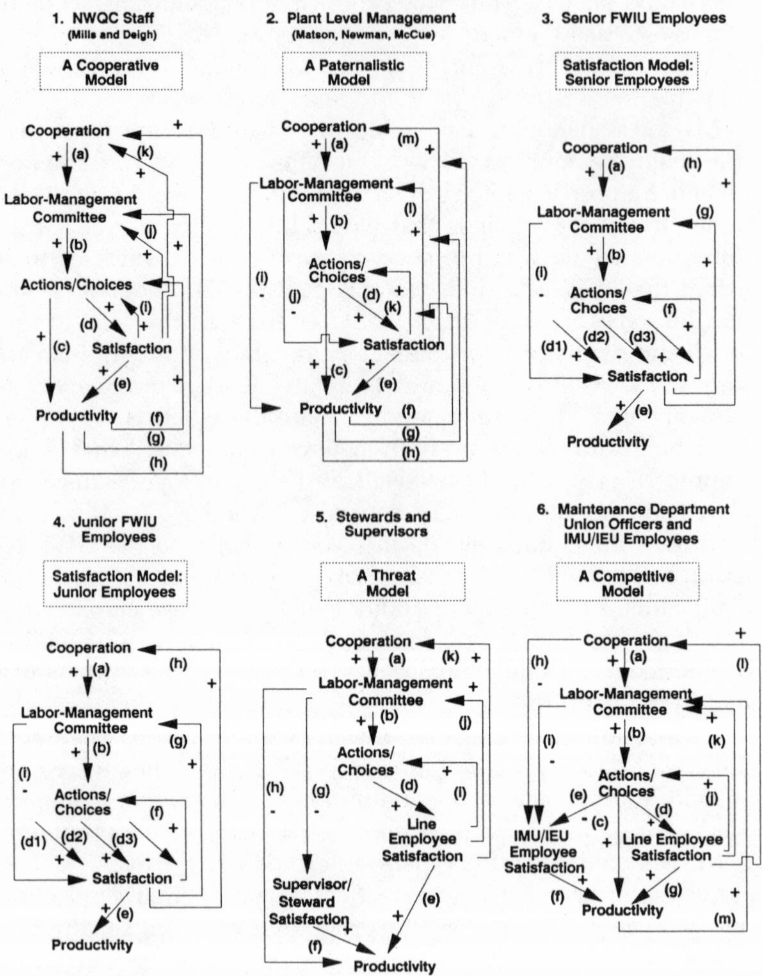

be accompanied by gains in productivity if they were to have an impact on QWL activities, on the strength of the local committee, and on the overall level of cooperation in the plant.

Satisfaction Models

Models illustrating the perspectives of old and young FWIU employees are presented as "satisfaction models" in Figure 4-1, models 3 and 4. Both junior and senior FWIU employees seemed to agree that greater cooperation was desirable. They also agreed on the establishment of a local committee as a means of realizing cooperation (a). Effective functioning by the committee would result in actions (b) that could increase employee satisfaction (d) and thereby boost productivity (e). There was little evidence, however, that FWIU employees viewed the program as an opportunity to find ways to improve productivity in the plant. Their suggestions and complaints were directed toward improving the quality of their own life at work. Employee satisfaction was the critical factor to be taken into account when assessing the adequacy of committee activities (f), evaluating the local committee itself (g), or determining the value of labor-management cooperation in the plant (h). Productivity improvements would come as a byproduct of increases in employee satisfaction (e). By implication, therefore, primary concern lay with satisfaction rather than with productivity.

Models 3 and 4 in Figure 4-1 indicate that realizing gains in employee satisfaction would not be a simple accomplishment. Some actions of the local committee might increase satisfaction for both junior and senior employees (d1). However, if the local committee initiated a job rotation or another program that reassigned jobs on some basis other than seniority, senior FWIU employees would respond negatively. This is indicated by arrows (d2) and (d3) in model 3. If the committee did not implement such a program, younger employees might respond negatively. This is indicated by arrows (d2) and (d3) in model 4.

This opposition created a dilemma for the QWL program. If the EJEC instituted a job rotation program, they could reduce the satisfaction levels of older FWIU employees. If they did not introduce such a program, they would not increase the quality of work life experienced by younger people in the plant. Any satisfaction increases arising from other QWL projects might be outweighed by the fact that young people could view the committee as siding with senior workers. On the other hand, if the local committee introduced a job reassignment program, productivity gains due to increasing satisfaction of young employees might be outweighed by productivity losses from less satisfied senior people. Moreover, rising levels of satisfaction that might be translated into increased support for cooperation (h) and for the local committee (g) by one group could be balanced by declining satisfaction and decreased support for cooperation by the other group.

If this problem were not troublesome enough, the committee seemed to be running out of time. Some FWIU line workers were already upset that too little had been accomplished. Members of the local committee were consuming resources that came partly from union dues. This was a source of irritation (i). Unless satisfaction were raised to compensate for this loss, employee support for the local committee could begin to decline (g), and the opportunity for greater cooperation could be lost (h).

The Threat Model

Assumptions underlying the perspective taken by stewards and supervisors are depicted in model 5 of Figure 4-1. It seems fair to say that at least initially, supervisors and stewards saw the program as a threat. They did not contest some of the primary tenets of the QWL model: Labor-management cooperation was desirable and a QWL committee an appropriate means (a). Moreover, the local committee might develop programs (b) that would increase the satisfaction of line employees (d), and this might, in turn, increase productivity (e). However, there was no indication that supervisors or stewards thought that they might benefit from the program themselves.

The local committee was seen as an alternative to both union and company management in this model, an alternative that was difficult to justify without assuming that company supervisors and union stewards were not doing their jobs. The very presence of the local committee, therefore, was disquieting at best (g). At its worst, the committee would distract employees from doing their regular jobs (h). Actions taken by the local committee, moreover, were intended to increase satisfaction among line employees and to receive or be denied support as a consequence [(i), (j), (k)]. Neither supervisors nor stewards seemed to view the program as a means to increase productivity or efficiency and thereby to make the supervisors' jobs easier or the supervisors themselves more effective. Worse, if the program actually decreased the satisfaction of stewards or supervisory personnel, it could indirectly decrease plant productivity (f).

The Competitive Model

The last players in this drama were the IMU/IEU employees in the Maintenance Department. Their perspective, depicted in part 6 of Figure 4-1, is the least compatible with Mills and Deigh's QWL assumptions. Many of the maintenance personnel viewed their relationships with FWIU employees as competitive. They feared that their union would be absorbed by the FWIU and that they would then lose their power and perquisites in the plant, particularly those relating to job assignments. Projects undertaken by the local committee could therefore decrease IMU/IEU employee satisfaction even as they increased FWIU employee satisfaction.

The local committee would be strengthened by greater labor-management cooperation (a). The stronger the committee, the more actions they could take (b) that would increase productivity directly (c) or indirectly (g) by increasing the level of satisfaction of FWIU employees (d). However, the greater the cooperation between the FWIU and company management, the *less* satisfied IMU/IEU employees were likely to become (h). The stronger the local committee became, the more concerned IMU and IEU people were likely to become (i). Every increase in FWIU satisfaction from local committee programs would make IMU/IEU employees more likely to feel deprived (e).

IMU/IEU people may have believed that despite the central role of FWIU satisfaction as a measure of program success [(j), (k), and (l)], the project would succeed or fail as a function of its effect on the bottom line (m). If so, the program's treatment of the IMU/IEU employees might be critical. If maintenance employees were to become sufficiently dissatisfied [(e), (h), and (i)], they might be able to force a termination in the program (m) by threatening to disrupt plant activities significantly (f). Because these employees played a critical role in maintaining equipment in the plant, this possibility was not unrealistic.

We do not claim that these six models, together with the top management model presented in Figure 3-1, correctly capture the variety of assumptions about the QWL program in Reginal. They do, however, reflect the range of beliefs that were present in the plant. The important issue at this point is not the accuracy of the models. The key point is the fact that whatever model most accurately depicts the causal assumptions generated by a particular perspective will implicitly or explicitly influence employee responses and subsequent behavior. Change agents should therefore try to identify the cognitive models operating in the client system and to develop strategies for dealing effectively with them. Our models should be understood as hypotheses that will be supported or altered as the story unfolds. Without these models we would be left with little guidance regarding what to look for and what to ignore. We do not want to mistake a map for the territory (cf. Weick 1979), but neither do we want to embark on a long journey without some navigational assistance.

Deigh appeared to maneuver among these competing perspectives skillfully, neither confronting them nor attempting to convince employees in the plant to see the QWL program from his point of view. As it was presented to the employees in Reginal, the program was to be locally managed, yet personnel affiliated with ISR were on site along with the assistant coordinator. The program also called for an outside consulting firm to be hired. Like members of a family, even as contentious a family as this one, the employees were suspicious of outsiders and saw little reason to have them around. Deigh, however, did not say that they were required by NQWC's funding source or by requirements that the intervention be comparable with those going on in other places. These were factors beyond his control and mentioning them might have undermined the assumption of local autonomy. Rather, he sought by various means to get the program up and running, presumably so the people in Reginal could experience it and judge for themselves whether the program was delivering its promises.

Deigh described the role of the outside resources as essentially consultative. He did not explain why consultants were necessary, but said they would help local people identify real problems and ensure fairness. As a result, he left the impression that outside resources were necessary for reasons that could not be explained. Deigh relied on his ability to establish rapport with FWIU employees and with plant management. He seemed to be saying, "Trust me. I know what I'm doing but I can't say why."

Perhaps Deigh had the right approach. At this point, being explicit about critical problems facing the program might have doomed it to early failure. By buying time, Deigh and the external consultant would have the opportunity to evaluate the various perspectives guiding plant employees. Deigh had tried to create a new understanding of employee grievances by distinguishing between low-level grumbles and metagrumbles, and he and a competent consulting team might subsequently be able to increase local management's tolerance for complaints and decrease local FWIU employees' inclination to generate them. By starting successful activities, perhaps local FWIU employees could begin to think more about productivity issues, and local and national management could begin to understand the meaning of autonomy for the plant-level committee.

If the program could survive its initial start-up period, perhaps IMU/IEU employees would find they were benefiting from it. Seeing how local committee activities could increase productivity and satisfaction would increase the perceived value of cooperation. This in turn would increase support for the functioning of the local committee. Under these conditions, perhaps the contending factions could be encouraged to change their points of view. Perhaps even supervisors, stewards, and Maintenance Department employees could be convinced to support the program. These changes, however, would take time and would require common experiences interpreted by a skilled facilitator. Therefore, although Deigh was probably correct in delaying confrontation with the various constituencies and perspectives right away, such confrontation was only being postponed. It could not be avoided.

5

Alternative Realities, QWL Projects, and Double Binds

The FoodCom bakery used a strict accounting control system that, despite Kochems's early assertions, was difficult to subvert. The plant had to produce a prespecified number of pounds of each product every week. Each ingredient was weighed when it entered the plant, and the number of pounds expended per week was reported to central headquarters along with unit production figures. The number of labor hours also had to be reported so that headquarters could compare these figures with a labor-hour-per-product standard. Each month headquarters issued an efficiency ranking for all plants in the division, and the Reginal plant had a history of being consistently at or near the top of this list. Efficiency figures posted weekly and sometimes daily within the plant represented the primary control mechanism. Declining efficiency was bound to bring inquiries and sometimes division level troubleshooters to Reginal. It also generated considerable energy during staff meetings as department heads and staff personnel attempted to appropriate praise or avoid blame.

The QWL project was beginning to consume an increasing amount of staff time. Supervisors and workers who otherwise would have been on the floor helping production and avoiding waste were now attending QWL meetings. Management believed that this caused either decreased production due to the reallocation of labor or increased labor hours as new employees were called in to replace EJEC members missing on the lines.

The QWL program staff, on the other hand, assumed that resources would be made available to allow for widespread employee participation. QWL advocates claimed that such expenses would be more than repaid through increased long-term productivity. In contrast, management's efficiency orientation emphasized short-term cost minimization. The tension between these two perspectives became evident as a series of EJEC projects were initiated during the winter of 1977.

The Plantwide Survey Project

The program evaluation design called for three administrations of a plantwide survey. These surveys were to be conducted at one-year intervals and contain questions that would allow the assessment team to compare employee attitudes and perceptions across time. The survey would assess such factors as employee satisfaction, perceptions of productivity, the quality of communication within and between groups, the distribution of influence, job characteristics, and intrinsic motivation (Seashore et. al. 1983). EJEC members intended to distribute the questionnaire instrument as employees left the plant at the end of each shift and to accept completed surveys the next day. The assessors, however, believed that if employees were asked to complete the questionnaire on their own time too many would decline to do so and would thus compromise the evaluation. In addition, there was a potential problem of response contamination, as employees could easily discuss their answers before responding to the questions. Finally, the assessors believed that employees might have questions about the survey and that these questions could only be answered during an on-site administration.

But on-site administration presented management with a severe problem. Most employees worked on the lines and could not leave their posts without imposing undue burdens on fellow workers who would have to work much harder to keep up with the line in their absence. Matson refused to consider shutting down lines in order to administer the survey. Arguing that each line produced a profit for only the last few minutes each day, he suggested that employees arrive early or stay late to fill out the questionnaire. The assessors opposed this alternative, believing it impractical. They thought that employees would not arrive early or stay late just to complete the questionnaire. Matson continued to reject any approach that increased costs to the company.

The assessment coordinator drafted a letter to Deigh in which he outlined the problem and described some ambiguities that had crept into the definition of the assessors' role. This letter is available as Exhibit 5-1. Tension between the plant's efficiency orientation and the proposed plantwide survey, he argued, represented a generic problem, not one restricted to the issue of questionnaire administration. The demands for short-term efficiency would continue to conflict with the QWL program unless some programmatic solution were found. Deigh responded rapidly by scheduling a meeting with management members of JQWLAC to discuss the issue.

EXHIBIT 5-1 The Assessment Coordinator's Letter to Tim Deigh Concerning Problems Confronting the QWL Program Assessment Effort in Reginal

February 26, 1977

Mr. Tim Deigh
National Quality of Work Center
Washington, D.C.

Dear Tim:

As you know, we spent last Thursday and Friday in Reginal at the FoodCom bakery. It was a marvelous experience for us; people were in general very cooperative and helpful, and we were able to get a great deal of valuable information. Our first questionnaire will be much more useful as a result. During our visit, however, I ran into some things which should be dealt with if our assessment efforts are to proceed smoothly. By mentioning them now I don't want to indicate that we have significant problems at this point; however, it is always good to anticipate. The first issue involves our lines of communication and authority. The second concerns the pressures that are on management at the Reginal plant.

First, it is important that the evaluation team be clearly under the direction of the local committee in Reginal. There were a couple of times Friday when this channel of communication/ authority got obscured. First, as you know, there was the matter of our dress. Before going further on this, let me say that I feel it is important for us to be responsive to the needs and wishes of the people at the site regardless of their position and that we try to conform to requests made of us whether or not they are made by the local committee. This is why we were more than willing to upgrade our dress, even though we are a bit concerned that it will inhibit out rapport with hourly employees. By responding to such requests, however, we can risk obscuring the fact that we are essentially under the direction of the local committee. I don't know whether Roger Matson was expressing primarily his own concerns or those of others; the first we heard of the problem was from you through Horace Seldon. The problem is that we may have set a precedent and established some expectations which might be difficult to live up to in the future. Roger and I could work this out together; however, if he was reflecting the wishes of others, such an accommodation is likely to be only temporary. This general problem of communication/authority was not limited to the issue of dress. For example, Roger would like to have copies of documents we produce for the committee. I feel uncomfortable about providing these without the committee's endorsement, so I'll be sending Roger's copy to the committee for them to distribute. The problem is that this might not be what Roger had in mind. He has expressed concern lest the committee fail to circulate all documents properly.

The second major concern we might anticipate involves pressures on management at the Reginal plant. As you know, the plant is run on a strict accountability basis. Foreman often pointed out that the name of their game was efficiency, and they frequently brought out the figures by which they were judged. They were under considerable pressure to maintain their efficiency. Paraphrasing a bit, the sentiment "We're maintaining 100 percent efficiency and that's what counts" was voiced frequently. Roger also made it clear that efficiency was the ultimate criterion by which all activities are judged. He also noted that lines run at a profit for only a few minutes each day and that even a relatively minor disruption can have serious implications for overall plant performance. I saw nothing which would indicate otherwise.

The absence of slack in the plant is likely to create two types of problems for the assessment team. First, we do take employees' time, and there is no doubt that this hinders department, shift, and plant efficiency. Those responsible for getting the product out may begin to resent our intrusions. This is made somewhat more problematic by the fact that some departments and shifts have more people than others and some employees are more "detainable" than others. This means that we of necessity affect some departments and shifts more than others. The resulting differential impact on department/shift efficiency could lead to resentment on the part of management.

We are facing our first case in point. We will be applying our baseline questionnaire early in April. This instrument takes about one hour to complete, but employees, including supervision, are not free to fill it out. Some plants have shut down production to provide their employees time to complete our questionnaire. Roger has made it clear that such a procedure is not realistic at Reginal, since this would create losses which could not be recovered. On the other hand, if we hand out questionnaires to arriving employees, we are likely to have a very low response rate. Most employees generally do not have sufficient free time (breaks or pauses in their work); even when they do, our experience is that they do not return the questionnaire. Sometimes the response rate is so low that the information gathered is worthless. Is there a way to introduce some slack into the system so that supervision will feel better about sustaining additional costs which may be associated with assessment? One model, of course, is to discount such costs in efficiency estimates. There are others, however, such as providing funds for overtime pay for employees to complete the questionnaire and to participate in other assessment activities (e.g., interviews, informal discussions). This will become a more critical problem as time goes on, and by April we will have to have some strategy for dealing with it.

The absence of slack at Reginal may present the assessment team with another problem. This one is a bit more subtle. Several of the foremen, general foremen, and supervisors told us that the employees who work for them were often slow, childish, lazy, or downright dishonest. Many of the hourly employees indicated that distrust between employees and supervision was a significant problem. As evaluators, we will be talking to hourly workers as well as to supervision. We have some indication that at least some of the lower-level management staff view this as allowing the wolf to guard the chicken coop. If so, they may feel that our activities can inhibit their ability to control their subordinates. Although it doesn't happen very often, activities such as ours can stir up issues and disagreements which have been covered over or sometimes long forgotten. Employees may feel they have a new lever over management, and they may try to test management control. This would be natural; however, there may be real costs for supervision. Such testing may have a direct negative effect on their efficiency ratios. If this happens, foremen, general foremen, superintendents and others may become suspicious and resentful of our presence. This not only will make our stay in Reginal less pleasant; it also will deprive us of a channel of information which is essential for a balanced assessment. Should supervision come to view us as a challenge to their control and as a threat to their effectiveness, we simply will not be able to do our job.

Summing up, we had a good couple days in Reginal, and our trip was quite successful; however, I spotted some potential problems which should be discussed. First, the lines of communication/authority have to be clear. We want to make sure that we don't obscure these lines by responding to individual requests. Second, the tightness of the Reginal operation presents us and lower-level supervision with some problems. If we take the amount of time necessary to conduct a detailed assessment, we are likely to inhibit efficiency. Since supervision is graded so closely, they may come to resent our presence. This problem might be made worse by distrust between employees and lower-level supervision. Supervision may come to view us not only as an inconvenience but as a threat to their control. These problems are not unusual, nor are they more prevalent at the Reginal plant than at other places we have visited. If they are not dealt with early, however, they could become significant roadblocks in the way of a detailed, comprehensive, and correct evaluation of the change attempt. I hope we can begin a discussion through which solutions to these problems can be found.

Sincerely,

Michael Moch
Site Coordinator
Assessment Team

While Deigh was waiting to discuss the "efficiency-first" orientation with the members of JQWLAC, the assessors continued to develop the questionnaire. They identified ten categories of issues that had been mentioned during the on-site interviews and mailed this list to Reginal. The list is presented as Exhibit 5-2. Joe Gromanger, concerned that Matson might think he had not been properly informed, left him a copy of the list. Gromanger then took a copy to George Newman at union headquarters and left additional copies with the EJEC cochairpersons for distribution to the other committee members.

EXHIBIT 5-2 Topic Categories Recommended for the Survey Questionnaire

1. Communication:
   a. Vertical: Questions . . . would deal with . . . communication between foremen and their employees, between management and superintendents, between superintendents and foremen, etc.
   b. Horizontal: . . . communications among people of similar work. Especially important here will be communication among co-workers.
   c. Union-Management–Union-Employee: . . . communication between the local Union and management, between the local and its FoodCom members, between the local and the international, and between the international and its FoodCom members in Reginal.
2. Interpersonal Relations: . . . relationships between people working on the same shift in the same department. Management (assistant foremen to superintendent) would be asked about their relationships with other managers. Nonmanagement personnel would be asked only about their relationships with other nonmanagement personnel.
3. Intergroup Relations
   a. Vertical: . . . relations between management and employees and between different levels of management. (It is likely that we will need different versions of the questionnaire for management and for employees.)

b. Horizontal: . . . relations between departments such as baking, packing, and maintenance.
c. Union: . . . how people feel about their union (local and international). We also might try to get at how people think their union officers feel about them.

4. People's beliefs about the people that work in the Reginal plant: . . . whether employees are discouraged or encouraged, how much pride they have in their work, and so on.
5. Training and Role Clarity: Many of the people we talked with felt that they or others really didn't have a clear idea about how to do their jobs. Some people felt that they often couldn't tell what was expected of them. Questions about these sorts of issues might be included here.
6. Influence: Some people felt that they weren't listened to. Some others wanted hourly workers to take a greater part in decision-making. Questions which get at these things may go in this category.
7. The nature of the jobs at FoodCom, Reginal: . . . questions concerning how jobs are assigned, whether people feel they have the proper equipment and support, whether employees feel their jobs are monotonous, etc.
8. Safety and Health: Several employees had suggestions dealing with health issues (such as flour in the air when the mixers are blown out) or safety (such as the way the mixers are cleaned and how the parking lot is secured). Questions dealing with these concerns could go here.
9. Policies: Several people expressed disagreement with some policies which appear to have been made by the union and FoodCom management. For example, there were frequent comments concerning classification, seniority, and changing shifts. Some other concerns seemed relevant only to management (such as not replacing people on sick leave). Others appeared to concern only the union (some feel they protect employees who should be let go). All these kinds of issues should fall in this category.
10. Miscellaneous: We will need to know several things about each of the respondents, such as age, race, sex, tenure with FoodCom, tenure at the Reginal plant, and so on. . . . The respondent's knowledge of and opinions about the EJEC might also be included here.

Deigh met with FoodCom corporate management at world headquarters on the same day EJEC members started working with the assessors' classification scheme. Coy had asked Pond and Farr to be present but did not invite any staff people. Deigh introduced the agenda as a discussion of "emerging glitches" and sought to establish two ground rules for dealing with them. First, he argued that the emerging problems should be interpreted positively. Having surfaced early, they could be rapidly addressed to avoid hurting the program later. Second, he asked those present not to take action on the problems without first talking to him. He expressed concern that any cure they might come up with might be worse than the disease.

Deigh then described the problems associated with efficiency constraints and with Matson's insistence that everything go through him before being disseminated. Farr and Coy both said that they had been monitoring the project very closely. They had told Matson that he was on the cutting edge of change at FoodCom and that Frank Struthers was watching his progress. The previous Thursday, the day before Matson had gotten angry because he had not been given a copy of the list of problems and questions, headquarters had told him to prepare a speech about the QWL project to present at the next plant managers' meeting. At this time there had been no let up in productivity standards. Matson had effectively been trying to staff the QWL program without securing additional workers. Coy recognized the problem and promised to ask the accounting people to find a way of allocating labor hours for QWL program activities. He and the others were less flexible when it came to allocating time for the survey. Coy, Farr, and Pond thought that they were being asked to incur costs that had not been mentioned in the initial proposal. Deigh sympathized with them, but disclaimed responsibility for the poor communication. He had not been on staff when the initial contract was negotiated. A bit disgruntled, the managers agreed to pay straight time for an extra hour before or after each shift so employees could fill out the questionnaire. Deigh returned to Washington believing that the management members of JQWLAC had made a significant accommodation. Management was, in his terms, "beginning to recognize that they are creating several problems for their plants in their efficiency-first mode of operation."

The next day Coy called Deigh to tell him that the company had changed its mind. No funds would be made available to enable employees to take the questionnaire after hours. Deigh immediately drafted a memo to Pond, Farr, Coy, Seldon, and Kochems. He began by noting that "the pressure for 'efficiency no matter what' had already begun to create pressures on the effort to bring about meaningful change. . . . With the formal and informal reward system of FoodCom . . . so closely tied to efficiency, even the most minute potential interference with that all-important figure produces great pressures and stresses throughout the system." He reminded FoodCom management that Ted Mills had told them to expect a temporary decline in efficiency, "even though all our efforts are, at least in part, attuned to the need to make any such downturn minimal and for the shortest period possible." The efficiency-first-and-foremost orientation was creating a situation, Deigh argued, in which "no matter how much local Reginal management may want to work to ensure success of the (QWL) project, such pressures from 'on high' make real progress extremely difficult—there is no way they can perceive that 'investing a dollar today to make five dollars tomorrow' will result in positive recognition for them." The efficiency-first perspective placed plant management in Reginal in a difficult if not completely untenable position. The local management was expected to encourage the development of new processes and techniques without even temporary decline in the plant's previously high levels of efficiency. Deigh reiterated that handing out questionnaires and picking them up the next day or handing out the questionnaires in the morning and picking them up that afternoon was unacceptable. He suggested shutting down lines or paying straight time for an hour before or after each shift. He concluded by noting that the company was planning to invest $250,000 in a project that could well be diffused throughout the company. The cost of shutting down lines would run about $6000 and generate data that could be critical for the success of the program. The cost of three surveys would not exceed $20,000, which was less than 10 percent of the total program budget and a small price to pay for an activity that promised so much for FoodCom worldwide.

Meanwhile, EJEC members, unaware of this problem, continued to develop the questionnaire instrument. Susan Sheffer suggested that employees might resist requests to report on their interpersonal relationships. George Newman did not want to include questions on union intergroup relations. He argued that the important parts of this issue could be covered by a set of questions on communication in general. Several EJEC members pointed out, however, that the questionnaire might help identify union problems that might otherwise go unnoticed. The committee decided to retain questions about union intergroup and interpersonal relations.

When the assessors sent the list of ten issue categories (Exhibit 5-2) to Reginal, they also sent a list of ideas that did not fit neatly into any of the categories. In their interviews with the assessors, employees had made a variety of concrete suggestions. The assessors sent a list of thirty-three of these to the EJEC along with the issue categories. They are presented in Exhibit 5-3.

EXHIBIT 5-3 Suggestions Made by Employees at the Reginal Bakery: Supplement to the Problem Category List

1. There should be more mop sinks on the lower packing floor.
2. Some people never get to see Mr. Deigh.
3. The clocks should have a light on them so people can see them from far away.
4. It would be helpful to have something to protect lungs and ears from cookie meal.
5. It would be good to have some different scenery in the cafeteria.
6. Some respondents wanted to have athletic facilities available.
7. Twenty minute lunch breaks are insufficient.
8. Packers should not have to crawl under packing lines.

9. Alter lockers in the change room to facilitate cleaning them.
10. Crumb catcher on oven #3 should be made wider to allow easier removal of crumbs.
11. Some on third shift would like to start on Sunday night rather than Monday night.
12. Salt from overhead conveyor gets into hair and clothes.
13. People should put their names on their uniforms.
14. Uniforms should be changed more frequently.
15. The uniforms are old, uncomfortable, indecent, and sometimes a safety hazard.
16. More pants should be distributed.
17. The cafeteria should be opened for the third shift.
18. There is too much improper parking and littering in the lot.
19. People take too long on breaks.
20. Some want a new refreshment area in the lower packing area.
21. Some want a no-smoking area in the cafeteria.
22. There is insufficient consideration for company property.
23. The rest rooms should be made more comfortable.
24. Ink on the end seals can cause rashes.
25. Food services could be improved.
26. A four-day, ten-hour day week could conserve gas.
27. The laboratory personnel should get their own samples.
28. There should be more social activities such as bowling leagues, dances, and so forth.
29. The plant is not a social club; there's too much socializing.
30. The temperature is uneven. It's too hot in some places and too cold in others.
31. The clothing room is understaffed.
32. The time clocks all have different times. It's difficult to know when to return from breaks.
33. Packers have only 20 minutes for lunch, and management takes too long ordering. They hold up the line.

Vince Keeley thought that quick action on some of the issues on this list could provide the QWL program with some badly needed momentum. In particular, he thought that the committee could arrange for proper coordination and placing of the clocks and for a nonsmoking area in the cafeteria. He proposed these projects to his fellow EJEC members.

The EJEC members continued to prepare for the first plantwide survey. Deigh had informed Gromanger that there was some doubt about whether the questionnaire would be administered at all. Without telling EJEC members that FoodCom had yet to approve the survey, Gromanger advised them to postpone consideration of questionnaire administration, saying the planning was "a bit premature."

Vice-President Struthers called a meeting of QWL program personnel at the FoodCom world headquarters to resolve the questionnaire administration issue. Matson flew in from Reginal for the meeting, which Seldon and Kochems also attended. Pond and Coy represented corporate management. Deigh and the assessment coordinator were also present.

Struthers opened the meeting by stressing the importance of the activities in Reginal. He said that the QWL program was a very high priority project, but then revealed that he had personally reversed the earlier decision to use company funds to administer the questionnaire. He had done so, he said, because of the expense involved. Cost was an extremely important concern. Disagreeing with the spirit of Deigh's memorandum, Struthers emphasized that the absence of slack in Reginal was a critical determining factor in the plant's performance. The fact that employees did not have enough slack time to fill out a questionnaire was desirable, not deplorable. He believed in running a tight ship and took personal exception to the implication in the assessment coordinator's letter that a concern for efficiency was bad. Pond said that he, too, took personal exception to the memo. He particularly resented the implication that his concern about minimizing costs meant that he didn't care about people.

Struthers asked the assessment coordinator whether a 60

percent response rate would be adequate. The coordinator believed that an accurate assessment required a response rate considerably in excess of sixty percent. Struthers disagreed. He said he knew about marketing surveys, and they seldom had response rates higher than 60 percent. Pond advised that employees should fill the questionnaire out at home on their own time. Coy suggested that the company mail the questionnaire and pay five dollars for each one that was filled out and returned. Kochems thought it would be possible to put an assistance booth up in the plant. Here employees could get answers to their questions about the survey and receive reassurance about the confidentiality of their responses.

Those present were provided with copies of questions used in other sites. Looking at these, Pond questioned the utility of the seven-point scales used to quantify responses. He argued that many of the problem responses the questionnaire would measure are very difficult to quantify. Struthers then criticized the entire process that had made the meeting necessary. He thought it was inappropriate to communicate by sending memos back and forth.

At that point, Deigh expressed his frustration at having the earlier decision to pay employees to take the questionnaire reversed overnight. Kochems responded that the decision hadn't been reversed, because "we" (the top management) hadn't agreed to the plan in the first place. He and the other staff members hadn't even been invited to the meeting at which the decision had been made.

Finally Struthers declared that the company would provide the resources to pay employees to take the questionnaire. He reiterated his commitment to the program: "It's got Frank Struthers' name on it, and it's going to succeed!" Then he turned control of the meeting over to Dalmar Pond and left. After an uncomfortably long delay, Pond asked Matson exactly what the EJEC was going to do in Reginal. Pausing a little, Matson said "autonomous work groups—management of the eighties!" Pond then concluded the meeting by telling Matson that the company was counting on him to make the program in Reginal a success.

Deigh Won the Skirmish but Lost the Battle: Funds Were Provided for the Plantwide Survey, but the Control Perspective Was Reinforced in the Process

In the previous chapters we argued that QWL programs are likely to affect and be affected by the schemata through which organizational members give meaning and coherence to organizational events. We also noted that organizations are likely to have a variety of schemata and that different groups in organizations can be expected to view events through systematically different—and possibly opposing—interpretive lenses. In FoodCom's case, there were at least five distinct perspectives. These corresponded to differences among top company management, local plant management, junior FWIU workers, senior FWIU workers, plant supervisors and stewards, and IMU/ IEU personnel. All of these perspectives differed in significant ways from the view advocated by the QWL program staff.

The control model presented in Figure 3-1 reflected inferences drawn from observations of top company management. Although Pond, Coy, and the others seemed to accept the possibility that the QWL program could increase cooperation between labor and management, they emphasized productivity outcomes. Improvements in employee satisfaction could be justified only if they had a positive impact on the bottom line. The risk was that the program might actually reduce productivity. It could stir up old animosities and actually decrease employee satisfaction. Similarly, it could consume resources without creating commensurate increases in output.

FoodCom management had not been told they would be asked to pay for a plantwide questionnaire to be administered on company time. Their attempt to avoid the cost of administering the questionnaire is consistent with the control model specified in Figure 3-1 (model 1). If the questionnaire was not going to increase productivity, the cost of administering it could not be justified (f). Looking at the situation over the long term, if the first survey was administered and failed to produce the desired effect, then plans for the second and third surveys would have to be reassessed (f).

The QWL perspective advocated by Mills and Deigh (Figure 3-1, model 2) did not concede that the program could have a net negative effect on productivity, although Deigh acknowledged that there might be a short-term productivity decline. Any temporary decline in productivity, however, would be more than compensated for by long-term improvements. In effect, he argued that his model and the one held by top management could be reconciled by taking time lags for effects into account.

Thus the assessors had initiated a sequence of events that culminated in Deigh's challenge of top management's control model. Deigh attempted to reconcile the QWL and the control models by introducing the concept of lag times, but Struthers rejected this accommodation. Though he ultimately agreed to pay for the plantwide survey, Struthers reinforced the control model and objected to the process that brought about the challenge in the first place.

The assessors had enlisted Deigh's help, and Deigh had challenged top management. Struthers, though acquiescing in the case of the survey, chastised Deigh and the assessors for initiating the challenge in the first place. As an observer, Matson might have taken this admonition to heart. He was being given the responsibility for making sure the program was a success. It seemed evident, though, that he better not share his burden with Deigh if Deigh would respond by challenging the thinking of top management. An efficiency-first orientation was good, Struthers emphasized. It was not to be changed. Moreover, problems arising from within the program were to be resolved within the constraints established and maintained by the necessity of minimizing costs.

When people believe they see clearly using one particular perspective, they are often unable to appreciate the potential utility of a different one or even to realize the extent to which another perspective might have validity in its own right. The control model employed by top management, consistent with the general choice model presenting in Figure 1-1, had served the company well. There seemed to be no need to change. Management's goal should therefore be to get all involved to share the control perspective. If this could be accomplished, then everyone would accept activities consistent with the control model as rational and appropriate.

Deigh seemed to have felt a parallel frustration with his own model. The QWL model could work, but people in key positions weren't accepting it. If they could just see the critical role that employee satisfaction played in determining productivity, they would provide more support for the program. They gave no evidence, however, that they understood this. They gave Deigh what he needed—money for conducting the survey on company time—but they withheld the more critical element. They made no concessions to the cooperative model advocated by the QWL program.

The meeting participants' failure to reconcile their different perspectives placed considerable pressure on Matson. His superiors expected him to make the QWL program a success while simultaneously maintaining short-term efficiency standards, even though Deigh had explicitly stated that this might be impossible. Yet none of the participants in the meeting described above, including Deigh, seemed able to transcend their own perspectives sufficiently to see the other perspective. No one explicitly contrasted the two points of view and analyzed their costs and benefits. At the end of the meeting, success still meant greater long-term productivity and short-term conformity to efficiency standards for some participants. For others it meant greater long-term productivity and quality of work life with acceptable short-term efficiency losses. The meeting did nothing to reduce this ambiguity. It concluded by placing heavier responsibility for the program's success on the plant manager without giving him the resources necessary for the program to succeed. Moreover, it may have decreased the likelihood that he or Struthers's other subordinates would ever challenge the control model, even when more significant administrative problems presented themselves.

When he returned to Reginal, Matson told the assessors he was very angry that they had gone around him and written directly to Deigh about the problems they were having with the assessment. Matson also was concerned that the questionnaire would open old wounds. Nevertheless, he and the plant personnel director, Greg Charlton, began to make arrangements for administering the survey. The plan to administer the survey affected not only Matson, but also the newly chosen consultants from the Center for Organizational Design. Almost as soon as they were hired, Drew, Ferrer, and Sholl from COD had to respond to the planned plantwide survey—

a significant intervention by an outside group over which they had little control in a program that was about to become their responsibility. Drew was concerned that the questionnaire might raise unrealistic expectations, but he had no choice other than to make the best of the situation.

The assessors sent a draft questionnaire to the EJEC on March 21. Gromanger conducted a pilot application that indicated that the questions would take approximately one and one-quarter hours to complete. Matson and Charlton decided that administering the questionnaire before and after shifts would be too cumbersome, and after considering other alternatives, finally decided to shut down lines to allow workers to take the survey. A detailed schedule was worked out that allowed an average of thirty employees to be free during each hour over a three-day period. Matson used regular weekly management staff meetings to communicate this plan to department heads. The department heads were to advise lower-level supervisors who would in turn inform their subordinates. The questionnaire was therefore to be administered through the traditional management hierarchy rather than through the EJEC or the union.

At a JQWLAC meeting on April 13, union representatives said they wanted the survey to include questions that would assess the feelings of the Reginal employees regarding their union local and international leadership. Management representatives wanted questions about employees' perceptions of plant management. Deigh resisted, arguing that any JQWLAC request would only increase the pressure on Newman and Matson. He urged that the choice of questions be left to the local committee.

In Reginal, Newman urged Ferrer and Sholl to keep questions about the union and local union leadership out of the questionnaire. Reflecting Drew's previously stated concern, Sholl was worried that the survey might generate unrealistic expectations and make his job more difficult. Meeting with Deigh and Sholl in Reginal on April 18, the assessment coordinator offered to draft a letter to employees that would describe the purpose of the survey and hopefully allay fears that the information would be misused. Deigh supported the idea, but said that the letter should come from the EJEC. It should stress the diagnostic functions of the survey and emphasize that there would be no evaluation at this time. Rather, the survey would identify problem areas and gather baseline evaluation data.

The assessment coordinator drafted a letter from EJEC to Reginal employees. The letter stressed that responses would be kept in strictest confidence and that averages—not individual responses—would be fed back to employees. Responding to the commitment to provide feedback, Drew drafted a memorandum in which he outlined several alternative feedback designs. These designs ranged from simple data hand-back to detailed discussions within diagonal slice groups or organizational families. Diagonal slice groups would be composed of employees from different areas and lines. Organizational families were groups of employees who worked together every day. In accord with typical survey feedback procedure (e.g., Nadler 1977), Drew also suggested that the results might be shown first to top management and then disseminated from supervisor to subordinate down the organizational hierarchy.

Drew agreed with Deigh that whatever feedback method was adopted, discussions of the data should focus on interpreting the meaning of the responses rather than on evaluation and blame. He believed that even though the survey was the project of the EJEC, to identify the problems and respond to them would essentially be a management task. "If managers begin to feel that the survey problems are going to be taken care of by the EJEC, then I think we will quickly hit a stone wall," he said. Drew saw the EJEC as a "catalyst for the formation of appropriate task teams, joint union-management committees, or appropriate actions or interventions through the management hierarchy."

Deigh had met with several groups of IMU and IEU employees during March and had encouraged them to join the QWL program; however, they had reaffirmed their decision not to participate. The EJEC therefore decided to make the questionnaire available to maintenance department employees on a voluntary basis. A week before the questionnaire was to be administered, Charlton gave the maintenance department superintendent a questionnaire sign-up sheet that he posted in the department office. Several department employees interpreted this as management coercion, however, and the sheet was quickly removed.

The questionnaire was administered on schedule. Four days later, on May 24, Drew sent a memorandum to Matson in which he stressed that plant management should respond to the results of the survey and that the results should be shared with all plant employees. He stressed that plant management would be crucial in determining the success or failure of the feedback activities. In particular, he noted that "many of the survey data issues will be evaluated and acted upon by management and in many areas this is as it should be."

The Clocks

As noted earlier, the EJEC members were feeling pressure from their constituents to act more quickly to improve working conditions. Accordingly, Keeley appointed subcommittees to investigate several of these suggestions the assessors had obtained from plant employees during the on-site interviews (see Exhibit 5-3).

Some employees had complained about the clocks, which were not synchronized. Employees leaving for break at the right time according to the clock in their department might find the cafeteria clock ahead or behind. If it was ahead, they would lose break time. If it was behind, they would be "chewed out" by their supervisors for taking too long on break. In addition, some thought the clocks were poorly placed. Their view of the nearest clock might be blocked.

Keeley appointed himself and Bobby Clayton to look into this problem. He spoke to the maintenance department employee responsible for setting the clocks and asked him to be sure they all showed the same time, and then he and Clayton toured the plant and identified optimal clock locations. They then wrote a memorandum to Matson on behalf of the

EJEC asking that seven new clocks be purchased. The memo included information about where each clock should be located, with each location ranked in order of importance.

The Keeley-Clayton memo was forwarded to Matson on March 28. The next day Matson confided to Joe Gromanger that he was feeling considerable pressure from corporate management to accomplish something on the QWL project. The outside facilitators were going about things in the wrong way, Matson said. Instead of letting the EJEC members decide what needed to be done, they should tell the EJEC what projects to undertake. Specifically, he argued that the EJEC should implement an autonomous work group plan on one of the assembly lines.

On March 30 Matson complained to those attending his weekly staff meeting that if the EJEC subcommittee on clocks had pursued the facts, they would have discovered that it was impossible to keep all the clocks on the same time. With Keeley present, he suggested that the EJEC contact "someone like IBM" and investigate purchasing an entirely new clock system.

Soon thereafter Keeley received a request from another subcommittee, one appointed to develop a proposal for improving the restrooms. This subcommittee asked Keeley to request three additional clocks, one for each of the first floor restrooms in the packing department and one for the men's lounge in the bake shop. Keeley did so, and Matson approved a purchase order for these and for the seven clocks requested earlier. However, he did not notify the EJEC. All Keeley knew was what Matson had reported during the staff meeting.

By late June maintenance workers had synchronized all the clocks. Within two weeks, however, the synchronizing device broke and the clocks were again uncoordinated. An outside contractor delivered the new clocks to Wally DeLeo, head of the maintenance department. DeLeo, apparently unaware that Keeley and Clayton had already identified locations for seven of them and that the other three were reserved for restrooms, decided to use them to replace old clocks. Such decisions were well within his traditional area of discretion, so he did not even think of informing Matson. As late as the third week in July, therefore, it appeared to EJEC members that nothing had been done on their request concerning clocks. Keeley gave the project up, believing that the EJEC proposal had not been approved.

A Nonsmoking Area for the Cafeteria

Soon after receiving the assessor's list of thirty-three recommendations, Keeley drafted a proposal for a nonsmoking area in the cafeteria. He forwarded it to Matson on behalf of the EJEC. Matson, consulting Charlton, responded that the EJEC needed to state how they expected to police the proposed no-smoking policy in the restricted area. Keeley thought that peer pressure would be adequate. Matson and Charlton were concerned, however, because the new area would occupy space to which some group had already laid claim.

If the new area included the tables under the window, Charlton thought it unlikely that maintenance employees who smoked would willingly go sit with packagers or bakers. If the new area included tables by the telephones, where would the female packagers sit who wanted to smoke? It was likely, he speculated, that the women would remain in the nonsmoking area and smoke rather than upset the established social patterns in the cafeteria. If this were to happen, it could reflect badly on the credibility of the QWL program.

On March 17, despite his reservations, Matson issued a work order to the maintenance department requesting that a nonsmoking area be cordoned off in the cafeteria. The EJEC asked that a "No Smoking" sign be posted in the area. When the area was cordoned off, however, no sign was posted. As a result, it took awhile for employees to find out why the area had been sectioned off. When they found out, there was further confusion because the restricted area was taken primarily from the space used by black employees. Some blacks who wanted to smoke moved elsewhere. Others, resenting the intrusion into their space, remained and continued to smoke. Nancy Daly petitioned the EJEC on behalf of these employees, claiming that the new area reflected racially discriminatory behavior. Soon thereafter someone—no one was sure who—reduced the size of the new area by about half. Keeley and

Clayton suspected that Matson had ordered the change, and resented the fact that they were not consulted. By the third week of June, the smaller nonsmoking area was in place and, with varying degrees of accommodation, accepted. However, it remained without a sign.

Restroom and Cafeteria Projects

Exhibit 5-3 included recommendations that the cafeteria be open during third shift, that there be a refreshment area in the lower packing area, that the restrooms be made more comfortable, that food services be improved, and that there be some different scenery in the cafeteria. Accordingly, Keeley appointed EJEC members to two subcommittees, one to examine the cafeteria problem and the other to evaluate the restrooms. Bobby Clayton and Patricia Roper became the cafeteria subcommittee, and Mark Dalton and Louis Young were assigned to the restroom committee. The company had a contract with an outside company, Reliable Foods, to operate the cafeteria. Clayton and Roper, therefore, had to deal with a firm the company could not directly control. They told Reliable Foods that their machines frequently ran out of product on third shift. Reliable Foods promised to install a larger pastry machine and to instruct their employees to restock the other machines more frequently. Clayton and Roper also asked Reliable Foods to remain open during third shift, but Reliable Foods refused, saying that remaining open would only pay if there were more than 125 employees working that shift.

The restroom committee requested and received new or repaired shower heads for the restrooms and a lock for a dirty clothes hamper in the women's dressing area. They also drafted a proposal for refurnishing the lounge areas. Having completed these assignments, Dalton and Young were reassigned to a newly constituted cafeteria and restroom subcommittee, along with Clayton and Roper. Johnny Pepin became chairperson. Wayne Sholl of COD visited the Reginal plant on April 4. He checked in with Matson upon arrival and was told that the EJEC subcommittees were developing proposals in areas that he, Matson, had already studied. In some cases, Matson said, he even had a budget worked out and approved. He wanted the subcommittees to investigate these areas without his input, however, because these were to be EJEC programs, not management projects. He thought that the subcommittees would come to the same conclusions he had and develop proposals in areas where he already had budgetary approval.

Sholl responded that Matson's withholding of information forced the EJEC to "reinvent the wheel." They would waste their time studying projects that management had already concluded were not feasible or too expensive. Matson disagreed, saying he would take the matter up with Deigh.

On May 11 the cafeteria and restroom subcommittee members sent a proposal to Matson requesting an air conditioner for the restroom in the mixing area. They also recommended that a lounge attached to this room be opened to women, with sex restrictions applying only to the actual bathroom area. On May 17 they requested that a table, chairs, and ashtrays be placed in the restroom in the bake shop.

During the first week in June Matson confided to the assessors that he was feeling pressure from several directions. He thought that the program was in trouble because it had not been sold to management before it had been introduced into the plant. Moreover, it should have been initiated by the IMU, rather than the FWIU, because the machinists were "feeling second fiddle." Supervisors also were wary. Some were beginning to fear that the program would reduce their roles. Matson had told them that they would be coaches rather than supervisors, but this had not seemed to help. Wayne Sholl was little help. Sholl was too "dormant," according to Matson, and had tried to turn assistant manager Billy Youngman against him. Accordingly, Matson had told Sholl not to speak to Youngman unless he, Matson, were present. Deigh, he said, whom employees were looking to as "God-Almighty," had been relaxing on the project. As a consequence, Matson thought the QWL program could easily "go to hell."

Matson noted that many of the changes proposed by the cafeteria and restroom committee had been included in the previous union contract. Money had already been allocated for a new restroom in the packing department and for air conditioning in the bake shop restrooms. The only new proposal the subcommittee had offered was the request for chairs in the restrooms. He rejected that proposal on the grounds that the requested chairs were too expensive and that the employees would cut them up. He did approve cheaper padded chairs. Wally DeLeo, who was responsible for buying them, ordered even cheaper plastic chairs.

Matson said the cafeteria subcommittee was also pursuing ideas that were being developed before the QWL program arrived. He had personally developed plans for a complete renovation of the cafeteria, but was frustrated because the subcommittee had resisted his plan to make the cafeteria look like a nice restaurant.

On June 6 Farr visited Reginal to help Matson find a way to deal with these and other problems associated with the QWL program. He confided to Matson that he knew QWL projects would be difficult to implement, so he shouldn't be too afraid to fail. He also encouraged Matson to delegate more responsibility to his subordinates. Accordingly, Matson requested that the cafeteria and restroom subcommittee meet with himself, Charlton, Youngman, and DeLeo.

This meeting took place on June 23. The cafeteria and restroom subcommittee members hoped to present their requests and receive cost estimates from management. They recommended an acoustical ceiling for the cafeteria, new paint for the walls, a carpet, a place to store employees' lunch boxes, a new arrangement with Reliable Foods for more frequent servicing of the vending machines, and an updating of the food service. For the restrooms, they recommended air conditioning, new chairs and tables, ashtrays, mirrors, new paint for the walls, and ventilation for the first floor restroom in the packing department.

Matson challenged several of the specific recommendations. He thought that a carpet would be too difficult to maintain, and suggested that the walls be paneled or papered rather than painted. Instead of a space for lunch boxes, he proposed a chute arrangement. He also concluded that he could not decide about any of the requests until the subcommittee provided accurate cost estimates. The subcommittee had expected management to assume the costing responsibilities. When Matson began to assign responsibility for determining costs to different subcommittee members, Pepin complained that they were not capable of making such technical judgments. Youngman sarcastically asked Pepin if he expected management to make the cost estimates, and Pepin did not press the issue further.

After the meeting, subcommittee members returned to an EJEC meeting in progress at the time. They were disappointed that they had been unable to make greater progress. Louis Young concluded that they had tried to move too fast, and Bobby Clayton thought that it would take more time to get things done than they had expected. However, confiding to the assessors, Gromanger said he thought he detected anger and frustration directed toward plant management:

> [Some members of the subcommittee] began to realize that Matson has an entire plan for the cafeteria in his head and is trying to get the cafeteria subcommittee to keep shooting in the dark until they hit upon a plan which is similar to his. What made them madder was the fact that Matson would give them no indication of how much money the company might be willing to spend on the project. They felt it was ridiculous to go shopping around for costs on all of these recommendations without some idea of their budget constraints.

Some EJEC members who had not been present at the meeting, particularly management representatives, began to complain openly that Matson was systematically ignoring the problems with which they had been grappling. Keeley suggested that the EJEC find ways to communicate their frustration directly to the JQWLAC. Perhaps they should start to take detailed notes to document their case should they ever have an opportunity to present it to higher company and union management.

EJEC members agreed that they should not assume the responsibility for estimating the costs of their suggestions. This, they thought, should be a management function. At

Sholl's suggestion they conducted a plantwide survey to document employee preferences. This would provide them with ammunition to press their cause. For example, they could clearly show employee preferences for painted or papered walls, Musak for the cafeteria, or better food service. If management failed to respond and the documentation of employee preferences was compelling, JQWLAC could not help but side with them against plant management.

The cafeteria and restroom subcommittee reconvened on July 6. Pepin had attempted to secure cost estimates on various music systems for the cafeteria, but had found that he couldn't get cost estimates without first establishing the size of the room, the number of available electric outlets, possible antennae locations, and a variety of other features. He also had no idea how much money management was willing to spend. On July 7 members of the subcommittee filed into Matson's office to meet once again with him and Charlton, DeLeo, and Youngman. Drew and Sholl had advised them to state their position clearly and to maintain their solidarity. This they intended to do.

Pepin began by explaining that the subcommittee saw its role primarily as a communication link between employees and plant management. It did not believe that its functions included cost estimation. Each subcommittee member then presented a section of the survey results indicating that the employees wanted better vending machine service, fresh food on all shifts, cleaner cafeteria facilities, and quicker line service. Issues associated with the cafeteria decor fell far down on the list.

Matson discouraged the committee from pursuing better food service, citing inevitably higher costs. He said that he too had surveyed the employees and that they were interested in changes in decor. Subcommittee members reviewed their data to the contrary and said that employees might be willing to pay the higher costs if they received better food service. Matson argued that Reliable Foods would not be receptive to food service suggestions, because it would become more difficult for them to make a profit. Youngman added that he wouldn't install new machines if he were Reliable Foods, because the employees would pound on them and damage them. A subcommittee member retorted that employees pounded on them because they didn't work properly.

At this point DeLeo interjected that he and Matson had been working on a cafeteria decor project for some time. He seemed genuinely surprised that the employees preferred food service improvements to changes in decor. Matson studiously ignored DeLeo and quickly agreed to consider food service issues. He would contact the vendors and arrange a meeting between them and the subcommittee, and he promised to have cost information regarding food service improvements within two weeks. The subcommittee members were surprised, pleased, and skeptical. They carefully documented Matson's statements by entering them in the EJEC minutes. They also drafted two articles for an EJEC newsletter to be sent to all employees on July 18. The first, titled "EJEC Survey, Cafeteria Results Surprising," is presented as Exhibit 5-4. The second, "Cafeteria Being Discussed," is presented as Exhibit 5-5.

EXHIBIT 5-4 July 18 EJEC Newsletter Article Titled, "EJEC Survey, Cafeteria Results Surprising"

The results of the EJEC survey and the cafeteria survey showed some interesting patterns in employees' desires regarding their work-life here in the Bakery.

From the general EJEC survey, the committee and the subcommittees were able to establish a priority for different projects based upon the strength of the employees' responses to different items. By far, the parking lot came out as the most worthwhile issue for the EJEC to consider, and a parking lot subcommittee was established to look into it. The condition of the cafeteria and restrooms also emerged as areas which people would like to see improved. Though there was not a majority of the people expressing an interest in the various social activities listed, there was enough interest to warrant the social subcommittee to set up softball games, picnics, and bowling leagues. On the other hand, the people expressed a negative reaction to the idea of rearranging the present relief schedule to allow more time for lunch, so the EJEC dropped this as a possible project.

As mentioned, there was an indication that the employees would like to see some changes made in the cafeteria. The cafeteria subcommittee speculated that the desired changes might be in the area of atmosphere and decor. However, from the results of the cafeteria survey, they found that employees were more interested in items relating to food service and cleanliness. From this information, the subcommittee changed its emphasis to food service issues, such as improved vending machine service and improved food service on second and third shifts.

EXHIBIT 5-5 July 18 EJEC Newsletter Article Titled, "Cafeteria Being Discussed"

The EJEC cafeteria subcommittee and a management committee including Messrs. Matson, Youngman, Charlton, and DeLeo have been meeting the past several weeks to discuss possible changes in the cafeteria which are designed to improve the food service and atmosphere of the cafeteria.

Ideas for improvements which were submitted by the EJEC subcommittee were obtained from a survey it initiated. About 150 employees were asked what sorts of improvements they would like to see implemented in the cafeteria. Most of the suggestions dealt with improving the steam table and vending machine services. Also high on the list were such items as cleaner cafeteria facilities and requests to schedule relief periods for employees in the bakery such that long counter lines are avoided.

The cafeteria subcommittee, headed by chairman Johnny Pepin, presented the results of the survey to the management committee and requested that, in accordance with employee desires, both committees arrange their objectives to concentrate on food service and related items.

The management committee is currently scheduling meetings with Reliable Foods and other vendors to discuss food service improvements. The EJEC subcommittee will be communicating the employees' desires at these meetings.

In addition to food service and cleanliness issues, the EJEC and management committees will also look into improvements relating to the cafeteria decor and atmosphere.

Matson did contact Reliable Foods. The company agreed to look into the costs of fresher food for second shift, canned soda machines, and a candy machine, and to get back to Matson within two weeks. The next day, Matson met Gromanger in the cafeteria line and told him he was very upset with the outcome of the meeting with the cafeteria subcommittee. He said he was going to hire another consultant, since Sholl was not teaching EJEC members how to "assist management." Sholl should be teaching them how to draw up designs and estimate costs, he insisted. The subcommittee had been rude, especially Johnny Pepin. Matson then moved down the line to the area where Patricia Roper was waiting. Roper was a member of the cafeteria and restroom committee and had attended the meeting the previous day. Matson told her that he liked her work and that he was going to give her a raise. He then asked her whether she agreed with him that Pepin had been out of line the day before.

Roper later explained that Matson had "cussed and screamed at Johnny, because Johnny got a little smart (at the meeting the day before)." However, she thought Matson had acted in good faith by contacting Reliable Foods and by agreeing to make cost estimates for improving the food service. She also said that Matson could not do everything by himself. For example, he had to rely on the maintenance department to carry out any changes in the cafeteria or the restrooms.

The Parking Lot

Another issue raised during the assessment team's February interviews (see Exhibit 5-3) involved security in the plant parking lot. This had been mentioned most frequently by employees in the maintenance department. One of them had surprised a young man who was breaking into an employee's car. The maintenance worker had given chase, only to be gunned down by another youth who was waiting in the bushes. The weapon used had been of a high caliber, and the maintenance employee had come close to dying.

In March Keeley created an EJEC subcommittee on parking lot and uniforms composed of Dalton, Matson, Leticia Sanchez, and Jack Resler. This subcommittee began acting soon after it was established. Within ten days a guard responsible for plant security apparently complained to Billy Youngman that a subcommittee member had come to him demanding that the guards keep better watch on the parking lot. Youngman complained to Matson, and Matson, in Gromanger's words, came down on him and Keeley.

The subcommittee addressed several problems with the parking lot, including frequent thievery, too few parking spaces, traffic jams at the end of the first and second shifts, and the danger of employees having to dodge moving traffic. They also considered several possible solutions, such as closing the parking lot and posting a guard at the gate or requiring an automobile identification sticker. The survey the EJEC had sent to employees included a question about the parking lot. Ninety-eight percent of the FWIU employees who responded were dissatisfied with the parking facilities, and twenty-nine of thirty-four maintenance employees who responded were also dissatisfied.

After Farr's June 6 visit, which inspired Matson to meet with the cafeteria and restroom subcommittee, Matson called for a meeting with the parking lot and uniforms subcommittee. Drew advised the subcommittee members to assume the role of employee representatives during the meeting. He advised them not to try to be design engineers or cost experts.

The subcommittee, accompanied by Sholl, presented its recommendations to Matson, Charlton, Youngman, and DeLeo immediately after the cafeteria and restroom subcommittee had made its second appeal to that group. They recommended installing an area for visitor parking, widening the rails that bordered the main driveway, rearranging parking spaces to allow for more slots, hiring security guards for all three shifts, and obtaining ID cards that would activate electronically controlled gates at the lot entrance.

Matson responded that he would need more detailed recommendations and reliable cost estimates before he could determine whether to support the subcommittee's proposals. He told the members that they would have to submit blueprints of their proposed design changes. Moreover, if they wanted to widen the main drive they would have to redesign the way it intersected with the city street. This meant they would have to contact the appropriate city officials to find out which city regulations applied and how to petition the city to allow for construction.

When the subcommittee members returned to the EJEC meeting room, members of the cafeteria and restroom subcommittee were already there. Members of both committees were very disappointed with Matson's response to their proposals. Some suggested that Matson had changed the rules of the game on them. Mark Dalton went so far as to say that for the first time since he had come to work for FoodCom, he felt like quitting.

The next day Sholl met with the EJEC executive committee. He told them he believed that the QWL program was involved in a political struggle. The rules had changed, and the situation required political tactics. Consequently, he reinforced his earlier contention that the subcommittees not provide the design specifications and cost estimates associated with their recommendations. These involved considerable technical detail and should be a management responsibility. He advised EJEC members that instead of providing design specifications, they should carefully document employee preferences through surveys and other means and record the events as they took place.

Subcommittee members made some attempts to comply with Matson's request for detailed information. They contacted the appropriate city official, but he was out of town. They generated a preliminary drawing of the design changes they sought for the parking lot. Joan Franks' son, who had drafting skills, helped Franks develop the drawing on her own time. On July 14 the EJEC handed out a parking lot improvement checklist with employees' paychecks. In a newsletter to employees sent out on July 18, the EJEC described the situation in a tactful but politically incisive manner. The article in the newsletter, titled "Parking Lot Studied," is presented in Exhibit 5-6.

EXHIBIT 5-6 July 18 EJEC Newsletter Article Titled, "Parking Lot Studied"

Messrs. Matson, Youngman, Charlton, and DeLeo have been meeting with the EJEC parking lot subcommittee to study various improvements related to security and traffic flow. Recently, these committees have been raising questions and exploring the legal aspects of altering the parking lot. Now that these legal questions have been reviewed, the parking lot committee will be designing a checklist survey to submit to the employees.

On the checklist survey, a number of items will be listed and employees will be asked to rank their preferences among these items. Items will include security alternatives such as erecting a guard hut by the entrance to the plant building, extending a chain-link fence along the guard rails leading from Scottsdale Boulevard, and requiring identification stickers on FoodCom Employee cars. Traffic flow items include widening the Scottsdale Boulevard gate, rearranging the parking spaces to allow for more available spaces, and extending the guard rails for improved traffic flow. Committee member Joan Franks has already had drawn up a diagram for increasing the available parking, which indicates possible sites for a guard hut.

New Uniforms

The assessment team's February interviews revealed considerable discontent with the uniforms. Some employees said the uniforms were too old, uncomfortable, too revealing, or, at times, a safety hazard. Accordingly, Keeley appointed an EJEC subcommittee to develop a proposal concerning the uniforms. As noted in the preceding section, this problem was combined with issues concerning the parking lot and given to Dalton, Matson, Sanders, and Resler to address.

FoodCom had been planning to issue new uniforms to its employees throughout the country. Plans were well underway and sample uniforms had already been ordered. Matson thought that by giving EJEC credit for the new uniforms he could bolster its image, so, in his words, he "threw them in" and agreed to EJEC participation.

On May 30, Dalton received samples of the new uniforms. They were sent to him not because he was a member of the uniforms subcommittee but because he was superintendent of the environmental services department. He immediately called Matson, who asked that the samples be brought to his office. Matson then called in Patricia Roper, Susan Sheffer, and Johnny Pepin, all management members of the EJEC. However, no union representatives on the EJEC were asked to review the uniforms, and the management representatives called in were not on the EJEC subcommittee responsible for uniforms.

Matson asked Pepin to display the samples in the packing department office and to call the shop stewards together to review the samples. When asked why he had not asked union members of the uniforms subcommittee to participate, he replied that the stewards were becoming envious of all the attention being showered on the EJEC. He also did not want union members of the EJEC involved, because they would have to take the employees' sizes and this would require that they work out of their classification.

The Project on Line 4

Product freshness was a critical problem for FoodCom. The company maintained a significant market share in part because its superior packaging preserved the freshness of its products. The competition had recently been making inroads in this area and the company responded by developing better packaging technology. One problem was that no matter how well a product was packaged initially, it would lose freshness as soon as the customer broke the package seal. Consequently, FoodCom had developed a new packaging process for one of its major projects that allowed customers to reseal packages easily after they had been opened. The process required new technology, which corporate headquarters decided to implement in Reginal.

Matson was responsible for testing and installing the new process; however, Youngman was in charge on a day-to-day basis. Matson and Youngman sought the advice of department superintendents and general forepersons. Pepin, the general foreperson in the packaging department, was surprised and pleased that plant management had asked for his input and had followed up on some of his ideas. Employees that far down the line had never before been allowed to have such an early say in the adoption of a new technology.

Pepin thought it would be a good idea to open the discussion even further. He raised the issue with Sholl and Gromanger and together they decided to get the EJEC involved in disseminating information about the new technology to hourly line workers. When they raised the issue, Matson was skeptical. He was certain Youngman would not like the idea and would resist anything that would take credit away from management. In addition, he thought that implementation was primarily an engineering problem. "Employees can't read blueprints," he said. However, it might be beneficial if discussion sessions with hourly workers were designed to disseminate information and if these sessions were run by management. EJEC people would be restricted to an advisory role.

This discussion took place in late April. On May 3 Pepin publicly threatened to quit the EJEC because management wouldn't let him disseminate the information to the hourly employees. Later that afternoon, Matson asked the EJEC executive committee if the EJEC would introduce hourly employees in the packing department to the new packaging process. Pepin remained on the EJEC.

The next day Matson used the weekly staff meeting to announce EJEC's new role. Johnny Pepin agreed to take administrative responsibility for running the training sessions, which were to start immediately. Afterwards, Youngman told Gromanger privately that the QWL program should get more involved with issues associated with efficiency, productivity, and machine down-time. He also said that Pepin had come on "like gangbusters" to get the EJEC involved.

Pepin conducted the first training session on May 10. He described how the EJEC sought to have employees become more involved in making decisions about their work. He explained why the change was taking place and went into some detail about the process itself. He presented blueprints for the new line, explained where the new machinery would be put, and described the design of a new switch system. He avoided telling workers that the new process would most likely eliminate three jobs.

Employee reaction was generally favorable, and Pepin soon found others willing to conduct training sessions on other shifts. Youngman consistently resisted EJEC involvement. He thought it was premature and preferred to postpone the training until the new equipment had been installed in August. Pepin nevertheless continued the sessions. By June 22 ten sessions had been run for groups of seven to twelve employees. After several sessions, Pepin began to describe how the process would eliminate several jobs; however, this did not seem to bother anyone. Some wanted to know if the new jobs would be easier. Nancy Daly asked why employees were being informed at such a late date and why the sessions hadn't been run earlier.

By the beginning of July the EJEC executive committee was considering how the QWL Program might become even more involved in the line 4 project. An article in a newsletter sent to plant employees on July 18 reviewed the training sessions. This article, titled "EJEC and Bakery Management Get Together on Plastic Film Conversion in Packing," is presented in Exhibit 5-7.

EXHIBIT 5-7 July 18 EJEC Newsletter Article Titled, "EJEC and Bakery Management Get Together on Plastic Film Conversion in Packing"

At the request of Bakery management, the EJEC assigned to the Packing subcommittee the responsibility of exploring ways of educating the people in Packing about the effects of the new plastic film being used to package materials. The plastic film is a superior packaging material and is replacing the cellophane which was previously used.

Working in cooperation with Leonard Duffield and his staff, the packing subcommittee scheduled meetings with small groups of employees to explain and answer questions relating to the plastic film conversion process. Part of the purpose of these meetings was to facilitate the communication between employees and supervision in the Packing Department. This is one of the goals of the quality of work life project here at the Reginal Bakery. When the opportunity presents itself, the EJEC will be attempting, with management's cooperation, to further enhance the communication and cooperation between groups in the bakery, not only between employees and supervision, but also between departments and union groups.

During the meetings in Packing, employee groups were also

> introduced to diagrams of the new packing line 4 and diagrams of the control buttons for this line. This, again, had the purpose of improving communication and providing the opportunity for employee involvement in the new packing line. Through the sharing of information, rumors regarding the new packing line were dispelled.

This newsletter also reviewed the progress of the cafeteria and parking lot subcommittees and announced that a joint meeting of the EJEC and JQWLAC would be held on July 20. The article in which this announcement was made, titled "Top Management, Union Officials Meet with EJEC" is presented in Exhibit 5-8. The meeting had been planned for some time. Several EJEC members saw it as an opportunity to document their own efforts and to expose Matson's lack of support. If they could show that the plant manager had been blocking progress, corporate management might have to take action.

EXHIBIT 5-8 July 18 EJEC Newsletter Article Titled, "Top Management, Union Officials Meet with EJEC"

The Joint Quality of Work Life Advisory Committee (JQWLAC) and the EJEC have planned a meeting at the Reginal Bakery for July 20. Attending from the JQWLAC will be Messrs. Coy, Farr, Seldon, and Pond from FoodCom, Inc. World Headquarters and Messrs. Scigliano, Papp, and Premater from the FWIU International.

Discussions will focus on a number of topics. The EJEC will be reviewing its organizational structure and how this structure has evolved over the past six months. Subcommittees will be reporting on their progress to date and on the methods they employ to increase the involvement of the people in the bakery in decisions affecting their work life here at the Reginal Bakery. The EJEC will also be exploring prospects for future activities aimed at increasing employee involvement and participation. Another issue which will be discussed is the results of the plantwide questionnaire conducted by the evaluation team and possible methods of feeding back the results of this questionnaire to the employees at the plant in order that it serve as a learning experience.

In addition to reviewing the EJEC activities for the past six months, the EJEC will be using this meeting with the JQWLAC as an opportunity for more direct contact with top management and the international union officials.

The Maintenance Department and the Maintenance Department Subcommittee

On March 11 Chuck Josephson, the nonvoting supervisory EJEC representative from the maintenance department, decided to resign. The other supervisors in his department were upset that their representative couldn't vote, and Josephson believed that none of them would take his place. When the EJEC discussed his resignation, Newman vetoed the idea the Josephson vote in place of any absent management representative, but both he and Matson decided to become nonvoting EJEC members. They hoped this would make Josephson feel better. Their resignations as voting members also opened the possibility that another FWIU member could be elected, which would mean that Josephson could be appointed to the open management position. Josephson agreed to remain on the committee temporarily until a decision about another union member was reached.

In the meantime Deigh made another attempt to enlist the IMU and IEU locals in the QWL program. He met with several groups of maintenance workers on March 21 and 22. After introducing himself, describing the NQWC, and reviewing the history of the project in Reginal, he presented the QWL program as an opportunity to establish a new form of labor-management relations in the Reginal plant.

Deigh argued that the QWL program presented workers and management with a "win-win" situation. Both parties could benefit by identifying areas where their interests overlapped and then by working to further these interests. Most of the maintenance workers' responses were cynical. They described the FoodCom suggestion system as an example of how management could not be trusted. The system provided bonuses to employees whose ideas were implemented within a certain amount of time after they had been suggested. Several machinists felt that management had intentionally postponed implementation to avoid paying the bonus. Consequently, the workers had stopped making suggestions.

Deigh argued that QWL program would be like the suggestion system, but that it would be set up so that everyone could trust it. At this statement, many employees openly questioned Deigh's competence. They asked him what he was going to do to make sure the QWL program was administered impartially. Deigh described his role as a third party facilitator. His questioner then said, "It sounds to me like you're not gonna be doin' nuthin'!" After a brief silence, another maintenance worker said "Somebody's gonna get fucked." An older employee stood up, red-faced, and claimed that before anyone tried to cooperate with anyone, management had to be willing to clean its own house. Others rallied to his support.

Two days later the chief steward of the IEU local, Neal Drinan, reported that his workers were ready to participate in the QWL program. The millwrights (IMU members), he said, were still "playing politics." He added that there were only eleven electricians among the ninety-odd maintenance department employees and that the IEU couldn't bring the whole department along by itself.

On March 28 Scott Lowry was accepted by the EJEC as the official IEU voting representative. Neal Drinan was installed as Lowry's alternate. With the addition of a new union member, Josephson was given full voting status. It was no longer necessary to elect an additional FWIU representative. Newman and Matson retained their nonvoting status partly to avoid having to redraft the EJEC rules, which limited the total number of management members to eight.

Drinan advised the EJEC to move quickly on some of the issues facing the maintenance department, suggesting that the millwrights would join them if it became clear they were "missing out on some action." On April 4 EJEC Chairperson Keeley established a maintenance department subcommittee consisting of Josephson and Lowry. Within a week this committee proposed the purchase of a new file cabinet for electrical blueprints. Matson immediately approved a purchase order for this cabinet along with one for a cabinet for machine diagrams for the machinists. He thought that by treating the machinists and electricians the same, he would show the IMU workers that their interests were being considered and that they too could benefit from the QWL program.

By the end of April management had promised the maintenance department subcommittee additional clerical help, a new two-person Cushman scooter, and a lockable metal tool cabinet. This committee had also ordered and received a new suggestion box for the QWL program, which they mounted next to an EJEC bulletin board. Finally, Josephson had experimented with new sodium vapor lights and was proceeding with plans to place them throughout the plant. They appeared to give off greater illumination and cut energy consumption by roughly 75 percent.

Drinan resigned as Lowry's alternate within three weeks of his installment. He thought that EJEC took too much time to make decisions and that the decisions weren't being implemented. The new scooter and tools, for example, had not yet arrived. Lowry and Josephson pushed ahead, replacing shower heads and valves for the restroom subcommittee and designing EJEC decals to be placed by each new EJEC accomplishment.

Josephson ensured that EJEC projects received priority and would often do them himself. However, his dedication to EJEC projects meant that other maintenance personnel were more burdened than ever. Some of the regular work (such as the line 4 project) had high priority as well, and DeLeo felt overburdened. Subsequently, during a staff meeting on May 25, Matson announced that the maintenance department was not to work on any EJEC work orders he had not personally signed. In addition, he asked DeLeo to keep a log of all EJEC projects and their associated costs.

Within a week Josephson and Lowry were complaining to Gromanger that DeLeo was sitting on EJEC work orders. Moreover, the list of tools they had requested had been changed. Some had been deleted. When confronted, DeLeo said he had held up all work and purchase orders until more people were involved in EJEC projects.

Sholl, Gromanger, Keeley, and Clayton met on June 6 to try to find a way to break the logjam in the maintenance department. They decided to monitor the progress of EJEC work orders so they could document the lack of progress and attribute it to maintenance personnel. Sholl suggested a three-step procedure. First, EJEC projects would be tracked during regular staff meetings. Department superintendents would be expected to explain why projects were being held up. Second, EJEC members would meet occasionally with Wally DeLeo to check on the status of EJEC projects. Finally, the EJEC would keep copies of all EJEC work orders. Each one would have Matson's signature, so when a project was being held up, EJEC would be able to document the authority behind its request for priority treatment.

The variance Matson had received from top management allowed him to charge EJEC time to an account funded by the FWIU. The FWIU, however, could not pay for the time spent by an IEU worker and Matson was not willing to ask corporate management for another variance. As a result, Scott Lowry had to charge the time he spent on EJEC activities to the maintenance department, and DeLeo had to absorb Lowry's time against his own efficiency score (e.g., employee hours for line changeovers).

EJEC work orders continued to receive low priority ratings in the maintenance department. By June 20, several EJEC members had become pessimistic about ever having good relationships with the maintenance people. Alan Quane, for example, thought that "they have no feeling for us at all. . . . There's some open animosity. . . . They get all the work and all the overtime. I wish it could be the electricians, but it's the mechanics. That's what hurts!" Lowry was equally discouraged: "We asked for things they should have done years ago. . . . We had a meeting Thursday with Matson to turn in a tool list. They deleted a couple of items. They (had) agreed to buy a two-man scooter, but they (now) appear to want to buy a one-man. I don't know how much cooperation we'll get. . . . We turn things over to Wally DeLeo, but don't have much authority. . . . If the maintenance department superintendent can say no to a (EJEC) decision, this can't work."

Marie McCarthy, the EJEC member whose husband was a steward for the IMU local, rejected the idea that the machinists were being intentionally uncooperative. She said they were "snowed under with the work they have to do. Our projects are not top priority. Redoing line 4 is priority." Joan Franks agreed. "The big slowup is the maintenance department," she said. "They've just got so many people and the (EJEC) can't be the first priority. The problem isn't EJEC, it's just that they don't have people to do the work." Bobby Clayton thought the machinists would not cooperate with the QWL program until the EJEC and the FWIU stopped blaming them for the slow progress. "Once they get the message we're not pointing (at) them, they'll come into the program," he said.

Meanwhile, Wayne Sholl continued to advise the EJEC to document the progress of each project. He and Gromanger believed they might be able to identify problems that had been addressed by EJEC subcommittees but ignored by management and list them in an EJEC newsletter. They hoped to have the newsletter out before the joint EJEC-JQWLAC meeting.

Was Roger Matson the Problem? An Alternative Explanation

Matson seemed to be sending two opposing messages at once. As a member of the EJEC, he supported the subcommittee activities. As the plant manager, however, he criticized the subcommittees' activities and demanded more from them than they were prepared or perhaps able to deliver. In an attempt to reconcile EJEC projects with the need to avoid additional expenses, he sought to merge EJEC proposals with the company plans for which budgetary approval had already been obtained. In the process, however, he had to oppose those aspects of each EJEC proposal that were not included in previously approved plans. Even when projects and established company plans were identical, he appeared to be duplicitous, supporting projects as EJEC initiatives when it was clear they were going to be implemented with or without EJEC sponsorship. He supported the EJEC's recommendation that the plant acquire new uniforms, yet they had already been ordered. He pressured the cafeteria subcommittee to recommend changes in decor, when many of these recommendations had already received corporate approval. He did not want the subcommittee members to try to improve food service and was certain he could convince EJEC members that recommendations concerning decor were their own ideas. If they found out that recommendations on decor were already in the works, this would be more difficult to do. So when DeLeo announced that considerable progress had already been made on a plan to improve the cafeteria decor, Matson abruptly terminated the discussion and agreed to pursue food service issues with Reliable Foods. Soon thereafter, however, he openly criticized Sholl and some of the subcommittee members for not "assisting management."

As long as EJEC recommendations could be accommodated within approved expenditure plans, they were approved. When EJEC recommendations involved new activities or acquisitions, however, they frequently ran into trouble. The survey encountered considerable opposition. The new clocks were not mounted in the locations recommended by the EJEC subcommittee, the sign requested for the nonsmoking area in the cafeteria was never made, and the space reserved for nonsmokers was mysteriously reduced. Specifications for changes in the restrooms were resisted, and less costly recommendations were made without the knowledge of the EJEC subcommittee. Recommendations made by the parking lot subcommittee were considered unacceptable because of lack of documentation, yet Youngman resisted the idea that management provide such documentation. Matson himself resisted EJEC involvement in the line 4 project until Pepin threatened to resign from the EJEC. Movement was slow on maintenance department subcommittee requests until Drinan resigned from the EJEC; Josephson then had some success moving EJEC projects ahead, primarily because he implemented them himself. However, this success was short-lived. DeLeo resisted moving rapidly on EJEC work orders and progress slowed to a halt.

It is tempting to attribute these events primarily to managerial incompetence and duplicity. Farr's presence in an advisory capacity suggests that FoodCom management might have been concerned about Matson's competence.

However, although a more capable manager might have been able to push EJEC projects ahead and avoid suspicions of duplicity, he or she would still have had to overcome obstacles and confront different constituencies that had divergent, if not completely opposed, points of view. It would be hard to argue that Matson was not being Janus-faced. If we are to help change agents address this sort of problem in the future, however, we should try to determine why he was so deceptive. If Matson's duplicity can be traced at least partly to characteristics of his situation, we might be able to recommend ways to alleviate his problem as a way to get QWL programs facing similar obstacles back on track.

A Situational Explanation

As described earlier, the plant operated on a strict labor hours-per-pound-produced basis. Corporate management eventually provided Matson with accounting variances for the survey activities and for EJEC members' attendance at meetings, but not without a struggle. However, there was no way to account for hours expended because of other QWL activities.

Thus Matson was in a difficult position. He was expected to make the QWL program a success. His career, or what was left of it, depended on this. His standing with top management, however, also depended on his ability to control costs. When an EJEC subcommittee reported to him, he therefore had two choices. He could support the recommendations, but if they involved expenses or the allocation of labor hours, they would be resisted by supervisors who would have to generate greater output per labor hour to avoid falling below standard. If the recommendations involved IMU personnel, there was the additional danger that resulting work orders would be carried out by people who had a vested interest in subverting them. Alternatively, Matson could deny the recommendation. This would risk alienating EJEC members and the outsiders participating in the project.

When EJEC members pushed hard for their projects, Matson tended to give ground. EJEC involvement on line 4, for instance, was a direct result of Pepin's persistence. Progress on the maintenance department recommendations came soon after Drinan's resignation. When the outsiders persisted, they too were accommodated. For example, the assessors were given the survey time they requested, even though they were scolded and, in essence, told never to act that way again. Matson was being held responsible for the success of the QWL program and for dealing with the threat to short-term efficiency that it seemed to represent. He therefore seemed prepared to reject the EJEC projects that increased costs unless the QWL program itself was placed in jeopardy by his rejection.

One way he sought to avoid this dilemma was to find EJEC projects that did not increase costs. The cafeteria was scheduled for renovation, and new uniforms had been ordered. Matson therefore encouraged, prodded, cajoled, and coerced EJEC members to support these projects. They, however, had different ideas and a strategy for implementing them. EJEC members, with Sholl's concurrence, decided to employ a tactic similar to the method used by the assessors to gain approval for the on-site survey. They decided to go directly to Matson's superiors. They would document Matson's resistance to their proposals and present this documentation to top management as evidence of noncompliance.

It might have taken a plant manager with considerable leverage with his or her superiors to resolve the problems Matson faced. Matson, however, was at the end of his career and had little influence with his superiors. He also had seen firsthand how Struthers was likely to handle appeals for help. Perhaps he could not envision another solution to his problem. He did not appeal to Deigh or to COD personnel for counsel; rather, he appeared to view them as a principal source of his problems. Consequently, he continued to implement two apparently contradictory policies: He expended the resources required to keep the program alive and rejected proposals that might have made it a success.

Relationships among Alternative Conceptions of How the QWL Program in FoodCom Would Work: The Resulting Decision Process

It is possible that the dilemma Matson faced might have been anticipated. It was to be expected that EJEC members would identify projects that would increase their levels of satisfaction and that they would evaluate outcomes on the basis of the extent to which the quality of their life at work was improved (Figure 4-1, models 3 & 4). Improving food service in the cafeteria and security in the parking lot could help achieve this aim.

Projects designed to increase satisfaction among FWIU employees, however, would not necessarily increase satisfaction levels among other constituencies. Nor would they increase productivity, at least in the short term. Many of the EJEC's proposals either increased supervisors' work loads, decreased the resources available to supervision for maintaining weekly efficiency standards, or did both. Supervision (Figure 4-1, model 5) could therefore feel greater pressure (g) or lower their expectations for productivity (h). However, few aspects of the EJEC proposals were likely to increase either their satisfaction or their subordinates' short-term productivity.

As Figure 4-1, model 6 shows, several of the proposed improvements in the quality of work life for FWIU employees could also be viewed negatively by IMU workers. Improving the accuracy of the clocks could deprive them of one of their maintenance functions. They also might be expected to be more punctual when returning from breaks. The maintenance workers had little interest in whether FWIU employees received new uniforms.

The EJEC did address some of the IMU workers' concerns. For example, IMU employees were interested in improving security in the parking lot, and seemed to support the projects Chuck Josephson had proposed. It is possible, therefore, that the interests of IMU and FWIU employees were not as diametrically opposed as model 6 in Figure 4-1 suggests. This interpretation is supported by Marie McCarthy's defense of the IMU employees. The demands of the project on line 4, along with their other duties, had made it difficult if not impossible for them to move rapidly on EJEC work orders.

Matson was caught in the middle. He might appeal for new accounting variances, but top management had shown it was not receptive to such appeals. Top management insisted on control (Figure 3-1, model 1), though Deigh advocated cooperation (Figure 3-1, model 2 and Figure 4-1, model 1). Plant management sought to reconcile the requirements of productivity with a strong sense of paternalism (Figure 4-1, model 2); FWIU employees, on the other hand, were primarily interested in acquiring amenities to enhance their satisfaction at work (Figure 4-1, models 3 and 4). Supervisors saw the QWL program as a threat to their prerogatives and to their access to resources needed to fulfill the requirements of their jobs (Figure 4-1, model 5). Finally, although the thesis might have to be softened in light of subsequent events, IMU employees thought that they benefited from competition rather than cooperation with the FWIU and with plant management. Any program designed to enhance cooperation, therefore, could undermine their position (Figure 4-1, model 6). The result was the development of a very complex decision

Figure 5-1 Combined Decision Model for QWL Project Proposals

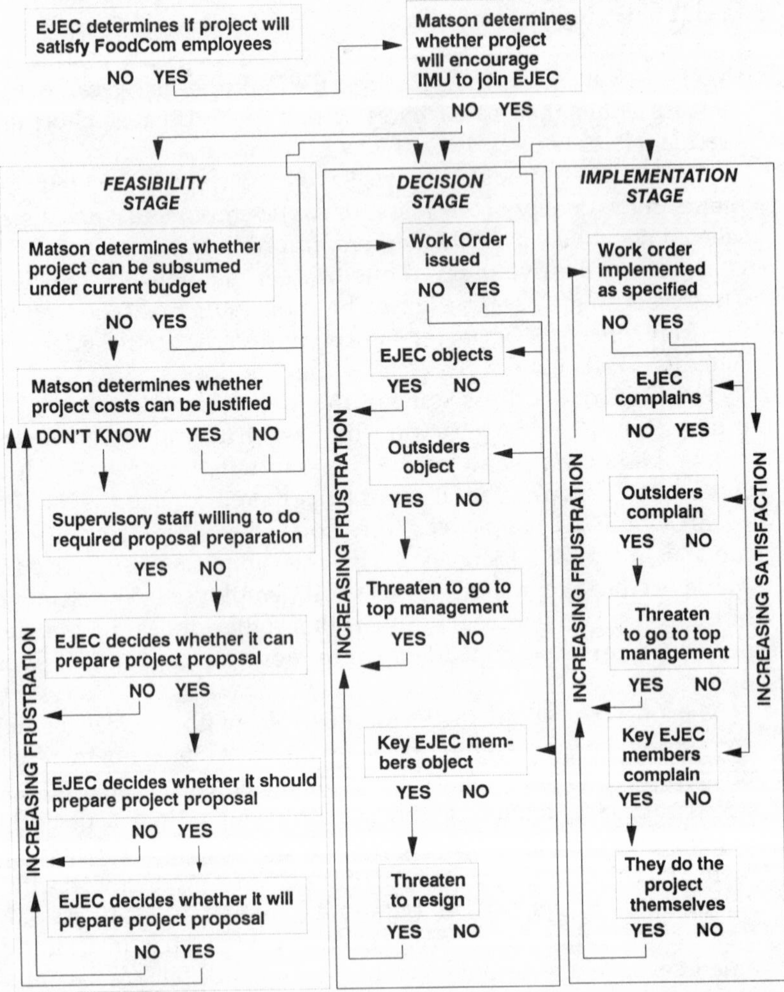

process. Figure 5-1 presents a model that attempts to depict this process as it evolved in Reginal.

As this decision model suggests, QWL projects were typically initiated by the EJEC and then proposed to plant management. Projects might have been directed toward increasing plant output, reducing costs, increasing quality, or any number of alternatives that might have been more compatible with management's wishes, supervisors' needs, or IMU fears. However, the first proposals were primarily for amenities. This is consistent with FWIU employees' initial understanding of the QWL project (Figure 4-1, models 3 and 4).

Once a project was proposed, Matson had to deal with the problems created by IMU resistance and his own supervisors' skepticism. The decision model in Figure 5-1 specifies that he evaluated proposals on the basis of whether they were likely to increase IMU support for the QWL program. Most proposed projects had to go through a lengthy feasibility study. Projects for IMU personnel, however, such as the new file cabinets, the scooter, the lockable tool cabinet, and the vapor lights, were declared feasible almost by definition. Work orders for these items were issued soon after the items were proposed. Like proposals for IMU employees, projects that did not imply additional costs were moved directly to the decision phase. These included the project on cafeteria decor and FWIU employee uniforms. Proposals requiring additional expenditures, however, had to be justified by arguing that they would pay for themselves in terms of quality, productivity, or both. Expensive proposals had to be approved by controller Steve Quin, who, as we noted earlier, believed the bottom line was the critical criterion. Proposed expenditures that could not be justified on the basis of their return could be approved, but documentation was required to show that they were needed and that costs had been minimized. Proposed projects that could be cost-justified, such as the clocks, were approved; accurate clocks were required to ensure that employees arrived and left on time and did not extend breaks. Proposals that could not be cost-justified were rejected.

Problems arose when detailed analysis was required to determine whether proposals could be justified and how. Matson depended upon supervisory personnel to detail proposals well enough to justify them to corporate management. Few of these supervisors, however, supported the EJEC proposals. Moreover, they were busier than usual with the line 4 project and had little time to detail proposals for improvements in food service, for altering the parking lot, and so forth. If supervisors had been willing and available, Matson would presumably have received competent advice and been able to evaluate the proposed projects. As it was, he had to tell EJEC members to provide their own cost-benefit analysis. EJEC members frequently felt unable to provide such technical advice. Even if they had been able, many members thought that they should not be asked to do this extra work, so they simply returned the somewhat modified proposals to Matson. Without recourse, Matson would reinitiate the sequence, and it would to through another loop. Each loop, however, would lead to greater frustration with the process.

Several projects either avoided or survived the feasibility stage. Having done so, however, they were not automatically approved. Approval was granted to conduct a plantwide survey on company time only after the assessors had appealed to top management. Pepin had to threaten to resign from the EJEC before he was given permission to conduct training sessions on the line 4 project. Drinan's resignation appeared to stimulate movement on the maintenance department projects. Only the new clocks, the uniforms, and the nonsmoking area for the cafeteria were given the green light without significant pressure being applied by EJEC personnel. Of these, only the uniforms were obtained without problems occurring at the implementation stage.

During implementation, the Cushman scooter request was downgraded from a two-person to a one-person model. Several of the requested tools were deleted from the request list. Specifications for the chairs for the restroom were downgraded. The new clocks were used to replace old ones instead of being mounted in the new locations as requested by the EJEC. No sign was ever made for the nonsmoking area, which itself was reduced in size. Once the assessors had demonstrated their willingness to appeal to corporate officials, no significant implementation problems were encountered by the questionnaire subcommittee. The other projects, however, seemed more vulnerable.

The generic model presented in Figure 5-1 does not account for all the particular events. We propose it only as a guide to be altered if and when contrary evidence presents itself. At this point, it seems to capture many of the decision-making patterns observed across EJEC projects. It also offers a plausible explanation for the fact that so few of the proposed innovations moved successfully from the proposal stage to implementation and for the increasing frustration EJEC members felt with the process.

The model is closely tied with the way different groups in the plant viewed the QWL program (Figure 4-1). It hypothesizes that Matson, rather than being the problem, was caught between opposing forces. If he could not justify supporting a proposal, he had to rely upon staff personnel who were reluctant to provide this support or upon EJEC members who were incapable of providing the necessary documentation. If EJEC members were unwilling or unable to implement their proposals, he had to rely upon the same staff or upon equally uncooperative IMU employees. To make matters worse, Matson thought with some justification that he could not appeal to corporate officers for additional resources.

It is possible that a more aggressive or subtle plant manager could have overcome the problems diagrammed in Figure 5-1. The situation Matson faced, however, is generic. Many managers find themselves caught between groups with conflicting demands, groups on whom they depend to accomplish their required work (e.g., Kotter 1979, 1985). Some find ways to solve this problem, but many do not, and change agents must then deal with the consequences.

COD staff, notably Drew and Sholl, decided to pursue a political strategy. Sholl advised EJEC members to document Matson's ambivalence in order to support an appeal to his superiors. This strategy is supported by the model diagrammed in Figure 5-1. By complaining to higher-ups, the outsiders might increase the chances that EJEC projects would be successfully implemented. Whether this would actually happen and subsequently increase the productivity and quality of working life in the Reginal plant, however, remained to be seen.

The First Annual QWL Conference

Beginning in 1977, the NQWC sponsored conferences for representatives of all the organizations that had participated or were participating in QWL experiments. The conferences consisted of group discussions and presentations by leaders such as Ted Mills about the underlying philosophy of QWL programs and about specific organizational arrangements, such as gain sharing or flexible work schedules, that might result from them.

FoodCom was eligible to send three management and three union representatives to the 1977 conference, which took place in Washington, D.C., on May 20–22. In April, the management members of the EJEC elected Susan Sheffer, Vince Keely, and Johnny Pepin as representatives. The union members of EJEC elected George Newman, Bobby Clayton, and Louis Young.

After FoodCom's conference representatives returned to Reginal, they included a brief description of the workshop in their May 1977 progress report. This description is available as Exhibit 5-9.

EXHIBIT 5-9 Excerpt from the May 1977 Progress Report Titled, "First Annual American Quality of Work-Life Association Conference"

From May 20–21, six members of the EJEC participated in this quality of work-life conference in Washington, D.C. In all, seventeen company and union groups were represented. Participants came from a wide variety of organizations, including auto plants, coal mines, hospitals, school districts, city governments, and engineering firms, to name a few. All were at different points in their projects, and had some very interesting stories regarding the quality of work-life projects in their organization. Two of the organizations had, for various reasons, terminated the project, and had some insightful explanations of the problems which led to the termination of their project. There were several reactions that the FoodCom people shared regarding the conference, including:

A. It became clear fairly early that the quality of work-life project at FoodCom is proceeding much more rapidly than projects which are four and five years old. Part of this relatively rapid progress is probably due to the fact that we have the experiences of other projects to rely upon when organizing our project. However, it is felt by most of the participants that the main reason for this rapid advancement lies in the fact that the union and management here have established a good relationship which facilitates working in a cooperative framework needed for an effective quality of work life project.

B. Through the sharing of experiences, we learned a good deal about the problems and snags other programs had come up against and how they solved these problems. Several issues which were of particular interest were: 1) the necessity of involving all members of the organization in the program as early as possible, especially middle management and the shop stewards; 2) the establishment of trust as being the essential first step before any quality of work life effort can truly be successful; 3) the need to have top management and union's commitment to the program and the need to communicate this commitment to the employees in the organization; and 4) how to continue a quality of work life program once the original participants left the site committees or there was a change in either managerial or union leadership. Associated with this process of problem sharing was a learning experience that occurred when people discussed the solutions they implemented successfully in their program.

C. Finally, we got a clearer idea of what exactly is meant by "quality of work life." We had a feeling for the wide range of changes that could occur in a quality of work life project and the complexity and difficulty of the task facing us.

Feeding Back the Survey Data

After the assessment team conducted the plantwide survey, the EJEC and COD began to consider alternative ways of processing and feeding the data back to Reginal employees. The EJEC asked the assessment coordinator to provide them with frequency distributions of responses by department, shift, and level (union and management). COD's Drew advised the EJEC members to clarify their role in the feedback process. They could act in a traditional role, as a catalyst or facilitator, by administering feedback sessions. Alternatively, they could act as a "strong, independent subsystem which can push for certain kinds of actions which are in the best interests of both union and management." As facilitators, EJEC members would not draw conclusions from the survey data, but as members of an independent subsystem, they would draw their own conclusions and develop action plans based upon the survey results.

In a memorandum to Matson in which he outlined alternative feedback strategies, Drew expressed a preference for the catalyst, or facilitator, option. Whatever role EJEC adopted, however, he thought that the survey results should be fed back quickly. Delays would only lead to leaks and rumors. He also thought that the EJEC should involve non-EJEC people in the questionnaire interpretation process.

On June 6, Sholl and Gromanger met with Matson to discuss Drew's memo and to begin to design a survey feedback procedure. Matson seemed not to listen as Sholl outlined the different possibilities. The next week Matson, believing Sholl was trying to turn Youngman against him, told Sholl he could no longer meet in private with his assistant manager. Youngman seemed to concur with Matson, saying "It's divide and conquer. I've seen it before."

Two days later Drew arrived to speak with Matson. He told Matson that an agenda was being prepared for a meeting between the project staff and the JQWLAC that would take place just before the EJEC-JQWLAC meeting. Drew told Matson he would describe events in Reginal as they actually occurred and would pull no punches. He would describe, for example, how Sholl had been prevented from speaking with Youngman. Matson was not invited to attend. Matson responded by immediately agreeing to let Sholl speak directly with Youngman. Drew then raised the survey feedback issue, and Matson agreed that EJEC members, management, and union employees should be trained to conduct survey feedback sessions.

Drew then met with the EJEC executive committee and advised them to feed the survey data back to employees as soon as possible. He stressed that management and union representatives should be given data relevant to their needs and that feedback sessions should include both supervisors and their subordinates. These sessions should be run by EJEC members and possibly non-EJEC supervisors and union stewards. Only selected data in histogram form would be presented during these sessions, but response frequencies for all questions would be available for reference.

Later that same day Drew met with the entire EJEC. Chairperson Keeley presented what he termed "the most feasible method" of feeding back the survey data. He recommended baiting employees with selected data summaries that could be posted on a bulletin board or passed out with employees' paychecks. EJEC would then offer voluntary feedback sessions for those employees whose interest had been piqued. EJEC members responded favorably and some suggested handing back data summaries rather than conducting feedback sessions. Drew recommended the feedback sessions, emphasizing their diagnostic and therapeutic potential.

The EJEC executive committee met again on June 23. Drew was not there, but Sholl continued to press for feedback sessions. He argued that designing feedback so that employees could communicate directly with each other about the survey results made it possible to minimize distortion and initiate real attitude change in the Reginal plant. The executive committee, however, was not convinced that FoodCom would underwrite the costs associated with this sort of program. Sholl recommended that the EJEC draft a proposal for feedback sessions and submit it to plant management. He presented several possibilities, including the following:

1. Meetings could be scheduled at the beginning and/ or end of each shift.
2. Several meetings could be scheduled over a period of several months. Each meeting would address a different problem area.
3. Written summaries could be generated and given to participants.
4. EJEC members could be trained to lead feedback discussion sessions.
5. Discussion groups could range from fifteen to twenty employees in size.
6. Fifteen minutes could be taken from the beginning or the end of each shift. Employees wanting greater involvement or more detail could stay on their own time.
7. Summary data sheets could be handed out. No meetings need be held.
8. Nothing at all need be done about feeding data back.

The assessors mounted the survey data on their computer. To analyze the data, however, they needed to know what to do with the responses from thirty Maintenance Department workers who had voluntarily filled out the questionnaire. Should these responses be included? Should the Maintenance Department be singled out even though they were not part of the QWL program and had a low response rate?

The EJEC decided to raise these issues with the chief IMU steward, Andy Gleason. The letter to Gleason, drafted by the assessment coordinator and edited by the EJEC Executive Committee, is presented in Exhibit 5-10.

EXHIBIT 5-10 Letter from the EJEC Executive Committee to Mr. Andy Gleason, Chief Steward of the IMU Local in Reginal

June 28, 1977

Mr. Andy Gleason
Chief Steward
IMU

Dear Andy:

As you know, on May 18–20 the Quality of Work Program administered questionnaires to employees at FoodCom-Reginal. These questionnaires asked employees to express their opinions on a variety of bakery-related issues such as the quality of supervision, the ability of employees to communicate with each other and with management, the ability of work groups to work closely together, etc. So far, 421 employees have filled out this questionnaire, and follow-up sessions are being conducted for those who were out on sick leave, vacation and lay-off.

The Employees' Joint Enrichment Committee supervised this administration in conjunction with an assessment team from the Institute for Social Research. The assessors participated because they have had extensive experience conducting this type of survey and because they could provide employees with complete confidentiality.

Approximately thirty Maintenance personnel participated in filling out the questionnaire. Since the Millwrights decided not to participate in the Quality of Work Program, the rate of participation in the Maintenance Department was below that of other departments. This was expected. The fact that so many Maintenance people filled out the questionnaire, however, presents us with a problem.

We feel that the information they provided should be made available to EJEC members and to all plant employees (in summary form, of course, to protect confidentiality). Several Maintenance employees indicated that they also wanted their answers sent to management people at International Headquarters to provide them with information about how things are in Reginal. While their concerns are understandable, we have no way of telling whether the feelings of the thirty people who took the questionnaire accurately reflect how all Maintenance employees feel. It is unlikely that the Maintenance results accurately reflect the opinion of members of that department. Consequently, we are reluctant to take these responses as expressing the opinion of the people in the Maintenance Department. This problem is made a bit more complicated by the fact that the FWIU, unlike the IMU employees, can control how the survey information is used in the bakery. As things stand now, IMU members don't have this kind of control, and we are reluctant to use their information without their participation and say-so.

We are not trying to say that you ought to join the EJEC. Neither are we saying that more Millwrights ought to take the questionnaire. You know you can join the EJEC any time you want. Likewise other Maintenance people can take the questionnaire any time they want. This is and should be completely voluntary. We do want to find a way to work with you, however, to find a way to properly assess and use the information those thirty Millwrights provided. Millwrights are the only ones who know whether this information accurately reflects how other Millwrights feel. You are also the people best qualified to control the use of this information. This is why we are seeking your cooperation. Simply put, we would like you, and other Millwrights if possible, to assess whether the responses we have represent the feelings of the Maintenance Department as a whole and to offer some direction for what we should do with this information now that we have it.

The EJEC Executive Committee currently is going over the answers people gave to the questionnaire items. The assessors have provided us with the number and percentage of people answering this way or that way. They also have provided us with this information by department. That is, we know how many people in Baking feel this way or that way about any particular question. Since only 30 percent of the Maintenance people took the questionnaire, we did not ask the assessors to provide this information for the Maintenance Department. We wanted to wait and first get your opinion regarding what we should do. We are prepared to work with you, with other stewards, with a committee you appoint, or in any way you feel is appropriate. The survey uncovered some interesting things, and we need you Millwrights if proper use is going to be made of it.

Cordially

EJEC Executive Committee
Vince Keeley
Susan Sheffer
Bobby Clayton
Marie McCarthy

During July the weekly statistics indicated that plant efficiency was declining. Matson voiced concern about the decline at a staff meeting on July 6 and said he was uncertain why it was occurring. The next day Keeley, Sholl, and Gromanger asked Matson to meet with him to decide on a format for feeding back the survey data to employees. Matson said there was only one option: Employees could meet on a voluntary basis on their own time.

On July 8 Matson met with the EJEC Executive Committee, Pepin, Newman, Youngman, and Sholl to discuss the survey feedback. He started the meeting by reiterating the need to minimize costs. Before he could finish, Newman interrupted, calling upon Matson to "Cut the bullshit!" Matson asked Sholl what he would do if he were responsible for the business. Sholl replied that if he had run such an expensive survey, he would be willing to have employees spend time in feedback sessions in order to get as much use out of the data as possible.

Matson became conciliatory. He said he would support the idea of having feedback sessions on company time but had insufficient authority to approve this sort of expenditure. He suggested that Keeley and Clayton petition the JQWLAC. George Newman argued that if Matson really wanted to have feedback sessions he would ask the JQWLAC himself and suggested that he and Matson jointly ask the JQWLAC. Matson declined but said the EJEC could say he supported the idea as an EJEC member.

The next week Matson received a copy of Drew's tentative agenda for the proposed meeting between the JQWLAC and

QWL Program staff (shown in Exhibit 5-11). With the agenda in hand, Matson sought out Gromanger and told him that if the survey data were to be fed back properly, feedback sessions should probably be conducted in the same way the questionnaire had been administered.

EXHIBIT 5-11 Memorandum to Roger Matson from Eric Drew Outlining Proposed Topics for Meeting between QWL Staff and Members of JQWLAC

Last time we met, I mentioned that I would like you to have an opportunity to review our agenda for the joint meeting in Reginal on the 19th. Wayne and I will be giving a report on the progress of the Regional project from the "outsiders'" point of view. Here, briefly, are the areas we intend to cover. Wayne will talk them over with you to be sure that we are in agreement on the key issues.

Summary of Progress Report (tentative)

Progress to Date. On balance, we feel this project has been moving along better than most we have observed or studied. The Employee Joint Enrichment Committee is now an established structure within the plant and has initiated projects aimed at improving the quality of work life in the plant. At this point, we will briefly run down the projects that have been worked on over the last several months.

We (the consultants) want to emphasize that Committee participants have been active, committed and cooperative in getting this program underway.

A Turning Point. We feel the project is now at a turning point. Now that a well-established structure is in place and the Committee has demonstrated its capacity to work together on personnel and employee-related problems, it is now necessary to shift gears into areas which can have a more direct impact on job satisfaction and the quality of work life. We feel strongly that all of the parties (particularly corporate and international [union]) need to address the fact that participation, involvement, productivity, quality of work, supervisory relations and union-management relations are all interrelated. Therefore, EJEC must become more than a "personnel" or grievance committee and must begin to tackle more increasingly significant and task-related problems.

The Focus for the Future. There are now a series of issues that provide good opportunities to genuinely and fully pursue the quality of work life approach. Here are issues we see as upcoming and important:

1. *Review of Survey Data.* A great deal of information has now been collected (through the assessment team) which pinpoints areas of concern and can provide a basis for more meaningful interaction between supervisors and employees and between the management and the union. Discussion formats are now being developed and we feel the climate of opinion in the plant, although highly positive, still reflects a desire and readiness on the part of employees to become more involved in improving the quality of their own work life as well as the effectiveness of the organization.
2. *Cafeteria.* The cafeteria presents an opportunity for genuine decision-making involvement in an area which does not encroach upon management prerogatives or contractual issues. Informal surveys of about 150 employees have already taken place and an opportunity for an employee-centered project is good.
3. *Quality of Work (Product Quality).* EJEC participants attended an NQWC meeting in Washington and came away with a great many new ideas. Among them was the possibility of committee work on waste. If the committee were able to launch a program that impacted on product quality, this would be an extremely valuable contribution to all of the parties. Any project of increased quality and direct or indirect involvements in productivity opens the issue of how gains from such improvement would be dealt with. The prospect of "gain sharing" needs to be explored openly and realistically.
4. *Clarification of Roles and Functions.* In conjunction with specific task activities, it is essential that the role and function of the Committee and its relationship to Management and the Union should receive continuing attention and clarification. Here are some of the issues that need to be worked on:
   a. The relationship between the Committee and the Management team (both as a group and as individuals). Individual

managers have different perceptions of the committee. Some see it as an extension of Management. Some see it as a separate unit with no direct responsibilities that has to sink or swim on its own. Some see EJEC projects as reflections on Management competency; i.e., if EJEC has to step in on an issue, it implies that some manager has been remissive. Obviously, these perceptions are linked and it should be clear that there is an underlying commitment to cooperation.

b. The Union's perception of the Committee evidently varies also. Some employees see the committee as a device to manipulate the work group; i.e., increased productivity, tighten up, etc. Others see it as an extension of Management. These are minority views and the more general opinion that the Committee is independent of both Management and the Union needs continuing reinforcement.

c. The consultant's relationship to line management is still somewhat unclear to some management members. Just as some employees and some managers are suspicious of EJEC, there are some who are suspicious of the consultant's role. The Committee members have shown increasing trust and cooperative attitudes toward the consulting staff and the quality of this relationship needs to be extended more broadly.

SUMMARY

Basically, we see this project moving along well and indications are that significant results are attainable. However, a significant shift in emphasis is needed if genuine improvements in the quality of work life and organizational effectiveness are to occur. The Committee must begin initiating more task and work related projects. Supervisors must become more involved in the process whereby these processes are launched, as well as in a review and deeper understanding of the meaning of Survey results. Union representatives have been highly cooperative. However, there are several projects where their role is not yet clear. More time needs to be spent with Union stewards by consultants and Committee members to clarify ways the Union can support efforts which benefit both the Management and the employee, (for example, clean up of work areas, increased participation in employee activities, etc.).

Roger, the above is a rather quick first run-through of some of the ideas we would like to pursue with you and with the Joint Committee. Wayne Sholl will meet with you at your convenience to discuss these ideas and I would certainly like to talk with you about them when we have a chance.

Hope things are going well.

Different Realities as Institutionalized Blinders: "Win-Win" Becomes "Win-Lose" in Reginal

As we suggested earlier, and as our description of the maintenance department issues reinforces, Matson was being asked to do something he may well have believed to be impossible. He was expected by his superiors to make the QWL program a success without expending additional resources. He was expected by the maintenance department to buffer them from EJEC demands on their time. Finally, he was being pressed by the EJEC to respond positively to proposals that demanded additional financial resources from headquarters and additional time from the maintenance department. At the same time he was being expected to accomplish all these things, several EJEC members were attending a national meeting in which new expectations were being introduced.

Drew and Sholl devised a strategy designed to force Matson's compliance. They told him they would present information to his superiors that would clearly indicate that he was blocking significant EJEC proposals and threatening the success of the QWL program. In the case of the survey feedback proposal, as expected from the model diagrammed in Figure 5-1, the strategy worked. After initially resisting the proposal, Matson reversed his decision and supported it.

Matson's suggestion that the EJEC executive committee petition JQWLAC directly about expenses for the survey feedback represented a significant departure from previous policy. His earlier statements were consistent with his mandate to make the program a success. He accepted the responsibility and he sought the credit. Now that he was being pressed on all sides, he was willing to share the responsibility if EJEC would relieve him of the necessity of confronting the efficiency-first rules of the company. However, neither COD nor the EJEC saw this as a meaningful concession. They took it as further evidence of Matson's resistance and lack of support for the program.

In this context Drew's memorandum to Matson (Exhibit 5-11) is instructive. Drew had told Matson that he would pull no punches in his report to the JQWLAC. Yet the memorandum was written in a constructive style and clearly provides a positive assessment of the QWL Program.

COD itself was vulnerable. Drew, Sholl, and Ferrer had spent a large proportion of their budget, yet had little by way of programmatic accomplishments to show for it. Perhaps as a consequence, their memo sought to emphasize the program's structural successes and its future promise. At the same time, however, they tried to raise the visibility of what they saw as managerial resistance and foot-dragging. The result was a document (and an agenda) that seemed internally contradictory. COD sought to claim praise and justify expenses even though it believed there were major program failures. There was no evidence in the memo that the consultants thought they had made mistakes or that management deserved credit for the structural successes.

Reviewing these events and the associated documentation, one might ask why neither Matson nor COD spoke their true opinions. The national conference the EJEC representatives attended had stressed the establishment of trust as an essential first step to a successful QWL program. However, neither Matson nor COD members acted as if they trusted each other very much. Why didn't Matson explain to Drew that he was trapped by his subordinates, the maintenance department, and the company's cost orientation? Likewise, why didn't COD confide in Matson that they needed to document QWL successes but felt blocked by management resistance? As we have suggested earlier, we suspect the answer is that neither party interpreted events in a way that allowed them to see the systemic nature of their dilemma.

COD appeared to believe that Matson really was the problem. And Matson appeared really to believe COD and certain members of the EJEC were responsible for the problems the program was experiencing. Moreover, these beliefs seemed to be driven by the participants' predispositions and by institutionalized constraints. Matson was predisposed to a familial or paternalistic system in which he played the central role. He also operated within a strict cost-control system. The COD consultants, particularly Sholl, operated within a system that required demonstrable short-term progress or good reasons for its absence.

Consequently, both parties moved toward the joint EJEC-JQWLAC meeting implicitly pointing the finger at each other. Had they been able to stand back and take a broader and less polemical perspective, Matson and COD might have been able to transcend their differences and develop a new foundation for trustful working relationships in the plant. As it was, however, they continued to play a game that QWL programs are designed to overcome. The "win-win" environment initially advocated by Deigh had become a "win-lose" situation characterized by Drew as the Reginal QWL Program "at a turning point."

6

The Enactment of Power by Lower Participants

The EJEC Secures Amenities, but Reinforces the Traditional Labor-Management Relationship

The EJEC executive committee met with Sholl on July 18, just prior to the JQWLAC's arrival, to complete planning for the meeting that would take place two days later. The executive committee members discussed the topics they would present and who would present them. Several were anxious about the presentations. They all agreed that their primary goal was to get the JQWLAC to clarify the scope of the EJEC's authority. Sholl said he wanted the JQWLAC to confirm the EJEC's authority.

The project staff, JQWLAC members, and EJEC members met in Reginal on July 19 and 20. On the afternoon of July 19, Deigh, Gromanger, Sholl, Ferrer, and the assessors met with the JQWLAC in a nearby hotel. Eric Drew had contracted a life-threatening illness and could not attend. He, Sholl, and Ferrer had prepared an eighteen-page report in which they reviewed QWL program events, outlined problem areas, and provided guidelines for the future. The report, titled "Quality of Work

Life, FoodCom-Reginal, Progress Review," was divided into four sections: (I) Status Report—Where Things Stand, (II) The Role of the Advisory Committee, (III) The Role of the Consultant, and (IV) Future.

The first section, "Where Things Stand," reported on EJEC activities. It noted that results from the plantwide survey had been reviewed by the EJEC and that "structures have been established for clarifying those results and beginning to feed them back to appropriate organization members." It described how the EJEC had established communication links between the operating departments and employees and reported that subcommittees were working on "recreational activities, the cafeteria, the parking lot and special problems that arise from time to time." It concluded as follows.

> The groundwork has been laid for continuing project activity. A committee structure has been established, subcommittees have been set up, communication links have been initiated and further communication and committee activity is planned. . . . The level of commitment and participation on the part of all committee members who attend regularly has been intense, serious-minded and cooperative. There have been frustrations and dissatisfaction along the way from both committee members (both union and management) as well as from employees, many of whom wish that the committee activities and end results could be sped up. The survey of attitudes toward the committee (conducted through the assessment team) shows generally positive attitudes towards the committee's efforts and toward its non-partisan role in union/management affairs. It must be said, however, that everything that's happened so far can only be considered as a "warm up" to more significant and meaningful activity. The warm up has been effective. Planned structures and processes have been developed by the committee and generally efforts have been seen as moving in the right direction. There have been occasional annoyances because of communication problems between committee members and various departments or groups and because of differences in expectations among various committee members and among some representatives of the union and some management people. These irritants are genuinely minor in comparison to other similar projects and have been worked through to satisfaction.

The report went on to state that "the (EJEC) committee could become an energizing and unifying force in plant affairs." The EJEC had not yet tackled any major issues but had "established a series of working relationships among its own members." If the QWL program in Reginal were to build upon this solid base, however, four problem areas had to be addressed. These are presented in Exhibit 6-1 as they were stated in the COD report.

EXHIBIT 6-1 Four Problems Identified by COD as Critical to the Success of the Reginal QWL Program

1. Role Confusion

The committee's role as a catalyst for Quality of Work Life projects is still not clearly defined by its members or by management or the union. It is neither critical nor pessimistic to say that the emergence of a new subsystem within a plant organization requires a great deal of effort and clarification if it is to survive and to contribute to plant operations. For example, if the committee attempts to improve the security in the parking lot, it is in danger of stepping on the toes of those who have direct managerial responsibility for the administration of the security force. Similarly, if the committee begins to redesign the cafeteria it may run into managerial interests in terms of cost as well as function, or it may find itself taking on a design role for which it is not technically qualified. Similarly, in projects of this type it may find itself making decisions for people that it, in some ways, has no right to make decisions for. There has been frustration among committee members around their inability to get certain kinds of tasks done. For example, work orders may get written but not followed up, or suggestions for improvement may be refused or turned down by operating managers who are in charge of the area in which the improvement is suggested. This is not to say that the management and the union have not been cooperative, but rather that the specific ways in which the committee initiates and implements action need clarification and continuing improvement.

2. The Management Team's Expectations

The local management team has mixed expectations of the committee. There are those who seem to feel that they should take a "hands off" attitude and let the committee do its own work or simply let the EJEC "sink or swim." There are others who seem to feel that the committee in effect is a competitor with management; i.e., if management is doing a good job then the tasks initiated by the committee won't have to take place anyway. There is a third view that the committee is, after all, in many ways an extension of management and its task is to carry out management functions by contributing new information, ideas, energy, etc.

3. The Union's Expectations

Up to now the Union's formal involvement (aside from committee meetings) has not been at issue. Current projects for the most part impinge upon the interests of management. That is, if the committee wants to install new equipment in the cafeteria or repaint a rest room or improve the parking lot, these activities do not for the most part impact directly on the interests of the Union. However, it's clear that when the committee begins to work on issues which are seen as management problems, then the Union does become a little concerned. For example, the question of clean up was seen initially as a "management problem" and therefore not in the province of the EJEC committee. It must be clear to all who are involved in this project that both the management's expectations and the union's expectations are for the most part positive and their behavior supportive. Difficulties are not arising from ill-will, lack of interest, or distrust. Rather, the few difficulties that have arisen require clarifying the role of the committee and the kinds of issues and tasks that need to be addressed if continuing progress is to be made.

4. Lack of Clarity of Purpose

The project's most significant problem has to do with the purpose of the Quality of Work Life endeavor. It would appear to us as outside consultants that both parties entered into this agreement with good intentions and positive expectations. As far as we can see as outsiders, neither party on its own or in joint sessions has deeply examined the potentialities of Work Life improvement. Do the parties anticipate the possibility of genuinely changing the structure of work within the FoodCom plant? Do the parties anticipate the possibility of providing new kinds of involvements in decisions affecting the work group? Do the parties intend to provide all employees (managers, union members) with increased opportunity to have influence on events affecting their own work and the quality of their life in the plant? If a way could be found to improve productivity or to reduce waste . . . , is the management prepared to engage in an innovative project which might result in some kind of sharing of the gains from such an endeavor? Is the union ready to cooperate in such an endeavor? Is the management prepared to make it possible for employees to design their own cafeteria, their own recreational programs, to have direct impact on various employee services that are made available through plant and corporate funds? The time has now come to decide clearly and firmly whether these options should be considered and pursued. By the time this meeting occurs, work will be quite far along in the development of the Survey Data which in many ways opens up these issues and a decision needs to be made immediately as to whether that "opening up" should be continued or shut off. For example, if one out of every three people feels they have nothing to say about what's going on in the plant, or if one out of every three people feels that the supervisors are not communicating effectively, then these issues must be opened up, discussed, and affirmative corrective action must be taken.

In summary, the rather hazy future has to be translated into specific targets, specific expectations, specific goals.

As noted earlier, COD staff hoped the joint EJEC-JQWLAC meeting would break the logjam of EJEC projects by enlisting JQWLAC support in overcoming plant-level resistance. The second section of their report raised the issue of the role of the advisory committee in the QWL program. This section is presented in Exhibit 6-2.

EXHIBIT 6-2 Section II in COD's July Report on the Status of the QWL Program in Reginal

II. The Role of the Advisory Committee

Now that the initial and basic work of the Quality of Work Life project is underway, a new series of issues is emerging which requires attention and support from the Advisory Committee. The issues can best be expressed in terms of questions:

A. What information does the Advisory Committee need to know in order to better judge the performance of this project and the EJEC operation?

B. What effect does participation in EJEC activities have on the future (career, employee support, union involvement, etc.) of committee members?

For example, in projects such as this it is often true that when individuals step out and take on leadership roles others become uncomfortable and distrustful. A supervisor or middle manager who is extremely active in committee affairs might begin to push for changes in plant operations. His behavior may be seen by senior executives as counter to established company policy or tradition. Similarly, a union member who is cooperatively and energetically involved in trying to improve relationships and processes of working with managers may be seen by rank and file members as "getting into bed with management." Local plant management, local union management, corporate management, and international union leadership need to provide a strong support system for people who are being encouraged at the local level to take risks, try new things, and enter into new levels of cooperation.

C. What role should the Advisory Committee play as increasingly significant decisions affecting budgets, standard operating procedures, traditions, and past practices begin to occur?

For example, one possibility emerging from some of the activities of EJEC might be in the direction of developing new programs for reducing (waste) or for improving the cleanliness of the work area, or for providing more participatory opportunities for employees on a given line to have some influence on how that line is run. These and many other similar kinds of projects should not be initiated unless there is at least tacit understanding of their potential and support for those who begin to explore possibilities in these areas.

The COD staff then discussed "The Consultant's Role." They noted that there were no corporate or plant-level OD professionals who could guide the QWL program's continued development. Though emphasizing their commitment to removing themselves as soon as possible, COD stated that "it is essential that as more important projects get underway that there is an existing support system to aid in those projects." This support, the staff said, should include (1) assistance in training EJEC members and others "to begin to create a more open climate," (2) support for those "who take risks to achieve improvement," and (3) help in developing "new problem teams to address new issues and tasks." Plant personnel would need assistance "to set up necessary discussions, to make available techniques for analyzing quality problems and, most importantly, to conduct these affairs in a way which insures the employees that they have something to gain by being involved in this kind of an endeavor."

The consulting contract called for a reduction in consultant time at the end of the first six months of activity. Four months had already passed, and Ferrer and Sholl were afraid they would have to decrease their involvement just as the program was moving into areas with the potential for "high pay-out for both the union and management." COD staff therefore recommended that time allocated for their involvement during the third six-month period of their contract be moved into the second six-month period. This would decrease their involvement during months thirteen through eighteen, but the resulting slack could be picked up "by staff people from local corporate management and from other forms of consulting help."

The report then outlined possible courses of action with respect to the cafeteria, waste reduction, and problems with the maintenance department. It noted that changes in the cafeteria could be administered (1) by management with the use of EJEC employee preference surveys, (2) by management with the assistance of small group meetings, or (3) by an EJEC committee given the discretion "to expend funds, make decisions, and take action in a decentralized fashion." Similar alternatives were outlined for projects designed to reduce waste, except that the decentralized option would not be managed by a single EJEC committee. Rather, quality control circles would be established so employees would perform quality control functions normally handled by supervisors or engineers.

Communications could be improved, COD staff members argued, (1) by developing work teams directed toward clarifying goals and objectives, (2) through supervisory training programs, or (3) by establishing work teams that would meet on a regular basis to discuss work-related issues. To deal with problems associated with the maintenance department, COD members recommended "further development of task forces dealing with (the maintenance department) and its relationship to line operations." They also suggested "the development of more specific and carefully organized ways of identifying critical issues affecting service and maintenance and consideration of the way in which priorities are established. This is now done through the management team and might need additional support in order to clarify the way in which the relationship is going."

Enacting Power by Calling upon Higher-Level Relationships

In earlier chapters we introduced the concept of linguistic skill. The language people use can achieve a variety of goals, including fostering particular interpretations of experience. To understand the functions of language in any particular situation, it is first necessary to understand the context out of which the language arises (Moch and Fields 1985). Thus it is instructive to explore some of the context for COD's report to the JQWLAC and then to assess the linguistic methods COD used to achieve the report's objectives.

COD's goal was to overcome local plant resistance to QWL proposals by appealing to a higher authority. As we noted in Chapter Five, the consultants, particularly Sholl, believed that they were in a power struggle with plant management and that the success of the QWL program in Reginal depended upon the successful application of political tactics. At no time, however, did their report state this belief. Instead, it concluded that the program had been successful and that problems encountered to date were less severe than those confronting other QWL programs.

COD staff may have been caught in their own double bind. By exposing the severity of the problems they were having with local Reginal management, they could be forced to confront their own impotence and ineffectiveness. This would have been awkward, because they wanted the JQWLAC to approve additional expenses for the next six months. Moreover, they had no reason to expect the management members of JQWLAC to readily accede to the political embarrassment of their own subordinate. The report is therefore replete with positive statements about the program and refers to problems as "occasional annoyances" and "irritants."

At the same time that COD staff sought to convey a positive impression of the program, they also implied that it would fail unless significant changes were made. These apparently contradictory impressions give the report a Janusian quality. COD staff attempted to reconcile these impressions through the "warm-up" metaphor. This image, however, implicitly devalued the QWL activities that had already occurred by suggesting they were simply practice.

COD staff members were vulnerable. Even though the initial survey feedback questionnaire had only recently been administered and the results were not yet fed back in the plant, consulting expenses and EJEC activity costs had been substantial. JQWLAC members might properly have expected meaningful results rather than simply a warm-up. Moreover, the proposal for greater consulting expenses during the next six months could easily evoke a negative response from cost-conscious FoodCom managers.

Perhaps sensing the problem, Sholl and Ferrer did not provide JQWLAC with advance copies of their report. Later, Ferrer explained that they wanted to wait until the meeting because the report "raises more questions than it answers." Indeed, the report appeared to be structured so the program would be judged to be on track in general but in danger of failure in all the particulars. The initial assessment is positive, but the explanations are abstract and are accompanied by few illustrations.

For example, the report claimed that groundwork had been laid that provided a solid base for future movement. When it came to specifics, however, the report only briefly mentioned the EJEC subcommittee structure and failed to describe subcommittee activities. With respect to survey feedback activities, the report noted that "structures have been established for clarifying those (survey) results and begin (sic) to feed them back to appropriate organization members." But it did not describe these structures. Alternative procedures for feeding the survey data back to employees had been discussed, but no structures had been agreed upon, and there was no approved implementation plan.

Having declared the program to date a success, the report went on to document a series of problems. Here the report changed format. Instead of being declarative it became interrogative, asking JQWLAC members where the program should go from there. As Moch and Fields (1985) have shown, interrogatives are useful as face-saving and attention-getting devices. They oblige listeners to attend to what speakers address and to reference the perspectives the speakers present. By using interrogatives (that is, by asking JQWLAC to draw conclusions based on a rather long list of specific questions), COD could try to gain leverage over plant management without having to admit that the QWL program was in serious trouble.

The questions provided JQWLAC members with the opportunity to choose between two alternatives. One alternative, however, was clearly inconsistent with QWL goals. For example, when asking JQWLAC to respond to the question, "What effect does participation in EJEC activities have on the future . . . of committee members?" COD could not have expected a negative response. In the context in which the question was asked, there could be only one answer. By asking the question, therefore, COD was implictly seeking JQWLAC support for the more active EJEC members as they confronted local management.

The review of the problems facing the QWL program was fairly comprehensive. However, these problems were described as possibilities when events to which they referred had actually occurred. For example, COD raised the possibility that EJEC involvement in cafeteria design might lead it into a design role for which it was not qualified. Although the problem is couched as hypothetical, it had in fact occurred. The use of possibilities rather than certainties is also a face-saving device (Moch and Fields 1985). Thus, it could also be a means by which COD could protect itself while simultaneously inviting aggressive JQWLAC action.

As one possibility under the heading "Role Confusion," the report noted that the EJEC was "in danger of stepping on the toes of those who have direct managerial responsibility." In fact, as noted earlier, Youngman had already complained to Matson that a member of the parking lot subcommittee had spoken directly with a security guard about how to do his job.

The inability of EJEC members to get their work orders processed through the maintenance department was mentioned. Again, however, the tone of the report was not historical but speculative. For example, it noted that "work orders may get written but not followed up, or suggestions for improvement may be refused or turned down by operating managers." In fact, both events had occurred repeatedly. To be historical would have been tantamount to accusing management of explicitly blocking EJEC activities, thus reducing the possibility that change could occur without direct confrontation.

The "Management Team's Expectations" section took on a harsher, more historical tone. However, the breadth of managerial resistance still had to be inferred, resistance being implicitly attributed to only "some" managers. For example, by noting that "There are those who seem to feel that they should . . . let the EJEC 'sink or swim'," the COD staff made no claim that these managers actually felt this way. Moreover, not all managers felt this way, only some. However, when the other perspectives were described, they were equally undesirable. This section seemed intended to leave the reader with the impression that there was little or no management support without having to state this conclusion explicitly.

When addressing the Union in the "Union's Expectations" section, the report takes on a distinctly historical and accusative tone. The FWIU local is taken to task for not supporting EJEC when EJEC members sought to address management problems. The report used the issue of "clean up" to illustrate the charge. A few weeks earlier some managers had attributed declining plant efficiency to an increase in the time it was taking to clean up the bakery after a product run. EJEC members speculated that they might be able to do something to decrease clean-up time, but George Newman had disagreed. He believed that this was a management problem, not a QWL problem.

As we noted earlier, George Newman was not a popular business agent. There was a good deal of union support for addressing management problems, so there was little risk associated with directly challenging Newman in the report. Unlike the EJEC members, however, members of JQWLAC, particularly management members, did not possess sufficient local knowledge to know that Newman was being singled out. They were therefore likely to take this section of the report as reflective of a balanced critical stance.

At the end of this section, COD staff reiterated that the few difficulties they were facing did not arise from "ill-will, lack of interest or distrust." By implication they were due to ambiguity. Presumably, members of JQWLAC could resolve these problems by explicitly defining the nature and functioning of the QWL Program in Reginal. This meant, again by implication, telling local management and union officials to respond positively to EJEC initiatives.

The "Lack of Clarity of Purpose" section was also presented in an interrogatory style. COD staff members did not state their opinions about what JQWLAC should and should not do at this point. Rather, they presented a list of problems and asked JQWLAC to draw the right conclusions. The section started by stating explicitly that in the opinion of COD personnel, neither the local management nor the local union had a deep appreciation for what a QWL program could be. The JQWLAC was then asked, in effect, to define this potential by answering a series of questions. Each one seemed a variant of a generic question: "Are you really serious about the QWL Program in Reginal?"

For example, the COD report also asked JQWLAC to decide whether the QWL program in Reginal could seriously consider whether employees could influence the decision making that affects work groups, whether employees could share in gains they had helped to realize, and whether employees would be given discretion to design their own QWL projects (e.g., the cafeteria). Together these questions begged a positive answer. A negative would constitute a substantial departure from the generally accepted QWL goals. Management members of JQWLAC, however, had not participated in forming these goals, so it remained to be seen whether their support would be forthcoming.

Tim Deigh called the meeting between the QWL staff and members of JQWLAC to order. The management members of JQWLAC had asked that Matson also attend, and their request was granted despite Drew's plea that Matson be excluded.

Deigh started by asking those present what they hoped to accomplish during their time together. Scigliano had previously been told that the meeting would attempt to raise the visibility of local management resistance, so he said that he hoped to get a project update that would document "the program's progress and lack of progress." Seldon, who had also been briefed on the problems associated with local management, wanted a "straightforward assessment." Farr wanted "to hear what's going on and to meet the people," and Pond simply wanted to discuss the project. Coy said he had no particular agenda, and Papp wanted to review the survey results.

Matson said that he wanted to know what the consultants meant when they said the project was at a turning point. Sholl, speaking for the consultants, replied that his intent was to answer questions at this meeting. Newman and Ferrer both thought that Sholl's goal was a good one. Deigh then said that in his opinion, the Reginal project was doing in six months what took other companies twelve months to accomplish. He turned the meeting over to Sholl, who presented selected results from the assessment team survey.

The survey results indicated that over 90 percent of the employees in Reginal agreed with the statement "In general, I like working here," and 82 percent agreed that "I am very much personally involved in my work." However, 40 percent disagreed when asked whether their superior kept subordinates informed. Almost half disagreed that "my superior encourages subordinates to participate in important decisions." Over 70 percent thought that "the conflict that exists between groups gets in the way of getting the job done."

JQWLAC members were pleased at the responses of the first two questions and expressed no need to explore them further. They generally agreed that employees believed that intergroup conflict was a problem because of the maintenance department. When it came to informing subordinates and allowing participation in decisions, however, participants had a variety of reactions. Newman said that employees didn't make the effort to keep themselves informed. Several management representatives, looking at the other side of the issue, believed it was inappropriate for line employees to participate in decision making.

Sholl reported that 45 percent of the respondents disagreed that "when management of this company says something, you can really believe it's true." Over half agreed that "The relationship between my union and the management is poor." Newman exclaimed that workers weren't really in a position to know the status of those relations. Matson opined that employees thought relations were poor because they didn't attend their union meetings.

Sholl then presented a histogram showing that 68 percent of the respondents agreed that "The Employees' Joint Enrichment Committee is needed here." Newman argued that this was because the employees were bored, but Scigliano cut him off, saying that the union would provide its interpretation later.

Ferrer then suggested the group consider COD's six month report. Passing out copies of the report, she said, "So far, we've been learning to work together. More complicated issues have surfaced, and we have to make some significant decisions." Seldon asked why copies of the report had not been circulated in advance. As noted earlier, Ferrer replied that sending advance copies would have generated frustration, because the report "raises more questions than it answers." JQWLAC members read the report, and Ferrer opened the floor for questions.

Scigliano, apparently surprised by the consultants' request to focus more of their time on the next six months rather than the final months, asked for clarification. Ferrer justified COD's request by reviewing the current activities that required direct COD involvement. Deigh supported the COD staff, saying that it was consistent with the spirit of the initial consulting agreement that called for COD to leave Reginal as early as possible. Pond asked what would happen if COD had not accomplished all it intended by the end of the second six month period. In response, Ferrer detailed proposals for conducting survey feedback, for reducing waste, for redesigning the cafeteria, and for dealing with the maintenance department. Reiterating her earlier argument, she explained that these projects were critical and that COD staff involvement was needed to bring them to a successful conclusion. Sholl claimed that COD staff had been working faster than they had anticipated, that they were now at a turning point, and that they simply couldn't "slacken up" at this point.

In an exasperated tone, Pond said he was worried the company was getting "a quick job." "You've been asking questions here that I wish you had the answers to. . . . We thought the EJEC would specify programs and costs, but now you come to us about projects!" Papp seemed to agree, asking,

"Why haven't these projects moved forward? Why aren't these things solved?" Sholl defended himself, claiming that the EJEC had needed setting up and that the proposed projects were complex. When Pond asked whether the EJEC had finalized their plans, Gromanger strongly responded, "yes!" A split second later Matson responded with equal emphasis, "no!"

Gromanger tried to explain that setting up a viable QWL decision making process takes a good deal of time. Sholl, in exasperated tones matching Pond's, complained, "This meeting has gotten into a consulting self-defense program!" Deigh asked Papp if Gromanger's explanation was satisfactory. Papp replied somewhat haltingly that he thought so, but that he wouldn't pursue it.

Matson then described how the EJEC had asked for carpeting in the cafeteria. He said he had to reject this proposal because "people have flour on 'em and they spill coffee." Ferrer explained "It's communication about things like carpeting that takes time and costs money."

Pond asked the consultants how one should handle communication problems like the one just described. Ferrer said it was difficult, and the meeting became a forum for complaints about communication problems. Seldon complained that the EJEC was supposed to make recommendations to the JQWLAC but that JQWLAC members hadn't heard a thing; Sholl responded that he and the EJEC needed to know what types of projects the QWL program could get into. Coy asked Deigh whether he had told them about their limits, and Deigh responded that they had been told to avoid contractual issues. Scigliano added that management members of JQWLAC would get involved when project proposals required financing. Sholl interrupted, saying, "The moon is available at a price! We're building involvement and responsibility! Employees need to learn. The Quality of Work project is going to give you more realistic people—more than a cafeteria!" Ferrer started to act as a facilitator, telling Sholl she heard that people were frustrated because the learning wasn't occurring.

Deigh, noting that the meeting had run 15 minutes over its time limit, asked what issues were causing people stress.

Seldon responded, "I'm being asked to make a decision and I don't know what it's about!" Sholl commented somewhat ruefully that perhaps the program staff should have met with the JQWLAC after the joint EJEC-JQWLAC meeting rather than before it. Resuming a more defensive posture, he said, "It takes time to build a new organization!"

The meeting continued, but no additional issues were raised. Ferrer said that EJEC autonomy had been both "a blessing and an albatross," and that members had difficulty working on projects without knowing whether they could carry them out. Matson detailed employee requests and the associated costs. Scigliano noted that the committee would have more information after the joint meeting scheduled for the next day, and Ferrer agreed to defer deciding on the issues raised in the COD report. When Coy asked whether the program had raised morale, Matson responded, "I don't see any changes for at least six months." Newman, however, believed that there had already been an upturn. He recommended that JQWLAC members not "be too critical of the (EJEC) Committee."

QWL Programs: Project Management or an Alternative Reality?

The EJEC proposals involved a series of amenities. In theory, however, QWL programs are aimed more at social and cognitive changes than environmental ones. They are designed to facilitate communication and understanding across groups and to offer qualitatively new ways of working together and interpreting events (cf. Bartunek and Moch 1987; Mohrman and Lawler 1985).

Sholl may have been trying to expose this by saying that a QWL program could provide more realistic people rather than simply a new cafeteria. If so, his appeal that such changes take time was well-founded. JQWLAC members, however, did not appear to be looking for significant social reorganization, but for specific content proposals to be sent for their approval. From their point of view, therefore, frustration over how long the program was taking was understandable.

From Sholl's perspective, the parking lot, cafeteria, and other projects were merely the vehicles by which new patterns of relationships and new ways of looking at the plant could be generated. Projects were not the ends, but the means. COD, from this viewpoint, was asking for more time to engage in a process of cognitive and social change, not for more time to develop and detail specific proposals. If this was the case, however, it was the first time COD had explicitly said so. When working with the EJEC, COD members gave the impression that they too were primarily interested in gaining amenities.

The interaction between COD and the JQWLAC illustrates a dilemma involved in trying to create a major change in interpretive lenses: Change agents may not fully understand what the new perspective they are advocating in theory means in practice. They may not fully understand, for example, how a QWL perspective is expressed in specific choices and actions. Thus, although advocating a new perspective (more collaborative social relationships), change agents may be reinforcing the old perspective through the activities they carry out (e.g., acquiring amenities such as new uniforms). The perspective Sholl advocated at the meeting and the perspective that appeared to have guided him to date seemed contradictory, and neither perspective was compatible with JQWLAC's efficiency and control perspective. It is therefore not surprising that in the meeting neither COD nor the JQWLAC understood the other's plans. If this is an appropriate characterization, we might well sympathize with Seldon's frustration: Perhaps he *was* being asked to make a decision and had no way of knowing what it was about.

The joint EJEC-JQWLAC meeting began early the following day. Chairperson Bobby Clayton characterized it as a regular EJEC meeting with JQWLAC members as observers. He therefore opened the meeting by asking the secretary, Susan Sheffer, to read the minutes of the last meeting. The minutes were read and approved. Chairperson Clayton then called upon Vince Keeley for some opening remarks. Keeley distributed copies of an "EJEC Organizational Chart," which is shown in Figure 6-1. He placed a large version of this chart on an easel in full view of the group and proceeded to describe the

Figure 6-1 EJEC Organizational Chart

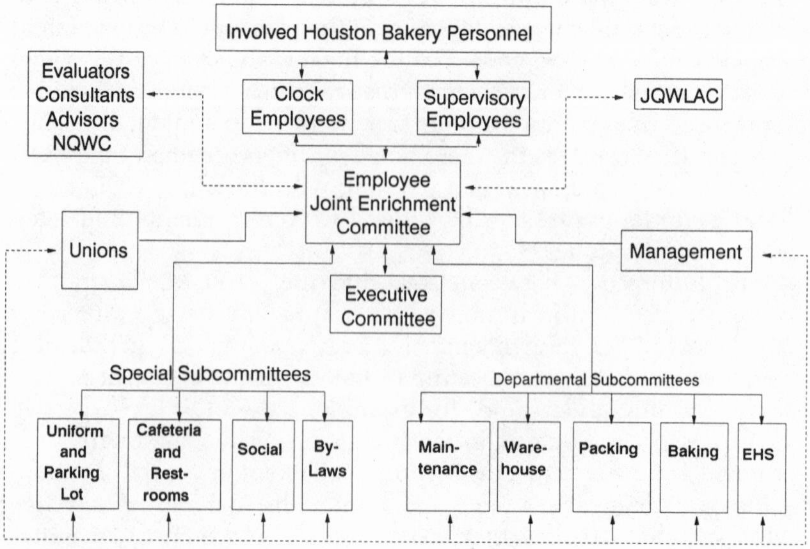

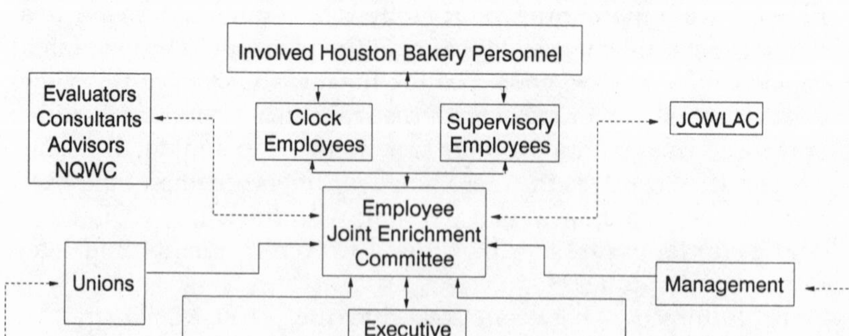

structure of the QWL program and review EJEC activities to date. Keeley's remarks, transcribed from tape, are available as Exhibit 6-3.

EXHIBIT 6-3 EJEC Cochairperson Vincent Keeley's Introductory Remarks to the Joint EJEC-JQWLAC Meeting

Each of you has a copy of our organizational chart. We felt that it might be beneficial for everyone to understand how we evolved to be where we are. Actually, we started right up here (points to EJEC box in Figure 6-1). And we found out that every time we came up against a problem or there was discussion on something with 16 people dealing with it and 16 people involved in any project, it became rather burdensome. So we developed into a subcommittee organization where the subcommittees could specialize in handling problems or projects or whatever the problem is. And when they had given this some preliminary thought, we could carry it up to our regular EJEC meeting and discuss it a little more intelligently. So this is basically how we arrived at these subcommittees.

We have a subcommittee for each department and the subcommittees for those departments consist of the people in those departments. There's two maintenance department representatives who comprise the maintenance department subcommittee, et cetera. Then we have our special subcommittees which will be in existence as long as they're needed. When we are done with any problems with the uniforms or our parking lot renovations, that subcommittee will be killed and we'll create another one as necessary and so on with the rest of them.

We've got lines of communication between the involved personnel, and the reason we say involved personnel is—even though they are kept aware of what's going on, they are not actually involved. We come down from involved personnel and supervisory and we have two-way communications there. The EJEC itself has direct lines of communication with the unions and management. We have a line of communication which is not quite as direct with the evaluators, et cetera, and with the Joint Advisory Committee.

We created the executive committee last actually to plan out our strategy for meetings, agendas, to serve as more or less a subcommittee dealing with things that the actual subcommittees don't deal with so we can think things out, make recommendations for the total committee, and expedite our whole operation. We have found ourselves being bogged down, tripping over our own feet, and we have made every effort to get our whole organization here as streamlined as possible and minimize the number of people that have to be involved in the initial stages of something, so that when we finally carry it out, we can get it further down the road and gather more people as we go along and get more opinions.

We have completed three projects so far. One is the no-smoking area in the cafeteria. This came about as a suggestion from one of the employees that felt that it would be nice if those who didn't want to smoke could sit where they didn't have smoke blown in their face. And we created an area—we have subsequently decreased it in size—and we think we have an area that suits the needs of the people. The packing subcommittee got involved with the packing department when they converted the plastic films to the new type and helped explain to the people exactly why it was necessary to convert to this film and made them aware of the problems involved, the problems they could anticipate, and we feel that that type of involvement—getting the people to feel that their point of view is also of concern to management—is what we feel is a very important function of this committee.

And then we sent out a general survey of eight questions looking for areas that we could get involved in, and the results of this have been very useful to our subcommittees in arranging some of their work. The projects we have in progress now, the cafeteria subcommittee is assisting management in providing information to help them to make the changes that the people are most interested in as we improve the cafeteria facilities. It started out looking more or less at decor and so forth. We went around to 150 personal interviews. The members of the committee talked to people in the bakery and we found out that the major concern was not the paint on the walls and so forth but the vending service and the food—the lack of food in the vending machines on the second and third shift—so we provided this information to the management to assist them in taking a course that will make the majority of the people more satisfied with the cafeteria's facilities.

The parking lot subcommittee made good use of the general questionnaire and found out that 87% of the respondents were not satisfied with the security or the traffic flow in the parking lot. Now this gives us some pretty good ammunition to go after the specifics. A survey is going to be sent out this week to find out specifically what the people are most concerned about. Is it security? Is it traffic flow, what would they want if they had their way about designing the parking lot? Of course we have to stay within the bounds of realism but at least to know what the concerns are we stand a much better chance of doing a proper job.

The social subcommittee is involved in planning various social and athletic activities and they're presently arranging a softball game between supervision and clock employees. We feel that this might actually make some people realize that people are people and that when you leave the confines of the building we're all ordinary folks and run around and play around together so we can develop a little better understanding between supervision and clock employees with that.

The bylaws subcommittee is in the preliminary stages of developing a set of bylaws. We feel that this is important. We have some information to go by but for the most part they're blazing a trail.

We got involved in a clock situation in the bakery and we recommended that 10 additional clocks be installed so that people are better able to see what time it is so that they're going on relief and getting back on time. Then we have the departmental subcommittees. The maintenance department has been the most active. They've suggested several items to improve the efficiency of the electrical department. They have requested a Cushman scooter which will give them a little better mobility, a number of new tools, a print file which will allow them to get the print of a piece of equipment more quickly so they can make the repairs more quickly. And these items are in the process of being [unintelligible].

They're also working on getting some constant running valves on the showers. We have a water pressure problem and all of a sudden your shower might change temperature on you real quick, so they have a valve which will maintain the temperature and they're apparently quite happy with that. The other departmental subcommittees are considering items that are causes of discontent within the department and the consensus has been so far that the major cause of discontent is chronically malfunctioning equipment. You're always fighting the same thing day in and day out and it keeps breaking down and we're looking more closely at that and we will get together with management in the near future and discuss some of these items.

We've also been involved with the assessment team and the questionnaire that they gave. We assisted in the developing and administration of that questionnaire, and we're now wrestling with the idea of how to feed that information back to the people. This subject I believe is going to come up later on in the discussion. Thank you.

When Keeley concluded, Bobby Clayton called on Marie McCarthy to discuss work methods and procedures. A transcript of McCarthy's remarks is available as Exhibit 6-4.

EXHIBIT 6-4 EJEC Executive Committee Member Marie McCarthy's Initial Remarks to the Joint EJEC-JQWLAC Meeting

I have part of it [the speech on procedures] and Johnny has part of it. The procedure we've followed to start with is to find trouble areas in the bakery. The way we find these is by the EJEC suggestion box, which was one of our projects, and sitting down and talking to the people by surveys on the questionnaire, and long-standing problems well-known to just about everybody here. And a second procedure we go through is the departmental subcommittees get together and decide what they want to work on. And then they bring it back to the entire committee, and we approve whether or not to do whatever it is. And special subcommittees are formed for specific projects like the cafeteria committee and the parking lot.

We've tried several different methods for how to get these problems taken care of. The first one we've tried was the subcommittees get together and they decide what they think is needed, like in the packing department. And the first thing they wanted was (waste) scales either changed or replaced. And work orders were requisitioned and whatever was written and this method completely failed, 'cause the time or mechanics or whatever was needed was not available to get the job done.

So we tried another method where again the subcommittees meet and get their ideas together and ask for a meeting with the appropriate people that could help us solve our problems. This method failed also, because we as a subcommittee failed to get a lot of the information we needed on our own and the information on cost and the time involved and things like this were not readily available to us.

The third method we've tried has worked pretty well and that's takin' surveys. The general survey that we took gave us a pretty good idea of what the people wanted us to work on first. And it gets the information right directly from the people. It just clearly outlines what they want and we don't have to guess about it. The second survey we took—the first one was written and it was given out with the paychecks—and the second survey was person-to-person. And as many of the EJEC Committee as could get free just went around and talked to people in the bakery and got our results from that.

We took this strictly for the cafeteria committee so they would have some information to take to Mr. Matson's committee with very clear ideas of what the people want. And these written and oral surveys it's been pointed out is a [unintelligible] of our committee. We would like the Joint Advisory Committee to give us some guidelines as to how these should be conducted and how we can continue with them. We'd like to know if the EJEC committee should be relieved to take oral surveys or if you want them written. Could the company and the union possibly alternate supplying paper, personnel, and things like that? These surveys are the best ways that we've found to get most people in this bakery to participate in the EJEC.

One other procedure we have to start projects are the long-standing problems in the bakery such as the rotation and training in the packing department for employees. Although this is primarily a contractual item—and we've had quite a discussion on it—we feel that we might come up with some recommendations that no one else has thought of that would be acceptable to both the company and the union. And after the preliminary work of the third method that we go through, we ask for meetings with the appropriate people to either help us get these projects started or to completely reject them, whatever. And Johnny's gonna elaborate on that a little bit.

Pepin then took the floor. His remarks are displayed in Exhibit 6-5.

EXHIBIT 6-5 EJEC Member Johnny Pepin's Remarks to the Joint EJEC-JQWLAC Meeting

Well, first of all, as we collect our information and what-have-you from the surveys or talking with the people or however we get it, we feel that in a written survey we get a better response from them. After we get these surveys as to what we want to tackle and try to get the information together as best we can, we have quite a few problems that we would like to get some advice from you about your committee. . . . If you want to stop at any one of these points and talk about it, that's fine. But I would like to bring up a few points that we're uncertain about. I don't know whether the Advisory Committee is as uncertain about it as we are or not, but we're sure uncertain. . . . For a good example, who provides technical information when we set out on a project? One good thing about this—that explains this—is we started on our cafeteria and we started talking about the decor and what-have-you in the cafeteria and about seating, walls, and so on and so forth. And talking to management we were to go out and see if we could get some information ourselves, and we found out real fast that we didn't know where in the heck we were. We couldn't very well find out anything as far as prices and time and this kind of thing. So we went back to the management after we had conducted the survey and found out that people weren't as interested in decor and what-have-you as they were in service and what-have-you according to shift. But we would like to know some advice so we would know, give us some guidelines as to how we should go about obtaining technical information for any project we set out to do. Other things that we would like to find out about and get some guidelines on is when we determine what a project might be, is there a way or is there a guideline . . . [unintelligible] how much money could be spent on a certain project or what would be rejected because of monetary values. And then we also need the cooperation of the company and the union both as far as this is concerned when it comes to any particular issue that people believe that is a big problem—when it gets to be a[n] issue of contractual type thing. I think you discussed this in a couple of meetings with George before. For instance, a good example of that is rotation and training policies. George contends that this is a contractual issue . . . except that we feel as far as our committee is concerned we do not want to interfere in any way with any contractual issues. . . . We do feel that our committee can help to obtain information from the employees to make contractual issues work, whatever they may be. And this is naturally where we need the cooperation of the company and the union with us to make these contractual issues work.

We also need guidance as far as governmental regulations are concerned. I think we have quite a few people that can help us along these lines—our advisors, Mr. Drew, and Mr. Sholl, and what-have-you—a very nice group of people that can help us along these lines, but we also want to work with the company in this regard.

And the other things that we would like to try to turn, some guidelines as far as we're concerned, so that we feel more comfortable about going about an issue so that we can resolve it whatever the issue may be. Is it—how can this committee after it's made a request, how can we get the decisions, how these decisions are made, where they're made, and how we are to report it back to the committee? [unintelligible] I think we need, when these particular issues are decided upon, that they will be or will not be. . . . Let's say they will be: we need designated responsible people, management, whoever, to actually follow through with the project to see that it's taken care of. And let's take the other side of the issue where an issue is rejected, whether it's rejected by local management or world headquarters or the union or whoever it got rejected by, if it is a very strong issue that people feel very strongly about does this committee have any right to appeal as far as the union and the company is concerned? In other words, how far should they go before they back off of it? Before we shut up? That's what it actually amounts to.

And then the other things that we would like to have some

guidelines on—and Marie's touched on them a little bit—we have, for instance, and Vince has also touched on them, we have our assessment team, which conducted that beautiful survey for the group and we want to get back to the people and have some meetings with them, and we would like a little bit, as far as this Advisory Committee is concerned, some guidelines as to how they feel our committee should be working with the people—whether they do it on their own time after hours, whether they work on work time; local management says okay you take the time and go do this, or we have allotted times. We would like some guidelines on this. I think that's about all I have. Thank you.

Chairperson Clayton summarized the first three presentations by noting that each speaker had discussed what the EJEC had done and how the QWL program was regarded at that point. He then called on Leticia Sanchez to discuss future EJEC activities. Sanchez's speech is available as Exhibit 6-6.

EXHIBIT 6-6 EJEC Member Leticia Sanchez's Remarks to the Joint EJEC-JQWLAC Meeting

Well, so far we've heard from Johnny and Marie and Vince Keeley on the projects that have been initiated and the areas we've touched. But now that we have the results from the survey and feedback, we'd like in the near future with your permission and your leadership to be able to get into some of the real guts issues that affect our daily work life and your profits. And by this I mean the human element, the issues that make our day either a good place to come out here and work or reject.

But I'm talking about getting more trust . . . improving our morale, improving our attitudes, developing trust. These are the issues that confront us day-to-day, and I know make an impact on our efficiency and on our work lives, and we'd like to know how do we relate these issues to the program? How do we make them work? And we'd like some answers and we'd like to be able to relate these with some of the ideas that were brought back from the [National QWL] workshop. And I really got some answers or some ideas that were brought back from the workshop. I might be able to relate these issues. But right now we'd like some commitment from you people . . . how do we go about with these human issues?

When Sanchez sat down again, Chairperson Clayton took the floor to elaborate upon her comments. His remarks are presented as Exhibit 6-7.

EXHIBIT 6-7 EJEC Member Bobby Clayton's Remarks to the Joint EJEC-JQWLAC Meeting

To get into this a little bit deeper, we have approached different ways of getting a job done. We've talked about some type of incentive program. We feel that if we can get in some type of incentive program to play out on our [waste rates], if we had some type of incentive program I feel that we could cut out a whole lot of this stuff. Waste, as far as labor is concerned, cut out labor if we get into some kind of incentive program. And one incentive program would be gain sharing. And people's askin' us different questions, and we would like to know from the Advisory Committee if its feasible for us to even talk about this kind of thing, gain sharing. Now, if we know from the Advisory Committee that we won't be able to get into gain sharing, then we'll know that we can't say that maybe after a while we'll be able to get into it. But these questions are being asked.

Some of these things may be contractual items, but they're also being asked, like a shorter work week. Can we get into something of this nature? We've been asked by numbers of people, would EJEC be able to get into a shorter work week? . . . And if we, this committee can get into something like this, then we'd like to know this. . . . We'd also like to get into . . . working on line 4, get it set up for better operations. We'd like to have some type of education program to let the peoples know why we're doin' what we're doin'. When we see these things happen somebody can say—somebody asks the question why is this being done? . . . Well, if we had some type of educational program to advise these people why this is happenin' it will be much better, this committee feels.

So, we've been asking a whole lot of questions. Now we'd like to get a little feedback from the—whoever can give us an answer on some of these things that we've been gettin' into, but we haven't really given you a chance to give us an answer on. So, before we can really open that to discuss any of these items that we've talked . . . [interrupted]

Clayton was still speaking when Gene Shapiro, an alternate EJEC representative from the Baking Department, interrupted him. To the obvious displeasure of just about everyone else in the room, Shapiro launched a broadside against the maintenance department. Claiming that the mechanics were incompetent and noting the three-week delays in repairs, Shapiro concluded by saying, "I'd like a little feedback on that!" Pepin immediately took the floor to tell the chairperson that a maintenance department subcommittee was looking into these issues and would submit proposals later. With a slight pause, Clayton recognized Dalmar Pond. Pond was the highest line official on the JQWLAC and usually stated the management position. His remarks are available as Exhibit 6-8.

EXHIBIT 6-8 JQWLAC Member Dalmar Pond's Remarks to the Joint EJEC-JQWLAC Meeting

I'd like to start off . . . and compliment the committee on very well-explained problems of a large organization. And I think probably you're handling probably your meeting better than we are in the Advisory Committee. It's been an interesting forty-five minutes. And you did put a lot of problems in front of us here that we have discussed to some extent, and they're good ones and they're most of the problems that come with large organizations. You've been asking questions here about advice or guidelines from the Advisory Committee. I don't know whether—I'm just saying something myself; the floor is open. . . . We think, that is we of the management, that we have a good working relationship with the union. We have a good operation. We have a mechanism through the foremen classification to the department head to the manager to get a lot of feedback and to know what's going on. We know that the organization doesn't work perfectly. We think we've done pretty well, but this project came into being of course. . . . The industry is going through changes . . . and maybe the straight line messages that didn't get through in the past have to change.

People have to be more satisfied with their jobs. They want to do better. So we feel—even though we think we're doing a good job from our side, the management side,—maybe we're not getting all the feedback that we can from the employees. Maybe it's not coming back up through the line. So our feeling was—at the time was—that we were putting the operation back into getting the voice of the people here in the plant through the EJEC committee to get recommendations to us. And what you've come back lately—that I've heard just now—a lot of problems have been thrown to us in the last ten years, and you know as you say poor planning on projects and do people really know the reason for this project or why this line is going in, why this project is going in and so forth, and some answers you get back—and it's a hassle [to] spend all your time doing this [unintelligible]. We have always had sort of a philosophy from the management side that the more the people understand what the job is and why they're doing it, the better they're going to do it. We're looking for methods and systems to solve these problems. The training and development we've talked about for years, and I know we've failed in some instances. We just get the feedback that we haven't done it. And we say here's three people that worked on this machine for three months, and you know this is an expert, and you go back there and ask them any question and they'll give it to you. But the other person doesn't seem to quite have the same knowledge of the machine, and she guesses at first. And these problems aren't easy.

How much you say we want to spend and what we want to do—we're willing to look at a program and if it's gonna take an extra person. . . . We could do it. If a training session can be set up here—and we've talked to a number of people about how best to deliver, and you get conflicting viewpoints from professionals that say . . . there's a difference of opinion. But then we're open, you know, from the management side here. You say what are the limits to the money we can spend? . . . We don't really know, haven't thought about it too much, but from our viewpoint of the company if it was in the operating or production or manufacturing then we won't spend any money unless we get it approved. To spend $10,000 on a machine, you've got to get a number on the machine and it has to be approved, you know. We have to tell them why we want it. Then it takes a little bit of time to do these things.

So, I just want to . . . compliment you, this group here, this committee, and I hope that you can give us the answers to some of these things also. I don't know how you—how else you want to get in here and discuss and have a number for us on each of them. The human element, that thought was very good. We're in a position to put down what we think about. Sometimes we take a little dim view of all this talk about the cafeteria, but we realize that these things, you know, we were thinking maybe some more of some issues of the person on the job, how to make the job more satisfactory, how to make the person on it come in here and do the job as expressed here, uh, by Leticia, was it Leticia? And it was a very good thought that you were thinking about that should come out of this committee. You should give us some ideas. . . . We want to do the job better. We want to make the company stronger. We want to make the jobs more secure. We think we're trying to do everything we can and if we're failing, we're willing to get the feedback.

Chairperson Clayton next recognized George Newman, who briefly noted that the QWL program had helped the local union by helping the stewards become more informed. Scigliano then rose to respond to what he had heard. As the senior union representative on the JQWLAC, Scigliano's comments usually stated the FWIU's position. His response is available as Exhibit 6-9.

EXHIBIT 6-9 JQWLAC Member Edward Scigliano's Remarks to the Joint EJEC-JQWLAC Meeting

First, I'd like to concur in what Dalmar Pond said, congratulating the committee and those that are helping, the consultants, Wayne and Tim.

Being that this is new to you, it's even newer to us. You know . . . your international officers don't have any experience in this field whatsoever. . . . We looked at a few situations over in a biscuit company who are competitors . . . but our experience is so limited that we felt that if there was a way of improving the quality of work for people, we were willing to try it. And when we go back and look at the initial meeting we had down here with our shop stewards, and many doubts that were raised, and suspicions about what the whole thing was about, was it a company trick, was it . . . a method to get more production out of the people? All those questions that were raised initially here seem to be well behind you now and that there is an understanding in my judgment from the work you've done that you are attempting to tackle the problems to improve the quality of work in this plant.

Our committee, when we first got organized, said that we wanted to give as much autonomy as possible to this committee here in Reginal. In other words, we didn't want to have a situation where they say well, we don't know that we can do this. We'd better check. We've got that other committee looking over our shoulders, and they may say no to this, and we wanted to give as much freedom as possible to the committee to operate. The two areas that we said we wanted to get involved in, and that was, number one, if what you were proposing and agreeing on here involved a change in the contract, then we would definitely want to have it approved. And I think you can understand that, because you are one of some fifteen plants that are under contract with our union, the same contract. That was one area that we said prior to being made effective, we would want to take a look at. And then, of course, and this mostly refers to the company where there's expenditures of money involved, I'm sure that the company Advisory Committee naturally has to get approval before they can proceed in that area. You don't have any problems with the union when it comes to spending the money of the company. We don't have to agree that they can spend as much as they want. But, I think you realize that they have a responsibility to get approval in these things.

Some of the questions that were raised here, we're going to be meeting this afternoon and certainly gonna take up the questions—all that I've noted. I'm sure my colleagues have noted some of these questions. Pretty difficult to give an off-the-cuff answer: You're going to be talking as one individual. However, I would say on a couple of things that were raised, such as the shorter work week, would this committee consider it. Well, you know, you're talking about a very big bombshell when you're talking about a shorter work week. Obviously, then you have to use common sense on the things you can accomplish. I'm sure, we've been trying to get a short work week from this company ever since long before I was around. Using the strength of collective bargaining nationwide, and not only this company, but practically no companies we deal with except the west coast have agreed to it. So, I don't know how the committee here in Reginal can engender that kind of pressure to get a shorter work week.

Now, I would say that on the issue that there are many, many other areas that you should address yourself to—than something that, well, I would say earth-shaking. . . . You wouldn't get a no from the union again on this, but look from a practical standpoint, the shorter work week, the first question I think would be asked is, is there any reduction in pay? Naturally, we wouldn't be recommending a shorter work week with less take-home pay. So, an area, an issue such as that, I would put somewhere back on a back burner.

However, when you talk about [the] rotating of workers in the shipping room, in the packing department rather, I think this is a more practical area, that even though it may infringe on the present contractual relationship, I think it's possible to be worked out. Now, here in Reginal, you have in the past made some changes in the contact that was negotiated nationally to fit your particular situation. Not anything drastic, but you do have a couple of areas where you operate a little bit differently than some of the other plants which was agreed to mutually by the union and the company and there haven't been any problems with that. So, I would say, you know, on the rotation, that would be in my judgment, a much more practical way to proceed and get something approved.

It's not the Advisory Committee's role to try and blunt or thwart any progress that you're making, and we want to try and be helpful. But, very frankly, we have not had anything much referred to us to this date. Now, we're gettin' quite a bit referred to us here, and that's why we're here, to get it referred to us, so we can start getting in and giving you some answers to this area.

Now, about the only thing I think referred to us was the question of payment of lost time which our officers in the International Union agreed to do. Don (Premater) and I went to the General Executive Board to get the approval on this project, and we are very dedicated and our desire is to see that it works, and I can understand that you can't make progress overnight, because these kind of programs involve the people. You know it's not like a committee can sit in a room and make a decision and that's it. The whole idea is involving all the employees and, therefore, it takes time to get their opinions, to sift out what's practical and what is not practical.

And I know that we're gonna be addressing ourselves to questions that were raised here, such as guidance on taking the surveys, what help you need, is there an appeals procedure on some points that you feel strongly about, the human issues, how do you go about it, the points Leticia raised. My own judgment on that is I think we have to rely very heavily on our consultants in that area. They have the expertise in that area to assist in translat-

> ing human issues into living things. But I appreciate the openness of the discussion and, frankly, if there are more things that you want to relate to us for our consideration, we're certainly, that's what we're here for, to try and be helpful.

After Scigliano sat down, Seldon asked the chairperson whether the EJEC needed any specific technical information at this time, since FoodCom had experts in certain areas. The company specialist in security, for example, might be able to help the parking lot subcommittee. Chairperson Clayton responded that the EJEC needed expertise, but then Premater indicated that he wanted to speak. Clayton recognized him.

Premater said he had expected the EJEC to relay recommendations to JQWLAC, but that not much had been sent up to date. He urged the EJEC to establish priorities and to concentrate first on the issues that the people in the plant thought were the most important. Marie McCarthy argued that the EJEC survey had already allowed the local QWL Committee to establish priorities. The parking lot and cafeteria projects were being pursued not because they were top priority items, she said, but because members were feeling pressure to do *something*. The parking lot and cafeteria projects were ways to get the QWL program going until higher priority projects could be initiated. The problem wasn't that the EJEC had not established priorities, but that they could not get needed assistance when they sought to address the problems they had wanted to correct. She continued:

> The reason we took up the parking lot and the cafeteria was because most of us on the committee are getting this 'What in the world are you people doing?' So we took this survey to find out what they would like and started on the parking lot and cafeteria while we were waiting on this questionnaire. So it's not that the parking lot and the cafeteria are first in priority, it's just that we had to have something to work on. As part of the information that we needed, that we couldn't or didn't feel like we would get, what we couldn't find out is where do you get cost estimates? What's it gonna cost to put the drapes in the cafeteria? How to go about that? That's what we mainly need.

Premater responded that FoodCom cafeterias were being renovated in plants all over the country. If the EJEC members had proposed a cafeteria project to the JQWLAC, JQWLAC would have give them access to experts and to ideas generated at the other plants.

Seldon then asked the chairperson to clarify Pepin's comment about the EJEC's need for help with government regulations. Clayton told him that the parking lot subcommittee had run into problems when it recommended that the plant access road be widened. Apparently there were regulations governing the width of access roads that intersect with city streets. Matson attempted to clarify the issue:

> Actually, what it is they said they wanted to widen the driveway. I said there was a regulation on it. You can only open it up so wide; otherwise, you have to get a special permission to widen it out any further. But [looking at Clayton], for your own desire and protection, this much, go down and find it out, right? Because a lot of times when we acquaint these things, you know, you have your doubts whether the management is telling you the truth or is just trying to point, uh, money. . .

Pond interrupted Matson to explain that FoodCom had regular procedures for such things as widening driveways. All the EJEC had to do was tell the JQWLAC what it wanted and the proposals would be handled in standard fashion at the corporate level. The problem was, he said, that the JQWLAC "didn't know what you wanted. . . . Tell us what you want, draperies, a dropped ceiling. But so far we haven't seen anything in the Advisory Committee." He elaborated:

> If it gets up to be $100,000, frankly, to tell you the truth, in some cases I can't tell Roger to go ahead and spend this. We have . . . a budgeted amount of money we can spend each year. If we don't have it this year, maybe we can say we'll do it next year—provide the funds for this. We have to put a statement in and explain very clearly what's the present situation that we want to spend this money and what we can get for it. If we just want to improve the decor and make it a pleasant surroundings for employees, we can put it in and get an approval, but . . . does that mean the steak

> isn't cooked just right or is the hamburger—do you want a top grade or somethin' . . . It's a big problem these days. We've been wrestlin' with it. And we feel—I do—we don't know exactly what you want.

Johnny Pepin took the floor. He argued that the EJEC Committee needed help from experts to detail their proposals sufficiently. He reviewed the problem with the access road and added details about the cafeteria. There were, for example, Occupational Safety and Health Administration (OSHA) regulations governing fire-fighting sprinkling systems for cafeterias. He seemed to imply that the EJEC members knew what they wanted, but needed help developing their proposals in sufficient detail. Seldon responded that FoodCom had experts on OSHA and other government regulations. "The problem is," he said, "and it's very apparent, I think, the further we talk, that we on the Advisory Committee are not at this point conscious of what your problems are. We're learning this morning."

John Papp said that OSHA regulations were very complex and, at times, ambiguous. The advice the EJEC would get from company experts, moreover, might differ from what the union would provide. He recommended that the EJEC and the JQWLAC exchange information and ideas more frequently so that proposals could be developed in sufficient detail and with sufficient expertise. Farr interjected that at the beginning of a project, no one knows the answers. However, once the committee had gone through the process once or twice, they would have the expertise needed for future projects.

George Newman responded that the EJEC members had not known that expert help was available and that they would avail themselves of it in the future. Vince Keeley then stood and, referring to the organizational chart that was still standing on its easel (Figure 6-1), began to draw a solid line to replace the broken line connecting the EJEC with the JQWLAC. As he modified the chart, he said, "I think I've seen something we need here in our organizational chart. I think what we have to do is get this line from a broken line [to a solid line]. . . . In other words, we've gotta restore communications with the Advisory Committee. And I think we can do that."

The meeting began to build upon this new level of communication. Pond, for example, explained how management had been trying to build up employee training programs in response to OSHA pressure. When OSHA investigates an accident, he said, the company must document that it did all it could to train the employee in proper job procedures. He asked EJEC to develop better ideas for how to deal with this problem.

Pepin responded with the complaint that the job classification system that had been negotiated with the union caused delays and significantly increased training costs. Employees who were perfectly capable of doing a job were not allowed to do so, and those who could not had to be trained even though they would do the job for only a short time. Pond jokingly said he would like a more flexible classification system, but was afraid to recommend it: If *he* recommended it, the union would be sure to resist it. Everyone laughed. Pepin said he didn't want to change the contract; Premater responded that contractual changes would require union approval at the national level. Pond, seeing an example of a dilemma he had been dealing with for years, said, "We've been wrestling with this problem. We need the EJEC to solve it!" He was laughing, and the laughter was contagious.

Leticia Sanchez brought the meeting back to the issue of survey feedback:

> Since you people initiated this program and brought it down here to us, we're a pretty determined bunch. And we want to see it work. And you people spent a lot of money getting the assessment team to conduct surveys. And now we're at a point where we got feedback from these surveys and you people are gonna advise us, so we'd like a little advice. . . . How do we initiate something to make use of the feedback? How do we get into the human element issues? We'd like some advice, you know. This is—you know—we're new.

Premater recommended that the EJEC members tell the company what they want. If they need help, they should seek it from the JQWLAC. Sanchez didn't think this answer was responsive, but didn't know what to do next. Marie McCarthy tried to help:

> What Leticia's tryin' to find out is that we've had (I'm on the Executive Committee that takes care of the questionnaires) and we did have a meeting with Mr. Matson, and we did ask him how we would go about feeding this back and getting the information from the people about what the priorities are. And what we were told to do was write a letter to the Advisory Committee to find out if we could go about feeding this back the same way we took it, or shut down an oven at the end of the shift and feed back this information, and start in on this project. Where it stands here right now, we don't know how to feed it back to the people and this is one of our commitments is that we get back to the people on the floor. We didn't write the letter, because we knew you were coming in.

Matson responded, somewhat defensively: "What I did say, Marie, was this. I went along with your recommendation and I would submit it to the world headquarters and the Advisory Committee." There was a pause in the dialogue. Seldon broke the silence, saying that the JQWLAC should not tell the EJEC how to feed the survey data back to the employees. Keeley then offered his opinion:

> Mr. Chairman, just to clarify that a little bit. We do have a concrete suggestion on how we would like to feed this information back. What we are looking for is, is this suggestion acceptable to the Advisory Committee? Because it will be a rather expensive method of feeding that information back. Our recommendation basically is to have groups of employees on company time to discuss the information and the results of the survey and in turn try and find out reasons for the answers.
>
> We know what the answers were. Now we want to go a little deeper and find out why. Why is it when we asked supervision "do you treat your people fairly?" for instance, we have this graph form and . . . 76.1 percent of the supervision felt that they were always fair with their subordinates. But we cannot [and] do not feel we can do that efficiently and effectively if we just post a notice and say at 3:15 we're gonna have—you can come if you want to, and, well, we're going to discuss the results of the

questionnaire. Because at 3:15 people are going to be going out the door to beat the traffic, and so the question is, how far are we able to do that?

Seldon asked how much the group sessions would cost. Keeley responded that the committee was asking for an hour of each employee's time, which, as Pond commented, was the same method in which the survey had been taken in the first place. Matson confirmed this. Pond then said simply, "Okay." Matson shouted, "Just go ahead with it?!!" Clayton said, "We'd better make a note of that," and there was general laughter. Pond asked if it was correct that the feedback method being proposed was the same one used to take the survey in the first place. Matson again confirmed this, and Pond nodded approval.

The meeting turned to other projects. Keeley commented that the QWL program would have to move quickly to gain the confidence of line employees and said that the EJEC had initiated the cafeteria and parking lot proposals to gain visibility for the program. Matson interrupted and told Keeley, somewhat defensively, that it would take six months to get started on either project. He explained that he had asked the appropriate EJEC subcommittees to meet with him so the projects could get underway.

An alternate EJEC representative underscored the importance of gaining the support of the maintenance department. George Newman then launched into a detailed criticism of the mechanics and was joined by Shapiro who added some fresh illustrations. Premater tried to change the tone of the discussion, claiming that the problems the EJEC had encountered would have been avoided had the mechanics been consulted before the QWL program was introduced. At this point everyone seemed to have an opinion, and the meeting degenerated into simultaneous mini-discussions.

In the midst of all this, Marie McCarthy looked across the table at Matson. In a voice that could be heard clearly above the din, she asked, "Where are our clocks?!!" The mini-discussions ceased immediately and all eyes turned to Matson. In sheepish tones, looking at the floor, Matson explained that the clocks had arrived but had been used to replace old ones. They had not been put in the locations requested by the EJEC. Leaning forward, McCarthy admonished him, "Why didn't you tell us about this?!" Matson softly explained that he himself hadn't been told.

Pepin seized upon the issue as an example of how people in the plant do things without orders and don't bother to tell others what they are doing. He said that EJEC involvement in the line 4 project was intended to facilitate such communication. With proper communication, everyone in the plant would know what was going on. Matson again interrupted. He told Pepin that he had asked him to postpone the line 4 project because the company was preparing a training film to deal with it. After a pregnant pause, Farr made a brief statement about the importance of getting many people involved, and Chairperson Clayton adjourned the meeting.

Immediately following the meeting, Scigliano called a meeting of the JQWLAC. Matson was excluded. As the members filed into the room, they took traditional bargaining positions: labor on one side and management on the other. Sholl sat with the union representatives. Deigh, Gromanger, and the assessors sat at tables connecting the two parties, at right angles to both of them.

The initial discussion focused on ways to provide the local committee with more consultation. Soon, however, Scigliano announced that he was going to make a pretty serious charge. He told members of the assessment team to stop taking notes. Then, in no uncertain terms, he accused Matson of blocking the progress of the QWL Program in Reginal and stated that if Matson continued to be involved, the project would "fall flat on its ass."

Deigh suggested that Matson might be caught between the resistance of the maintenance department and the reluctance of his own subordinates to support the program. Management members of JQWLAC were conciliatory. Pond, Coy, and Farr thought that they could get the plant manager straightened out and asked for a two-month trial period. Scigliano obliged, apologizing for injecting himself into a management problem.

The meeting then turned to specific EJEC requests. Survey feedback would proceed according to the plan proposed by the EJEC, and the line 4 project would receive full Advisory Committee support. However, proposals for a shorter work week and gain sharing were not supported. It was not practical to reduce working hours without a corresponding reduction in pay. Gain sharing would involve the union and the company in contract disputes nationwide, so it could only be considered on a nationwide basis. Management members of JQWLAC could not come out formally against this proposal, because Struthers had been pressing for it. JQWLAC, however, would advise against it.

The next morning the assessment coordinator met with Matson, who was extremely depressed. He used to be religious, he said, but the more religious he got, the more of a hell his life became. He felt like that now. He didn't know what was going on.

Matson said he was willing to do what he could to overcome problems with the maintenance department. He would try, for example, to curb George Newman and keep him from publicly attacking the machinists. The IMU local had come close to joining the program, he said, but "Deigh screwed it up." He couldn't elaborate, however. He thought that he had not really had enough time to talk to people. He was very hurt that people were complaining about the program's slow progress, especially since he had had to "drag 'em in here [his office] to talk about it." Most supervisors wanted to quit the program after the first six months, and "I was the one who kept 'em there," he said. Some would never change. They would always take the "I'm-the-boss approach." In fact, a union petition was being circulated to stop the program. Matson said he would "grab the guy who started it and try to educate him!"

The biggest problem, however, was supervision. Keeley and Dalton weren't doing their jobs, and their subordinates were feeling forced to do superintendents' work. Matson wasn't sure how to handle this. Farr, who had once managed the Reginal plant, had agreed to come down next week and bring experts in parking lots and cafeterias. Maybe he could help out.

The week ended with a Friday staff meeting. Matson presented several of the frequency distributions that Sholl had shown the JQWLAC. Staff members were particularly interested in the high proportion of employees who thought that conflict between groups was getting in the way of getting the job done. They all agreed that this corresponded to the tensions between baking and packing on the one hand and with the maintenance department on the other. Matson said he wanted to reduce tensions between the two unions. He wanted to make this a plant goal for the year. Youngman, concurring, said he was concerned that Shapiro's comments during the joint EJEC-JQWLAC meeting might make matters worse. Matson said that the "complaining asshole . . . should be raked over the coals like I was!" Keeley and Pepin quickly pointed out that Shapiro had been acting on his own and apologized for his behavior.

Content versus Process Realities: Gaining Content Changes Can Actually Reinforce Traditional Processes

We have focused on the use of language for conveying meaning throughout our study. Symbols may be used to accomplish similar purposes (cf. Dandridge 1983). Keeley's initial presentation of the EJEC organizational chart (Figure 6-1), which set the stage for the rest of the JQWLAC-EJEC meeting, illustrates this very well. When this chart stood unchallenged, much of what subsequently happened was accorded legitimacy. Yet the chart was unprecedented in the FoodCom system.

Two aspects of the chart stand out. First, it gives the EJEC a central role in decision making in the plant. It is the sole representative of supervisory and clock employees. Management is accorded a facilitator's role. No direct lines link clock employees with the unions or supervisory employees with management. Had someone complained about the absence of these lines, Keeley would doubtless have apologized and added them. It is instructive, however, that these lines were absent in the original chart and that no one challenged this radical implication that neither the local union nor local management should play the primary role in representing plant employees in areas not covered by the collective bargaining agreement.

Second, the chart places the maintenance department on equal status with other departments and overlooks the IMU. Yet the IMU local had not agreed to participate in the program, and it was widely known that the maintenance department played a key role in deciding whether or not to pursue QWL projects. The EJEC appeared to ignore the IMU by not including it in the chart. When Shapiro and Newman raised the issue, it was quickly placed on a side rail.

By placing management in a facilitator's role, Keeley effectively reversed the model Matson had implicitly advocated by criticizing the EJEC for not "assisting management." Now it became the plant manager's responsibility to respond to EJEC initiatives, rather than the opposite. The rest of the meeting was a well-orchestrated working-out of the implications of this new assumption. As a result, the EJEC received support for its projects from corporate-level management and succeeded in disseminating the belief that the plant manager had blocked EJEC progress.

Keeley's presentation did more than simply set the stage. By reviewing all the QWL program projects, Keeley gave JQWLAC members the impression that the QWL program had developed considerable momentum. By characterizing the cafeteria project as oriented toward food service rather than decor, he legitimized EJEC's perspective on what was in fact a hotly contested issue between the EJEC and plant management. By explaining EJEC's reliance upon employee surveys, he justified a process used primarily to provide ammunition with which to confront plant management.

Keeley's presentation effectively legitimized the EJEC's social functions as well. He distinguished supervision from management in the plant by avoiding using the term "management" for superintendents and those higher-up, notably the assistant managers and the manager. As Keeley described them, the social activities were designed to reconcile supervisors and clock employees. The term "managers" was notable in its absence.

Mention of the projects added to the impression of momentum, but also provided the seeds for future dissension. EJEC had requested new clocks; however, no one on the committee knew at the time what had happened to them. Likewise, specifications for the scooter, tools, and print file requested by the maintenance department had apparently been altered. By discussing defective machinery, Keeley implicitly raised the issue of the maintenance department in general. Finally, Keeley noted that the EJEC was "wrestling with the idea of how to feed that information back to the people." In fact, the EJEC had a fairly clear proposal, but it had been rejected by plant management. The EJEC was wrestling not so much with an idea as with Matson. The trick was to make this fact visible without appearing to challenge the traditional power relationships in the plant, despite the fact that EJEC was hard at work doing just that.

McCarthy's presentation built on Keeley's. Working on the assumption that the EJEC activities were legitimate and had developed momentum, McCarthy attempted to explain why these proposals had yet to move forward. The first approach failed because mechanics or time or "whatever was needed" was not available. The second approach failed because the EJEC lacked sufficient expertise "on our own." The third approach, taking surveys, worked.

What McCarthy did not mention, although her presentation legitimized this perspective, was that the third method was in effect an information conveyor, with executive functions left exclusively to management. Both McCarthy's presentation and Keeley's chart presented the EJEC as a device for communicating the wishes of supervisors and line employees to top management. Failure to detail or implement proposals, therefore, lay at management's feet.

Pepin continued to develop this theme. He explained that members of the cafeteria subcommittee had presented proposals to management only to be sent back to get prices and estimate completion times. This was beyond the subcommittee's capability. The members then tried surveys and found out exactly what employees wanted, he said, but they still lacked technical expertise. How should they get the needed information? The problem was not restricted to the cafeteria: It also plagued the parking lot subcommittee. Pepin also contrasted the EJEC's position with that of local union management. George Newman thought rotation and training were contractual issues, Pepin noted, but couldn't the EJEC get into these types of concerns?

In his statement Pepin came close to stating explicitly the essentially political nature of the EJEC members' appeal to the JQWLAC. Positive decisions on EJEC recommendations simply weren't being made. How could EJEC force the issues it felt strongly about? What Pepin failed to mention, and perhaps was unaware of, was that simply by mentioning these issues, he was forcing them. The content of his request was inextricably bound up with the process. By asking for a review of the content, he was effectively altering the process by which they were considered.

Having established the legitimacy of their efforts and presented information that they were making little progress, EJEC members turned discussion to the future. Sanchez stated a widely held belief that trust and positive attitudes would lead to high employee morale and high profits. The QWL workshop that several EJEC members attended had given them concrete ideas for ways to increase trust in Reginal, and Sanchez appealed to the JQWLAC for a commitment to deal with these human issues.

Chairperson Clayton described the kinds of programs in which EJEC might involve itself in the future. Could they implement gain sharing? Was a shorter work week a possibility? (Although this may seem impractical, a work-reduction program had in fact occurred at another QWL site and was probably discussed at the workshop.) Finally, Clayton mentioned EJEC's involvement in the line 4 project.

The first three or four presentations might have been condensed into a few declarative statements. First, the EJEC had accomplished a great deal during its first six months. Second, there were few concrete accomplishments because local plant management had rejected, blocked, or delayed EJEC projects. Third, the JQWLAC should tell Matson to be responsive to EJEC suggestions and tell Newman that EJEC can develop proposals that address contractual issues. Given the political nature of this message and the context in which it was conveyed, however, the communication took an interrogatory rather than a declarative form. The EJEC presented the data and asked for help. The data might have been interpreted in several different ways, but EJEC left it up to the JQWLAC to interpret it correctly and provide the desired assistance. Pond's initial statement, for example, indicates that he was skeptical of much of what had been suggested but was unwilling or unable to state his reservations explicitly. He started off by attributing the stated problems to the size of the company. Management had done well, but now employees had to be satisfied on the job. Moreover, neither the EJEC's suggestions nor general employee criticisms were new. Picking up on the line 4 project, he suggested that informing employees was a time-consuming "hassle." Training was also a problem.

These allusions and indirections contrasted with Pond's statements that management was open to subordinates' views and to receiving feedback about their failures. He did seem genuinely interested in receiving suggestions about how to address the human element and was candid about his opinion of the cafeteria project. Finally, it is important to emphasize that like his plant manager, Pond was also constrained by cost-control procedures. Even the chief manufacturing officer of a division that had fifteen plants nationwide could not approve expenditures of more than $10,000 by himself.

Scigliano acted much more supportively. He noted that the QWL program had gained broad local union support and counseled EJEC members not to expect overnight success. He also attempted to address specific issues. He advised the EJEC to drop the shorter work week proposal and to focus on a more manageable issue like job rotation. However, he seemed to interpret the EJEC's request for assistance as a request for specific project suggestions: He noted that the EJEC had been given autonomy and that it was not the JQWLAC's responsibility to become closely involved with specific projects. He restricted JQWLAC's role to evaluating proposals that involved contractual changes, required significant expenditures, or both.

Seldon interpreted EJEC's call for help as a request for technical assistance that could be provided by corporate staff personnel. This was important and helpful, but it did not address the problem EJEC members believed they were facing. EJEC members did lack technical expertise, but they thought it was management's job to generate detailed specifications based on EJEC's preferences.

To Premater, EJEC's lack of progress could be traced to the fact that they had too many projects going on at once: The members needed to establish priorities. McCarthy corrected him, saying that the EJEC knew its priorities. The problem was that they were being asked to do things of which they were not capable. Premater then suggested they take advantage of corporate-level experts, which reintroduced Seldon's interpretation. Matson seemed to sense the EJEC's tactics. He stated that EJEC members might think management was simply trying to put up roadblocks in order to save money and urged Chairperson Clayton to check out the regulations for himself. Explicitly raising the issue of trust, however, was as unseemly for management as the issue of power and politics was for the EJEC, and Pond quickly interrupted his plant manager.

Pond's response exhibited the same tension between his indirect allusions and his direct statements that had characterized his initial remarks. He began by reminding EJEC members that he could not approve significant expenditures by himself, but implicitly restated his disapproval of the cafeteria project by asking whether employees thought their steaks weren't cooked just right. No one had mentioned an issue like this.

At the conclusion of his presentation, Pond said he was unsure what the EJEC was really implying. Pepin tried to help by raising another technical issue. Seldon again suggested the use of company experts, but now he too wondered out loud whether he understood what the EJEC members were really trying to say. After Papp's comment indicating difference of opinion between the union and management, Keeley told the JQWLAC what EJEC members were seeking. They wanted a direct line to JQWLAC—symbolized by the straight line in the organizational chart—for the approval of their projects.

The drawing of the straight line led the two committees to enact the proposed new relationship for a few moments. Pond admitted that for him, training was primarily useful as a means for dealing with OSHA. Pepin raised the issue of the restrictive job classification system, and Pond explained why he might be less than candid about his real feelings on the subject. His admission that he had not been able to solve the problem seemed genuine: The contagious laughter certainly was.

But there was still unfinished business. Sanchez reminded the group that they had made no progress on the survey feedback issue, and Premater again insisted that he thought the problem was one of priorities. McCarthy talked directly about Matson, telling the JQWLAC that he had not approved the EJEC's proposal about the survey feedback. The issue was therefore up to JQWLAC to decide. Matson then either brazenly lied or distorted the truth in his own mind. He said he had agreed to submit the EJEC's proposal to world headquarters, when in fact he had agreed only to let the EJEC submit its own proposal with his support as a member of EJEC.

The subsequent pause seemed necessary for EJEC members to grasp the fact that Matson had so clearly distorted the facts. Seldon, however, still needed to grasp the EJEC's message. He interpreted McCarthy's statement as a request for help in designing a survey feedback program until Keeley again spoke up to make the issue crystal clear. The EJEC had a concrete proposal that simply needed JQWLAC's approval. After a brief discussion of costs, this approval was given.

Matson's surprise was evident not only in his statement, but in his demeanor. After exclaiming, "just go head with it?!!" he leaned forward and, open-mouthed, looked at Pond for what seemed a very long time. It was as though he thought Pond had been looking to him all along to minimize the costs of the QWL program, yet Pond himself had just approved an $18,000 to $20,000 expenditure as though it were a minor expense.

There were still unanswered questions. The issue of the mechanics was being avoided again, so McCarthy demanded to know what had happened to the clocks. Matson's response focused attention on his own failings. Pepin attempted to generalize the issue to abstract communication problems, but Matson seemed to interpret Pepin's intervention as an attempt to gain support for the line 4 project. Perhaps it was. In any case, Matson's subsequent comment that he had delayed the line 4 project was tantamount to an admission of guilt. He stood tried and convicted of obstruction, and the meeting was adjourned.

Matson himself had now become an issue, and if the management members of JQWLAC though they might avoid it or postpone dealing with it, they were wrong. Scigliano was adamant. The EJEC had therefore succeeded in accomplishing its goals: It got support for the cafeteria and parking lot proposals, and survey feedback would proceed immediately according to the EJEC's wishes. Most importantly, the EJEC had moved to the point at which the JQWLAC was seen as the primary reviewing body for its proposals.

A closer look, however, might have revealed potential future problems. No substantial process changes occurred or were even considered. The set of relationships had changed somewhat, but the assumptions upon which they were based remained intact. Matson apparently increased his resolve to push the QWL program through, despite resistance, and management members of JQWLAC resolved to help their plant manager. However, despite the fact that Deigh had explicitly raised the issue, JQWLAC management representatives did not provide Matson with help in dealing with the maintenance department or in addressing resistance among his lower-level subordinates.

More importantly, management members of JQWLAC did not seem to grasp the importance the EJEC placed on dealing with the human issues of openness and trust. Even as the local committee resorted to indirection and allusion to get their projects approved, management members of JQWLAC were themselves unable or unwilling to deal openly and directly with their own superiors. To avoid responding positively to the EJEC's gain-sharing proposal, they had to attribute its rejection to the union members of the JQWLAC. Otherwise, they would have had to oppose a project which their superior, Struthers himself, had been seeking to implement. The inability to address issues directly therefore went far beyond the Reginal plant.

The joint EJEC-JQWLAC meeting may actually have reinforced this pattern of indirection, a point which further reflection on the metaphor of language might help illustrate. If we take grammar as a reflection of the patterns of speech, then it will be clear that what is taken to be grammatically correct arises out of daily speech. Grammatical patterns are reinforced or changed through applications, through speech itself (e.g., Giddens 1979). The more the patterns are followed, the stronger the rules become; the more the patterns are violated, the looser the rules become.

Similarly, in conforming to patterns of indirection and allusion in order to gain approval for their projects, the EJEC may have actually reinforced one of the primary barriers to dealing with trust and openness. The cafeteria, parking lot, and survey feedback projects were not particularly high-priority items. They were "fillers" designed to give the EJEC momentum. However, to get them approved, the EJEC adopted tactics that ran counter to their longer-term goal of increased openness and trust. They therefore might have won the battle but precisely in doing so forfeited the war.

Miles Farr and company experts on cafeterias and security visited Reginal the week of July 27. By the end of the week Matson asked EJEC members where they wanted the new clocks. Electricians put in the necessary wiring. The air conditioner requested for the baking department restroom was installed, and the parking lot and cafeteria subcommittees met in Matson's office with the experts from world headquarters.

New vending machines were ordered for the cafeteria, and Reliable Foods promised that fresh food would be available for second shift. Reliable Foods also agreed to consider keeping the cafeteria open during third shift if there were a minimum of 125 employees in the plant. A new microwave oven was ordered, and an old one replaced. Architectural plans for cafeteria renovation were submitted to the EJEC for consideration. The parking lot committee succeeded in getting approval for a covered walkway to the plant entrance, ID stickers for the cars, and picture IDs for employees. A "park-at-your-own risk" sign would be removed, a guard station would be constructed outside the building, and the parking lot would be resurfaced.

Sholl continued to stress the need to document all agreements and to monitor and record progress. Periodic reports were to be sent to the JQWLAC. Matson thought the reports were unnecessary, because he regularly sent such reports to corporate management, and the EJEC sent minutes of their meetings to the JQWLAC. Matson was also concerned about mounting costs. He estimated the cost of the ten new clocks at $30,000 and said that the bill would be sent to the JQWLAC.

Progress on requests made by the maintenance department subcommittee lagged despite all the other plant activity. The subcommittee requested a meeting with Matson to review the problems, but Matson declined on the grounds that Wally DeLeo was too busy. Three days later Gromanger brought him a memorandum from the subcommittee requesting a meeting to review maintenance department projects and reminding him that DeLeo had stated that most of the items would be completed within thirty days. Matson scheduled the meeting to follow a staff meeting on August 3.

At the August 3 staff meeting, Matson announced that the plant had failed a recent company inspection. It had failed this same inspection ninety days earlier, and employees had apparently not made the necessary improvements. Plant efficiency also had fallen. It had been declining for several weeks, but now was down to 87.9 percent of standard. Matson asked his staff to find out why. Anyone blaming the Maintenance Department, however, would be seen as trying to pass the buck. Youngman suggested that efficiency was down because many supervisors were attending too many meetings when they should have been dealing with production problems.

After the staff meeting, Gromanger tried to gather the members of the maintenance department subcommittee for their meeting with Matson. Josephson said he was too busy to attend. Matson himself had forgotten about the meeting, but said he would contact DeLeo to find out how the EJEC projects were coming along. The next day work on the installation of the new clocks stopped. DeLeo had ordered the new scooter for the maintenance department, but had not followed up on the other requests. He had no idea when they would respond to those requests.

That weekend, the EJEC social subcommittee sponsored a softball game pitting hourly employees against supervisors. The teams split a double-header. Gromanger umpired "to maintain my third party status." Matson didn't attend, because as he put it, he had sneezed his dentures out at his future son-in-law's stag party and had to spend the weekend at the dentist's office.

Sholl continued to press for documentation. He wanted to send a progress report to JQWLAC on September 1, so he asked each EJEC subcommittee to document its activities by time. Gromanger integrated the activity-by-time information into an overall program-by-time chart. Sholl also tried to meet with Youngman, but Youngman declined, citing other pressing obligations.

The maintenance department subcommittee finally met with management, but Matson could not attend. DeLeo claimed that he had not ordered the requested tools because of poor security in the area in which they would be stored. He agreed to order some of the heavier items, because these would be difficult to steal.

The EJEC decided to make a greater effort to address some of the problems causing declining efficiency in the plant. Pepin approached Carl Schwab, the manager of the plant office, and requested the productivity and cost data needed to pinpoint problem areas. Schwab refused to release these data without Matson's or Youngman's permission. Matson was in San Diego for contract negotiations, so Pepin went to find Youngman. He found him just as Youngman was being informed that the baking department was sending overweight products to packing. When Pepin asked for permission to see the productivity and cost data, Youngman exploded. He thought that Keeley's involvement with EJEC projects was one of the reasons the bake shop was sending out overweight product. Youngman accused Pepin of waiting until Matson was out of town and then going to Schwab behind Matson's back to get information. If Pepin had to look at office data in order to identify efficiency problems, he clearly didn't know his own job. Pepin decided to wait for Matson's return before pursuing the issue further.

On August 16, the JQWLAC sent the EJEC a formal response to their July 20 meeting. It is available as Exhibit 6-10.

EXHIBIT 6-10 Memorandum from JQWLAC to EJEC Regarding the Joint Meeting on July 20, 1977

TO: EJEC
SUBJECT: Joint JQWLAC/EJEC Meeting, July 20, 1977
FROM: JQWLAC
DATE: August 16, 1977

Please accept our compliments for the outstanding manner in which you conducted our recent joint meeting and for the remarkable progress that you are making in this extremely complex and oftentimes stressful endeavor in which we are all involved. We commend you for your candor, professionalism, growth and development which you evidenced during our visit. We received yet another lesson in the complexity of this project and the need for all of us to maintain a mode of thinking that encourages learning and movement towards more effective relationships. It was very clear that we, the JQWLAC, and you, the EJEC, have not stayed in touch with each other about activities, to the extent that we should, in order to provide you with the resources, support and guidance necessary to you.

Listed below are our suggested solutions/answers to the specific issues that you so brilliantly raised during our meeting.

1. Availability of Resources to EJEC

We suggest that EJEC formulate its project outlines looking to local management in a local union leadership for information, cost data, estimating, detail design, etc.; and, where special expertise is required, Mr. Matson will make the necessary arrangements. In the event either FoodCom or the FWIU is unable to locally approve a proposal, it should be passed on to JQWLAC for review and disposition. If local management and union resources are not available and/ or adequate to fulfill the needs of the particular EJEC recommended activity, we suggest the EJEC forward a request to the JQWLAC for assistance. The full resources of the FWIU and the FoodCom corporate organization can then be brought to bear on the specific task/project. It is the view of the JQWLAC that the EJEC should not be expected to develop fully researched project proposals when expertise and resources are available at both the local and national levels that can materially assist in the development of proposals for more rapid disposition.

2. EJEC Project Priority

We suggest that all EJEC projects having been approved/ adopted for implementation by all appropriate parties be placed on the formal project list of the local bakery. Implementation and follow-up mechanisms within that system can be engaged to ensure implementation at the appropriate pace. If the approved project(s) fall outside the authority of the local management and/or union leadership, such proposals should be transmitted by the EJEC (with local management and union endorsement) for action by the appropriate person(s) at the JQWLAC level.

3. Closer Liaison between JQWLAC/EJEC

We recommend that the EJEC in conjunction with Wayne Sholl, Teresa Ferrer, et al develop a monthly project status report to be forwarded by the EJEC to the members of the JQWLAC. The JQWLAC can then be better informed of potential delays and can respond, as needed, to facilitate progress on these projects.

4. EJEC Member Surveys of Employees

You indicated that you have learned, through your experience, that oftentimes the most effective method for involving all Regional bakery employees in the development of projects and their priorities is for EJEC members to conduct small group and one-on-one surveys of employees. You requested that JQWLAC give you guidance on that issue. So long as the time required to conduct such surveys is kept to a reasonable level (which we are onfident you will do as you have demonstrated in the past), such time may be accomplished on company time, during the period when consultants are involved. We caution against excessive survey work which serves to raise employee expectations beyond realistic levels. In addition, we recommend that you continue to utilize short, written surveys and checklists via paychecks when that method is appropriate.

5. Job Descriptions

Job descriptions of the type you suggest are not in place within FoodCom. Since the development of job descriptions is a long and arduous process, we suggest that you provide the JQWLAC the kinds of problems/issues for which you feel they are needed prior to embarking on this project. There could well be other items currently available that could provide the response to problems/issues prompting your request.

6. Education and Training

We recommend that the EJEC become involved in assisting local management and union leadership in dissemination of information regarding changes and innovations. Assisting local management and union leadership to share information and suggestions on better implementation of changes through employee meetings seems to be well within the charter of the EJEC. We encourage the widest possible communication of all information available to both local management and union officials and suggest that any mutually agreed upon methods (that you may locally determine) would be of benefit to all concerned in easing tensions and anxieties generally caused by lack of understanding and information about changes. At the same time, management remains responsible for in-plant training and will want to be involved for consistency of approach.

7. Human concerns are clearly a project area in which the EJEC could/should become involved.

The planned feedback of the assessment team's questionnaire data (as you suggested) is an excellent start in clarifying areas of concern and development of priorities in this and other areas, as well.

8. Questionnaire Data Feedback

As indicated above, we agreed that the same methodology as that used in the administration of the initial questionnaire can be utilized to feedback the results of that questionnaire and to begin the process of further involvement of all employees as well as clarifying issues and priorities. These feedback sessions may be conducted on company time so long as they are conducted in such a way as to minimize (as much as possible) production interruptions.

It is our understanding that the items listed above were those that you submitted for our guidance. Please let us know if we have missed anything.

Again, our congratulations on your progress. With your help, we have renewed our commitment to be as facilitative as possible in your efforts. We will attempt to meet jointly with you (as we did on the 21st) again in the future in order to foster continued coordination of our two committees. If there are other actions that you feel are needed on our part, to further assist you in your efforts, please don't hesitate to call on us.

How the QWL Program in Reginal May Have Reinforced the Adversarial Patterns It Sought to Replace

At first, EJEC members felt their meeting with JQWLAC had been a success. Some of those present at the meeting were euphoric. Although he cautioned that advocates of the program should continue to document compliance with their wishes, Sholl also was optimistic. The program had received support on all of the contentious items. Pond had agreed to support the survey feedback process, even though it would cost $18,000 to $20,000. More than this, JQWLAC members had agreed to a "solid line" relationship with the EJEC. Future project proposals seemed destined to receive a fair assessment.

A more penetrating look might have revealed several problems lurking just below the surface. Coy, Pond, and Seldon did not agree to take Matson out of the decision-making process, although they did agree to provide him with help. Several of Matson's post-meeting statements and behaviors indicated he had not had a change of heart. He was bitter that he had been "chewed out." He was critical of the clock project. He declined to meet with the maintenance department subcommittee and forgot about the meeting when it was rescheduled. His supervisors had also not become more supportive. Youngman continued to be critical of the time the QWL program was taking from his supervisory staff. He and Pepin almost came to blows when Pepin asked him for productivity data. DeLeo continued to postpone implementation of the maintenance department projects. More than this, plant performance appeared to be declining. Such a decline could reinforce the cost-minimization mentality that had plagued the program from its inception.

The joint EJEC-JQWLAC meeting resolved none of the process problems the QWL program was designed to address. While progress had been made securing amenities, the process by which decisions were made in the plant, diagrammed in Figure 5-1, was left essentially intact. In fact, as was noted earlier, by going though the elaborate appeal process, the meeting actually may have reinforced the established procedures.

New processes, based on participation and trust, were not mentioned. There is no evidence that participants were even aware that such alternatives existed. By successfully appealing to top management, moreover, EJEC may have increased local management's resolve to maintain established procedures. The plant-level decision making procedures, outlined in Figure 5-1, were as strongly in place as ever. However, the vertical component of the appeal process, noted in the "DECISION" column in Figure 5-1, became more visible. A diagrammatic rendering of these procedures is presented in Figure 6-2.

THE VERTICAL APPEAL PROCESS AT FOODCOM

Figure 6-2 depicts the vertical appeal process observed at FoodCom based on our observations of the QWL project. The process was initiated when a decision maker at any level received a project proposed from below. The primary concern seemed to be costs. The first task of management, therefore, was cost control, and the first question asked in the process was whether or not new unbudgeted resources were required. If not, as we saw in Figure 5-1, the proposal could be approved without further delay. If new

Figure 6-2 The Vertical System Considers EJEC Proposals

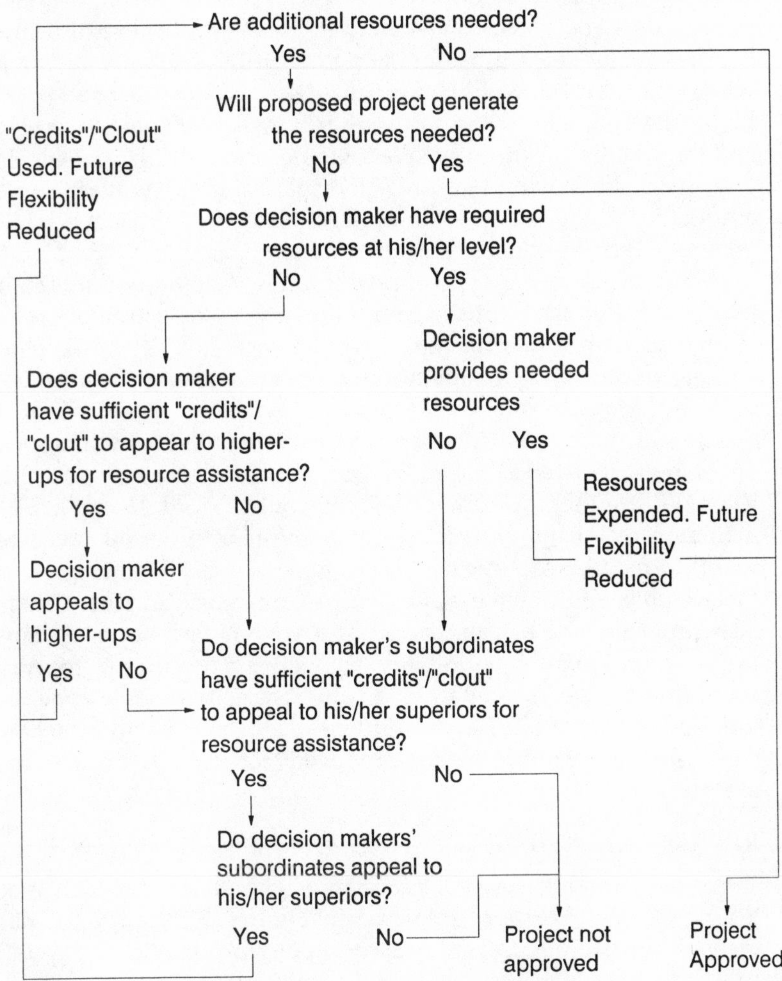

resources were required, however, the project was reviewed to determine whether it would result in resource savings sufficient to pay for itself. Alternatively, the project might generate new resources to cover its costs.

Either way, a project that promised to pay for itself could receive rapid approval. If the project was not likely to pay for itself, or if a credible argument could not be made to this effect, the decision maker could provide the needed resources on his or her own account. Alternatively, he or she could appeal to higher-ups who could approve additional expenditures. We saw this decision sequence in Pond's case. He could approve certain expenditures, but he had to refer those greater than $10,000 up the hierarchy where his request would reinitialize the decision sequence at a higher level. In the case of the $18,000 to $20,000 survey project, Pond seemed sure the controllers would approve his request. We can infer, however, that this sort of approval would not be automatic. If Pond frequently applied for these funds, he would, presumably, experience greater and greater resistance. Matson may have been in this type of position. He was in his last job and had little influence with the company, so he was extremely reluctant to make appeals on his own. Likewise, the funds he could allocate under his own signature were very limited.

When Matson refused to provide available resources or to appeal for help, his subordinates launched their own appeal. Struthers's insistence that the program succeed provided the leverage. Neither Matson nor Pond could afford to have EJEC members resign in protest. Pond therefore responded favorably to EJEC members' appeals. Had Quin rejected his request, he presumably could have appealed to Struthers. Struthers might have appealed to his superiors, and so on. Each appeal, however, would expend credibility as well as resources, for in a cost-oriented system like FoodCom, there was only one criterion against which expenditures—even in the long term—could be justified: pounds produced for each resource unit expended.

REPRESSING AND THEREBY PERPETUATING CONFLICT

There are obvious dangers associated with using decision making processes like those depicted in Figures 5-1 and 6-2. There are substantial disincentives associated with moving proposals upward in the hierarchy. Conflict resolution is also essentially a political process. Outcomes are determined on the basis of the past behavior and current influence of those making the appeal. This places great pressure on the individual decision makers. The system itself generates different perspectives and conflicting interests. Unless decision makers can resolve conflicts without appealing to their superiors for assistance, only the most pressing are likely to get addressed. To make matters worse, the decision process observed at FoodCom seemed incapable of evaluating itself. Many problems were attributed to conflict among groups. However, any attempt to address this problem explicitly was declared "out of bounds." While he might have been more politic, Shapiro's attempt to raise the issue of the maintenance department was universally rejected. Matson admitted he did not know why plant efficiency was declining; however, he would not accept attempts to attribute it to the maintenance department. With the exception of Shapiro's intervention, for which EJEC members later apologized, there was little mention of intergroup conflict during the joint EJEC-JQWLAC meeting. Yet it provided the foundation for the entire process.

Mintzberg could have had FoodCom in mind when he described the generic form of a machine bureaucracy (1979: 314). According to Mintzberg, machine bureaucracies tend to be old and large. At the time, FoodCom was over sixty years old. As with FoodCom, machine bureaucracies tend to face simple and stable environments. They have highly formalized and specialized jobs, and coordination occurs primarily through the standardization of work. Their essential characteristic, however, is an "obsession" with control. "A control mentality pervades it from top to bottom" (319). Mintzberg quotes Parkinson (1974: 60) to the effect that machine bureaucracies are characterized by "Fordismus," a German word that "conjures up the epitome of maximum industrial efficiency." This was certainly true of FoodCom.

Mintzberg explains that machine bureaucracies are "ridden with conflict: the control systems are in place to contain it." They accept conflict as a necessary consequence of implementing policies required to maximize efficiency. The problem as it is defined in a machine bureaucracy, therefore, "is not to develop an open atmosphere where people can talk conflicts out, but to enforce a closed, tightly controlled one where the work can get done despite them . . . 'Conflict is not resolved in the machine bureaucracy; rather, it is bottled up so that the work can get done" (321).

Machine bureaucracies may outperform other forms under certain conditions. It may even be true that under these conditions, the costs of conflict are more than compensated for by the benefits of cost minimization. Whether or not this is true is a concern for organization designers. For those implementing QWL programs in such settings, however, it is enough to realize that some participants may implicitly or explicitly believe that a control mentality saves more revenue than openness and trust can generate. As both Struthers and Pond reiterated during the meeting that was called to resolve the first questionnaire administration issue, cost control was perceived as good, not bad.

JQWLAC members were reluctant to support EJEC proposals for gain sharing. It was bound to create conflict between plants in the FoodCom system. Because Struthers was pressing them for just such a project, however, they decided to repress rather than confront the issue. It wasn't even mentioned in the JQWLAC's August 16 memorandum (Exhibit 6-10), and, as we will see later, management members of JQWLAC failed to tell Struthers of EJEC's interest in a gain-sharing proposal. The strong norms to avoid dealing explicitly with the maintenance department and the extreme care EJEC members took to maintain the appearance of hierarchical propriety during their meeting with the JQWLAC seem to point to the same thing: the Reginal Bakery and, perhaps, the entire bakery division, was not designed to address conflict. It was designed to implement one solution to the problem of minimizing production costs. And part of this design called for stringent controls, which, in effect, acted to prevent the organization from becoming "sidetracked" by efforts to resolve conflict or to find new solutions to production problems.

The accounting control system perhaps was not the most effective of these controls. Being explicit and visible, it could be (and on at least one occasion was) changed. The tacit cognitive control—the taken for granted understanding about dealing with conflict by controlling its expression (Scott 1987; Zucker 1983)—was more penetrating. It effectively prevented participants from confronting conflict as a problem. When participants acted, therefore, they adopted political rather than problem-solving strategies, strategies that contained but also perpetuated the underlying conflict-ridden process. Ironically, then, the QWL program in Reginal, designed to communicate a new vision of cooperative labor-management relations, had actually reinforced the adversarial patterns it sought to overcome. Deigh's initial strategy—getting the QWL program going in Reginal and then attempting to generate experiences through which his vision of cooperative labor-management relations could be communicated—had not changed these patterns. By gaining entry and seeking to stimulate change from within, the QWL program seemed to be making more accommodations than the system it was designed to change. Whether or not it would continue to do so remained to be seen.

7

A Process Model for Developing Intervention Strategies in Machine Bureaucracies

As we commented in Chapter 6, many participants in the QWL program in Reginal were very satisfied with the outcome of the joint EJEC-JQWLAC meeting. However, the meeting had served to reinforce, rather than challenge, already established patterns. The adversarial mentality underlying labor-management relations was still very much in place. No attempt had been made to neutralize or otherwise address the control mentality that had proved to be such a difficult obstacle. Relationships among members of different unions were more contentious than ever. Many projects remained unimplemented. Substantive progress in Reginal, therefore, was more apparent than real.

The QWL change agents at this point had the opportunity to choose among three distinct intervention strategies. First, they could have accepted as given the adversarial mentality underlying labor-management relationships and continued their efforts to secure amenities for employees, as presented in models 3 and 4 of Figure 4-1. This most likely would have required a continuation of the essentially political decision process on a project-by-project basis as depicted in Figures 5-1 and 6-2. It would not have changed labor-management relationships in the direction of greater cooperation.

Alternatively, they could have challenged the existing patterns of relationships, directing their efforts toward implementing the QWL vision of a qualitatively different cooperative form for labor-management and labor-labor relations in the plant (Figure 4-1, model 1). Finally, they might have attempted to surface the multiple perspectives that existed in the plant and to help members of the client system become aware of the diversity of perspectives from which they might choose. Taking this approach, program managers would have helped the client system develop the ability to identify the alternative perspectives present, to select from among them, and to implement the chosen alternative.

If QWL program managers in Reginal wished to select the second course of action—implementing the cooperative perspective—there seemed, on the surface at least, to be two ways they could act. They might try to implement the QWL vision aggressively through political means, or they might attempt to adopt an open, facilitative method of implementation more in keeping with the participative spirit of QWL (cf., Dunphy and Stace 1988).

In the first part of this chapter we will suggest an approach for implementing the QWL vision that might have been used in Reginal. We will develop an alternative model of decision making that contrasts with the processes depicted in Figures 5-1 and 6-2 and that is more consistent with the participative prescriptions characteristic of QWL programs. However, we will also suggest that the simple presence of such an alternative model is insufficient. Implementation of such a model represents a major challenge in itself. In particular, we will discuss some of the problems that will likely face change agents who attempt to implement the QWL concepts reflected in the model, and we will use the experience in Reginal as an illustrative case in point.

These problems arise from the following dilemma: Change agents attempting to implement a QWL perspective in machine bureaucracies will almost certainly be misunderstood, distrusted, or both. If they attempt to implement a more open and participative perspective using confrontational, controlling methods, they may be seen as duplicitous, because they are engaging in behaviors that will be seen as inconsistent with the change they are advocating. However, if they implement the change using strategies consistent with their values, such as increasing employee participation, they risk being misunderstood. Participants are likely to initially use their new-found influence to enact the perspective the change agents are trying to replace or transcend, because they are unfamiliar with any other perspective that could guide their action.

One might conclude that those who seek significant cognitive change in established organizations such as machine bureaucracies may be attempting the impossible. Perhaps they are best advised to restrict themselves to implementing changes that do not conflict with established cognitive assumptions, which we have elsewhere called first-order changes (Bartunek and Moch 1987). Had Deigh, Sholl, and the EJEC decided to spend the remaining QWL program resources securing amenities, they would have opted for first-order change. In doing so, they would not have provided an alternative to the decision making process in Reginal (Figures 5-1 and 6-2). They would simply have continued to try to advance EJEC members' preferences using the established patterns of decision making.

There is evidence, however, that although significant cognitive change is very difficult, it is not impossible (cf., Bartunek and Franzak 1988; Schaubroeck and Green 1988). For example, in Jamestown, New York, representatives of management and labor from several different companies came together to address an economic crisis in the city. They initially saw the crisis from contradictory perspectives. With effort and some real difficulty, however, they finally came to understand each other's perspective and to develop a qualitatively new, shared perspective that changed the image and reality of Jamestown's labor-management relationship (Meek 1983; Meek, Nelson, and Whyte 1983a; Meek, Nelson, and Whyte 1983b; Trist 1986). Later in this chapter we will suggest strategies by which

QWL change agents might help facilitate the development of alternative perspectives in organizations.

An Alternative Decision Making Process for Reginal

The QWL vision specifies a very different type of choice process than the hierarchical problem-containing process used in Reginal and represented in Figures 5-1 and 6-2. There are undoubtedly several alternative decision processes consistent with the QWL vision. We present a process in Figure 7-1 that can be considered representative of the larger set.

At Reginal, the major type of QWL activity involved the implementation of particular projects. Consequently, the decision making process we suggest is aimed at this type of activity; although decision making processes obviously extend beyond project implementation. The process specified in Figure 7-1 is initiated when any constituent of the QWL program proposes a project. At this point each of the three primary constituencies—the JQWLAC, local labor, and local management (the latter two as represented in the EJEC)—render judgments concerning the project's appropriateness and feasibility. If they disagree, their judgments are routed to each constituency along with a presentation of the reasons behind their opinion. The process of considering the proposal is then reinitiated and proceeds through a series of loops until consensus is achieved. If the constituents agree that the proposed project should not be pursued, it is dropped. A positive response, however, requires commitment of program funds to develop the proposal and assess its feasibility.

This approach to assessing the feasibility of proposed projects involves representatives from different constituencies and levels in the organization. The plant manager, so central to the process illustrated in Figure 5-1, is only part of one of the three constituencies represented in Figure 7-1. The scarcity of resources, which constrained the decision process described in Figures 5-1 and 6-2, is not overcome in the proposed process.

Figure 7-1 A Model Decision Process Specified by the QWL Vision

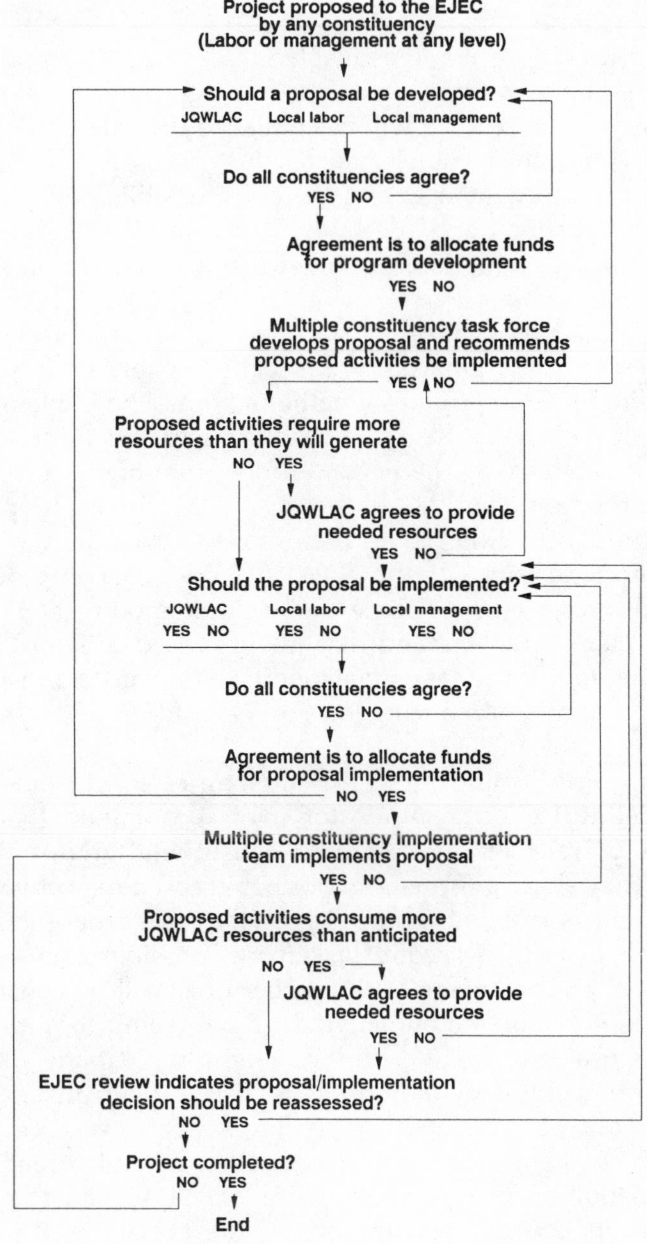

However, resources are made available—if at all—immediately after agreement on the value of the proposal rather than only after considerable frustration and multiple appeals to higher-level personnel.

Once funds are made available for developing the proposal, a task force is to be established to guide the development process. This task force will be similar to the cafeteria or parking lot committees established by the EJEC. However, it will have much more say over and more responsibility for the eventual specifications and the budget for the project. As in the case of project initiation, the plant manager would play a less central role.

If the proposed project, as specified by the task force, involves only marginal expenses or is capable of paying for itself, the EJEC determines whether it should be implemented. If it will cost more than it will documentably return to the plant, it must secure the needed funds from higher-level company or union sources. If the JQWLAC agrees to provide these funds, the EJEC could then move to consider the implementation decision. If the JQWLAC does not approve the expenditures, the task force must either modify and resubmit its plan or recommend that the proposed activities not be implemented. If the task force modifies its plan and resubmits it with explanatory documentation, the EJEC and JQWLAC must reconsider it.

Both the EJEC and JQWLAC must agree to implement the proposal and allocate funds for it or recommend that it be altered or rejected. If the three constituent groups do not agree, they share information, opinions, and perspectives until agreement is reached. If they agree that the proposal should be implemented, a second task force, possibly composed at least partly of members of the earlier one, will be constituted to guide implementation activities. By agreeing to implement the proposal, the EJEC, with top labor and company support, will commit implementation funds. If cost overruns are minimal or can be generated by greater than expected revenues created by the proposed program, they do not threaten the implementation process. Otherwise, JQWLAC must agree to increase its commitment or reroute the project to the EJEC.

At this point EJEC must reconsider its earlier implementation decision.

Figure 7-1 calls for continuous or periodic EJEC project review, for shared responsibility on the part of the various participants rather than purely "top-down" responsibility, and for a multiple constituency task force to provide the managerial functions. It therefore represents a radically different approach to decision making and administration in the plant than is identified in Figures 5-1 and 6-2.

This process is likely to be cumbersome and time-consuming. Its strength, however, lies in its insistence on collaboration and consensus before any decision can be made to proceed at either the feasibility or the implementation stages. This enables all the multiple perspectives and realities represented to be considered in the decision making process and is similar to the process of consensus-building among different constituencies used in many Japanese companies (e.g., Takeuchi 1985). The requirements for collaboration and consensus create difficulty in decision making because they require communication among representatives of different perspectives. However, this is not an insurmountable obstacle; several ways of facilitating such communication have been introduced, including strategic assumption surfacing, dialectical inquiry, and devil's advocate approaches (e.g., Cosier 1981; Mason and Mitroff 1981; Schweiger, Sandberg, and Ragan 1986).

This type of approach is consistent with QWL principles, but its basic premises of collaboration and shared responsibility among different groups must be accepted for it to succeed; otherwise, the collaboration it implies is likely to be deceptive. We turn now to problems experienced in Reginal with implementing such collaborative premises.

The Implementation Dilemma Facing Managers of the QWL Program in Reginal

The FoodCom story to date suggests that the participants in the QWL program in Reginal came to understand the program in terms of the perspective the program was designed to replace. Those advocating QWL precepts in similar settings elsewhere may therefore become as frustrated as Deigh was during the meeting concerning the first survey administration proposal or as perplexed and angry as Sholl became during the JQWLAC-QWL project staff meeting just before the joint EJEC-JQWLAC meeting in Reginal. Deigh tried to confront Struthers, Coy, Farr, Seldon, Kochems, and Matson with the limitations of their "efficiency-at-any-cost" mentality, but his efforts were interpreted as a challenge to the company's cost-minimization and control functions. Sholl told management members of JQWLAC that the QWL program could give them more than just a renovated cafeteria. It could build involvement and responsibility and give employees more realistic understanding of FoodCom's management. However, Sholl was perceived merely as trying to extend his contract and give the company a "quick job." It seemed that all of Deigh or Sholl's actions were judged on the basis of cost criteria or their consistency with established values. Actions consistent with the existing (and valued) perspective of coordination and control were supported. Those that appeared to be inconsistent with this perspective were resisted.

Deigh operated on the collaborative assumption that members of the client system are the best judges of what will facilitate or hinder productivity and the quality of working life in Reginal. He therefore implemented a decision making process that gave local participants authority to enact their interpretation of QWL. If he had articulated the process he had in mind, it might not have been significantly different from the one depicted in Figure 7-1.

Unfortunately, when the consultants introduced this new decision process into a system whose members were steeped in a tradition of distrust and the repression of problems, the participants responded in the only way they knew. They became focused on the short-term and on external rewards—amenities—rather than on long-term collaboration for a more jointly satisfactory work environment. Yet, amenities as such were not on Deigh's or Sholl's initial agenda. Moreover, one might argue that amenities are usually inadequate goals for

QWL projects. This meant, in effect, that the consultants' understanding of an appropriate collaborative QWL process significantly interfered with their achieving an appropriate QWL content and that the QWL perspective became coopted by traditional patterns of understanding.

This problem is likely to present itself any time one tries to implement a program that calls for significant cognitive change using a participative procedure such as the one EJEC employed. The newly empowered participants in the QWL program in Reginal interpreted the program in terms with which they were familiar. The program provided resources for local expression, assuming that they would be used to fulfill employees' needs for meaningful and challenging work and for satisfying social relationships. In contrast, the employees sought amenities and employed change strategies based on advocacy and political maneuvering. It therefore seemed that Deigh and Sholl were being forced to choose between one of two sides in a central dilemma: to accept the local definition of what constituted a QWL program (first-order change) or to act in ways that were inconsistent with their participative schemata. If they took the latter approach, they were likely to be misunderstood, or to be seen as duplicitous.

Sholl seemed more willing to accept the employees' interpretation of QWL as amenities than was Deigh. Yet he had been hired to help the local committee find ways to facilitate cooperative labor-management relationships. Partly because he seemed to accept the employees' emphasis on amenities, he came to be judged not in terms of how he facilitated labor-management cooperation, but in terms of the number of amenities acquired within the time period specified by his consulting contract. To meet these demands, he acted as if he had to challenge and overcome the resistance of local managers politically. Far from facilitating cooperative labor-management relationships, he then became a key architect of a decision process that further alienated these two constituencies.

Deigh, on the other hand, seemed more willing than Sholl to continue to press for significant cognitive change. But the more he pressed for a participative decision process, the more the EJEC decisions reflected the perspective he had sought to change. At some point, program participants might learn from his example. However, there was no evidence that this point had been reached or that it was reachable in the time frame allotted for the experiment.

Several EJEC members urged the QWL program to address the human issues. However, the EJEC members too fell prey to short-term concerns. Leticia Sanchez frequently urged the EJEC to consider human relations issues, for instance, but she became distracted by the process of acquiring clocks and better food service. Marie McCarthy noted that the search for amenities had been a stopgap procedure. As a stopgap, however, it was consuming the vast majority of EJEC members' time and energy. It was becoming critical, therefore, that those managing the program either accept this definition of the QWL program in Reginal (first-order change) or move to introduce the QWL alternative (second-order change, cf., Bartunek and Moch 1987). A third alternative would be to work to develop the client system's awareness of the dilemma itself—to engage in what we elsewhere have called third-order change (Bartunek and Moch 1987)—by introducing the client system to a perspective on perspectives. We describe the second-order and third-order alternatives below.

Second-Order Change: Implementing the Change Agent's Preferred Alternative

In general, second-order change can be defined as the conscious modification of schemata in a particular direction. Research that has been conducted on this process suggests that second-order change begins with a dramatic event or perceived crisis strong enough to unfreeze the established or institutionalized perspective (e.g., Gemmill and Smith 1985; Gray, Bougon, and Donnellon 1985; Palazzoli et al. 1986; Tushman and Romanelli 1985). For second-order change to be carried through, change agents must strongly advocate a clear alternative to the present way of operating—that is, a new perspective (Bartunek and Moch 1987; Belgard, Fisher, and Rayner 1987). If a new perspective is forcefully presented, then conflict, ambiguity, and power struggles surrounding it are normal. This happens partly because the new perspective is likely to be seen at least initially as a negation of the original perspective rather than as valuable in itself (Bartunek 1988; Child and Smith 1987).

We will describe this process more fully later in this chapter. Here we simply note that because the targets of second-order change are unlikely to understand the new perspective without it being strongly presented, and because presentation of the new perspective is typically accompanied by conflict and power struggles, change agents advocating greater openness, trust, and participation as alternatives face an especially difficult choice. On the one hand, they might attempt to impose their vision. However, this is most easily done through essentially confrontational strategies (which seem inconsistent with participation). They might instead communicate through example, which may not seem very forceful. Deigh appears to have chosen the latter strategy, Sholl the former. Both, however, encountered problems.

Sholl appeared to be duplicitous. He advocated a closed political decision strategy for implementing a program designed to facilitate openness and trust. Had those who sought to understand his perspective focused on his example, they might easily have concluded that he was committed to maintaining an adversarial process in the plant. In contrast, Deigh seemed to rely on the QWL process to carry the message about its content. His strategy was not so much political as educational. However, he too gave the appearance of being duplicitous. As employees were deciding to accept the QWL program in Reginal, he explicitly promised not to change established patterns of collective bargaining, participant benefits, or promotion possibilities. Yet he was attempting to alter the cognitive foundations upon which each of these patterns were based.

Third-Order Change: Advocating a Perspective on Perspectives

A third alternative available to the QWL program managers in Reginal was to try to acquaint the company with its own cognitive diversity and with the limits to change imposed by its structure, its institutional history, and the mechanisms it employed for coordination and control. This change strategy was not attempted in Reginal, so we can speak about it only speculatively. Introducing it here, however, provides a useful context for the discussion of first- and second-order change. It also suggests that a broader variety of types of change is available than is often realized.

The intention in third-order change is not to impose the QWL or any particular alternative perspective. Rather, it is to help members of the client system develop their own diagnostic capabilities in order to be aware of perspectives out of which they are operating—to "have," rather than "be" these perspectives (Kegan 1982) or to be able to "change [their] point of view and see [their] situation in a new light" (Smith 1984, p. 488). Clients then can select and implement alternatives of their own choosing (such as cooperation or control or some alternative perspective). This does not necessarily imply that the change agent is neutral with respect to the alternatives being considered. In fact, by explicitly accepting or rejecting some of the alternatives personally, the change agent may provide a role model useful for instructing the client system in how a perspective on perspectives might be applied. In the final analysis, it is members of the client system, not the change agent, who select, adopt, and change the interpretive schemata.

In third-order change, change agents explicitly communicate a perspective on perspectives. They attempt to explain what they are trying to do as they do it (Bartunek and Moch 1987). Because third-order change is designed to allow members of the client system to participate in choosing the perspective to which they will eventually adhere, the change agent does not impose a particular point of view. Rather, he or she works to help members of the client system become aware of the nature and functioning of cognitive schemata so they might gain a measure of freedom from and control over them.

A change agent, for example, may prefer a vision that focuses on the meaningfulness of work and/or work relationships and evokes a participative decision process. He or she, however, would present this alternative as one among many. In addition to introducing members of the client system to a QWL vision and its associated decision processes (e.g., Figure 7-1), the change agent could also present the closed hierarchical perspective and its decision processes (e.g., Figures 5-1 and 6-2). We have described the hierarchical perspective using the QWL alternative and the Reginal plant as references. This may have led the reader to view it in a negative way. However, many believe machine bureaucracies have their place (Mintzberg 1979). The ability of machine bureaucracies to provide goods and services in a cost-effective way may more than compensate for the human and social costs they incur. They may well be acceptable to organizational members who choose to focus on external rewards rather than upon internal or social values.

A third-order change strategy may allow change agents to be more consistent—some would say more ethical. It encourages change agents to respect clients' freedom to choose particular alternatives. However, although it may liberate participants from the bonds of particular schemata, such a strategy must somehow introduce them to a schema of schemata. And this simply raises the dilemma associated with change and the ethical issue of freedom of choice to a higher cognitive level. Although the change agent is up front in advocating a perspective on perspectives, he or she is likely to have to engage in activities that significantly disrupt established routines in order to bring members of the client system to the point where they can understand what is involved (cf., Torbert 1987). The disruption, moreover, cannot be justified on the basis of some preferred specific alternative perspective. It must be justified on the basis of the need to gain freedom from any specific perspective.

In this section we have introduced second- and third-order change within the context of the dilemmas experienced in Reginal. We now expand on this introduction by describing characteristics necessary for second-order change toward the QWL perspective to occur.

Characteristics of Second-Order Change

The QWL vision advocates two-way communication and shared responsibility based upon openness and trust. It is predicated upon a variety of fairly explicit values and beliefs: for example, the beliefs that most individuals are capable of making a high level of contribution to the attainment of organizational goals if they are provided with supportive and challenging organizational environments, that solutions to most attitudinal and motivational problems in organizations are transactional, and that "win-win" solutions to conflicts are possible and desirable (cf., French and Bell 1984). As such, it represents a point of view that contrasts sharply with both machine bureaucracies' obsession with control and with designs that contain conflict but actively resist conflict resolution. The patterns are so different that some people (e.g., Lavoie and Culbert 1978) question whether OD can be implemented in such systems.

Given the very different perspectives held by QWL advocates and those involved with machine bureaucracies, change agents seeking to implement the QWL vision in such organizations must necessarily engage in second-order change. How might they attempt to achieve this change? To address this issue, we discuss dilemmas QWL change agents experience in such systems and ways they might see these dilemmas. Then we describe processes of second-order change more fully and, concurrently, suggest strategies change agents might use to help achieve their desired outcomes.

Dilemmas and Paradoxes Associated with Second-Order Change

We noted above that QWL change agents experience a central dilemma in trying to implement a high quality of working life characterized by open collaboration in machine bureaucracies. Their normal stance to achieving such change is likely to be facilitative. However, facilitation can reinforce already existing interaction patterns rather than change them (cf., Dunphy and Stace 1988; Elden 1986). Consequently, instead of taking a facilitative approach, change agents may attempt to implement their perspective forcefully, and perhaps coercively (Dunphy and Stace 1988). Employees, however, are likely to interpret this type of action as inconsistent with collaboration and therefore as deceitful.

A dilemma such as this represents a paradoxical situation (cf., Cameron and Quinn 1988) in which two contradictory and even mutually exclusive elements such as "facilitation" and "forcefulness" appear to be present. It doesn't seem possible for change agents to be forceful advocates of collaboration and simultaneously facilitate organization members' collaborative achievement of their own goals. Forcing organization members' open, collaborative participation is likely to be seen as contradictory by both change agents and organizational members.

Paradoxical situations such as these have begun to receive some analytical attention (e.g., Quinn and Cameron 1988; Smith and Berg 1987). These analyses have focused on successful and unsuccessful ways of dealing with paradoxical situations. They indicate, first, that a common (though frequently unsuccessful) pattern for handling such dilemmas is splitting the competing perspectives, acknowledging that only one has validity (Smith and Berg 1987), and then setting them in a competition with each other in which one perspective wins and one loses. This might be done by change agents who acknowledge the validity only of facilitation or forceful advocacy and try to establish conditions that disallow the other approach. This approach does not allow the dilemma to be surfaced openly. Instead, the underlying conflict between the Two approaches is likely to be displaced onto other issues or people, who then become the focus of attention. In Reginal, for example, the plant manager became the object of concern.

How might dilemmas such as these be addressed more productively? This requires a kind of Janusian thinking (Rothenberg 1979) in which both poles of the dilemma—the two apparent opposites—are considered to be equally and simultaneously operative and true. For example, Rothenberg described creative composers who could conceive of simultaneous dissonance and harmony in a chord and artists who could paint tension and rest in the same scene. The viewing of the two poles of the dilemma as simultaneously valid enables the viewer to join these two poles rather than split them from each other. It further enables the viewer to foster a dialectical interaction between the two poles, one that eventually allows the paradoxical situation to be transcended (Ford and Backoff 1988). That is, the two poles of the dilemma eventually may come to be seen within a larger framework, within which they are complementary rather than contradictory.

Dealing with Forceful Advocacy versus Facilitation. How might forceful advocacy and participation come to be seen within such a larger framework? This dilemma may be considered analogous to dissonance versus harmony in a musical chord. From a Janusian perspective, forceful advocacy may be an effective means of facilitating open expression. In fact, one might argue that these perspectives necessarily reinforce one another: How can we advocate the expression of viewpoints for others without claiming it for ourselves? A Janusian approach suggests that an appropriate role for QWL consultants is forceful introduction and fostering of the types of schemata, structures, and processes (such as joint labor-management committees with truly shared responsibility) that encourage members of a client system to present their own opinions, even if these are not consistent with open collaboration.

It is often true that change agents and others do not have the cognitive capacity to simultaneously advocate a particular perspective and facilitate the expression of others' opinions. Argyris (1985, 1988) has continually focused attention on this problem. However, there is no underlying reason why people can't do both, and the primary intent of much of Argyris' work has been to help people develop this capacity.

In the FoodCom case as we have described it to this point, the QWL change agents seemed unable to see the two approaches as simultaneous possibilities. Instead, Sholl appeared to enact a forceful advocacy approach that was not very consistent with open cooperation, while Deigh attempted to facilitate cooperation in a way that wasn't very confrontational. The two approaches were not coordinated in such a way that something new and transcendent could be created from them. Instead, they remained split—distinct and, at least in appearance, contradictory.

Other Dilemmas Encountered. Forceful advocacy versus facilitation was not the only dilemma the change agents faced. Related dilemmas included the QWL cooperative perspective versus the control perspective of top management and the QWL cooperative perspective versus competitive intergroup rivalries in the Reginal plant. Before the JQWLAC-EJEC joint meeting, the change agents had not handled these dilemmas in a way that would eventually allow them to be transcended. Rather, in the case of the cooperation versus the control perspective, they found themselves drawn into a win-lose power struggle between their perspective and that of top management. This was particularly evident in situations involving decisions about the survey administration and attempts to get accounting variances. The control perspective seemed to win in these struggles. Over time, Sholl's actual approach, if not his words, came to reflect the control perspective more than the cooperative one, as Sholl covertly led the EJEC into a political power struggle against the plant manager. One result was that while several activities took place at Reginal prior to the JQWLAC meeting and some comparatively superficial changes occurred (such as the implementation of the no-smoking area in the cafeteria), no significant changes in underlying patterns of relationships—the major purpose of the QWL program—were achieved.

Deigh approached the dilemma of cooperation versus intergroup rivalries in a different fashion. Rather than establishing win-lose power struggles between the two perspectives, he seemed to work hard to avoid the issue. Deigh did this, for example, by promising different groups different outcomes from the QWL project. Like the more competitive style, this type of approach, by keeping the perspectives separate, also had the effect of splitting them (Smith and Berg 1987).

As is the case with forceful advocacy versus facilitation, the consultants need not have pitted cooperation against control or separated cooperation and intergroup rivalries. It would have been possible for them to conceive of these apparently opposed schemata as simultaneously true, perhaps to see all of them as representing valid concerns. However, without the type of perspective we are advocating here, this outcome would have been very difficult for them to achieve. Seeing this type of dilemma requires that change agents be aware of the underlying schemata present in a situation and able to grasp the dilemmas that arise as schemata confront each other and interact in concrete settings. It requires change agents to confront their own commitments to the point at which they are comfortable advocating their chosen sen alternative and simultaneously being open to others in contexts where they are seen as experts. In the process of doing this, they will be forcefully providing a model of facilitative open behavior.

The Role of Client Misunderstanding in Change. We noted above that clients are likely to misunderstand change agents' attempts to create cognitive change. This misunderstanding may become an integral part of the change process, not simply be a block to it. For example, family therapists who make use of paradoxical therapeutic strategies often find themselves misunderstood (cf., Siporin and Gummer 1988). However, these therapists distinguish between their own understanding and that of the families with which they are working: They know the underlying coherence of their activities even if the families involved cannot understand it. They often consciously prescribe activities that do not make sense within a family's frame of reference precisely to help family members become aware of the limitations of their present understanding. In this way therapists help family members move toward second-order change in their relationships with each other (Watzlawick, Weakland, and Fisch 1974).

Organizational change agents may deal with misunderstanding by creating a context and structures in which members of the client system grapple with the alternative perspective long enough to begin to understand it. Because this activity is usually very difficult, maintaining the context can be a challenge in itself, as Mills discovered when he attempted to initiate the QWL program in Gorland. Deigh discovered the same thing when he encountered restrictive obstacles in Reginal. Change agents need to take care not to compromise their own perspective in order to buy time for the change activities. This, perhaps, was a critical flaw in Sholl's strategy. They also must strongly advocate their point of view even when it threatens to generate resistance sufficient to destroy the change attempt itself. Failure to do so seems to have been a crucial flaw in Deigh's strategy.

A Process for Achieving Second-Order Change

We noted above that second-order change involves a discontinuous change in schemata, a qualitative shift in the way some phenomenon is understood. We also noted that one crucial characteristic of the process of this change is a paradox-based interaction between competing perspectives. Now we move beyond presentation of the characteristics of second-order change to a description of the overall process of such change.

Identification of Schemata

The first task of a change agent in such a change is to identify the schemata initially present in an organizational setting. In Chapter 4 we suggested some ways of identifying schemata, especially through attention to the language and to the metaphors organization members use. Here we add an additional dimension to our earlier analysis: We clarify the type of schemata of particular concern in QWL interventions.

Organizations have at least two types of schemata. One addresses organization members' understandings of the organization's overall identity and work. This might include, for example, AT&T's understanding of itself as a high technology company. The second type of schemata addresses organization members' understandings of relationships among various organization members and groups. The QWL paradigm and QWL interventions directly address this latter type of schema.

There are many types of schemata regarding relationships that organizational members might hold. We have described several of them, including the cooperative QWL schema (e.g., Mohrman and Lawler 1985) and the managerial control schemata (Feldman 1986; Hanlon, Nadler, and Gladstein 1985). The paternalistic understanding present at Reginal (Chapter 4) is one version of the managerial control schema (Feldman 1986). Another different type of schema about relationships is an "autonomy" schema, such as is present in many educational settings (e.g.,Bartunek and Reid 1988; Weick 1976). In these settings, the different academic units typically expect to be left to act quite independently, with very little coordination. We develop the role of these schemata in more detail elsewhere (Bartunek and Moch 1989).

Organizational schemata do not exist in a vacuum; they are expressed and embodied in the organization's structures, norms, resource allocation patterns, and ways of handling conflict (Bartunek 1984; Bartunek and Reid 1988; Ranson, Hinings and Greenwood 1980; Tushman and Romanelli 1985; Tushman, Newman, and Romanelli 1986). These structures and patterns in turn maintain the schemata (Giddens 1979). For example, the control schema at FoodCom was expressed in a machine bureaucracy structure, a strict internal accounting system, and a damage-control style of handling conflict that contained rather than resolved problems in a way that reinforced and maintained the hierarchical control perspective. Attempts to change schemata must therefore address the behavioral patterns and structures through which the schemata are expressed; otherwise, existing schemata will continue to be maintained, and alternatives will be discarded.

Challenges to the Initial Schemata

We suggested earlier that for the second-order change process to begin there must be a very strong challenge to the initial schema. That challenge must be dramatic and forceful enough to create a sense of crisis in powerful organization members regarding the original perspective. In the FoodCom case, for example, for second-order change to begin (at least at the level of the JQWLAC), the challenge to the control perspective and its expressions would have to be strong enough to cause JQWLAC members to feel a sense of crisis about the adequacy of this perspective.

Successful challenges to an entrenched schema are difficult to achieve. Organization members are likely to experience strong negative reactions to challenges to the initial perspective, including defensiveness, shock, and a sense of loss (e.g., Tannenbaum and Hanna 1985; Tunstall 1985). Consequently, unless they are convinced that the crisis necessitates change, they may pay lip service to the challenge and find ways to subvert it in practice (Bartunek 1988). How might a sufficiently strong challenge take place?

There have been some descriptions of ways such challenges take place during naturally occurring second-order change processes. The challenges occur due to poor organizational performance, managerial succession, powerful subgroups' interests no longer being served by the present perspective, managerial practices no longer succeeding, or a major environmental shift that renders the present understanding inadequate (e.g., Bartunek 1984; Gray, Bougon, and Donnellon 1985; Hedberg 1981; Pondy and Huff 1985). Change agents attempting to initiate second-order change might make organizational personnel aware of any of these potential problems. For example, they might build on the fact that some organization members' interests are not served by the established perspective or point to environmental conditions that require entirely new approaches. Alternatively, they might employ adapted versions of the paradoxical procedures family therapists use to initiate change in troubled families (e.g., Palazzoli et al. 1986; Siporin and Gummer 1988; Smith and Berg 1987).

There are two general categories of these strategies: symptom prescription and paradoxical reframing. Siporin and Gummer (1988, p. 215) describe symptom prescription as including "permission, modification, exaggeration, or redirection of symptomatic behavior, and the prediction or prescription of release [from the symptoms]." For example, families in which a particular troublesome behavior pattern is present might be told they must carry out that particular behavior but only at specific times and places. Paradoxical reframing, according to Siporin and Gummer (1988, p. 216) includes "the relabeling and redefinition of behavior and situations, as well as the subsequent stimulation of different relationships, rituals, and rules." The relabeling must include some illogical or contradictory feature. For example, a family therapist might relabel a family's quarreling as an expression of family members' needs for closeness and understanding.

Paradoxical strategies like these have been used relatively infrequently in organizations, primarily to deal with problems relating to individuals or small groups (e.g., Hirschorn and Gilmore 1980; Steier and Smith 1985; Woodruff and Engle 1985). Ways these strategies might be used to achieve substantial organization-wide change are just beginning to be explored (e.g., Palazzoli et al. 1986). It would seem, however, that they would be applicable to the initiation of second-order organizational change. For example, change agents who wish to challenge a managerial control approach may encourage its extreme use, but only for particular types of problems. Change agents who wish to deal with intergroup rivalries might demand that various groups interfere with each others' efforts. Finally, these change agents might relabel the disagreements as extremely beneficial for organizational functioning, suggesting they are necessary for any communication at all. These types of change agent actions, if sufficiently dramatic and contradictory, might begin to loosen the initial perspective from its moorings.

The Presentation of an Alternative Perspective

Challenging the initial perspective, though necessary, is not sufficient. An alternative vision or perspective for the organization must also be presented. Moreover, the presentation of this alternative must include structures and norms consistent with it; otherwise, the crisis will not lead to change because there is no clear direction toward which the organization might change and no new structures to counter existing patterns of behavior.

Some general methods by which alternative perspectives to a schema may be introduced have been suggested. Gooding (1989), for example, suggests that advocates of change focus on raising the visibility of negative outcomes and then identifying alternative schemata capable of explaining the outcomes without contradicting the real or presumed "facts" of the situation. Related to this idea, Gioia and Manz (1985) suggest developing models or exemplars for new types of behavior for responding to situations that evoke the original schema. Bartunek and Ringuest (1989) describe how these new behaviors might be received. They describe what some of the effects of these new behaviors might be, both on the people who do them and on the organization undergoing change. The innovators they studied were less likely to be given significant organizational assignments and were more likely to leave the organization than their less innovative counterparts. However, those who remained came to feel they had been influential, at least more influential than their less innovative coworkers. Bartunek and Moch (1989) also suggest that change agents identify and categorize schemata along multiple dimensions and then focus attention upon both similarities and differences between established and alternative schemata in order to introduce the client system to their differences. This approach would also require attention to ways the schemata are enacted in practice.

The QWL perspective was an alternative to the control schema present at FoodCom. The labor-management committee was an associated structure that could, if properly utilized as an open, collaborative venture, provide a counterpoint for established adversarial relationships. However, this alternative perspective had to be strongly presented to have an impact.

The new vision was not articulated clearly at FoodCom, and the challenge to the organizational control schema was, at best, only weakly expressed. Although Deigh questioned the control perspective (for example, in conjunction with the administration of the plantwide survey), there is no evidence that he succeeded in getting the JQWLAC members to appreciate the value of cooperation. In fact, Deigh's approach was to downplay any potential crisis. During his introduction of the program at Reginal (Chapter 3), for example, he told the employees that the Reginal plant was chosen because it was doing well, not because there were problems. Although this approach helped get the program voted in by the Reginal employees, it severely limited the type of impact the program would be able to have later.

Moreover, the consultants did not forcefully introduce the EJEC to a way of operating that focused on shared responsibility between labor and management. Rather, as in the case of the parking lot and several of the other projects (Chapter 5), the consultants reinforced the committee's expectations developed from the control perspective that the EJEC should ask for particular outcomes and management should be required to carry out the work necessary to achieve these outcomes.

Interaction and Conflict between Perspectives

When an initial perspective has been brought to a crisis point and an alternative introduced, additional steps are required. At this point there are at least two perspectives present (in some situations there may be many more; cf., Child and Smith 1987). As we noted before, however, organization members who hold strongly to the original perspective are unlikely to see an alternative perspective in its own terms. Rather, they are likely to focus on its challenge to their traditional ways of understanding and to therefore act defensively, resisting the new approach. The normal course of events includes considerable ambiguity and conflict between the different perspectives and the people and groups espousing them. Moreover, as we suggested above, one normal way such conflict is expressed is in a win-lose struggle between the perspectives, with advocates of each perspective trying to establish it to the exclusion of the other. These win-lose struggles sometimes retard potential changes (Bartunek and Reid 1988).

As we hinted earlier, there is an alternative to a win-lose conflict between perspectives. This alternative, a paradoxical one, implies a dialectical interaction between the perspectives in which both are considered to have a proper place and in which both are seen as having the capacity to inform each other. For this type of interaction to be present, there must be some people involved in the change process who are capable of "holding" each perspective, regardless of whether this is the perspective out of which they would operate themselves. That is, some participants in the change process need to appreciate the simultaneous validity of the different perspectives.

During naturally occurring second-order change, this role is typically played by organizational leaders (Bartunek 1984). During QWL interventions, it may be played by change agents who are capable of paradoxical thought and action. These change agents would be capable of both operating out of the QWL paradigm and appreciating values underlying the control perspective. This might mean that they are not hesitant to advocate a QWL perspective: that is, they work to establish the cooperative schema and accompanying labor-management committees and other structures (e.g., Figure 2-1) that foster a high quality of working life. However, they also encourage structures and processes that allow both the control and QWL perspectives to inform each other.

Outcome of the Change Process

A dialectical interaction between perspectives has the capacity over time to lead to a creative new synthesis, one that could not have been imaginable to the participants in advance (cf., Bartunek and Moch 1987; Gemmill and Smith 1985). It has the capacity to lead organization members to create new schemata that transcend any of the initial schemata, either of the organization or the QWL change agents. The schemata might, for example, encompass appreciation of the roles of both control and cooperation.

What does this suggest about the implementation of a cooperative decision making process such as that shown in Figure 7-1? It does not suggest that such an effort should be abandoned. This decision process reflects a pattern consistent with the QWL perspective and is an important alternative to more control-oriented change processes such as those in Figures 5-1 and 6-2. However, it also suggests that when QWL change agents introduce such a decision process they should not reject challenges and uncertainties out of hand, but should instead work with the client system. They need to help clients—and top management in machine bureaucracies—identify the underlying beliefs out of which the decision process is being challenged and to let the underlying values of the two approaches inform each other. The end result of this process should be a model for decision making that goes beyond any of the models we have presented, including the one in Figure 7-1. By advocating a particular model and then enabling its development, consultants can act in a manner that is simultaneously forceful and facilitative.

Realizing Third-Order Change

Implementing third-order change in machine bureaucracies presents many of the same problems as second-order change (and more difficult ones). Although change agents are not committed in advance to any particular perspective, they are committed to a perspective on perspectives. As was the case in second-order change, participants interpret change activities in terms with which they are familiar. It is not realistic to expect them to understand experientially a perspective on schemata until they have experienced steps leading to it within their own organizational setting. Consequently, systems that have undergone multiple second-order changes are likely to have the greatest capacity for third-order change.

Strategies for third-order change in machine bureaucracies may not initially look very different from those that direct second-order change in these settings. The difference is that the change agent's approach is more educative, because the change agent attempts to help organization members understand the underlying processes associated with second-order change. The consultant is especially helping organization members understand dilemmas and the opportunities they provide for ongoing schematic change.

There are several possible tactics for introducing the client system to experiences that facilitate third-order change (Bartunek, Gordon, and Weathersby 1983; Bartunek and Moch 1987; Torbert 1987). For example, Bartunek and Moch (1987) suggest that one way to induce this type of change is to establish structures (such as matrix-like structures) that consciously enable people to operate using different perspectives. These structures are not introduced to create an environment conducive to the adoption of a preferred alternative point of view, but to give members of the client system the experience necessary for gaining a perspective on a variety of points of view, a perspective on perspectives.

The decision making processes described in Figure 5-1, 6-2, and 7-1 could be used to introduce third-order change. For example, a change agent might begin a third-order intervention by presenting these three models to organization members as alternative decision schemes. Initially, organization members would be likely to adopt the perspective most consistent with their established view. With its implementation, problems would arise. The change agent might then use these problems to confront the premises of the process (cf., Bateson, 1972). Managers might then choose another. With its implementation, new problems would arise. The consultant might use these problems to confront the premises associated with this new approach, and a third alternative might then be selected, used, and challenged.

At some point, most likely after a very long period of time, members of the client system would have sufficient experience to recognize that any decision process selected has costs and benefits. Moreover, they might then be in a position to discover that the criteria used to evaluate decision processes can change as a function of the underlying perspectives used to generate the processes in the first place. At this point, they might have undergone what Bateson (1972) called "learning III" and might be converted to a perspective that views schemata themselves as problems or as solutions. Perspectives can then be grasped in and of themselves, and members of the client system thereby freed from the tacit unexamined assumptions that constitute perspectives per se. We should note that this type of change is extremely difficult for individuals to achieve (Bateson 1972, p. 301). It is even more difficult for organizations. Nevertheless, it seeks a valuable outcome: freedom from the bondage of any particular point of view (Bateson 1972, p. 304).

Those familiar with top or middle level managers in machine bureaucracies might be quite skeptical about the ability of such systems even to begin movement toward third-order change. If it was difficult to get Struthers to move away from his commitment to the cost or control perspective, how long might he endure the development of a perspective on perspectives? How could Matson ever be brought to the point of understanding that the control mentality, the QWL vision, or any other point of view are simply examples from a much larger set and that he and other people in his plant might develop the ability to identify, analyze, select, and change them? Expecting this amount of change is perhaps unrealistic. If so, second-order change (if that) may be all that could possibly be expected from those socialized into one and only one vision of how their organization might function. On the other hand, machine bureaucracies facing increasingly turbulent times might have to learn to change. They might even have to develop the capacity for never-ending change. If so, they may have to begin to develop third-order change skills in order to remain viable.

The costs of developing third-order change capability are likely to be substantial. This process requires participants to experience confrontation and multiple points of view continually. If every phase in the proposed process were followed, change agents would be required to allow several difficult decision processes, each of which would be challenged at the schematic level (Figure 1-1) in order to introduce the client system to another point of view. If the first confrontation generates confusion and suspicion, the second may eliminate any chance for eventual recovery. Consequently, support from top management is crucial. Without long-term understanding and support from above, there would be virtually no chance a program for third-order change would survive at middle and lower levels.

8

Managing the Dialogue Among Competing Perspectives

Feeding Back the Survey Data

During the joint EJEC-JQWLAC meeting, JQWLAC members had agreed that the EJEC could conduct survey feedback sessions using the procedure employed to administer the questionnaire in the first place. Employees would be given release time from work during which they could attend group discussions of the questionnaire results. From August through October, EJEC members and the consulting staff designed and then carried out these survey feedback sessions.

A Survey Feedback Model Aimed at Initiating Second-Order Change

While carrying out the feedback sessions, the EJEC members and consultants did not attempt to manage cognitive social change. Despite the popularity of the survey feedback technique, there are few models for how to apply it to this type of change. Thus, the feedback sessions in Reginal did little more than raise well-known issues and highlight differences among contending groups. Discussing these sessions, however, can help illustrate how a change agent may be a simultaneous advocate of the QWL framework and a moderator for the dialogue between it and established alternatives.

To make this discussion productive, we will first review a standard model of survey feedback. With this as a baseline, we will present a model of a feedback process designed to facilitate second-order change toward a QWL perspective. We will then assess the survey feedback events, constrasting them with those prescribed by this model.

The most prominent current model of survey feedback is that developed by Nadler (1977, 1979). He suggests (1979, p. 309) that the purpose of feedback is to alter behavior and that this purpose is achieved as follows:

> Through feedback, a group may obtain information about the quantity and quality of its output as well as knowledge about the effectiveness of the methods used to achieve desired levels of performance. Feedback serves as an error correction device and, therefore, as a stimulus to begin problem identification and solution.

As an "error correction device" and "stimulus," feedback serves both motivational and directional (or "cueing") functions (Nadler 1977, ch. 4). It has a motivational component in that it may serve as a reward or sanction by signaling how effective a particular behavior is or by leading to perceptions that changes in behavior will be rewarded or sanctioned. It has a directional component in that it gives cues about appropriate types of behavior or directs organizational members to further diagnoses or ways of learning about what the underlying problems really are. For these functions to be successful, the behaviors required for successful change must be feasible and the feedback must clearly specify correction or search routines.

This feedback model is consistent in many ways with the problem-solving model we presented in Figure 1-1, which suggests that the presentation of negative feedback about outcomes of action is likely to lead to changes of some type. In Figure 1-1, we suggested that four possible types of changes might occur: in actions, means, desired conditions, and if none of these is successful, in schemata. The standard feedback model implicitly and, to some extent, explicitly, focuses on first-order changes in actions, means, and sometimes the desirability of particular conditions. This focus is shown in its specification of what a cueing function might achieve, as well as its assumption that to be successful the feedback must imply clear correction or search routines. As we noted in Chapter 7, second-order change is typically not achieved through clear routines.

Not surprisingly, survey feedback is typically most successful with groups already operating out of a QWL orientation. For example, Neilsen (1984, p. 209) suggests that individual organizational members who "share a clear affinity to the consensus orientation, which we as OD consultants try to model, will see the feedback process as consistent with how they prefer to work in general, and will find the results interesting and useful." Neilsen adds that these individuals will be much easier for OD practitioners to work with than individuals who operate out of other orientations such as dependence or apathy.

An initial attempt has recently been made to use feedback to surface organizational schemata, thus moving slightly beyond discussion of action, means, and ends. Bernstein and Burke (1989) have described statistical methods that can be used as part of survey feedback to make organizational schemata and implicit causal relationships among schemata more explicit. However, their method stops with identification; it is not aimed at fostering second-order change in schemata. We now turn to ways survey feedback may help achieve this type of change.

Our model of a survey feedback process designed to facilitate second-order change is presented in Figure 8-1. It is based on (1) the problem-solving model presented in Chapter 1 (Figure 1-1) and (2) the prescriptions in the previous chapter. As we indicated earlier, Figure 1-1 posits that schematic cognitive change will come after outcomes have been assessed negatively and less costly alternative solutions (in actions, means, and ends) have been exhausted.

Figure 8-1 is based on an assumption that, at least initially, participants are unlikely to be aware of schemata out of which they are operating, but that those schemata will affect responses to the data they are fed back. In the case of the Reginal plant, as we suggested in Chapter 7, the paternalistic schema substantially influenced the interpretation of the QWL intervention. For example, it led to expectations that amenities should be provided, rather than that responsibility for improving the quality of life at

Figure 8-1 Processing Feedback Data to Facilitate Second-Order Change

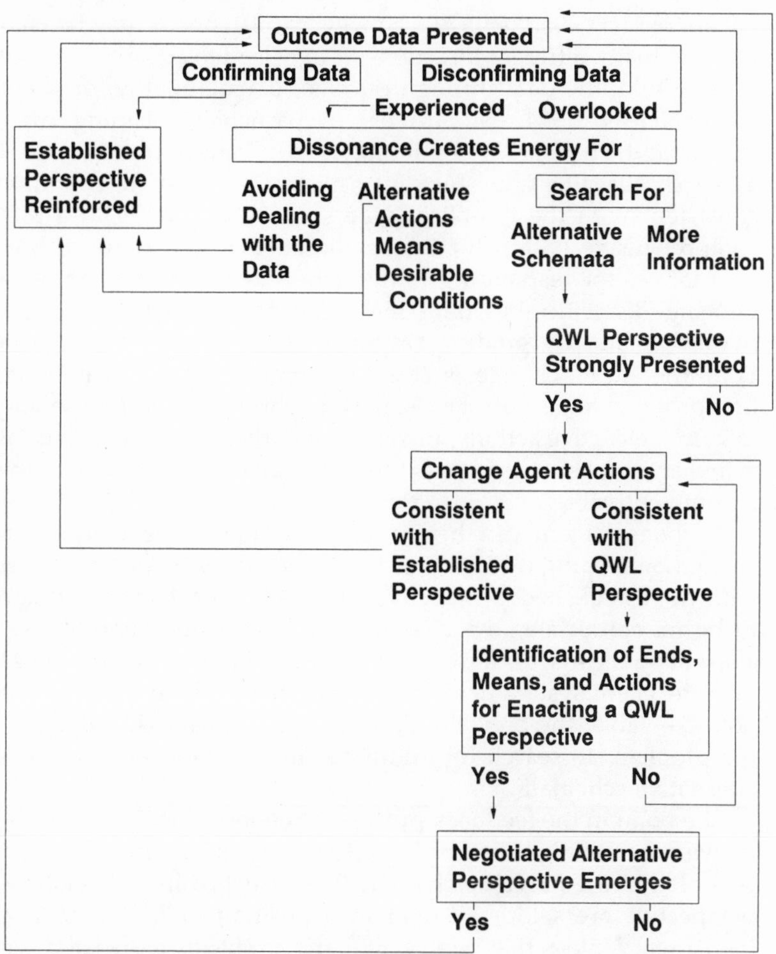

work should be shared. In addition to affecting perceptions of the data, schemata affect perceptions of, for example, what types of actions should be taken, and by whom, in response to negative information.

Consequently, when presenting feedback, the change agent should be conscious of whether the data are likely to be seen as confirming or disconfirming existing assumptions and schemata. Confirming data are likely to reinforce the established perspective.

Disconfirming data may easily be overlooked or ignored. If an incongruity between the data and established points of view is actually experienced, it might pass unnoticed or it might generate energy (cf., Nadler 1977). However, this energy may be channeled in many different directions. It may lead to actions that avoid dealing with the data through outrage, denial, apathy, or skepticism (Neilsen 1984, ch. 10) or, in particular, blaming rituals (Moch and Huff 1983). Preferably, an incongruity will lead to a search for alternative actions, means, or desired conditions consistent with the established perspective or simply to a more comprehensive search for information. Finally, if none of these alternatives for responding to the data is seen as adequate, experiencing disconfirming data may lead to a search for alternative schemata. By guiding responses to disconfirming information, therefore, change agents can initiate a process in which first-order change can be achieved (through directing energy toward alternative actions, means, and ends consistent with established schemata) or a process through which second-order change becomes possible.

A change agent can help a client system achieve first-order change by helping it identify actions, means, and ends consistent with the established perspective. If suggested actions are judged to be inappropriate, the change agent can help clients develop alternative means. If these are assessed negatively, he or she can help the client system determine alternative ends. If these are also not acceptable, the only alternatives may be to avoid dealing with the problem, to search for additional information, or to consider alternative schemata.

The point in the feedback process when introduction of an alternative schema might be appropriate represents a critical juncture. As noted in the previous chapter, those steeped in an established perspective are seldom if ever in a position to transcend it on their own. Unless this perspective and problems associated with it are surfaced, and unless an alternative is strongly presented, participants will simply continue to interpret new information in already familiar ways. They may blame individuals or conditions, or change actions, means, or ends without considering the underlying schema that generates these alternatives. Change agents can facilitate the process of grappling with schemata rather than with these more surface issues. One way they can do this is by making use of disagreements and problems that arise to surface inadequacies with the original schema. If they are to be successful, however, the model specifies that they must also present an alternative schema—in this case, the QWL perspective. Otherwise, the client system will have little alternative but to understand the data within its already existing schemata, rather than work to make new sense of the data that generated the energy for change in the first place.

Change agents must not only introduce the QWL perspective, but also act in ways consistent with it during the feedback session. If they act in terms the client system already subscribes to, they will reinforce the established perspective by their own example and thereby make change that much more difficult to accomplish in the future. At this point, in other words, change agents must become moderators of the process as well as advocates of the QWL point of view. While presenting the QWL perspective, they must exhibit openness and receptivity, *even to perspectives they seek to change*. And they must engage members of the client system in a dialogue made meaningful because it would have the potential to change the change agent's own preferred vision.

In addition to introducing the QWL perspective and acting in ways consistent with it, QWL change agents need to help the client system identify ends, means, and specific actions that enact this perspective. This will help the client system understand ways the perspective may be expressed—instantiated in concrete activities. In addition, if and when activities arising from the feedback session encounter difficulty, the identification of actions, means, and ends consistent with a QWL perspective will help clients adopt a problem-solving attitude within this perspective.

By iterating this type of feedback sequence, members of the client system should make progress toward understanding the QWL alternative and toward developing their own new synthesis from among competing perspectives. If a new synthesis does emerge, it will then become the guide for the established order.

Third-order change requires the acceptance of ongoing cognitive alterations. That is, once a *new* synthesis emerges, the change agents' role will be to strongly present a new alternative—to challenge the newly installed established order. This process of ongoing creation and recreation would continue until members of the client system gain the knowledge and ability to transcend any particular perspective, including the one operating at any given time.

COD contracted Max Summers, a former training officer at another company, to conduct the survey feedback sessions. Summers visited Reginal on August 18 and met with Charlton, Schwab, and Orlandon. Youngman was too busy dealing with production problems, and Keeley, Pepin, Sheffer, Dalton, and Roper all were feeling pressure to concentrate on production rather than on the EJEC. Matson explicitly forbade Keeley and Dalton from taking any formal role in the survey feedback process, citing problems they were having with their duties as department superintendents.

After Summers' visit, Farr called Deigh and told him that some of Reginal's management had interpreted the visit as an opening salvo for an attack on supervision. Josephson, in fact, had stormed out of a meeting with Summers because he believed the survey feedback sessions could turn into a forum for abusing supervisors and members of the maintenance department. Consequently, Farr and Deigh visited Reginal on September 15 and held several meetings with supervisors and shop stewards. Those attending voiced little opposition to the QWL program or to the planned survey feedback activities. Encouraged, Deigh returned to Washington.

The management members of JQWLAC had reported to Struthers that the QWL program in Reginal was in trouble because of ineffective consulting by COD. They had also told him that Scigliano had resisted gain sharing. Meeting with Struthers and Coy, Deigh argued that the COD consultants had been doing a good job. Moreover, Deigh made it clear that despite what Struthers' subordinates had told him, the management members of JQWLAC had resisted the EJEC's gain-sharing proposal. Hearing this, Struthers, a champion of gain sharing, became enraged and offered to visit Reginal personally to help straighten out the QWL program. Deigh counseled caution, arguing that no one can create a revolution from the top and that these issues had to be worked out locally.

Lack of Knowledge of Schemata Can Be Costly

The potential that survey feedback interventions offer as a way of stimulating cognitive change is not likely to be realized if those people implementing the intervention have little knowledge of the schemata operating at the particular site. As Figure 8-1 implies, change agents must be able to distinguish between QWL and alternative perspectives in order to manage the dialogue between them. Perhaps because of his lack of familiarity with the Reginal plant, Summers quickly exhibited behaviors consistent with the established machine bureaucracy perspective. When he visited Reginal he spent a large proportion of his time with plant management. In addition, there was no attempt to retrieve Keeley and Dalton for the feedback activities even though these two managers represented important bridges between the machine bureaucracy mentality and the QWL vision. Without their participation, managing the feedback process would be much more difficult.

Even the idea of having survey feedback sessions created energy that might have been channeled in constructive ways. Some employees in the maintenance department and in supervision were upset that the sessions would provide lower-level bake shop and packaging personnel an opportunity to debase them. To see that this concern was not particularly farfetched, we need only to review the joint EJEC-JQWLAC meeting. The energy that came from this concern, however, was diffused in ways characteristic of machine bureaucracy operations. Deigh met only with those who were voicing concern to determine whether their opposition was sufficient to preclude survey feedback activities. He did not raise the possibility of a confrontation with the FWIU workers. He simply concluded that the resistance could be contained and moved on to other matters.

Deigh also avoided confrontation over gain sharing. Management members of JQWLAC had advised the EJEC against gain sharing. Then they blamed EJEC's decision not to pursue it on Scigliano. They also blamed the lack of progress in Reginal on COD. In typical machine bureaucracy fashion, Struthers offered to solve these problems hierarchically. At this point, Deigh might have strongly advocated the QWL alternative. By visiting

Reginal, Struthers might have had the opportunity to learn about QWL firsthand. His presence might have provided a context in which he might have been able to contrast consensual with hierarchical decision making. However, Deigh again opted to diffuse the tension.

Company consultants working to redesign the cafeteria sent preliminary drawings to Matson. He rejected them without notifying the cafeteria subcommittee, arguing that they didn't reflect the wishes of the EJEC. The EJEC itself rejected proposed plans for a redesigned parking lot because they contained alterations that plant employees had not requested. Company consultants generated revised proposals.

On September 22 JQWLAC members met in Washington to review QWL activities. Farr and Coy reported that they had done everything they had promised after the July meeting. They were meeting with Reginal management, and the situation was improving. Matson and DeLeo were building an "atmosphere of cooperation" to deal with the craft problem, and EJEC members were, in Coy's terms, "happy as the dickens." The first issue of the plant newspaper was about to come out, and a seminar reviewing the line 4 project was planned for October.

Seldon thought that COD had failed miserably because it hadn't kept JQWLAC informed. Scigliano said this wasn't part of COD's job, and Deigh agreed. COD had been hired to help the EJEC, not the JQWLAC. The EJEC, moreover, was performing admirably. Deigh presented a project-by-time chart prepared by Gromanger that documented over forty projects completed or in progress. JQWLAC members decided they could keep better tabs on the program by sending a two-person team to Reginal on a month-by-month basis. The JQWLAC then reviewed the results of the plantwide survey. A summary of their meeting, sent to the EJEC on October 7, is presented as Exhibit 8-1.

Survey feedback sessions were scheduled to begin the week of September 26. COD staff explicitly counseled that the sessions should focus on interpreting employee responses. Personalities were not to enter into the presentations, and neither individuals nor groups were to be singled out for blame.

Each feedback session was to be run by one management EJEC member and one union EJEC member. There were thirty-six of these sessions, held two at a time and lasting one and a quarter hours each. Either Summers or Gromanger was in attendance for all sessions. They ran an overhead projector, which cast bar graphs reflecting employee responses onto a screen. They also acted as moderators, attempting to clarify employee questions for the session leaders and providing appropriate commentary.

EXHIBIT 8-1 Memorandum from JQWLAC to EJEC Regarding JQWLAC's September 22 Review Meeting

TO: EJEC
SUBJECT: JQWLAC Meeting, September 22, 1977
FROM: JQWLAC
DATE: October 7, 1977

At our meeting on 9/ 22, we discussed a number of items related to the project in Reginal and your activities in that regard. We would like to share with you our thoughts and would appreciate your letting us know any reactions that you might have.

1. EJEC and Project Progress

We reviewed time-line charts on the project and the many activities in which you have been engaged. We are delighted by the energy and action taken by the EJEC. We are even more committed to providing you with the resources, advice and any action that may be appropriate to assist you in your efforts and to facilitate the prompt resolution of any problem areas that you may face.

2. EJEC/JQWLAC Liaison

Hopefully, you realize how valuable the experience was for the JQWLAC to visit with you in joint session, in July. During that meeting and in subsequent communications, it has become very clear that we, the JQWLAC, must maintain closer contact with you and your activities. The COD team has been helpful in the reporting procedures that they have recommended. As effective as these types of communications may be, they will never replace the value of face-to-face discussion.

You clearly indicated your desire for continued contact with the JQWLAC and we to the EJEC. With this in mind, we would like to request permission of the EJEC to authorize a periodic visit of a joint labor-management subcommittee from the JQWLAC to Reginal and the EJEC. We would like to suggest that these visits, with your prior approval in each case, be conducted so that this JQWLAC subcommittee could visit immediately prior to our fall JQWLAC meeting. Our next meeting is scheduled for early November. We have requested that Tim Deigh coordinate details to determine the specific times for such a visit which will be to the best advantage to all concerned.

Please discuss this suggestion at your next EJEC meeting and let us know how you feel about periodic visits from a subcommittee of the JQWLAC (one from FWIU and one from FoodCom). Tim Deigh can then work out schedules if you concur.

3. Innovative Work Designs and Projects

Apparently during the joint EJEC-JQWLAC meeting our response to the potential involvement of EJEC in innovative work processes, gain sharing, etc. was interpreted that we, the JQWLAC, were against any such involvement at any time. In our meeting, 9/22, we discussed this matter in depth. It is the position of the JQWLAC that there are a number of activities/projects currently in various stages of completion by the EJEC in Reginal. We caution the EJEC against getting too many things going lest there be dozens of half-finished activities and the other labor and management employees in Reginal see the EJEC as ineffective.

As soon as the EJEC, with the advice of the COD group, Joe Gromanger, and others feel that it has made sufficient progress on existing activities to enable it to take on work design, etc., types of projects, we will be happy to review your plans and give our counsel on embarking into these kinds of activities. The JQWLAC feels strongly that it is EJEC that should determine the activities in which it should be involved. We wish only to provide guidance and the necessary resources to enable you to accomplish the goals of the project. Innovative work design, creating a more open and

> responsive work climate, investigating new ways of doing things together, in ways that meet the needs of the company, the union and the employees are clearly within the scope of the charter of the EJEC. We simply wanted to caution against "getting too many irons in the fire" at the same time. We trust that this will clarify this situation. Please advise us whenever you are unclear on this or any other matter relating to your activities. We will do anything we can to clarify them.

Eric Drew had prepared a detailed script for session leaders. At the beginning of each session, the leader was to state the purpose of the meeting as follows:

> Our objective today is to review the questionnaire that most of you filled out. We're here because every plant, every organization, every group can find ways of working together so that people get more satisfaction from their jobs and feel better about what they're doing. EJEC is a group which is designed to find out more about how everyone in the plant feels and thinks and to identify ways in which we can make this a better place to work. Specifically, today then, we're here to look at a survey. . .which is our first organized attempt to find out how people feel about the plant and about ways in which we work together.
>
> We are not here today to solve any particular problems nor to identify specifically "who's wrong." In other words, we may find as we look at the survey results that some people are dissatisfied with certain aspects of the work situation. Maybe they feel they don't get enough information to do their jobs properly; maybe they feel that they don't have enough to say about what's going on in the job, and so on. Today we don't want to try to figure out who's to blame for these problems; rather, we want to get a deeper and more complete understanding of the nature of the problem. . . . Our goal is to understand and clarify ways in which this could be a better and more fulfilling place to work, recognizing that there is already a great deal of satisfaction with what's going on.

After completing the initial statement, the session leader was to write "Why do we see things differently?" on a board or newsprint so all could see. After a brief discussion underscoring the fact that different people can respond to the same things in different ways, the session leader was to present the overhead bar graph showing employee survey responses to a question asking them to rate the extent to which they agreed or disagreed with the statement, "In general, I like working here." This bar graph is presented in Figure 8-2. The leader next was to show a series of graphs indicating positive employee perceptions (examples in Figure 8-3) and then present an additional series "where there are indications of opportunities for improvement or change" (examples in Figure 8-4). These graphs were intended to stimulate discus-

Figure 8-2 Employee Responses to the Question, "In general, I like working here."

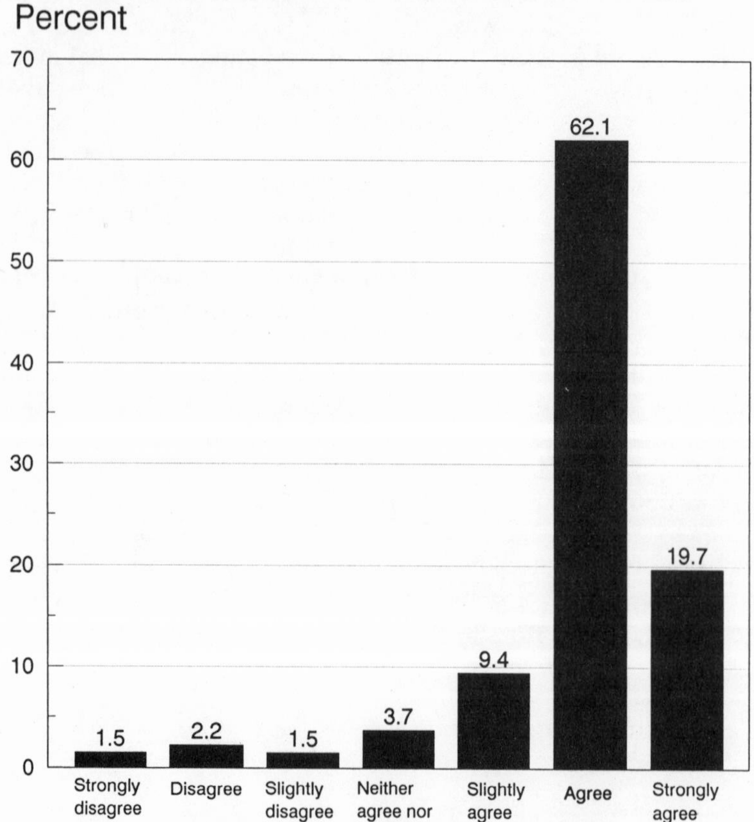

Figure 8-3 Employee Responses to Questions Eliciting Positive Employee Attitudes

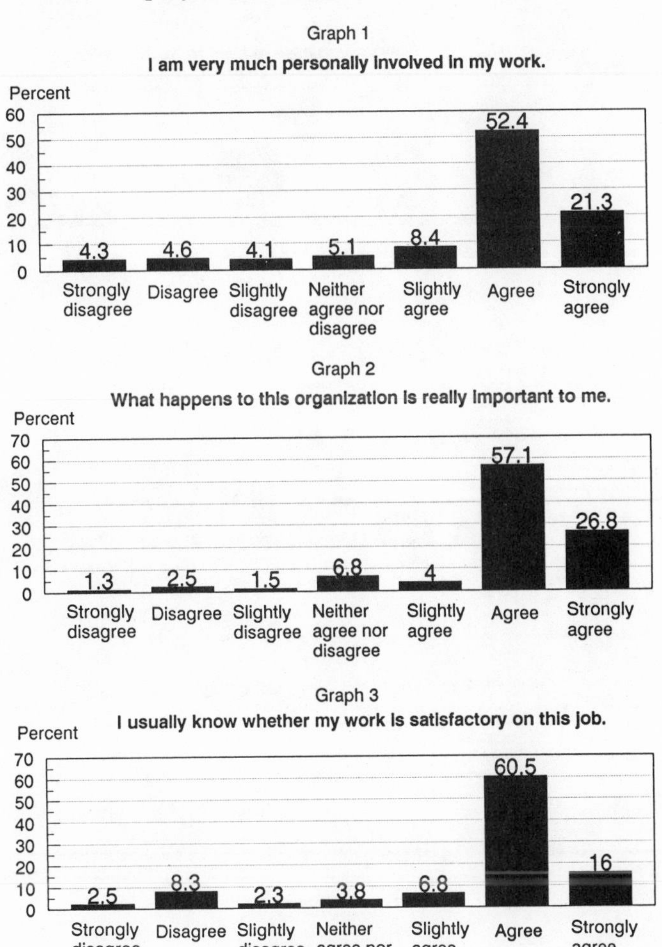

sion and requests for additional graphs (illustrated in Figure 8-5) that could be selected from a list of questions given to the participants at the beginning of each session.

In general, session leaders initially had difficulty following the prepared script. During the first few sessions, Summers and Gromanger frequently intervened to correct deviations from the script, and the sessions began to go more smooth-

Figure 8-4 Employee Responses to Questions Eliciting Negative Employee Attitudes

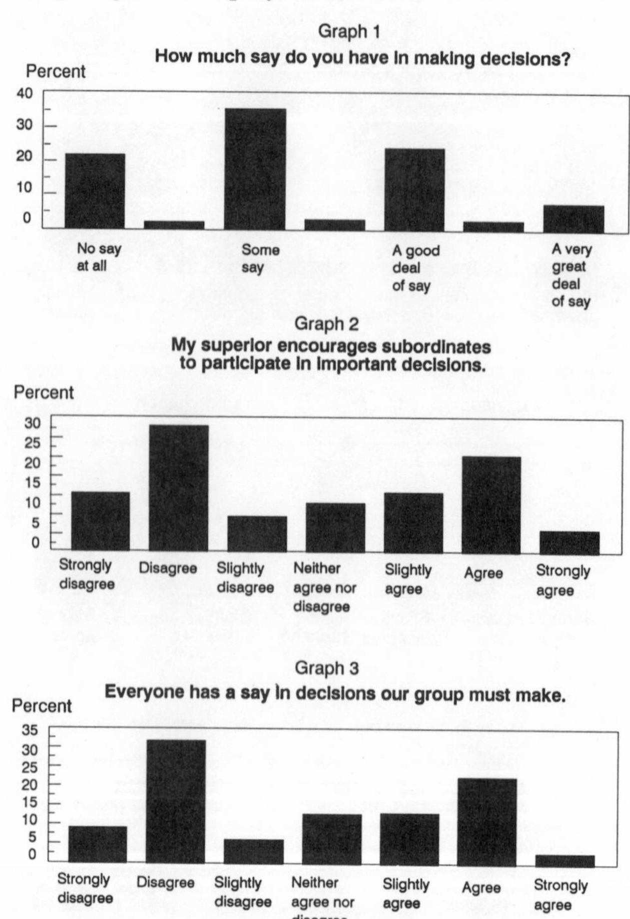

ly. Summers contributed to the smoothness of the operation by asking leaders who had succeeded in avoiding rancorous conflict without stifling participant participation to lead subsequent sessions.

Employee comments on the graphs reflected the same critical orientation the assessors had encountered in their initial interviews. Everyone seemed to have their favorite target, the most popular being supervision, the maintenance

Figure 8-4 (continued)

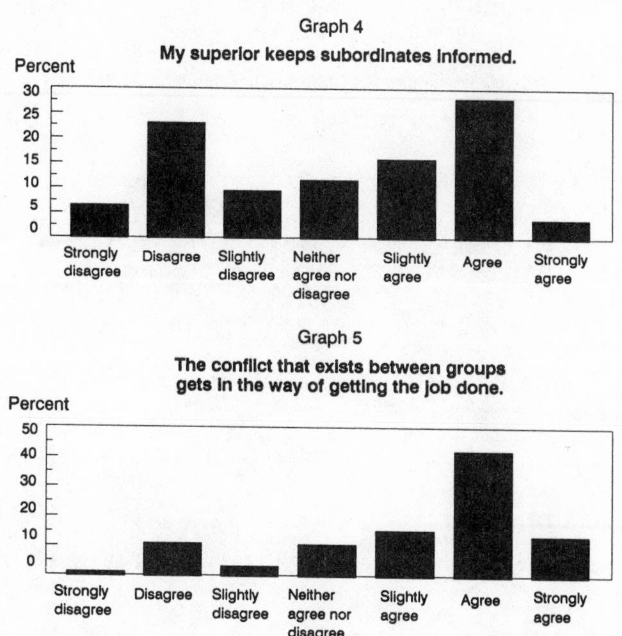

department, and local union officers. Those attending the sessions were seldom challenged to reconsider their own opinions or perspectives and often responded to data that was contrary to their views by questioning the validity of the data or the questionnaire. When discussion became heated, Summers would replace the graph being considered by placing another one on the projector and asking employees to offer their interpretations of the new overhead. Gromanger would let contentious discussions run longer but made no attempt to encourage them.

Several of the feedback design prescriptions went more or less unheeded. There were few attempts to understand how or why different people see things differently, but several attempts to blame individuals or groups for the survey results. A good deal of energy was generated when some individuals found specific data presentations to be confirming at the

Figure 8-5 Employee Responses to Questions They Could Select

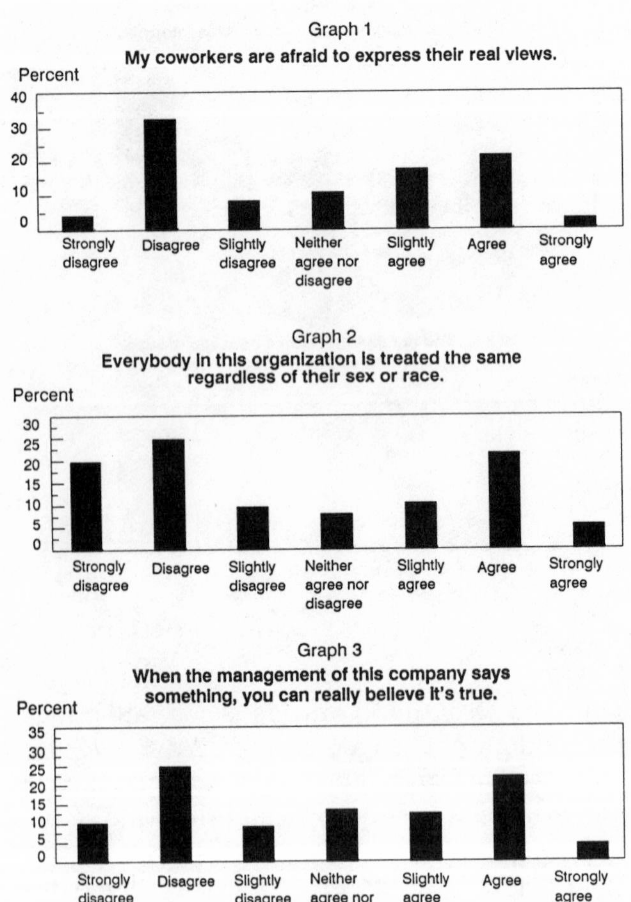

same time that others found them disconfirming of their particular set of assumptions. Many responses therefore seemed to stem from the participant's initial perspective; however, little attempt was made to encourage dialogue among these perspectives with an eye to generating an alternative that would transcend them. At no time was the QWL alternative strongly presented.

Figure 8-5 (continued)

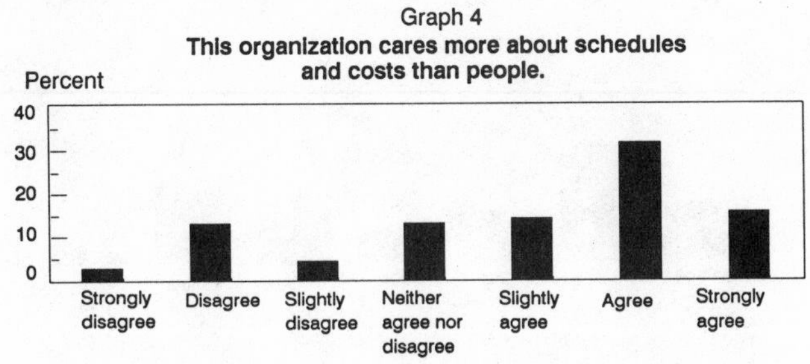

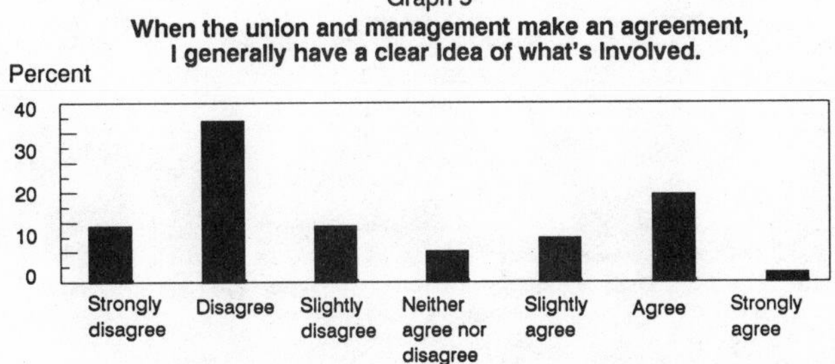

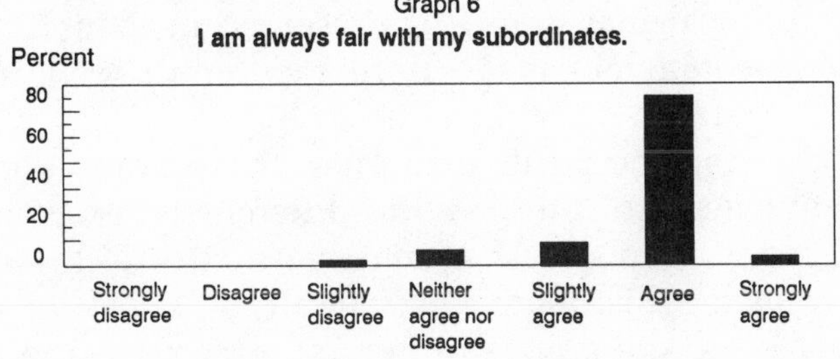

The assessors were asked not to tape record the feedback sessions. Several EJEC members felt taping might keep some employees from expressing their true feelings. Samples of responses to representative graphs therefore represent the assessors' handwritten transcriptions. The assessors frequently could not keep up with the comments being made; their notes, however, do represent a time sampling of participant responses. A sample of the types of comments made in

Figure 8-5 (continued)

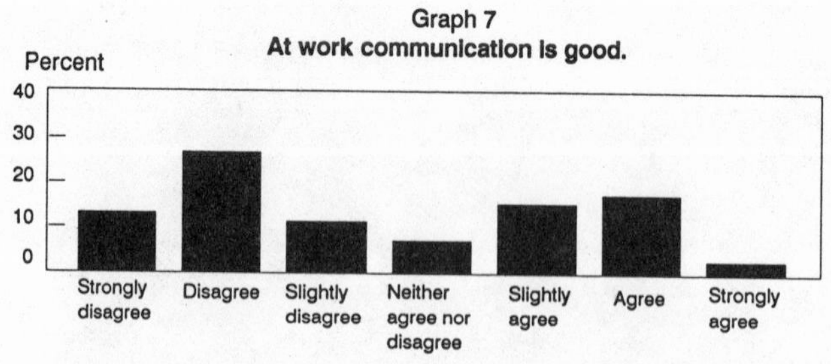

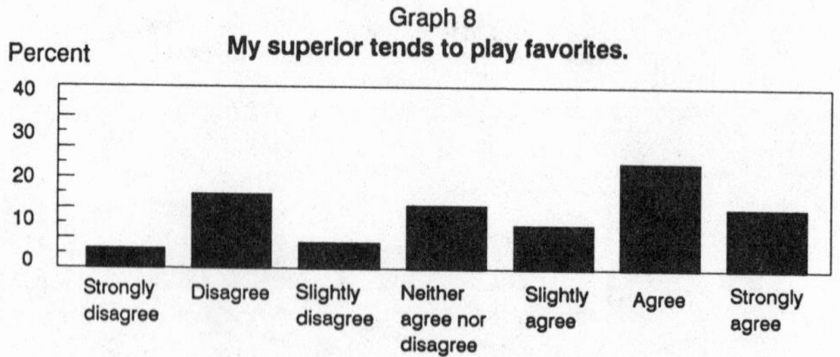

response to particular graphs is presented in Exhibit 8-2. Sequences of comments made during different feedback sessions are separated by broken lines.

After showing the positive and negative graphs, the leader asked employees to interpret the different types of responses. Then the leader asked employees to select particular graphs from the distributed list (Figure 8-5). A sampling of the responses to the graphs in this list is presented in Exhibit 8-3.

EXHIBIT 8-2 Selected Employee Comments to Positive or Negative Graphs

In general, I like working here. (Figure 8-2: 91.2 percent more or less agree.)

Respondent 1: People are not telling the truth. Not 91%!
Respondent 2: I like it. I've been here since 1945.

- -

Respondent 3: Me, I like working here because of the pay.
Respondent 4: It's air-conditioned and has uniforms.
Leader: Why are 5 percent of the people dissatisfied?
Respondent 5: There are some who would never be satisfied no matter where they were.

- -

Leader: Why are 5 percent dissatisfied?
Respondent 6: Some you can't please with anything. Their home life. Maybe they don't want to work, but they just have to.
Respondent 7: The conditions they have to work under and the cooperation they get affects that.

I usually know whether or not my work is satisfactory on this job. (Figure 8-3, Graph 3: 83.3 percent more or less agree.)

Respondent 1: Well, we've all been here a long time, and we know when we do well. But it would be nice.
Respondent 2: What about when we do something wrong? Then we hear about it!
Respondent 3: If they recognized us, that would make us work harder to satisfy them. It would also be recognizing a large group like a line.
Respondent 4: Some time back we've started not caring about the people on the line. That's got to reverse.

- -

Respondent 5: They don't take the time to tell us we're doing a good job.

How much say do you have in making decisions? (Figure 8-4, Graph 1: 22 percent say not at all.)

Respondent 1: So true!
Respondent 2: Right!
Respondent 3: They don't ask us to participate much. They just put us where they need us.
Respondent 4: It looks like most people want to be more involved.

My superior encourages subordinates to participate in important decisions. (Figure 8-4, Graph 2: 49 percent more or less disagree.)

Respondent 1: (a supervisor) There's not a whole lot of decisions to be made on the line.

Respondent 2: If we put our minds together, we can get together. Sometimes we are able to decide things.

- -

Respondent 3: Some people don't know who the superior is. I didn't know when I took the test.

Respondent 4: Break out departments. Do these separate.

- -

Respondent 5: We can argue, but they don't pay any attention.

Respondent 6: They don't care about us.

Respondent 7: It depends on your department. Our superintendent comes around and asks us what we think.

Respondent 8: (sarcastically to Respondent 7 above) How long have you been here?

Respondent 7: Three and a half years.

Respondent 8: You can't count on your supervisors. I want to be able to count on them when they tell me something. They change their minds.

- -

Respondent 9: This question doesn't take into account that this is a factory and that decisions are made weeks in advance. You have to have management to run it. But it would be good if there was a better feeling about it.

Everyone has a say in decisions our group must make. (Figure 8-4, Graph 3: 50.2 percent disagree.)

Respondent 1: I think I'm listened to, but I'm not always right.

Leader: Do you think that any of the 48 percent who disagree are from the bake shop?

Respondent 2: Ninety-nine percent of the time they'll listen to you and try to get it going right.

- -

Respondent 3: You say everyone has a say in decisions our group must make, but the only decision you have is to do your work the way they tell you.

Respondent 4: Yes, only the decision to dump (throw product out as not usable) or not to dump.

Respondent 5: If you wouldn't eat it, you shouldn't pack it!

Respondent 6: There are some decisions that people don't want to take. That's why we have supervision. I don't want the decision to dump cookies, because they'll just get down on me.

EXHIBIT 8-3 Employee Responses to Optional Graphs Selected from List Shown in Figure 8-5

My coworkers are afraid to express their real views. (Figure 8-5, Graph 1: 44.1 percent more or less agree.)

Respondent 1: Last week they fired someone, because her relative wasn't doing her job. They fired both of 'em. People were afraid to express themselves, so when it came down to it, people didn't fight this.

Respondent 2: (a supervisor) There's a lot of them that are afraid. But (looking in her direction and smiling) Martha's not! (general laughter)

Respondent 3: They know that they can tell these old girls anything. But the new girls make them afraid. The supervisors are afraid they'll meet them outside. It all comes down to black and white. It all comes down to the races. Supervisors are just afraid of some of the races.

Respondent 4: Most folks fear (for) their job.

Respondent 5: I don't understand that.

Respondent 6: They'll screw you. Don't think they wouldn't!

Leader: Why would they be afraid?

Respondent 7: (a trainee) I'm not afraid, but my supervisor often doesn't know.

Respondent 8: When I express myself, they say, "There goes Anne again, always griping!"

Respondent 9: I've had this trouble with the mechanics. I try to give 'em a hint about what's wrong with a machine and they don't always like it.

Respondent 7: We new employees aren't supposed to talk, because it's distracting. (Company policy prohibited talking to or by trainees.)

Respondent 10: After thirty days, people (trainees) don't get messed up (terminated) when others talk to 'em. So then I leave 'em alone.

Respondent 7: How do you think this makes the new person feel?

Respondent 11: (a trainee) You want to make friends when you're new. We only been here four weeks and those who know what they're doin' can't talk. Then I have to tell 'em to go away; I'm being tested.

(Trainees are on probation.) So they think I'm a snob.

Everybody in this organization is treated the same regardless of their sex or race. (Figure 8-5, Graph 2: 54.5 percent more or less disagree.)

Respondent 1: (female) The men have a better go of it. Isn't that what this means? . . . You know the men have it better!

Respondent 2: (male) It should be higher on the disagree side. People are afraid of the survey. They thought that their answers would be reported to the personnel office, and so they changed their answers. Communication is a long problem. Material things you can change, but constitutional things will take longer. You should let people know that you're not here to do miracles.

Respondent 3: (female) That's right! We have to do what men don't do.

Respondent 4: (female) I saw a man sleeping.

Respondent 5: (female) I've seen men helping women and not helping men.

Respondent 6: (male) There's a right sex and a right race.

Respondent 7: (male) That shoulda' been two separate questions.

Respondent 6: (male) I've seen what (a female employee) says. I've heard someone in supervision say the same thing; "Since she wants a man's job, let her do this. This'll really fix her!"

Respondent 8: You should have asked me some thirty years ago.

Leader: So that means there has been a big improvement?

Respondent 9: Nowadays, it doesn't matter, as long as you get along and do your job.

Respondent 8: If you act right with everybody, you'll get along fine.

Leader: When might our problem be on that one?

Respondent 10: (black male) It's very controversial.

Summers: In other organizations you know, is this high? (silence) People don't know?

Respondent 11: (black female) Race and sex are combined.

Summers: What we gonna do?
Respondent 10: Haven't been able to do nothin' for 200 years.
Respondent 11: It's a problem in this plant.
Respondent 12: (female) In packing, they try to pull the young men through. It's OK for a while, then there's a problem.

When the management of this company says something you can really believe it's true. (Figure 8-5, Graph 3: 35.2 percent more or less disagree.)

Respondent 1: From shift to shift they'll tell you different things.
Respondent 2: They never tell us nothin' whether it's true or not!
Respondent 3: Here's where it's happenin'!
Respondent 4: Don't know whether to trust supervision or not.
Respondent 5: I ask supervision, and weeks go by and nothin's done.
Respondent 3: This is one of the worst problems in the packing department. Every two weeks they change rules, depending on who you are.
Respondent 6: Can't believe that this was a true answer, those 40 percent who agreed. What they say goes for that day maybe, but after that it might have changed.
Respondent 7: (general laughter) It's a misrepresentation. The company posts things. The rest of it is people talking to people. You can trust it when it's posted. Some people talk and say it's from management.
Respondent 8: Not everyone believes in gossip.
Respondent 9: But sometimes gossip is true.
Leader: (general laughter) Do 40 percent really believe the statement's true?
Respondent 10: The question must have been at the end of the test. People were tired.
Summers: What can we do to change this?
Respondent 10: Communication. There's a breakdown in this company.
Respondent 11: (general laughter) The company's not in the habit of tellin' us their business to start with, so the question doesn't apply.
Respondent 12: It depends on the individual you're talkin' to.
Summers: So, what I hear is that management does not get the word and doesn't have the training. How

about the information that's put on the bulletin boards?

Respondent 13: If our supervisors had more information, it would help a great deal, but some of them don't even have enough information.

Summers: Let's go on.

The organization cares more about schedules and costs than people. (Figure 8-5, Graph 4: 64.4 percent more or less agree.)

Respondent 1: That was just a bad day.

Respondent 2: They don't want you to have time to break.

Respondent 3: Sometimes we're afraid to ask for a drink of water.

Respondent 4: That goes back to the fact that we don't have any choice about the kind of product we put out anymore.

Respondent 5: This is true. They don't care about people. The line goes too fast. Slow it down, and you'll get more production out.

Leader: Did people understand the question? Anything to add?

Respondent 6: If the company don't make money, I don't make money.

Summers: Wouldn't it be wonderful and progressive if you worked with a company that cared equally about costs, schedules, people, and all these things? . . . Do you think that a company could care but just not tell the people? One of the goals of NJEC (sic) is to develop an organization that cares about costs and people and all these things.

Respondent 7: That's a fact! The organization cares more about costs and schedules than people.

Respondent 8: (a supervisor) Our communication is so scattered over the country, the company is not getting across.

Summers: Wouldn't it be wonderful if people, costs, and schedules were equally important?

Leader: The organization has to make a profit.

Respondent 9: That's exactly why you get 64 percent.

When the union and management make an agreement, I generally have a clear idea of what's involved. (Figure 8-5, Graph 5: 61.1 percent more or less disagree.)

Respondent 1:	I agree with this. We think we know, but what it gets out there on the floor, it's something else. It's not clear until it hits us in the face.
Respondent 2:	They're always changing it around. I have to go to the union meetings myself if I want to know things.
Leader:	Why do 61 percent disagree?
Respondent 3:	Redoing agreements makes people unhappy.
Summers:	What about union meetings?
Respondent 3:	Bad attendance.
Respondent 1:	We hear word of mouth on the line.
Respondent 2:	You can't find a notice, and you never know when it'll change.
Summers:	How many read bulletin boards? (Many say they do.)
Respondent 4:	Things are done in conflict with the agreement, but that don't mean the agreement has been changed.
Respondent 5:	The local agreements are bad. You don't know about most things until it affects you.
Respondent 6:	When it gets to us, it's already been decided.
Respondent 7:	Yeah, it's been signed, sealed, and delivered.
Respondent 8:	The union allows different things on different shifts.
Respondent 9:	Communication. Communication all the way.
Respondent 10:	Usually, it's done under the table.
Respondent 11:	You find out things when you get your butt chewed out.
Respondent 12:	People don't read the bulletin board.
Leader:	Where's the breakdown? Is it on the bulletin board, or don't people read the bulletin board?
Respondent 13:	We don't got time to read the bulletin board. We gotta go on our breaks.
Respondent 14:	There's too much stuff on that bulletin board.
Respondent 15:	If we had a strong union, the company would listen, and then we'd have good communication. But the people don't care, so we don't have a strong union.
Respondent 16:	They don't stick to what they agree on. They're always changing it. I think they're in cahoots. (general laughter) It depends on whether the

union or company brings it up as to how it gets resolved.

Respondent 17: The membership doesn't really vote on these things.

Respondent 18: That's true!

Summers: How does the union communicate and how does management put out the work?

Respondent 19: It's usually hearsay.

Respondent 20: It's different things for different shifts.

Respondent 21: It depends on who you are.

Respondent 22: A lot of times you don't know until some problems arise.

Respondent 23: We don't communicate with our union, because our members don't care.

I am always fair with my subordinates (asked only of supervisors). (Figure 8-5, Graph 6: 91.3 percent more or less agree.)

Respondent 1: (after uproarious laughter) I couldn't talk to my supervisor. It would be out the door!

Respondent 2: (after general laughter) Bull!

Respondent 3: Oh Man! Wow!

Leader: Why do they say this?

Respondent 4: They believe they're right, but they're not.

Respondent 5: People don't admit when they're wrong.

Respondent 6: I guess there were 2 percent that were honest.

Respondent 7: When we judge ourselves, it's hard. The person who answered this probably really believes he was fair. I would too.

Leader: Does this go back to how we see things different?

Summers: Do you 'spose that if management were to take more time to explain what they're doing, things would be o.k.?

Respondent 8: They treat us as a clock and not a human being.

Respondent 9: Even management are dissatisfied with their boss.

Summers: Could you get a good answer from your children on this?

At work, communication is good. (Figure 8-5, Graph 7: 54.3 percent generally disagree.)

Respondent 1: You have to start with the top. Communication has to go both ways.

Respondent 2: You have to understand the problem with the other departments.

Leader: I was responsible for installing some equipment and was not told I was going to be doing it until I got a call to come in and load it from the trucks.

Summers: Why was there a communication breakdown?

Respondent 3: Maybe he didn't read things in the office. Maybe that's his problem.

Respondent 4: That's true of all the departments.

Leader: We have three communication channels—one for the union, one for management, and now a new one in EJEC—and all of them are lacking right now.

Summers: Its easy to blame the people at the top, but you have to solve your own [communication problems] first. I've been teaching communication courses for many years, but still with just the two of us in the house, me and my wife, we often don't communicate with each other. I don't tell her when I'm going to be out of town.

Leader: We have to move on.

Respondent 5: Communication between who? Employees and superiors?

Summers: Can someone summarize here?

Respondent 6: Lack of union-company cooperation.

Respondent 7: Or lack of supervision!

Summers: Weren't people asking to be involved more?

Respondent 8: I'd say the number one problem is communication. Between baking and packing, the company and the people, including our own supervision.

Respondent 6: There's no way shop stewards can be relieved to tell everybody.

Respondent 7: Two hundred fifty people in packing. How could they be contacted?

Summers: How can we make this right?

Respondent 6: Get some of 'em relieved.

Respondent 7: More information on the bulletin board.

Respondent 9: Why not have different questionnaires for each department and for each supervisor?

Summers:	The EJEC is trying to get a composite feeling.
Respondent 7:	Our department is run totally different. You're confined more and can't walk around and communicate.
Leader:	All departments have communication problems. Now EJEC has trouble communicating like the union and management.
Respondent 8:	The people have to take blame. I demand communication. I say, Bobby, I gotta know. Then he tells me what he needs and he gets it!
Respondent 7:	Should all 256 people go up there and demand?
Respondent 10:	Has communication got better since we started this program?
Respondent 11:	Why can't more people approach supervision?
Respondent 10:	Some people are like talkin' to a wall.

Unless the Ways Participants Understand Events Are Changed, Opening Lines of Communication Can Do More Harm Than Good

The survey feedback design had some characteristics in common with the model presented in Figure 8-1. It explicitly acknowledged that individuals see things differently. It proscribed blaming rituals, sought to avoid a discussion of personalities, and advocated "a deeper and more complete understanding of the nature of the problem." However, it was not directed toward identifying or changing schemata. In addition, there was no explicit attempt to advocate the QWL perspective. The problems identified therefore were those seen from the machine bureaucracy perspective.

The sessions, however, offered several opportunities for the initiation of a second-order change process. For example, disagreements might have been exploited to demonstrate how differences in individual attitudes can be a function of differences in perspectives. Different attitudes therefore can occur when the "facts" of the situation are identical. For example, Respondent 1, responding to the fact that 91 percent of the survey participants reported they like working in the plant (Figure 8-2), declared that participants were not telling the truth. Respondent 2 countered that he or she liked working in the plant. This clear-cut difference, however, was not exploited.

Many statements were taken as criticisms of management or supervision. These statements might have been used to help members of the client system understand the nature of a machine bureaucracy and the problems machine bureaucracies create. For example, the second respondent to Graph 3 (Figure 8-3), noting that 83 percent agreed that they generally know whether their work is satisfactory, appeared to be complaining that workers receive job feedback only when they are doing something wrong. This, however, was consistent with a machine bureaucracy concept. Machine bureaucracies attempt to minimize costs and, implicitly, to trade off humanistic values for productivity gains at work. Providing feedback for work well done, from this point of view, is counterproductive. Yet this perspective was not articulated. Those who might have been able to articulate it treated the comment as an attack on supervision rather than as a move toward greater understanding.

A similar dynamic occurred several times when the issue of lower-level participation was raised (Figure 8-4, Graph 1). Line employees generally supported the data showing they did not participate in decision making. The tone of their response implied that management and supervision should give them greater voice. Yet significant participation of line workers is not compatible with the machine bureaucracy concept. This concept assumes that efficiencies will be gained primarily by specifiying all jobs in advance and then by inducing compliance with preestablished rules and regulations (Mintzberg 1979).

On several occasions individuals—usually supervisors—articulated the machine bureaucracy perspective that would have explained many of the less popular policies and behaviors in the plant. Responding to Graph 2 (Figure 8-4), showing that 49 percent of the respondents disagreed that their superior encouraged subordinates to participate in important decisions, Respondent 1 (a supervisor) noted that there were few decisions to be made on the line. Respondent 2 disagreed with Respondent 1. Respondent 3 blamed the questionnaire for the discrepancy. Respondents 4 and 7 implied that the discrepancy was due to different supervisory styles, suggesting that the lack of participation may be blamed on individual differences among supervisors. Respondent 5 blamed management inattention for the lack of participation. Respondent

6 blamed management's lack of concern. Blaming rituals (Moch and Huff 1983) played a significant role in attempts to grapple with these data.

Respondent 9 provided the change agent with an excellent opportunity to foster understanding of how a machine bureaucracy works. This person pointed out that the plant scheduled activities well in advance and that this feature precluded much line participation. This statement reflected an appreciation for the underlying contextual problem facing the QWL program in Reginal. The control mentality that confronted the QWL perspective derived from a set of machine bureaucracy assumptions that presumed that control is required in order to enforce the production plan. The change agent therefore might have used Respondent 9's comment to help participants grasp the underlying machine bureaucracy perspective in order subsequently to contrast it with the QWL point of view. Yet the opportunity passed. Respondent 9's comments went essentially unheeded.

Looking at Graph 3 (Figure 8-4), Respondent 3 stated a central tenet of a machine bureaucracy as though it were abhorrent and disparagingly noted that "the only decision you have is to do your work the way they tell you." Many industrial engineers, however, would consider this an ideal state of affairs.

In order to facilitate a dialogue between such a machine bureacracy perspective and the QWL alternative, the change agent might have attempted to present the management theory and historical tradition underlying the machine bureaucracy concept. At the very least, this might have provided an alternative explanation for behaviors that were being attributed primarily to personality flaws. It may have preempted the blaming rituals and moved the dialogue ahead. For example, at this point the change agent might have asked whether meaningful participation can be reconciled with the machine bureaucracy notion. If not, the QWL alternative might have been strongly presented as an alternative model, one that might address problems of participation as well as effectiveness and efficiency.

The survey feedback intervention generally was exploited to reinforce intergroup hostility rather than to foster mutual understanding or to generate the greater degree of trust and openness characteristic of a high QWL environment. There were honest expressions of anxiety concerning racial and gender-related issues (for example, Respondent 3, Figure 8-5, Graph 1). When Graph 2 from Figure 8-5 was presented, Respondent 2 provided a superb opportunity for the change agent to introduce the possibility of a realistic long-term QWL activity designed to increase mutual appreciation among those of different sexes. This person distinguished between "material things," like the amenities the QWL program had been pursuing, and "constitutional things," such as increasing intergroup understanding and cooperation. Unfortunately, Respondents 3 and 4 interpreted these comments as supporting the idea that little can be done about the tensions between people of different sexes.

The change agent did nothing to retrieve the opportunity, even when Respondent 5 provided evidence that males have helped females in situations in which they would not have helped another male. In the absence of a strongly presented alternative perspective, participants had little alternative but to resign themselves to what they unanimously agreed was a bad situation. Respondent 10 implied that they should not believe they could make significant progress in Reginal if no one had "been able to do nothin' for 200 years."

The plant manager later expressed considerable dismay that over 35 percent of the survey participants thought that they could not really believe what management said (Figure 8-5, Graph 3). Laughter during the feedback sessions and skepticism concerning the 40 percent who said they believed management made matters worse. Yet there was little attempt to diagnose the reasons for these differing perceptions. Respondent 7 suggested that formal posted statements were trustworthy, whereas hearsay was not. Respondent 13 offered a more systematic interpretation. The problem was that supervisors themselves were not sufficiently informed. However, neither of these opportunities to explore the issue of trust and communication and to develop a programmatic alternative were pursued, and the dominant impression was simply one of blame and derision. On at least one occasion, Summers abruptly terminated the discussion by moving to another graph.

Other issues met with a similar fate. For instance, 64 percent of the survey participants agreed that the organization cared more about schedules and costs than people (Figure 8-5, Graph 4). From a machine bureaucracy perspective, this is as it ought to be. One might go so far as to say that, from this point of view, the relationship between the organization and its employees should be exclusively mutually instrumental. The employee is exchanging his or her labor for extrinsic rewards. Personal satisfaction and mutual caring are outside of the equation.

This perspective, however, was given little credence in the

feedback sessions by either the participants or the change agent. Management and supervision were therefore judged as lacking by criteria that were incompatible with their institutionalized position. The feedback sessions did not help them realize this, however, and they departed feeling they had been attacked personally. The change agent was given some openings. For example, Respondent 6's statement that "If the company don't make money, I don't make money" seems a peculiar comment during a discussion about organizational "caring." He seemed to be expressing the assumption that an instrumental relationship is necessary if the company is to remain competitive and profitable.

Summers countered by coming as close as he ever did to explicitly stating the QWL alternative. He idealized a company that could care about both extrinsic and intrinsic factors—about both people and costs. However, he did nothing to initiate investigation of whether this was possible. No activities, means, or ends were identified that would enact the QWL alternative and move the client system further along toward significant cognitive change. Summers eventually chose to avoid this issue, a response consistent with the established pattern of resolving conflicts. By doing so, he reinforced this pattern (cf., Figure 8-1).

With some exceptions, management and union leaders were explicitly or implicitly blamed for poor communication (Figure 8-5, Graph 5). Some charged them with being aligned against workers on the line. Comments expressing a willingness to assume responsibility for these problems (e.g., Respondent 23) generally went unheeded, and Summers's interventions seemed directed more toward identifying new solutions within the established perspective than toward presenting an alternative.

Supervisors' responses to the item "I am always fair with my subordinates" (Figure 8-5, Graph 6) tended to evoke a caricature of a blaming ritual. The laughter underscored what seemed to be an almost universally held assumption that supervision was somehow unable to acknowledge or even see their own shortcomings. Respondent 7 provided Summers with an opportunity to explore the possibility that one's perspective is likely to be a function of one's position. However, he chose to pursue activities consistent with established patterns of behavior rather than to emphasize differences among alternative cognitive schemes. The inference seemed to be that if supervisors took more time to explain what they were doing, they would be perceived as more fair. The deeper problem—suggesting that supervisory behaviors were grounded in a perspective that employees did not fully understand and did not value—was not addressed.

Summers came close to asserting the QWL theme of shared responsibility during a discussion of Graph 7 from Figure 8-5. Here over half of the survey participants disagreed with the statement: "At work, communication is good." He contrasted blaming rituals with responsible attempts by employees to solve problems themselves. His subsequent remarks, however, were only descriptive. He did not take the next step and describe actions, means, or ends for resolving communication problems in ways consistent with the QWL alternative, and any potential for greater understanding was lost.

Because Matson kept Keeley and Dalton from participating, Johnny Pepin was the highest-ranking management member to lead feedback sessions. By the day his first session was scheduled, many supervisors had begun to believe that the feedback activities were a calculated attack on them. Line employees, unwilling to take responsibility for problems in the plant, were blaming supervision and plant management. Pepin was aware of this when he started his session saying, "we're not here to solve problems or to blame anyone, but to find out why people feel differently." His session is presented in Exhibit 8-4.

EXHIBIT 8-4 Survey Feedback Session Led by Johnny Pepin

Jack Resler (present to help Pepin with the overhead) presents Figure 8-2, which shows that most people like working in the Reginal plant.

Pepin: Why 5 percent (disagree)? (silence). People have to make a living. Some people don't like to work at all.

Resler presents the positive graphs, such as those in Figure 8-3, and the negative ones, such as those in Figure 8-4. At the conclusion of this presentation, Figure 8-4, Graph 4 is left on the screen. It shows that 39.6 percent of the respondents more or less disagree that superiors keep subordinates informed.

Pepin: Who is the superior? (silence) What do we need to do?

Respondent 1: You hear only a month later from five different guys after a problem arises.

Pepin: (insistently) What do you mean? Tell me, what do you mean?!

Respondent 1: There were too many questions. . . . The same thing over and over again. It was a waste of time.

Respondent 2: People didn't stop to think about the question. This is why they disagree.

Respondent 3: Those 49 percent [not agreeing] are like peons.

Respondent 1: What is considered an important decision?

Pepin: How do we encourage people to be open and help people to make decisions? This company has to make a profit to help our jobs!

Respondent 1: There should have been another word in there. Add "about gettin' things done." I have told my people this and that will be done and come in the next day and it's not done. The guys in maintenance may have other things happen, but it doesn't get done.

Pepin: Would it help if they came and told you they couldn't get to it?

Respondent 1: Yes.

Respondent 4: I turned something in last Friday and it's still not done.

Respondent 1: The little people from the top to bottom deserve a hand for keeping this going. If there's not a bobby pin or a piece of cardboard or something, there'd be more down time than you can count.

Pepin: Would you like to hear about what's the other groups's (supervision's) problems?! That's communication! What should we do?! Teamwork!

Someone requests Figure 8-5, Graph 8, which shows that 53.4 percent more or less agree that their superior tends to play favorites. Resler presents the graph.

Respondent 5: When someone gets a day off, some people get to go first.

Respondent 6: How your superior treats you makes a big difference.

Pepin: Have you ever thought that this problem could be due to you! There are differences between people.

Respondent 3: Personality makes a difference.

Pepin: Why does everybody like Ben Ashley [another packing department supervisor] and not me? (general laughter) Why do you like Ben and not me? Someday we ought to change this, so you'll have a better feeling about me. Why does Ben have such a nice personality? (looking at Respondent 6) How do you feel? What's your name?

Respondent 6: Maureen.

Pepin: I know her name's Maureen.

Respondent 1: Why aren't the FoodCom rules carried on all three shifts?

Pepin: Why do you feel this happens?

Respondent 7: Rules are enforced on first shift and not on second shift. People on second and third don't always pick up their cookies. First shift follows the rules. Supervision doesn't enforce the rules on second.

Respondent 1: A rule's a rule. If people can't follow 'em, they should go to their superior.

Resler puts up Figure 8-4, Graph 5, which shows that 83.6 percent of the respondents more or less agreed that conflict among groups often gets in the way of getting the job done.

Pepin: What were the groups?

Respondent 8: (from packing) Bake shop and maintenance. If the crackers don't break [at the perforation], you can't pack 'em.

Pepin: If humidity [which affects the "breakability" of crackers] is wrong, bakers have limits too. If communication would be better, this'd be seen.

A participant requests Figure 8-5, Graph 7, which shows that 54.3 percent of the respondents more or less disagree that communication at work is good. Resler puts up this graph.

Pepin: What is communication?

Respondent 3: Knowin' what's going on. You in particular tellin' us peons what's happenin' (followed by general expressions of agreement).

Pepin: That's one of my faults. We on the EJEC hear constantly: What the hell you doin' up there [in EJEC meetings]. We say, how can we tell people what's going on so they'll know, so they'll tell us their thoughts, and we'll make this a better place to work. The only way the EJEC will succeed is for you people to tell us what the problems are, so we can deal with them.

Respondent 8: The bulletin board is too high. We don't have enough time anyway.

Pepin: What can we do?

Respondent 8: Run us off a copy to take home.

Respondent 1: Dennis [packing department superintendent] walks past and sees twelve trucks back up and says "do the best you can." Yet I need somethin' fixed, and that's maintenance, and they don't tell me what they're doin' with maintenance.

Pepin: Everybody can be doing their best, but we don't know it, so we blame someone.

Presentations Seen as Stemming from Particular Perspectives Are Likely to Be Misunderstood

Johnny Pepin was one of the most active members of the EJEC. Although he was also a supervisor, he had confronted Billy Youngman over whether the EJEC should become involved in training for the conversion of line 4 and had led the line 4 training sessions. When Pepin was leading feedback sessions, he was more than willing to confront the issues as he saw them. Like many other supervisors and union stewards, he believed that the QWL program might lead to greater employee satisfaction and, thereby, to greater productivity (Figure 4-5). However, QWL program activities were also having a direct negative effect on productivity by taking his and others' attention away from day-to-day production problems. As plant management became increasingly concerned about this problem, it put greater pressure on supervisors to focus more on their regular duties and, by implication, less on the QWL program. The survey feedback sessions exacerbated this problem. In addition to finding themselves under greater pressure, supervisors, it seemed, were being personally abused by line workers who took the opportunity during the feedback sessions to blame them for the legion of problems in the plant.

Feeling this tension, Pepin tried to get participants in his feedback session to see things from their supervisor's point of view (Exhibit 8-4). At several points, he attempted to get line employees to see and understand how he and other supervisors felt, insisting that communication includes lower-level people listening to those higher up.

He was openly critical of blaming rituals and stressed that lower-level employees needed to provide constructive inputs into the QWL dialogue. They also needed to listen. If they knew, for example, that humidity can affect the "breakability" of the crackers, they might be less inclined to blame the bakers when "unbreakable" product came down the line. He asked whether line workers themselves might not be responsible for their supervisor's "favoritism," implying that preferential treatment was given to superior employees. He claimed that the company needed more employee initiative and input in order to make a profit. His tone and demeanor indicated that he thought this initiative and input were not being given.

FWIU members in Pepin's session did not view the situtation the same way Pepin did. They believed that the QWL program had been designed to increase their quality of work life and that increases in productivity would be a more or less automatic consequence of higher morale (Figures 4-3 and 4-4). Pepin, moreover, was a member of the "opposition," and his demeanor was therefore intimidating as well as insistent. The first thing he said was that, in his opinion, some employees do not like to work at all. He *demanded* that Respondent 1, who had just blamed supervision for communication problems, explain himself. Respondent 1, changing the thrust of his argument, then blamed the questionnaire and the maintenance department. Respondent 3 implied that those who feel they are not informed are those who, because of their position, should not be informed.

Pepin was closely identified with the supervisory perspective. Even when he attempted to get others to see events from a different point of view than his, however, they responded to him in terms with which they were familiar. Some were ingratiating; others turned silent, keeping their opinions to themselves. However much he tried, he had difficulty breaking out of his own perspective; when he could operate beyond his limited viewpoint, others would interpret his efforts as though he were still operating in a parochial manner. Our notes do not indicate whether Summers and Gromanger were present during the feedback sessions Pepin led. If they were, they said nothing. Yet it seems that only an outside change agent—someone not identified with any of the contending perspectives—would have been able to help participants identify the dilemma they were in.

The EJEC executive committee met after Pepin had completed the feedback session reported in Exhibit 8-4. Meeting with them was Tom Gib, who had recently been hired by FoodCom as a corporate director of training and human development. He was visiting Reginal, he said, to help plan for the time when the outside facilitators would leave and to help diffuse the QWL program to other FoodCom plants. The assistance of someone from the corporate level had been requested by the COD consultants at the EJEC-JQWLAC meeting (Chapter 6).

The executive committee members started by reviewing the survey feedback sessions. After a few comments about employees' concerns with a decline in product quality and the lack of recognition for good work, Pepin said, "Everyone comes down on supervisors, but they don't know what problems supervision faces!" Susan Sheffer, a supervisor herself, counseled that supervisors should talk more, but Pepin disagreed. Looking at Sheffer, he said, "You always say communication! The givers of information feel they give out enough. The receivers want more. The supervisors don't always have the time or the knowledge!" Sholl asked how this problem might get resolved. Sheffer suggested "meetings between supervision and line employees at least once per week."

The meeting continued in this vein for some time. Clayton believed that union members had been willing to discuss some of their own shortcomings. Pepin, however, argued that they had not expressed much willingness to contribute to plant productivity and efficiency. The prevailing attitude among the workers was, "If I don't get something out of it, forget it!"

McCarthy and Sheffer said employees felt they had benefited from the survey feedback sessions. Pepin said that one-third to one-half of the people he had talked with after the sessions said they "were shit!" McCarthy said Pepin must have been talking primarily with supervisors. Clayton argued that a faithful few should work to get the ball rolling. Then others would "want to get on the bandwagon." Pepin was more critical. "When the people get on the bandwagon, what about supervision and the management of this company? Aren't *they* gonna get somethin' out of this?"

McCarthy turned to Gib and asked him if he could help the EJEC address some of the problems they were discussing. Gib responded that he would be glad to help, that he had "a whole bag of tricks." His only requirement was that he be accepted voluntarily by the EJEC and not expected to speak for management. Pepin told him the EJEC needed all the help it could get, but that the executive committee could not speak for the entire EJEC on this matter. The meeting then adjourned so that Pepin could run another survey feedback meeting.

After his second feedback session Pepin expressed considerable frustration. He still felt employees weren't willing to do their part in helping make the plant a better place to work. He was feeling pressure from management. A few days earlier, when a line had broken down, Matson had accused him of being more interested in the EJEC than in production.

Matson felt the feedback sessions had documented that employees wanted to be supervised, but supervised fairly. For example, he felt that some employees took too long on break just to test management's resolve. When they got away with this sort of behavior, other employees felt they were not getting the same breaks. Therefore, the survey feedback sessions had shown how management must enforce the rules. In addition, employees had said they were very satisfied with their jobs. Matson concluded from that statement that employees should be willing to put in a full day's work.

Youngman was the most vocal manager in his response to the feedback sessions and to the QWL program. After months of refusing to talk with the assessment coordinator, he agreed to a one-on-one interview. He had worked his way up in two other plants, he said, and had learned that you have to "mix with people." To gain influence, you have to take initiative and be willing to assume responsibility. Employees in Reginal, however, were asking for more say in decisions without being willing to do anything about it. The plant was "falling apart," because employees were unwilling to asssume the responsibility that comes with greater say in decision making.

Youngman argued that the QWL program had made a difficult situation worse. FWIU workers "hate supervision and they hate maintenance, because they make a few cents more." By responding to employee complaints about supervision and maintenance, the EJEC had converted employees' "problems" into management "projects." EJEC's perception of employees' problems, moreover, was of doubtful accuracy. "In the feedback session and on the questionnaire, you ask people whether supervision are liars," Youngman stated. "After the questionnaire, I sat down with a bunch of Mexicans. They didn't have any idea of what the questionnaire was about!" Youngman also complained about the outside facilitators who come "flying in here" and have "fancy dinners" when what was really needed was money to purchase better operating equipment.

During the feedback sessions, the management of the union local seemed to fare better than plant management; however, there were several implied criticisms of the union. For example, employee complaints about unfair job or shift assignments reflected badly on stewards responsible for policing the contract. Consequently, George Newman suggested that the stewards and plant supervisors meet off-site to address some of the problems raised during the feedback sessions. The EJEC subsequently invited FWIU, IMU, and IEU stewards to meet with plant supervisors on Saturday morning, October 22. By October 14, only four supervisors had agreed to attend. During a JQWLAC inspection visit, Gromanger mentioned the problem to William Coy. Coy spoke with Matson, who in turn spoke with supervisors. Shortly afterwards, the sign-up rate improved sufficiently for Newman to reserve meeting space in a nearby motel.

Established Patterns Reassert Themselves

Problems associated with the fact that local plant management, supervisors, stewards, and FWIU employees on the line subscribed to different interpretations of the QWL program (cf., Figure 4-1, models 1-6) continued to plague its implementation. Coy had to intervene for the Saturday meeting to occur, just as Deigh had previously had to intervene to overcome resistance to the plantwide survey and Pond had had to overcome plant-level resistance to the survey feedback sessions. For his part, Matson remained pinioned between his own managers and supervisors on the one hand and top management support for the QWL program on the other. By meeting with supervisors and union stewards, perhaps this impasse could be overcome.

By allowing the more diagnostic phase of the survey feedback intervention to be separated from a more prescriptive action-oriented phase, however, the change agents became vulnerable to having QWL activities be biased in favor of the supervisory, steward, or managerial perspectives—even as the feedback sessions were biased in favor of the FWIU employees' point of view. What might be prescribed, therefore, might not have a great deal to do with the complaints voiced by line employees. More critically, the decoupling might continue to preclude a dialogue between the divergent perspectives.

COD asked Summers to conduct the Saturday meeting. Newman was scheduled to make some introductory remarks. Sholl, Gromanger, and members of the EJEC executive committee arrived early and found that Newman had arranged the seating so that union and mangement personnel would face each other in typical bargaining style. Newman said he was planning to open the meeting with a direct attack on Matson for continuing to obstruct the progress of the QWL program. Sholl thought that perhaps this should be done, but the others disagreed. Gromanger thought the FWIU stewards would take their cue from Newman's attack and assume an aggressive posture. Moreover, he feared

Matson would react defensively and this would only make matters worse. McCarthy appealed to Newman to tone down his remarks.

Perhaps as a consequence, Newman's opening remarks were conciliatory. He described the purpose of the meeting only in terms of facilitating steward-supervisor communication. Matson was equally magnanimous. "It's a pleasure for me to be here, to see this fine group here to confer on areas of concern in the plant," he said. "We hope you'll give it your utmost this morning. I'm sure with this fine group today, you'll help solve areas of concern."

Bobby Clayton then summarized the survey results, noting that although people liked working for FoodCom, they wanted better communication, more involvement in what's going on, and better training. "It's not bad to have problems, but to have them and not do anything is bad," he said. Clayton then introduced Tom Gib, who recommended that participants think about what the plant would be like if the problems they were addressing were solved. He counseled union and management personnel to brainstorm solutions without regard to whether they were good or bad. Evaluating solutions would come later. The first problem was to get the suggestions out.

Participants then met in four small groups. To prevent them from being too responsive to top plant or union management, Matson, Youngman, Charlton, Schwab, Newman, and McCue constituted a distinct group, which Marie McCarthy was asked to lead. Supervisors and stewards were arbitrarily assigned to each of the other three groups, which were led by Bobby Clayton, Susan Sheffer, and Vince Keeley. Each group generated lists specifying what would be required to improve communication, training, and employee involvement in the plant. They then identified methods for making the improvements they recommended. The groups' suggestions, as submitted by their respective secretaries, are reported in Exhibits 8-5 to 8-8.

After the small group meetings, all participants got back together to review the results. Bobby Clayton promised to provide copies of the group lists to all participants. Keeley asked how people felt about the meeting. The response was generally favorable; however, some participants were skeptical that anything would come of the effort.

EXHIBIT 8-5 Summary of October 22 Discussions between Stewards and Supervisors:

Group Led by Marie McCarthy
(including Matson, Youngman, Charlton, Schwab, Newman, and McCue)

I. Communication: Methods
   A. Increase attendance at union meetings
      1. Refund money/ expenses
      2. Invite special guests
   B. Post summaries of meeting
      1. Write up reports to be handed out, mailed or placed on bulletin board
   C. Give out information on union-management meetings, agreements
   D. Company give out written answers to problems
   E. Grievance meetings
      1. Allow attendance by person involved
      2. Give consideration to personal problems, family situation
   F. Notice of union meetings passed out with paychecks, placed in plant magazine
   G. Notify supervision of agreements made in union-management meetings
   H. Keep a file of current information on union-management "understandings" in departments
   I. Give written notice on all grievance decisions to employee involved
      1. Immediately after union-management meeting
      2. When grievance is made
   J. Notice of current changes in agreement
      1. Have separate bulletin board
      2. These go into department file
      3. Notice placed in next company magazine
   K. One line production management

II. Training: Methods
   A. Training in all areas should be broadened
   B. Employees are afraid to take higher paying jobs
      1. Shift preference keeps people on jobs where they have seniority
   C. Use training films
      1. Management has fourteen training film libraries
      2. New films for packing department employees
      3. Film presentation expanded
         a. Operations of equipment
         b. Involvement of people
   D. Improve training of trainers
      1. Supervision class every two weeks
      2. Seminars for training
   E. Get more people involved in training

III. Involvement: Methods
   A. Improve information about the business
   B. Give people the opportunity to do new things
   C. Determine areas of concern and let people know when they can contribute
   D. Listen to employee suggestions and complaints and take some action
   E. Films of union activities for greater interest
   F. Orientation tours on total organization for employees
      1. Company supply information on union and union membership
   G. Comment: only a few people want to be involved in work changes
   H. Use colorful notices for new information
   I. Use flashing warning light to emphasize notices
   J. Question: involvement in what?
      1. Product quality
      2. Shift changes
      3. Complete say/ no say
      4. Where should we be?

EXHIBIT 8-6 Summary of October 22 Discussions between Stewards and Supervisors:

Group Led by Susan Sheffer

I. Communication
   A. Requirements of good communication
      1. Establish formal channels; identify areas where channels are needed
      2. Trained people who can listen to avoid defensiveness and other blockades to good communication
      3. Two-way communication needed in order to clarify messages, orders
      4. Need time to communicate properly and allow for clarification
   B. Methods
      1. Plantwide intercom
      2. Magazine
      3. Departmental blackboards for notification of changes

II. Training
   A. Requirements
      1. Inform employees of proper work procedures
      2. Establish systematic procedure for training
      3. Need employees and trainers with ability to understand training and to teach procedures
   B. Methods
      1. New employee indoctrination for general company policies
      2. Need personnel who can properly train employees
      3. On-the-job training

III. Involvement
   A. Requirements
      1. Need communication between all levels before involvement can occur
      2. People must be interested in issues
      3. Trust needed before meaningful communication occurs
      4. Need to encourage opinions of people
      5. Must give proper consideration to opinions so people feel they are meaningfully participating

EXHIBIT 8-7 Summary of October 22 Discussions between Stewards and Supervisors:

Group Led by Bobby Clayton

I. Communication
   A. Requirements
      1. Need better communication between top management and union officials
      2. Need continued follow-up to ensure messages understood, carried out properly
      3. Need communication to flow up and down in hierarchy and horizontally to all departments
   B. Methods
      1. Utilize present channels and systems
      2. Allow time for group meetings in departments to discuss problems, clarify assignments
      3. Need to encourage employees, recognize superior performance

II. Training
   A. Objectives
      1. Establish an organized program
      2. Improve product quality
      3. Improve technical expertise
      4. Improve safety
      5. Increase pride in job
   B. Methods
      1. Implement systematic training program
      2. Job rotation on experimental basis so replacing absent employees easier
      3. Allow time for proper training
      4. Establish qualification tests for job classifications

III. Involvement
   A. Objectives
      1. Improve employee attitudes
      2. Increase understanding of operations, others' problems
      3. Increase understanding of importance of job to company

4. Improve trust
5. Resolve departmental conflicts

B. Methods
1. Communicate with employees
2. Teach that each job affects another job

EXHIBIT 8-8 Summary of October 22 Discussions between Stewards and Supervisors:

Group Led by Vince Keeley

I. Communication

A. Objectives
1. Keep people better informed (especially why changes occur)
2. More communication allows for faster action
3. Better understanding in general
4. "Peace of mind" results from reduced uncertainty
5. Results: better attitude, efficiency, production
6. Improve records with written communication

B. Methods
1. More, better written communications
   a. Written safety rules
   b. Written agreements and procedures
   c. Upgrade record keeping forms
   d. Publish plant newsletter
   e. Update bulletin boards
   f. Start departmental libraries
   g. Consistency in policies; document policies
   h. Publish new employee booklet
   i. Electronic bulletin board in cafeteria
2. Verbal communications
   a. Arrange meetings with involved people
   b. Set up an information center
   c. Better inter- and intra-departmental phone system, pagers
   d. Train a communications coordinator to inform all concerned people of problems, decisions
   e. Plantwide P.A. system

II. Training
  A. Objectives
    1. Employees better informed of work procedures
    2. Reduce accidents
    3. Better qualified operators
    4. More flexibility when replacements needed
    5. Better efficiency, attitude
  B. Methods
    1. Make up training films
    2. Allow for one-on-one OJT for new and old employees
    3. Assign a coordinator to establish a systematic training procedure
    4. Checklists for job assignments
    5. Make explicit limits of responsibility
    6. Conduct job analysis interviews to determine all tasks associated with jobs
    7. Give labor allowance for training to departments
    8. Construct tests for qualification determination
    9. Allow for a reasonable qualification period on each job (if employee moved to another position)
    10. Utilize qualified people to train
III. Involvement
  A. Objectives
    1. More interest in work
    2. Contentment
    3. Reduce absenteeism
    4. Productivity, safety
  B. Methods
    1. Personal contact between superior and subordinate
    2. Equal treatment of all employees
    3. Encourage personal opinions
    4. Develop pride in work

The EJEC met the week after the supervisors-stewards meeting. They had sent out a survey asking employees for their opinions concerning job rotation. Of 209 responses, 49 percent favored job rotation and 49 percent were opposed. It seemed that younger employees with low seniority were in favor, while those with high seniority who held the most desirable jobs were opposed (Figure 4-1, models 3 and 4). Dalton reported that, in the interest of better communications, he had taken seven packing workers through the baking and assembly areas. The committee also scheduled a softball game. Most of the meeting concerned how the EJEC should respond to the supervisors-stewards meeting the previous Saturday.

The EJEC decided to create two new subcommittees, one for communications and one for training. A third topic addressed on Saturday, employee involvement, was tabled until it became clear there was a need for a subcommittee to deal with this issue. Each subcommittee was to have four EJEC members and four members selected from non-EJEC members who attended the Saturday meeting. Non-EJEC members were to be paid from QWL project funds. To minimize expenses, committee meetings would be held in place of regular EJEC meetings.

In a formal planning report dated October 28, 1977, the EJEC stated the purpose of the communications subcomittee:

> To improve the deficiencies in communications identified in the survey feedback sessions and supervisor-steward meetings and to achieve the following:
>
> 1. Better informed employees about the operations of the bakery
> 2. Reduce resistance to changes and improved efficiency
> 3. Quicker and clearer lines of communication
> 4. Improve overall understanding of interrelated functions of bakery personnel.

The purpose of the training subcommittee was:

> To improve the deficiences in training identified in the survey feedback sessions and supervisor-shop steward meetings and to achieve the following:
>
> 1. Better trained employees; better oriented and trained new employees
> 2. Improved job performance

3. Improved safety practices
4. More flexibility when replacements are required
5. Improved efficiency
6. Improved morale and attitude of workforce

Methods Used for Generating Solutions May Reinforce the Established Perspective

Choices that can have a significant impact on policies can be made with little forethought (Cohen, March, and Olsen 1972; March and Olsen 1976). The decision to involve supervisors and stewards in the prescription phase of the survey feedback intervention was made with the best of intentions. They had felt attacked during the feedback sessions, and their involvement and support were critical for effective implementation. However, the prescriptions that came out of their deliberations were highly selective from among the issues raised during the survey feedback.

The decision to focus on three topics—communication, training, and involvement—restricted the scope of deliberations. The decision not to establish a committee for the involvement issues restricted the QWL program's focus even further. Gone were the issues of creating more interest in work, instilling contentment, developing pride in work, increasing trust, encouraging people's inputs, improving employee attitudes, and giving people the opportunity to do new things. Emphasis now was to be given to writing more rules and procedures, publishing a newspaper, updating bulletin boards, improving the intradepartmental phone system, installing a P.A. system, making better use of training films, developing checklists for job assignments, giving departments a labor allowance for training, and establishing departmental blackboards.

These proposals, though specific and quantifiable, presumed that all employees shared the same interpretive framework. The implicit assumption seemed to be that established patterns in Regional were sufficient, if only all concerned were properly informed and given correct information. In short, the prescriptions, minus concerns about employee involvement, presumed that only first-order change was needed. By segmenting the decision process into line employee (diagnostic) and supervisor and steward (prescriptive) components, the change agents allowed those who had been less exposed to QWL concepts—many of whom had resisted the QWL program in the first place—to make the prescriptions that would henceforth guide the program.

By isolating top labor and union management into one of the four groups, the decision process was segmented even further. The plant manager had a poor track record distinguishing between his own ideas and those advocated by the EJEC. Not surprisingly, therefore, some of the ideas suggested by the top management group during the supervisor-steward meeting came to be implemented by management under the EJEC name. One of them, which later came to be called the "line-by-line" project, was to become one of the EJEC's most important efforts.

Segmentation of the decision process into groups whose members share a common perspective may help a QWL program develop concrete implementable proposals. However, it may do so at the expense of negotiation of a new shared understanding of the nature of work and of the work organization. As Kanter (1983) notes, it compartmentalizes actions and problems and thus retards change. It may allow decisions to be made, but it limits the dialogue among alternative perspectives that lies at the core of second-order change. As the perspectives of a subgroup come to guide decisions that affect the entire system, the goal of establishing a community of shared mutual understanding must be sacrificed. And if this subgroup is dominated by those who hold to the established perspective, the most one can expect is new actions, means, and desirable conditions that are consistent with the established framework (Figure 8-1).

The November EJEC newsletter contained a description of the survey feedback sessions. It is available as Exhibit 8-9. The newsletter also included a statement concerning the supervisors-stewards meeting, which is available as Exhibit 8-10.

EXHIBIT 8-9 Article from November 1977 EJEC Newsletter Titled: "Survey Feedback Sessions Identify Issues Affecting Work-Life in Bakery"

Beginning September 26th, the EJEC, in close cooperation with local management and the union, began reviewing the results of the assessment questionnaire with the employees in the Bakery. In all, 36 meetings were held, with employees from all departments participating in the discussions of the results of the questionnaire. EJEC members conducted the discussions and noted these topic areas most actively discussed. In quite a few areas, the workforce expressed strong positive feelings in regard to work at FoodCom. In general, the large majority of employees like working at FoodCom, are involved in their work, and are satisfied with the way people treat them. People at all levels expressed confidence and trust in their co-workers and felt they could get help from the people around them if they were in a bind. People in the feedback sessions also agreed, in general, that they were satisfied with their pay. Several areas emerged as needing (to be) worked upon, since there was general dissatisfaction conveyed regarding these areas in the feedback sessions. They included:

1. Communication: People felt that communication could be improved at all levels in the Bakery, between all departments, between the union and management, between the clock employees and the union officials, and between the EJEC and the employees in the bakery.
2. Training: People stated that there is a need for more training of new employees and of employees moved to different jobs in their departments.
3. In general, the people felt they were not informed enough about decisions and changes which affect their jobs and about the reasons for these changes. Also, the people wanted to be more involved in the decisions which affect their work-life at FoodCom.
4. There is a need to increase the understanding of work-related problems faced by people and of the operations involved in other departments, on other shifts, and between clock employees and supervision. The EJEC's next step, given these findings, is to try and find ways of correcting or alleviating these problem areas.

EXHIBIT 8-10 Article from November 1977 EJEC Newsletter Titled: "Supervision, Shop Stewards, EJEC Meet to discuss Survey Feedback Results"

On Saturday, October 22, 57 members of supervision, shop stewards, EJEC, union officers, and bakery management met to discuss the information the EJEC received during the discussions of the questionnaire results. The participants were divided into four groups consisting of supervisory, union, and EJEC personnel. One group was made up of top management and union officers. Members of the EJEC Executive Committee led the group discussions. From 8:00 A.M. to 12:00 P.M., four group discussions were held; two large group discussions and two small group discussions. The small group discussions were divided into two parts: First, three general problem areas, communication, involvement, and training, were presented and the groups listed what they hoped to accomplish by resolving these problem areas. Second, the groups developed specific procedures and methods which might be employed to resolve the problem areas. The large group discussions involved reporting to the entire group the results of the small group meetings and involved questions and answers to clarify objectives and suggestions. Over a hundred suggestions were made at these meetings. Included in these are the following for improving the problem areas:

1. Communication

   Arrange meetings between supervision and employees

   A plant-wide intercom

   Publish a plant magazine

   Written safety rules, work procedures

   Written notification of current union/management decisions and grievance settlements

   Departmental blackboards for notification of changes

2. Training

   Utilize training films

   Set up a systematic training procedure

   Construct tests for qualification determination

   Allow reasonable time to train and qualify on jobs

   Improve training of "trainers"

3. Involvement

   Arrange supervisor/ clock employee meetings

   Encourage personal opinions, listen to suggestions and act on them

   Improve information about the business

   Orientation tours for new employees

9

Reinforcing Old Patterns

Moving Toward First-Order Change

The off-site Saturday meeting between supervisors and union stewards produced several suggestions for ways of improving communication, training, and employee involvement. One of the recommendations of the management group at the meeting had been for "one line (or line-by-line) production management." This proposal involved establishing a line coordinator position that would be responsible for maintaining communication among those in different departments who worked on the same line. The position had been implemented in another FoodCom bakery and appeared to be working out quite well there.

Matson introduced the idea of a line-by-line project at a staff meeting a week after the supervisors-stewards off-site meeting, suggesting that the Reginal plant take one experimental line and coordinate everything on it from mixing to packing. He then presented the idea to the EJEC on November 3. The proposal, however, had been the product of the off-site meeting by a group composed almost exclusively of top labor and management officials, and few EJEC members had entertained the possibility of engaging in such a project. Most believed it was a management project and should remain so, and a motion was passed to that effect.

Teresa Ferrer from COD attended the EJEC meeting. The next day, Ferrer and the executive committee met with Matson to argue that the line-by-line project should remain a management initiative. Matson, however, was adamant that it was to become an EJEC project. Ferrer and the others then acquiesced, and the next day Ferrer drafted a memo outlining several suggestions for organizing the project, including the need for training, accurate and timely measurement of both cost factors and general climate, and the successful integration of all three shifts. She suggested that the EJEC attempt to build an "effective management support system" for the line coordinator and develop means to facilitate integration among people on the experimental line.

Bobby Clayton convened a special meeting of the EJEC on November 9. The only topic was the proposed line-by-line project. Matson introduced the project by saying it was a direct outcome of the EJEC's off-site meeting. There was general consensus that it would be best to begin with line 7, because there were relatively few product changeovers on that line. Vince Keeley moved that the project commence with a morning meeting during regular production time. The meeting would include mixing and baking people as well as relevant personnel from the maintenance department. Superintendents from these three departments were given the job of choosing the line coordinator, and initial discussion was held concerning performance measurement and feedback.

At a regular EJEC meeting held the next day, members expressed concern about the line-by-line project. Many believed that participating in it would require additional meeting time if they were still to work on their other EJEC duties. Matson assured them that any extra time they needed would be provided. Johnny Pepin moved to suspend regular EJEC business on November 17 and to take the entire afternoon to deal with the project. This motion passed. Chuck Josephson then moved to reverse the EJEC's earlier decision not to take responsibility for the new project. This motion also passed.

Joe Gromanger then drafted an announcement concerning the proposed line-by-line project, and the EJEC directed him to post it. It is presented as Exhibit 9-1.

EXHIBIT 9-1 Memo from EJEC for All Employees Announcing the Proposed Line-by-Line Project

November 21, 1977

TO: FoodCom Employees
FROM: Employee Joint Enrichment Committee
RE: Experimental Project on Line 7

1. Management and the FWIU have proposed an experimental project for improving communication, training, understanding, involvement and line performance while reducing waste on line 7 which the EJEC has accepted as an EJEC project.
2. The basic concept behind the program will be to assign the responsibility of the entire line to one member of supervision. This member of supervision will work through the supervision of the various departments (maintenance, mixing, baking, warehouse, environmental services, and packing) in achieving this objective.
3. At the present time, the proposal is being studied by the EJEC for the purpose of making recommendations concerning its implementation to management and the unions.
4. The EJEC will make every effort to involve the people on the line and other interested people in formulating its recommendations to management and the unions.
5. Group discussions will be held with the people on the line to define problems and to work towards acceptable solutions.
6. This is an experimental project. Line 7 was chosen as the test line; thus, there will be a temporary emphasis on Line 7. We do not want the personnel on the other lines to feel neglected. If successful, the project will be expanded to include the other lines. The cooperation of all the people in the bakery is requested during this trial period.
7. As further developments on the project take place, you will be informed.

At the November 17 meeting, Sholl recommended that the EJEC divide into four subgroups, each concerned with a different topic relevant to the project. One group was to deal with getting employees involved. A second group was given responsibility for determining what statistical data should be gathered to measure the project's success. A third was to design employee meetings for the project, and a fourth was to recommend personnel policies.

Each group met and returned their recommendations to the total EJEC. The Involvement group's recommendations included the following:

1. People on line 7 will start their involvement with the notification of the purpose and procedures for the experimental project.
2. The people on the line will decide regular meeting times and procedures and will aid in identifying problems and solutions on the line. Meeting frequencies will be determined by management and the coordinator.
3. Feedback on experimental line performance should be posted daily on blackboards in such a manner that no one area or department is singled out for poor line performance.

The statistical group gave two proposals:

1. Standard and actual production data should be displayed by department and by shift as soon as the data is available.
2. The line coordinator will be responsible for reporting data to the involved employees for feedback purposes and to management for necessary corrective action.

The meetings group suggested that:

1. The initial orientation to the project should take place in two meetings with everyone involved in the experimental project. The agenda for the first meeting will be a general orientation. The second meeting will provide more opportunity for answering employees' concerns about the experimental project.

2. After the orientation meetings, regular meetings on the line should be held on a weekly basis until they are felt not to be needed.

Finally, the personnel group reported two recommendations:

1. All departments should be involved to some degree in the line experiment. All people working on the line should be involved in the project. This includes people on all shifts on line 7.
2. Training on the line should be improved by having the employees help determine the training needs. Then the line coordinator would make recommendations to management for training improvements.

The EJEC members asked the packaging, baking, and maintenance superintendents—Keeley, Griffith, and DeLeo—to let them know their choice for coordinator by December 1. The orientation meetings were scheduled for December 13 and December 20. The project would formally begin on January 3.

On December 1 the superintendents had not yet selected a line coordinator for the project. None of them thought they could spare any of their people. DeLeo resisted the idea of assigning a maintenance person to the project because he needed all the people he had. Moreover, there was no job description for the line coordinator. Matson agreed to draft one for the next EJEC meeting, scheduled for December 8. EJEC members agreed to postpone the orientation meetings until the line coordinator had been chosen.

Meanwhile, Matson was confronted with serious production problems. The pounds produced per labor hour relative to standard during October showed that efficiency had dropped 20 percent from the same time the previous year. There were production problems with line 6, and figures could not account for 17,000 units of one of the products. Employee meetings on departmental safety and foreign substances had been instituted because of increases in the number of serious accidents and consumer complaints concerning foreign material in the product. However, attendance at these meetings was poor.

As management was grappling with these problems, the plant was scheduled for another health inspection. No one knew when the inspectors would arrive.

By the EJEC meeting on December 8, Matson had not found time to write the job description for the line coordinator position and did not even attend the meeting. The EJEC executive committee sent him suggestions detailing its conception of the line coordinator's role. Matson did not respond to this initiative, however, and the EJEC, concerned lest it lose face among employees, commissioned Joe Gromanger to post a notice explaining the delays.

Matson submitted his version of the line coordinator job description to the EJEC on December 15. It was very different from the description the EJEC had recommended to Matson. EJEC members had wanted a line coordinator who had line authority to give directions and make decisions. In Matson's version, the coordinator was to have no line authority. His coordinator had only liaison functions limited to facilitating communication across departments. Matson's description is available in Exhibit 9-2. Roper, Josephson, and Sheffer—all management representatives on EJEC who had expressed an interest in becoming the coordinator—withdrew their names from consideration. Without line authority, they thought they would have insufficient support and backup. So long as the coordinator would have no formal authority, however, there seemed to be no reason why regular FWIU line employees could not be considered for the job. EJEC members recommended that Bobby Clayton and Marie McCarthy be considered.

EXHIBIT 9-2 Line Coordinator Job Description, Management Version

The duties to be performed by the line coordinator will be over and above the normal supervisory complement. The objective is to coordinate the activities of all operating departments during the process of working with production employees in the problem solving and implementation procedure.

The first requirement will be the holding of informational meetings designed to bring production people involved in (product

> name) manufacturing up to date on all operating statistics such as efficiency, waste, downtime, etc.
>
> When this has been accomplished, and during the above meetings, the objective of the QWL experiment will be described and discussed: survey feedback, communications, training information, understanding of work-related problems, and encouragement of employees to participate in improving QWL.
>
> Plans will be made to hold sectional meetings on an "as needed" basis, each section being a group of employees of 3, 4, 5, 6 from a section in the line in the Bakery, during which problems specific to that section are reviewed with the group with all invited to participate in the discussions, with opinions as to trouble spots, possible corrections being covered. The coordinator will maintain a record of any changes agreed upon by the groups and be responsible to work with interested, responsible supervision at all levels in achieving implementation. The coordinator will hold repeat meetings as needed with the entire #7 (product name) crew to keep everyone up to date on the development and to get evaluative comments from all persons, etc. The coordinator will on a systemic running schedule give EJEC a brief summary of activity, suggestions made, decisions for corrections and/or change, and monitoring of implementation. In addition, he will check and record the improvement developed as the result of changes made.

On the same day these events occurred, the JQWLAC met at FoodCom headquarters. William Coy described the line-by-line project, and all present responded enthusiastically. They agreed that this was a very important development. Meanwhile, November's efficiency showed a precipitous decline. The plant was running at 89 percent efficiency. Matson instituted new restrictions on the use of overtime. The plant also failed to reach an important energy conservation goal. On the bright side, the plant did pass its health inspection; although its score indicating the presence of foreign substances was not impressive.

The first EJEC meeting of the new year took place on January 5. Chairman Bobby Clayton informed the committee that Matson had offered the line coordinator job to Ben Ashley, a packing supervisor. Ashley was perhaps the most popular supervisor in his department. He had accepted Matson's offer, and Brian Hurley moved that the EJEC accept Ben as the line 7 coordinator. The motion passed.

Joe Gromanger had developed a tentative schedule of events for the line 7 project, beginning with training. The training would take place in January. The project was to get under way in February. Tom Gib presented a training plan involving sessions for Ashley individually and for the line 7 employees as a group. Bobby Clayton asked for volunteers to assist Gib, and both Marie McCarthy and Susan Sheffer came forward.

Tom Gib met with Ashley on January 23 and 24. On January 25, they met with Susan Sheffer and Marie McCarthy to plan the line 7 orientation meetings. The first of these meetings focused on describing the program. There was relatively little employee discussion. The second meeting was more open for discussion. Employees identified seventeen problem areas (or projects) to be addressed:

1. Baking windows are welded shut; causes poor air circulation and excessive heat during summer months.
2. Improve communications between departments, improve understanding between departments and shifts.
3. Need clutch on #7 bundler.
4. Floor trucks which are half full of assembled cartons should not be left for first shift—good housekeeping.
5. Need better training procedures for people on the line.

Many of those present at the second orientation meeting believed that most group functions could be handled either by smaller groups or by the line coordinator or shop steward. Meetings of all line 7 personnel could therefore be limited to special cases. Information about important matters should be communicated by word of mouth. A steering committee, established to manage line 7 activities on a week-to-week basis, included representatives from all departments except maintenance. No maintenance department personnel attended the orientation meeting.

On February 1, Matson also announced a "concentrated training program for supervision." These sessions, not part of the EJEC program but also run by Tom Gib, were extensive.

Superintendents, assistant superintendents, and other management personnel met for training for two hours during each of five successive weeks. Lower-level management personnel met for training during each of six weeks.

Once the line 7 project began on February 13, Ashley began to call meetings of the steering committee on a weekly basis. During these meetings, the specific problem areas were discussed, and Ashley reported what had and had not been accomplished. For example, when pursuing employee complaints about excessive heat in the baking department, he found out that the windows in the bake shop had been welded shut to allow for more constant temperature and air moisture during the baking process. Because ventilation was not a problem at this point (it was winter), members decided to look into changing the direction of the fans but to postpone more ambitious solutions until the weather got warmer.

During a JQWLAC meeting held the next day, Tom Gib, William Coy, and Tim Deigh all reported on the progress of the line 7 project. All three considered progress to be excellent. Deigh cautioned members that the project might be gaining enough momentum to generate pressures to move the concept to other shifts and lines faster than the JQWLAC members might be expecting. The new project also made the headlines of the second edition of a newly instituted plant newspaper. The article described the project as "giving line personnel a voice in some production decision making and an increased understanding of procedural and operational problems." The role of the line coordinator was described. Ashley, it was said, "will oversee all production aspects of the line; that is, everything from mixing and baking to packaging as well as maintenance." The article concluded by noting that seventeen problems were already being worked on and that one aspect of Ashley's job would involve collecting production data and reporting on progress. It identified its information source as Joe Gromanger and noted that the project was "related to the Bakery's Quality of Work Life Program."

Matson was very enthusiastic about the line 7 project. In a talk to bakery managers in late March, he called the project "the most exciting and innovative program we have attempted through the Quality of Work Life project." He described the coordinator's position as "responsible for coordinating the activities of the entire line." On the issue of actual line authority, Matson noted that:

> Ben has not replaced the need for specialized supervisors in the departments. He works with the supervisors to correct problems and implement the (line) committee's projects. As Ben becomes more familiar with the operations of the (number 7) line, we feel he may be able to take on more of those responsibilities, enabling the departmental supervisors to concentrate on other lines.

Matson concluded by telling the managers that the experiment already had resulted in decreased waste and greater employee involvement in their work. He also asserted that if positive results continued to come in, the experiment would be expanded to other lines and other shifts.

By March 14, the line 7 steering committee agreed that the time had come to convene the entire group, communicate what had been accomplished to date, and ask for suggestions for additional projects. By this time, there were twenty-eight projects, eleven of which had been completed. Ashley reviewed these and presented several charts and graphs that showed line 7 productivity, with the exception of one particularly troublesome product, to be 98 percent of standard. He then asked employees for suggestions for additional projects. Seven were suggested.

An article appearing in the May issue of the plant newspaper was titled "No. 7 Line Experiment Doing Well," and discussion began concerning extension of the concept to other shifts. Matson, Charlton, Keeley, Griffith, and Gromanger met and decided to extend the project to the line 7 second shift. Matson asked Griffith to determine which supervisors might be available for the second shift coordinator position.

On May 2, the line 7 steering committee met and recommended that Susan Sheffer be assigned as the second shift line coordinator. However, Matson appointed Irene Jones, a packaging department supervisor like Ashley and Sheffer. Ashley was given the responsibility of training Jones, and an orientation meeting was scheduled for Line 7 employees who worked second shift.

Gromanger began this orientation session by giving a brief history of the quality of work program. Ashley summarized the results of the project to date, and Jones described the line coordinator's duties. The meeting was then turned over to the employees. Twelve concrete suggestions for projects were received, and a second shift steering committee was formed.

The second shift line 7 group pursued the same types of projects initiated by those on the first shift committee. For example, they concerned themselves with fixing a malfunctioning interdepartment telephone in the bake shop, insuring the evenness of the salt distribution on the product, and considering a buzzer system for signaling people on different parts of the line. These projects were generally completed with dispatch.

Established Patterns Reappear: the Imposition of a Participative Project

The proposed line-by-line project had many features that made it attractive to QWL change agents. By adding variety to employees' jobs and by giving the work group greater control over work activities, the project might increase employee satisfaction and internal motivation (Hackman and Oldham 1980). It could therefore enhance both employee satisfaction and productivity. Projects similar to this, such as autonomous work groups (Goodman 1979; Trist, Susman, and Brown 1977) and quality circles (Lawler and Mohrman 1985; Steel and Lloyd 1988) accordingly had broad appeal. These types of projects have been introduced in a wide variety of QWL programs (cf., Bushe 1988; Lawler 1986). Because of the way the line-by-line project was introduced in Reginal, however, much of its potential may have been lost.

Stewards, supervisors, and top management dominated the off-site meeting, and in addition, top managers were isolated from lower-level supervisors and union stewards. This segmentation gave those in a position to implement proposals in the plant the option of claiming EJEC support for their ideas without having to present them to a broader constituency. Without being exposed to other inputs, top management simply implemented the line-by-line project using hierarchical channels. EJEC members were therefore presented with a fait accompli by their plant manager who claimed legitimacy gained through the use of open QWL procedures. They therefore understandably rejected the project as an EJEC activity.

Like the program introductions in Gorland and Reginal, it seemed that a participative project was being imposed. Regardless of its objective compatibility with QWL principles, therefore, its implementation effectively reinforced the established order (Figure 8-1; cf., Elden 1986). When the QWL program itself was initially imposed or "sold" to line workers, it was possible to argue that imposition was required in order to initiate a dialogue among perspectives that could not have occurred otherwise. With the introduction of the line-by-line project, however, no such claim could be made. Nothing in the proposal called for dialogue directed toward significant changes in the nature of labor-management relations in the plant. Rather, the proposal was almost exclusively directed toward facilitating productivity and efficiency, and its implementation reinforced the assumption that decisions were going to continue to be made at the level of plant management. This point was further illustrated by Matson's disregard of EJEC recommendations regarding the line coordinator's authority and by his rejection of specific individuals recommended to fill that role.

Rather than create a line manager role that had significant authority, Matson opted to restrict the line coordinator to a liaison or communication link. Giving Ashley significant authority would have challenged the departmental structure and, most likely, would have been resisted by at least two of the department superintendents (Griffith in packing and DeLeo in maintenance). Appointing a union member to be line supervisor—even though the position did not include supervisory responsibility—also represented a significant departure, and Matson demurred. It was clear that there would be no significant changes in the structure of the organization, in the allocation of individuals to positions, or in the influence exercised by lower-level participants over work-related decisions in the plant. Changes, if they were to occur at all, would be compatible with the perspective of plant management. They would be first order changes (cf., Chapter 7).

Changes in Personnel

The schedule for the termination of COD's involvement, revised after the July 1977 EJEC-JQWLAC meeting, called for a substantial reduction in time commitment beginning in early 1978. Joe Gromanger's contract was due to expire during the summer of 1978. EJEC membership was also due to change. Its operating rules called for elections of new EJEC members every six months. Each election was to select half of the representatives, with each representative serving for one year. This meant that half of the EJEC representatives were to be replaced (or possibly reelected) in January. It had taken committee members a great deal of time to educate themselves in QWL concepts. There was concern that new members, unfamiliar with what had been going on, would fail to carry ongoing EJEC projects to completion.

In addition, the new demands of training, communication, and the line-by-line project were just beginning. EJEC representatives to the training and communications subcommittees had been appointed. Committee members who were not EJEC representatives could also be appointed, but there was no way to compensate them for their time. Management was not prepared to charge this time against its own budget, and there was no alternative category. On December 15, the JQWLAC decided that these representatives could be paid from project funds so long as total program expenditures did not increase. This meant that the time available for regular EJEC meetings would have to be reduced.

The EJEC members did not think they could postpone the coming elections. However, Chuck Josephson offered a motion to increase the term of service in the future to two years and to elect half the EJEC membership every year rather than every six months. He also proposed that the EJEC executive committee include the two cochairpersons, the secretary, and a member at large. Josephson's proposals were accepted.

Pepin decided not to run for reelection to the EJEC. He said Matson had told him he didn't want to see any general forepersons on the next EJEC. Matson denied this, saying their involvement was acceptable to him. He only wanted to support those who sought to leave the EJEC because they were feeling undue pressure. Several other union and management representatives also expressed a preference for not continuing.

The elections were held during the week of January 9. Six new members were elected to the EJEC. From supervision they included Warren Wilhelm (environmental services), Fred Baker (baking), and Joel Barrett (packing). From the union they included Curtis Talbot (baking), Marjorie Touchette (packing, first shift), and Barbara Bailey (packing, second and third shifts). These representatives joined Keeley, Josephson, Morse, Sheffer, and Roper (supervision) and Young, Franks, Lowery, Clayton, and Daly (union) to make up the new EJEC. Matson and George Newman filled out the committee as ex-officio participants.

The new EJEC members were installed on January 12. It was immediately clear to them that there was much to do. There were twenty-six projects underway as well as numerous standing committees (five department committees, the parking lot and cafeteria committees, and the newly added communications and training committees). Tom Gib was present to initiate discussions about starting training programs for both supervision and clock employees; meetings between Matson and three of the department subcommittees (cafeteria, warehouse, and baking) were scheduled; and a new member orientation was planned. The problem of reimbursing Scott Lowery for his time was reintroduced. Deigh, who was present at the meeting, committed himself to finding a way for Lowery to be compensated.

After the EJEC meeting, Deigh communicated to the JQWLAC that morale among the EJEC members was excellent and that both union and management support were good. He thought that Gib would be of great help during the phase-out of COD and that Gromanger was becoming more open to confrontation. This was important, because Sholl and Drew would no longer be playing this role.

The next EJEC meeting was held on January 19, and the new members were assigned to one or more of the standing committees. Young, Touchette, Barrett, and Josephson were appointed to the new communications committee; Keeley,

Bailey, Morse, and Franks were selected for the new training subcommittee. The EJEC members were asked to suggest names of people who were not on the EJEC but who might also serve on these committees. Finally, new officers were elected. Marjorie Touchette and Chuck Josephson became the new cochairpersons. Josephson was well known for his independent style. Touchette also took a proactive stance. At her first executive committee meeting she predicted she would get fired, "because we're here to get something done and they're (George Newman and Roger Matson) not serious." Josephson was to serve as chairperson for the first month. Joan Franks was elected secretary, and Susan Sheffer was elected member-at-large to the executive committee.

In addition to these personnel changes, there was a shift at FoodCom: Struthers was promoted to a corporate position. Several participants expressed concern that one of the primary supporters of the project had now become one more step removed.

In early February, the problem of paying Scott Lowery had been worked out. His national union, the IEU, would compensate Lowery for the time he spent on EJEC activities. The union then would be reimbursed by the American Center. Finding people who were not EJEC members but were willing to serve on the training and communications committees, however, proved to be more difficult. On February 2, the EJEC decided to fill the remaining slots with EJEC members if necessary.

Management Statements of Support for the QWL Program

The QWL program appeared to be gaining support among top management. Dalmar Pond offered a strong defense of the program via a videotaped presentation to company supervisors. His talk noted the following:

> Throughout the United States industry . . . there is a growing discontent among a good number of the employees who are not in

> the management organization. These employees probably number 90 percent of the total employees in industry. No matter how good the organization operates, no matter how good the supervision run their operations, as the majority of the people become dissatisfied with their work station, if they would like to have more decisions and more knowledge of the area in which they work, this feeling could grow and be counterproductive to the entire capitalistic system in American industry. This project, named the Quality of Work Life, is an attempt to deal with the problem in the FoodCom operations before it becomes a matter of fact. . . . We are very pleased with the efforts and with the progress of this project in the Reginal Bakery.

The JQWLAC met on February 28. Gib was present, and he, Coy, and Deigh all gave the project high ratings. Gib was making good progress on the training program, the line-by-line project was seen as getting excellent results, and there had been progress toward making the program more self-sufficient. Deigh thought that the reconstitution of the EJEC had been "accomplished in an outstanding manner resulting in an even stronger and more effective EJEC than prior to its reconstitution." An EJEC proposal for a second joint EJEC-JQWLAC meeting was received favorably by the group. The meeting was scheduled for June 13.

The second issue of the new plant newsletter was published in early March. Matson included an article thanking the retiring EJEC members:

> A lot of what [the new committee will] accomplish will be due directly to the outgoing committee members. . . . The first year's committee trod on unfamiliar ground and trekked into new territories. . . . They did well, and satisfied a great many expectations. For this, they earned our thanks.

Matson voiced his own support for the program. In a speech before fellow plant managers in March he echoed Dalmar Pond's earlier presentation, saying that:

> Throughout the United States Industry, there is a growing discontent among a good number of the employees who are not in the management organization. . . . . No matter how good the

> organization operates, no matter how good the supervision run their operation, as the majority of the people become dissatisfied . . . this feeling (of discontent) could grow and be counterproductive to the entire capitalistic system in American Industry.

He added:

> Though we do not expect overnight results from the quality of work life program in eliminating the discontent so many managers see in their work force, I feel that in the past year, the Reginal bakery's program has done a tremendous job in achieving the results we expected from the program, and we look forward to 1978 with increased enthusiasm as the committee works toward its goals.

The Issue of Break Time

Marjorie Touchette, the newly elected EJEC cochairperson, began to focus her attention on interdepartmental relations. She was angry because maintenance personnel, employees in the warehouse and sanitation departments, and some in baking were not as machine-paced as most of those in packaging. Consequently, they could stretch their breaks without forcing their fellow workers to work through their break time. Because their lines were machine-paced, however, packers had to remain on the line until they were relieved.

The maintenance workers came in for special attention. Because this was by no means a new problem, they had developed a standard defense. They argued that when they weren't working the equipment must be functioning properly. Packaging personnel should be happy when maintenance employees were in a position to stretch their breaks. A good measure of their effectiveness, they argued, was the number of them who could be found lounging in the cafeteria.

This explanation was not calculated to please the packagers, and it particularly upset Touchette. She began to push for an EJEC proposal to give packaging department employees five extra minutes of break time. At an EJEC meeting on March 9,

Chuck Josephson moved that the EJEC investigate the possibility of getting more relief time for "confined people." This clearly challenged the doctrine that the EJEC should not get into issues that were the subject of collective bargaining; consequently, Newman and Matson opposed involvement with the issue. Moreover, representatives from the less confined departments did not wish to expose the practice of break-stretching. The discussion became heated, and Josephson's motion was denied despite its endorsement by both committee cochairpersons.

The following week, Touchette suggested to her fellow workers in the packaging department that they show their concern over the issue of breaks by making suggestions through the EJEC suggestion box. She was chairperson of the EJEC meeting held on March 16 and spent more than fifteen minutes reading the resulting petitions. The discussion was again heated. Newman again expressed strong opposition to EJEC becoming involved in this contractual issue. It was then proposed that the EJEC direct its efforts toward finding ways to better utilize the fifty minutes of break time currently available through the contract and that this responsibility be given to the packaging department subcommittee. This proposal, however, was voted down. Newman opposed it on the same grounds that he had opposed Touchette's initial suggestion. Matson also opposed it.

Deigh was present at this meeting. He reported to the JQWLAC that this issue of relief time created conflict that was "difficult, but in my opinion healthy." He thought that the way the issue had been presented on March 9 had been unfortunate and that Matson and Newman's categorical rejection had angered some EJEC members. When the issue was again raised on March 16 and phrased in terms of finding ways to better utilize, rather than to increase, relief time, Matson and Newman had "slammed the door" despite the fact that the problem, as it was presented, was not a collective bargaining issue. Deigh reported that he had subsequently succeeded in encouraging all parties to be more responsive.

To defuse the relief time issue, Gromanger drafted a letter for George Newman addressed to Josephson and Touchette as cochairpersons of the EJEC. It explicitly rejected the idea that the total amount of relief time be increased but supported any effort to find ways to more effectively utilize the fifty minutes of relief time currently available. This effort, however, must not affect or change the present labor-management agreement, adversely affect the productive efficiency of the bakery, or adversely affect the relief schedules of other areas in the bakery.

Touchette reintroduced the issue on March 30. This time, Franks moved that the problem be defined as finding ways to more efficiently utilize the fifty minutes of break available through the current contract and to turn the problem over to the packaging department committee. This proposal was turned down. It was a close vote, nine for and three against (ten needed for passage). Josephson, who argued that the issue should be left alone until a JQWLAC observation team was present, cast one of the three negative votes. Touchette, already feeling alienated from many of the committee members, now felt undermined by her cochairperson.

By the end of March, Deigh felt the time was right to begin to address the issue of diffusing the quality of work project into other FoodCom plants. In a memo to JQWLAC members, he noted that events and growing experience with the project suggested that diffusion might be appropriate. The participants had more than fifteen months of experience with the formal EJEC structure, four months of operating with greatly reduced COD participation and help, and five months of experience with the new production organization on line 7. In addition, the assistant coordinator's role had become more defined, the JQWLAC had agreed to hire a replacement for Gromanger, and a variety of highly visible projects had been completed. Deigh suggested a step-by-step diffusion plan.

A JQWLAC observation team composed of Donald Premater and William Coy visited the plant during the week of April 3. The executive committee members met with Premater and Coy and suggested that a "nonprecedence memorandum" be agreed to by which the Reginal plant would experiment with giving more relief time to packaging department employees. This experiment would have no precedent-setting implications for the other plants. Coy and Premater opposed the proposal. Premater claimed that such activity would be "illegal," because the labor-management agreement on the quality of work program specifically stated that no contractual issues would become involved. They agreed, however, that the EJEC could make a recommendation to the local union council. The council then would decide whether to consider bringing up the issue within the context of changing the collective bargaining agreement.

After Coy and Premater left the meeting, Touchette and Josephson expressed considerable frustration. Touchette thought that all of the EJEC projects undertaken up to this point were essentially managerial and that the company should have taken care of such things in the normal course of running the business. EJEC members and plant employees were getting nothing in the way of a significant improvement in the quality of their working life. Josephson was angry that visitors from the JQWLAC thought they could unilaterally restrict EJEC activities. Both expressed considerable bewilderment that an officer of the international union would be so adamantly opposed to finding a way to give employees more relief time.

The EJEC met on April 5. Scott Lowery, Susan Sheffer, and Barbara Bailey were absent, as were their alternates. Scott Lowery was frequently the only electrician assigned to the packing floor, and it was not easy to find replacements for him. Pepin, Sheffer's alternate, was also often required to stay in the department rather than attend the EJEC meetings.

The topic quickly turned to the problem of relief time. Premater informed the members that they had no authority to get into contractual matters. Relief time was such a matter, and Premater argued loudly that the only way the EJEC could consider such a problem would be to make recommendations to the local union council. Keeley then moved that the issue focus on finding ways to more effectively use the amount of relief time already available and be turned over to the packaging department subcommittee. The motion was again voted down. Touchette then handed Joe Gromanger a note announcing her resignation from the EJEC. Bobby Clayton explained that the issue of effective use of the fifty available minutes was not a contractual issue: The motion was then put to another vote and passed. Touchette decided not to resign.

An Attempt to Address Labor-Labor Issues in the Plant

We commented in Chapter 4 that QWL projects focus on labor-management relationships but infrequently address labor-labor issues. Touchette's proposal was an attempt to address such an issue: to achieve greater equality between groups in the time allotted for breaks. This was an issue on which the perspectives of the packaging, baking, and maintenance employees differed substantially. For example, the changes in relief time that would satisfy packaging department members (equal amounts of time) were likely to decrease the satisfaction of other employees, particularly the machinists, who wanted to maintain superiority. Moreover, even raising the issue represented a threat. It raised the visibility of the practice of break-stretching.

As we noted in Chapter 7, problems between FWIU members and IMU members had been systematically avoided, and this had considerably limited the EJEC's ability to deal with their differences in perspectives. Publicly raising the issue of break time offered EJEC members a chance to surface and confront some of the different perspectives present in the plant. If carried out well, this confrontation might have had the potential to achieve significant changes in understanding and improvements in relationships. However, when the EJEC seemed on the verge of initiating this type of confrontation a familiar pattern reappeared: an imposition by higher level authorities who unilaterally decided the issue was out of bounds.

Touchette then exhibited another already established EJEC pattern, although she had probably not seen it in action before: She threatened to resign. As had happened in response to Pepin's and Drinan's previous threats, this threat succeeded to some extent. It got the relief time issue on the EJEC's agenda, albeit in an altered form that didn't challenge the collective bargaining agreement.

The new form was a step forward in itself. There is some indication that in successful QWL interventions, labor-management committees eventually move beyond "legalistic concern" with whether the issues they are considering are related to the contractual bargaining agreement and find ways to address these issues informally outside of the contract (Bushe 1988). It remained to be seen what would come of the EJEC's consideration of this issue.

JQWLAC Review of the QWL Program and Continued EJEC Activities

After their visit to Reginal, Coy and Premater could not reconcile their views concerning the nature and progress of the quality of work program there. They both had talked with Matson. Coy thought that although Matson had voiced complaints about the program, he basically supported it and believed it was having a positive impact. Premater, on the other hand, had the impression that Matson did not think the program was making a contribution. Matson had told him, for example, that the EJEC projects would have been accomplished without the EJEC.

Coy and Premater agreed that Newman was not optimistic about the future of the program. Newman told them it had little support among supervision and some aggressive resistance. EJEC projects should have been taken care of by management, he said. He was, however, enthusiastic about the line-by-line project and urged that it be extended to all three shifts.

Premater was not impressed by the EJEC, though Coy thought it was on the right track. They both saw it as proceeding in a cumbersome fashion, and they both reported that members were frustrated by the slow progress of the subcommittees and by difficulties associated with being relieved to attend EJEC meetings. Premater saw the EJEC as infringing on the grievance procedure. Coy thought that almost every topic was related to the correction of physical or operational problems in the plant, and he found this impressive. He saw progress in areas such as safety and security as enhancing the quality of working life in the plant. Premater believed that the morale of the workers and of supervision was at an all-time low. They concluded their report to the JQWLAC with the following summary:

> William Coy feels that the Quality of Work Life project is progressing satisfactorily, viewing the confrontations, adverse comments by parties involved who were really reacting to the need for change as they were personally impacted, (Matson, Newman, Supervision) as part of the process of change—and none of which should represent final roadblocks. On the other hand, Premater honestly feels at this time, that the Quality of Work Life program in Reginal is not working and that it will not work.

The Coy-Premater report was submitted on April 5. On April 17, Deigh contacted JQWLAC members and proposed that they meet on May 3. The suggested agenda included discussing of the Coy-Premater report, finding a replacement for Joe Gromanger, planning for the joint EJEC-JQWLAC meeting planned for June 13, and diffusing the quality of work program to other plants within the company. In preparation for the meeting, Jim Kochems contacted the assessors and asked for an update of any data they might have. He told them the company was planning a high-level review of the program. One of the options was to scrap the entire project, and he wanted all the information he could get in order to ensure that it would receive a fair hearing. In an aside, he expressed some resentment that Deigh was raising the issue of diffusing the program to other plants. He thought that Deigh had done this because the American Center needed additional funds.

As the program review was being conducted, EJEC activities continued. The training and communication subcommittees met, the line 7 project continued, and the EJEC planned for the joint EJEC-JQWLAC meeting. On April 20, Joel Barrett and Susan Sheffer were called out of an EJEC meeting to attend to business on the floor. This prompted the executive committee to write a memo to Matson noting that these people were critical to the effective operation of the quality of work program. Two days later, Matson urged his superintendents either to find relief for EJEC members or to let their alternates attend the meetings. Louis Young and Scott Lowery failed to attend the EJEC meeting later that day.

Several people at the EJEC meeting expressed resentment at plant management for restricting attendance and at George Newman for opposing their call for more break time in the packaging department. Some EJEC members expressed reservations about allowing Matson and Newman to attend their meetings. They argued that members weren't free to express their true feelings. Curtis Talbot moved that Matson and Newman be excused from attending regular meetings on a six-week trial basis. Roper seconded the motion, and it carried. Neither Matson nor Newman would attend an EJEC meeting until the second joint EJEC-JQWLAC meeting. They would then be considered invited guests.

At the next EJEC meeting, held on May 4, Josephson and Touchette were represented by their alternates. Touchette had not attended an EJEC meeting since April 5, when Premater and Coy were visiting. EJEC members attending this meeting voted to cancel EJEC meetings until June to allow members time to respond to a second plantwide survey, which the assessors were planning to conduct in mid-May. When the EJEC reconvened on June 1, Josephson, Sheffer, Talbot, Lowery, Daly, and Barrett were absent and had not sent their alternates. Touchette also was absent, but her alternate was present.

Members attending the meeting were told that Tim Deigh had interviewed dozens of prospective replacements for Joe Gromanger and had narrowed the field to two candidates. His first choice was Alfred Thayer, then a staff member at the American Center. Thayer thought that the FoodCom/FWIU project was "the most dynamic of all the Center's projects" and decided to submit his application for the job. Deigh's second choice was Margaret Tippett, a Ph.D. candidate in industrial/organizational psychology at a local university. She had been introduced to the quality of work projects during a colloquium and was excited by the possibility of participating in the Reginal program. The EJEC scheduled interviews with both Thayer and Tippett for June 22, a week after the second joint EJEC-JQWLAC meeting.

Subcommittee Activities and Associated Projects

As noted earlier, there were many EJEC subcommittees. Much of the EJEC meeting time during this period was set aside for the activities of these subcommittees.

The training and communication subcommittees established in response to the off-site meeting held their first meetings on March 3. Keeley was appointed chairperson of the training subcommittee, and Young was appointed chairperson of the communication subcommittee.

Both subcommittees submitted reports at the next EJEC meeting on March 10. The training subcommittee decided to conduct informal interviews with employees to determine their training needs. In the meantime, they recommended that training allowances be established for individual departments.

The communication subcommittee set about investigating ways to deal with communication problems discussed during the off-site meeting. Some members agreed to look into ways of improving interdepartmental communication. Others assumed responsibility for establishing a written record of all labor-management agreements and grievance decisions. The subcommittee as a whole agreed to look for ways to more effectively update plant bulletin boards and arrange the material placed on them in more readable form.

The written records of local labor-management agreements were to be kept in each department. Matson ordered binders in which these agreements could be compiled, and the binders arrived by April 20. On April 27, Matson sent them along with a memo to his superintendents. In the memo, Matson specified who could and could not have access to the documents: "As stated in the EJEC Meeting Minutes of April 20th, these books are to be made available to your department supervision and shop stewards in the event of a disagreement over an official agreement or company notices. They are not for use by other employees." The EJEC minutes did indeed note that supervision and shop stewards would have access to these records, but they did not limit access to these individuals.

The other projects of the communication subcommittee took longer to address. On May 18, the subcommittee issued a set of recommendations concerning other areas identified as needing improvement. These are reproduced in Exhibit 9-3. The EJEC accepted these recommendations; however, with the joint EJEC-JQWLAC meeting pressing closer, nothing concrete was done to implement them.

EXHIBIT 9-3 Report of the Communication Subcommittee

May 18, 1978

Communication Subcommittee Report:

1. Discussed the spiral notebooks for all departments and the agreements and notices that should be included in these. The notebooks have already been distributed to the departments.
2. We discussed safety films and safety rules. We recommend that the safety rules be posted in areas where employees can regularly familiarize themselves with the rules, especially in times of emergencies.
3. We propose that when there are any changes on the lines, such as mechanical changes or changes in the variety being run on the line, that the personnel on the line be called in for a meeting to inform them of these changes.
4. Improvements should be made to update the bulletin boards. We propose that in baking, EHS (environmental services), and the warehouse that plexiglass holders be installed to counter the humidity and dust in these areas. Also, it was suggested that part of the (bulletin) boards be used exclusively for current or "hot" items and the other part of the board be used for permanent items.
5. We propose that an interdepartment phone be installed in the mixing room to facilitate communication with other departments.
6. We suggest that graphs be placed in the machine man area, the baker area and the packing department that show the percent efficiency on each line.

Louis Young, Chairperson

The training subcommittee met on April 13 and reported its recommendations to the EJEC on April 20. Its members proposed that qualified clock employees serve as trainers for new personnel. Qualifications would be determined by a joint agreement between the company and union. Trainees would be assigned to the appropriate shift as an extra person and be paid on straight time. They also recommended that trainers be given a one-hour session in training by Tom Gib. The EJEC accepted the report.

Training subcommittee members met with plant management on May 18 to present their proposals. Pepin, as acting chairperson in Vince Keeley's absence, acted as spokesperson for the group. In his subsequent report to the EJEC, Pepin noted the following: "Mr. Matson still had a number of questions regarding the details of the proposal." These included the following: "Will films be used for training?" "If so, which ones?" "Will safety training be included in the program?" "What areas do we propose that the training start?" "Will a written description of the job be presented for the trainer?" "Who will do the actual training?" "How will the training be done?" "How many hours are sufficient for training?" "Who will train the trainers in training practices?" "Why is the training necessary?" Pepin concluded his report by saying that the training subcommittee was going to go directly to Tom Gib for assistance. Before anything could be done about this, however, the subcommittee members had to prepare for the second joint EJEC-JQWLAC meeting.

The Bake Shop Subcommittee

In November, the bake shop subcommittee had made several proposals, such as purchasing a new wire-cutting machine, installing an additional elevator, computerizing the entry of lard and water to the south box mixers, repairing leaks in the existing spray machine, installing a tub ejector on the spindle mixer, and completing work on a snack enrober and allied equipment. After the January EJEC elections a new bake shop subcommittee was appointed, with Vince Keeley as chairperson. It began its work with an introductory meeting with Matson and DeLeo. Matson opened the session by explaining to committee members that the JQWLAC had turned down their request for a second elevator. The committee, according to Matson, had failed to document the time lost due to elevator downtime and to show adequately that it really was dangerous to operate the old equipment. While Matson might have communicated with management members of JQWLAC about this issue, there is no record of it having been discussed by JQWLAC.

Next, the committee raised the issue of the proposed new wire-cutting machine. Keeley noted that a new cutter would be needed especially if a particular new product were to go into production. Matson said the new product was "in the hopper," but that there was no need for a new wire cutter. Keeley disagreed, and he and Matson engaged in a somewhat lengthy argument. Finally, Matson told Keeley to write the requisition but to document all of the problems that were arising owing to the use of the old equipment. Keeley agreed to do this.

The topic then turned to the committee proposal to computerize the entry of lard and water to the south box mixers. DeLeo suggested a plan for doing this that also involved motorizing certain scales. Keeley and Matson expressed their approval. DeLeo also took responsibility for thinking about installing a tub ejector on the spindle mixer and for reporting back concerning work on the snack enrober and allied equipment.

Attention then was given to earlier EJEC recommendations. New clocks had arrived. DeLeo said he didn't know where to put them. Keeley told him. DeLeo reported that the new cabinet requested for the maintenance department had arrived. All the tools originally requested by the maintenance department subcommittee could therefore be ordered, except for the oscilloscope. DeLeo said his department had no use for an oscilloscope.

After this session, members of the bake shop subcommittee

turned their attention to their other duties. The bake shop subcommittee simply stopped meeting.

The Packaging Subcommittee

The EJEC asked the packaging subcommittee to address several issues that had been the source of complaints. Some employees, for example, thought the duties of the line leader relative to those of the foreperson were not clearly defined. Another issue involved equity in the allocation of overtime. Overtime was supposed to be given to the most senior person capable of doing the job. Some claimed that this procedure was not being followed. Finally, as noted earlier, the packaging subcommittee was asked to find a way for employees to make better use of the fifty minutes of break time they had been given through collective bargaining.

In late March, the packaging subcommittee addressed a memo to Greg Charlton, proposing that overtime be allocated by posting a master sheet on which employees could request overtime. Assignments would go to the most senior person qualified to do the job. Charlton felt the proposal had merit but that the union might not support it. So long as the union would agree that anyone bypassed in seniority could not file a grievance, he thought the company would approve the proposal. On April 5, the EJEC passed a motion approving the posting of a daily overtime list in the packing department.

The packaging subcommittee met with Matson on April 27. Matson categorically rejected the subcommittee's plan for allocating overtime, claiming that Dennis Griffith and Johnny Pepin were working to develop a way to address the problem. The committee also proposed that packaging department employees could make better use of their fifty minutes of break time if they had their own lounge. This would eliminate the long walk to the plant cafeteria. Matson also rejected this suggestion. The packaging subcommittee members had other obligations, and, because management had assumed responsibility for developing the new overtime sign-up procedure and had vetoed the new lounge, they turned their attention elsewhere.

The Environmental Services Subcommittee

By early April the environmental services department subcommittee made five formal recommendations to the EJEC. It wanted a new procedure for distributing employee uniforms. It also requested a new small lawn mower and edger, a new vent in the steam room, a new floor sander, and a jack to aid employees in moving skids when they sought to clear an area. The EJEC accepted these recommendations, and the executive committee forwarded them to management.

The Warehouse Department Subcommittee

The warehouse department subcommittee submitted its recommendations to the EJEC on January 20. The subcommittee members wanted to install a restroom in the warehouse area, extend the receiving dock, and replace one of the older forklifts. On February 3, the committee met with DeLeo, Charlton, and Matson. Management agreed to extend the receiving dock but felt that more work would have to be done to develop the plan for a new restroom. Likewise, a new forklift could not be approved until it could be documented that the one to be replaced was inadequate. Subcommittee members agreed to generate the necessary documentation.

After this meeting, the warehouse department subcommittee members stopped generating new projects; however, they did identify a location for the planned new restroom. Eventually, a requisition for the purchase of the new forklift was written and approved, and an architect was scheduled to design the extension to the receiving dock.

The Maintenance Department Subcommittee

On February 23, maintenance department subcommittee members met with electricians, the lead carpenter, and forepersons.

They discussed several projects, some as old as the subcommittee itself. These included securing the electrical shop, completing the overhead cabinet, and acquiring a new work buggy. Management took responsibility for following up on these projects. On April 5, the subcommittee reported to the EJEC that progress had been made; however, the electrical shop still did not have locks on its doors. After this meeting, subcommittee members concentrated primarily on their other responsibilities.

The Parking Lot Subcommittee

At the November 3, 1977 EJEC meeting, the parking lot subcommittee had moved that window stickers, rather than bumper stickers, be used to identify cars of company employees. This would allow security personnel to locate cars operated by people who might be in the lot to rifle employees' cars. The motion carried, and the EJEC recommended to management that window stickers be made available to employees. With this single exception, there was no activity concerning the parking lot until early February. At this time, Matson announced that the funds had been approved for the parking lot and work was to begin, weather permitting, in early April.

The parking lot decals arrived in mid-April. Some stylistic changes had been made, and some EJEC members expressed annoyance that the EJEC had not been notified that these changes were being considered. As requested by the EJEC, however, window stickers, not bumper stickers, were to be used. At this time, work had still not commenced on the parking lot. With the exception of some increased parking space required because of a high level of employment, the parking lot remained as it had been during the first joint EJEC-JQWLAC meeting.

The Cafeteria Subcommittee

Work on the cafeteria was underway before the second joint EJEC-JQWLAC meeting. The cafeteria committee was active, not to deal with the renovation but to address other problems. For example, the organization responsible for operating and supplying the cafeteria, Reliable Foods, was not providing all shifts with sufficient utensils. It had also initiated a policy of charging for hot water, ketchup, and mustard and for the use of knives and forks. Moreover, a can of soda that cost thirty cents when purchased from the machine cost thirty-two cents when purchased directly from the cafeteria workers.

The cafeteria subcommittee met with Matson on January 20 to discuss these issues. They had been involved in improving the food service in the cafeteria and thought employees were blaming them for the new practices. Matson agreed to correct the practice of charging different prices for the same product and to discuss the other issues with Reliable Foods. The subcommittee members also received Matson's and the full EJEC's approval for writing a letter to the JQWLAC describing the situation and requesting their assistance. Joe Gromanger was commissioned to draft the letter.

At the February 2 EJEC meeting, Matson reported that he had met with Reliable Foods and had resolved most of the problems. Employees would not be charged for hot water if they used their own cup. There would be no charge for utensils. He also said he was working on eliminating the charge for tax on soda purchased directly rather than through a machine. At this disclosure, Scott Lowery became upset. The EJEC had taken responsibility for addressing the cafeteria issues and was in the process of communicating with the JQWLAC about them. He resented Matson's interference. He therefore moved to discontinue all EJEC subcommittee work until the JQWLAC delineated the extent of the EJEC's authority to implement projects and communicate directly with JQWLAC. The motion was seconded by Touchette but voted down by the EJEC. Members decided that the cafeteria subcommittee would investigate the facts and meet with Matson again before the next EJEC meeting.

The cafeteria subcommittee met with Matson on February

7 and agreed that any subcommittee member could contact Reliable Foods to report that the machines were empty. The subcommittee also agreed to come up with a procedure for estimating the total number of people working third shift, so management could contact Reliable Foods when the requisite number for a third shift operation would be present.

On February 23, the cafeteria subcommittee reported to the EJEC that the vending machines still were not being properly serviced. By March 16, work had begun on the cafeteria renovation; however, employees continued to complain of the lack of utensils on late shifts.

Old Patterns Reassert Themselves and Enthusiasm for the QWL Program Wanes

The distinctive ways different groups understood the QWL program in Reginal (chapters 3 and 4) continued to direct participant behaviors; however, time and resource limitations led participants to focus on projects that could enhance efficiency. Those advocating the acquisition of amenities became a smaller and smaller minority. To free up resources, EJEC meetings were cancelled. Several key EJEC participants chose not to run for reelection, because they felt pressure from plant management to give greater priority to production issues.

The established process of decision making (Figure 5-1) continued to characterize choice behavior. The EJEC and its subcommittees did not assume greater responsibility and authority as expected after the joint EJEC-JQWLAC meeting. Matson continued to play the central role. When EJEC subcommittees submitted recommendations, he would ask for additional documentation. In the case of the training subcommittee, he asked for detailed specifications and even questioned why the recommended training should be done. When the bake shop requested a new elevator and a new wire cutter, he asked for documentation that would show how the expense could be justified. Some projects were carried through to completion (e.g., a new cabinet for the maintenance department); however, implementation of projects was still problematic.

For example, DeLeo canceled the order for an oscilloscope on his own initiative.

Attempts by the EJEC to effect a choice process more in line with QWL ideals (Figure 7-1) and to deal with labor-labor issues proved ineffective. For example, members of the packaging subcommittee worked out a detailed plan, approved by the EJEC and Greg Charlton, for the allocation of overtime. Matson simply rejected the plan, choosing instead to use the traditional means for developing and implementing labor-management policies. He also vetoed construction of a new lounge as a way of dealing with the break time issue, thus summarily eliminating this issue from EJEC consideration.

Matson also interjected himself into the activities of the cafeteria subcommittee. For example, he took on the role of intermediary between the subcommittee and Reliable Foods. The subcommittee preferred to work directly with the JQWLAC and contact Reliable directly. Scott Lowery and other subcommittee members resented Matson's interference in the decision process. However, they could not convince their colleagues, and their proposal to halt subcommittee work until JQWLAC delineated their authority was voted down.

There were some new themes. On the positive side, EJEC subcommittees from the bake shop and packaging focused more on work-related and other substantive issues. Dalmar Pond now thought the QWL program might help resolve a crisis in worker attitudes that he saw as having the potential to undermine the captalist system.

Other new themes were not so encouraging. EJEC members became less willing to challenge management opposition to their proposals. Frustrated by management's lack of response to their suggestion for a new overtime assignment procedure and its opposition to their proposal for a new lounge, members of the packaging department subcommittee simply stopped meeting. Faced with multiple demands and no additional resources, the bake shop, maintenance, and environmental services committees became inactive. More importantly, perhaps, the EJEC began to experience severe attendance problems. Some members were frustrated by the lack of progress. Others were experiencing work pressures. As a result, EJEC meetings, already curtailed to free up time and money for subcommittee activities, became less and less productive.

The QWL program at FoodCom had been described as a new

approach to corporate governance (Chapter 2). After approximately eighteen months, the EJEC had been the catalyst behind several projects designed to increase productivity and efficiency and to make employees' work lives more comfortable. However, the EJEC had not succeeded in assuming greater responsibility for decision making, and plant management had maintained its executive role. Changes that had occurred had been behavioral rather than attitudinal or perceptual, and many of the projects (e.g., cafeteria renovation) and new behaviors (e.g., additional training and the line-by-line experiment) may well have come about had the QWL program never been launched.

Matson's behavior in the six months preceding the second joint EJEC-JQWLAC meeting bore many resemblances to his behavior prior to the first such encounter. Once again he put his own judgment above that of the EJEC. Once again he denied the committee critical resources. Once again he insisted that subcommittee members function as specialists in areas far removed from their areas of expertise. However, COD had phased out its activities, and Sholl was not present to orchestrate another enactment of power by the EJEC.

It remained for Deigh to assess the situation and prescribe future directions. He was hampered, however, by his "quality control" role. He could not take direct consulting responsibility for the program. He also sought to begin diffusing the QWL concept throughout FoodCom and consequently might have felt pressure to focus upon the successes rather than the failures in Reginal. As the time for the second joint EJEC-JQWLAC meeting approached, however, the future direction of the QWL program in Reginal was very much in doubt.

The Second Joint EJEC-JQWLAC Meeting: June 13, 1978

By June 2, the EJEC executive committee had developed a proposed agenda for the joint meeting and had assigned responsibility for different topics to individual employees. Each subcommittee was to be discussed, and Ben Ashley and Irene Jones were to give a progress report on the line 7 project. Several other topics were identified for presentation and discussion. One of these, titled "Areas for Overall Project Improvement by EJEC," included a discussion of training for executive committee members and members of the EJEC, the development of a procedures manual describing the assistant coordinator's duties, and treatment of issues relevant to the interface between the EJEC and other groups.

Other topics included four policy areas that the executive committee felt required attention. Chuck Josephson agreed to bring up the problem of EJEC involvement in what might be seen as contractual issues. Bobby Clayton was to talk about information flow and reporting relations. Clayton also agreed to discuss EJEC opportunities for assisting groups in dealing with problems they were having difficulty resolving. The fourth policy area concerned resources. Susan Sheffer was selected to discuss external resources that would be made available to the EJEC in the future.

Chuck Josephson was scheduled to round out the EJEC presentations. He was to outline plans and projected budgets for future EJEC activities. Then the meeting was to be turned over to a discussion of issues of concern to JQWLAC members.

As was the case for the first joint meeting, the activities of the second meeting were carefully orchestrated. Deigh prepared a format for each report. Each reporter was to inform those present of the composition of his or her respective subcommittee, the number of meetings it had had, and the number of recommendations it had submitted to the appropriate authorities. Reporters were to note the numbers of these recommendations that had been approved and implemented, approved and awaiting implementation, and disapproved. They were also to provide a project summary detailing specific projects. Reporters were then to describe briefly their subcommittee's future plans. In conclusion, each participant was asked to follow a prepared script. The scripts for the presenters other than those describing the subcommittees, reproduced in their entirety, are presented as Exhibit 9-4.

EXHIBIT 9-4 Scripts for the Second Joint EJEC-JQWLAC Meeting

FRANKS: EXECUTIVE COMMITTEE AND EJEC TRAINING

We feel that in some ways, with changes in composition etc. of the EJEC, that some additional training is needed. Training for both the EJEC as a whole and the executive committee as well. We have already begun with training from Tim Deigh and Joe Gromanger.

Thus far we have been able to cut in half the time required for regular Thursday executive committee meeting by learning to work more efficiently. We will work with Tim Deigh and Joe Gromanger to develop a listing of additional training that is needed and a place to accomplish such training utilizing Tim Deigh when he is here, Joe Gromanger and his replacement and also consider proposals for use of Gib.

FRANKS: PROCEDURES MANUAL FOR ASSISTANT COORDINATOR

We have also requested that during the approximately six week period in which we have two assistant coordinators here that they develop a procedures manual of all the methods we have developed and should utilize to make the operations of the EJEC more efficient and to help ensure that we are doing our tasks in a complete and easily understood manner. We will have a draft of that procedure manual completed by September 1. This draft will also include some areas, we are sure, that are not covered and are in need of further work and decisions. The draft of the procedures manual will then be given to all EJEC members, JQWLAC and Mr. Matson and Mr. Newman for their review and recommendations.

BAKER: EJEC-MANAGEMENT INTERFACE

We are well aware that the EJEC has not been as effective as we would like it to be in addressing the legitimate needs of both the management and the FWIU as organizations. We recommend from the management perspective two actions:

1. At regular meeting—include examples—in which management and supervision are present (including management representatives on EJEC) that at least once each month at such meetings that the management representative on EJEC be given about fifteen minutes on the agenda of such meetings to give a brief outline of what EJEC is doing and to ask their fel-

low supervision/management for areas in which they (management) are having problems in which perhaps EJEC could be of some assistance.

2. We also would like to ask Mr. Matson to write an informal note once each month to the EJEC outlining areas in which he feels the EJEC could be of potential assistance in resolving problems.

MARTINEZ: EJEC-UNION INTERFACE

Use the same type as above substituting Union terminology as appropriate; after noting that the EJEC could be more effective, replace the rest of the statement above with the following: We recommend from the union perspective two actions:

1. At regular meetings in which union representatives are present that the union representative(s) on EJEC be given about 15 minutes to give a brief outline of what the EJEC is doing and to ask their fellow union members for areas in which they are having problems in which EJEC could perhaps be of some assistance.
2. We would also like to ask Mr. Newman to write an informal note once each month to the EJEC outlining areas in which he feels the EJEC could be of potential assistance in resolving problems.

ROPER: EJEC-ISR INTERFACE

Another area in which we would like closer contact is with groups of employees—both management and union employees. We recommend that consideration be given to using the occasion of the survey feedback from the last survey in May, 1978, as an occasion to discuss in small groups the QWL program and what areas they feel it should be addressing more, which less, etc.

We have already had approved the same small group arrangement for the survey feedback and schedules for relief will be worked out to enable those to occur in, probably August depending upon when Mike Moch gets the data ready. We would like to recommend that an additional 30 minutes be allowed at those meetings to enable general QWL program discussions to occur.

A detailed planning report will be prepared shortly on this recommendation for review and, hopefully, approval by all appropriate authorities.

DALY: OFFSITE MEETINGS BETWEEN SUPERVISORS AND STEWARDS

As you know, in October of last year we held on off-site meeting with all supervision and union leadership of the plant that we all felt was very successful. We would like to recommend that at least two such meetings be held each year. We are presently preparing a planning report on this proposal as well.

BAILEY: PROCEDURES FOR PROJECT FOLLOW-UP

One of our major problem areas has been what many people both on the EJEC and in the bakery feel is very long periods of time to get EJEC projects approved. In many cases the projects were just of the type that take a long time. In other cases we—the EJEC—have done poor work in preparing for the project. In still other cases, poor follow-up has caused delays as well.

We are recommending a procedure to assist in making sure that approved EJEC projects are completed as quickly as possible. We will forward a detailed recommendation to all concerned very soon. Generally what we have in mind is a procedure on every approved project like

- Establish a schedule of time and due dates for each element of the project.
- Check that schedule with all appropriate parties to make sure we have a complete outline of events and to gain approval of the various steps and the names of those responsible for each—here in Reginal in management, the union or on the EJEC or in world headquarters, of FWIU HQ or wherever.
- Upon approval a schedule would be published with copies to all responsible persons with their due dates and to EJEC and JQWLAC.
- Each person responsible for some element of the project would then be asked to provide periodic status reports on his or her portion of the task with copies to all parties to ensure that we stay on track and know of delays and why they may be needed.

JOSEPHSON: EJEC INTERESTED IN CONTRACT ISSUES

Suggest here that Chuck [Josephson] say that we appreciate JQWLAC's action on our request for clarification of contract issues and EJEC's role in such actions. To ensure that we understand accurately your memo (reinforcing the need for EJEC to avoid getting into contract issues) I would like to tell you what we think your intent is and have you correct any errors that we may have—then go into the detailed memo and close with something like "of course we recognize and share your concern that we don't go off half cocked on some issue that is not what the people want or is something that clearly cannot be changed."

CLAYTON: INFORMATION FLOW

One of the general areas of concern for all employees in Reginal, management and union alike, has been what they see as lack of adequate information about changes that are occurring or are going to occur in the future. Not only was this very clear in the first survey data; it has been repeatedly brought to EJEC's attention since that survey was taken.

We also recognize that senior leadership of both the company and FWIU have in the past preferred to wait to discuss potential changes until all the details were known so that a clear picture can be presented. It is our view that not only do rumors get started about projects, innovations, and changes and local supervisory and union leadership are not informed sufficiently to squelch rumors but also we feel that employees (again supervision and hourly alike) do not have to have all the information about a change. For example, if a major change is being considered for a year from now a brief notice could be given saying what is planned and that details are not known at this time but will be provided as they come up.

In this way not only will a major need begin to be met but the EJEC would also know of planned changes and could then make recommendations of ways it might be able to help in not only reducing the resistance to change but also to suggest ways to involve supervision and employees in those changes to enable them to occur more efficiently in the future.

SHEFFER: CONFIRMATION OF EXTERNAL RESOURCES

Another policy area is in what external resources the EJEC can expect to have available for the balance of this year with Wayne Sholl phasing out, etc. We would like to confirm our understanding of what will be available to us.

We understand that a replacement for Joe Gromanger has been approved for a period of one year after Joe leaves. As previously reported by memo we are in the final processes of selecting a replacement at this time and hope to have that task finished by July 1 to enable Joe's replacement to begin work here about the middle of July.

We also understand that Tim Deigh will be visiting with us an average of twice each month for the balance of the year.

We also understand that resources from world headquarters and from FWIU international are available as we might request them.

Finally, we also understand that if additional resources are needed we can make recommendations to you for your consideration of those requests.

We would appreciate hearing from JQWLAC if these understandings are accurate.

JOSEPHSON: EJEC PLANS AND PROJECT BUDGETS

The EJEC would like to begin work immediately on preparing schedules and cost estimates for its activities for the balance of the year for submission to Mr. Matson, Mr. Newman, and JQWLAC.

Included in these projections will be our recommendations on costs and time involved in a number of areas.

- Off-site meetings mentioned by Nancy (Daly).
- The additional thirty minutes during the survey feedback meetings mentioned by Patricia Roper.
- Any books, magazines, and other materials that we might suggest.
- Recommendations in the areas of EJEC training and overall bakery training and communications as well.

We wanted you to be aware that we are planning to work on this type of project if you feel as we do that it would be more beneficial for our total planning purposes for this program.

On July 12 and 13, Tim Deigh conducted coaching sessions with each participant. The joint meeting began on the afternoon of the thirteenth. As had been the case the previous year, this was a formal EJEC meeting to which JQWLAC members had been invited. Other guests included the line 7 coordinators, Jones and Ashley, and the assessment coordinator.

Roger Matson and George Newman also attended as guests of the EJEC, because they had been excluded from direct EJEC participation. Touchette did not attend but had sent her alternate, Jose Martinez.

The meeting proceeded as scripted. Keeley reported two bake shop subcommittee projects completed, nine approved. Barrett reported nine recommendations from the packaging subcommittee, five completions, three underway, and one disapproved. The other subcommittee representatives presented similar information. Louis Young reported that the communications subcommittee had turned five projects over to the maintenance department for completion. Four projects were in process and six required more planning. Vince Keeley requested a labor allowance from the JQWLAC so that time allocated for training would not be charged against production labor hours.

Ben Ashley described how the first shift line 7 project had started with seventeen problem areas, but that this list had eventually grown to forty-five. Twenty-five of these had been addressed, thirteen were in process, and others had been dropped or postponed. Ashley presented several graphs reflecting changes in line 7 productivity over time. These charts showed that the first shift was more productive than the other line 7 shifts and had come closer to realizing standard package weights. They had lower waste rates and had dropped to almost zero absenteeism. George Newman asked why absenteeism on the line had dropped, and Scott Lowery volunteered that it was because the people were happier on the line.

Irene Jones then reported on the line 7 second shift project. They had nineteen projects, and three had been completed. Recently, the second shift employees had initiated a productivity competition with first shift and had defeated them on six of the eight days they had competed. Newman asked Jones whether the line was integrated all the way back to mixing. She answered affirmatively and noted that communication was better, because mixing employees were more involved and took more pride in what they were sending down the line.

Joan Franks and the other EJEC representatives then presented their prepared material. Josephson announced a coffee break following his presentation of EJEC plans for the future.

When members of both committees got back together, Josephson called for JQWLAC members to voice their concerns. Immediately, Premater asked EJEC members to report on how involved second and third shift employees were in the QWL Program. He noted that all EJEC projects started on first shift and that the other employees felt left out. Josephson admitted that there had been some resentment but that the line 7 project was now started on second shift. Premater said that this was just one project and asked whether there was more communication between the EJEC and second and third shift employees in general. At this point, Seldon broke in and congratulated the EJEC for their efficient reporting. Martinez asked Josephson to tell Premater that the EJEC had made an attempt to establish better communication with all employees by putting information sheets on tables in the cafeteria. Newman then commended the EJEC, saying: "There are intelligent people in the building. The EJEC thing is going to go. They've done a tremendous job."

Scigliano joined the chorus of those expressing support for what the EJEC had done. He said that when he had visited earlier, his shop stewards were suspicious of the program. They were, he said, suspicious no longer. The real question, he felt, was whether things had happened that wouldn't have happened without the Quality of Work Life program. The project was, in his opinion, worthwhile and had the potential of doing a great deal more. It would take time, but the EJEC members were making good progress.

Josh Atteberry asked whether the EJEC was going to develop a line 1 or line 2 project. Josephson, looking at Matson, asked "Mr. Matson?" Matson, smiling, said that the line-by-line concept would eventually be spread to all the lines. Premater offered his interpretation of Atteberry's question. He thought the line 7 project was suspicious, because it was not a difficult line, and recommended that the next line-by-line project be on a cookie line because "those people go home exhausted."

Matson agreed that line 7 had been selected because it was the easiest. Other employees were somewhat jealous, he said, but "there'll always be disgruntlement. Let the EJEC tell us what line to do next."

The topic then turned back to the original positive themes. George Newman told the members that Marjorie Touchette was very sorry to have missed the meeting and that she was very enthusiastic about the EJEC. John Papp complimented the EJEC members on their excellent and concise reports. He noted that the union was interested primarily in making jobs more enjoyable and that the management was mainly concerned about efficiency. Combining these two goals, he said, was something the JQWLAC really hadn't faced up to yet. Dalmar Pond tried to integrate the two goals:

> We're in business to be profitable, . . . and it depends, in part, on employees' attitude. But we're not perfect. It's difficult, for example, to give out all the information. This committee right here is a form of communication. We're not out to overwork people. We're concerned with productivity-quality. We're facing a market that isn't growing rapidly. With that type of market, you have to have quality. . . .

Nancy Daly noted that some of the people had not been properly trained. There also was resentment against all the attention given to first shift. Newman interjected at this point, asking Deigh to give his opinion of the Reginal project. Deigh felt that the EJEC had done "a hell of a good job." After additional discussion, Josephson thanked the JQWLAC members for their visit and closed the meeting.

After the joint session, JQWLAC members met privately. Their initial discussion revolved around bringing in a new assistant coordinator. Seldon asked Gromanger if he would submit a white paper before he left. Seldon was particularly interested in things Gromanger might have done differently if he had had the money and authority. Papp had heard that the program had to either take off or be terminated. He was optimistic about the future of the program, and claimed to have initially been "one of the negative people." Scigliano believed that there was so much talent in the plant that if "the positive people keep workin', the negative people [will] drop out."

Seldon had talked to several employees and everyone expressed a desire to continue the program. Deigh noted that tension over EJEC involvement in contract issues had lowered morale considerably. Premater felt that the program was at a crossroads. It would soon either succeed or fail. Deigh put the time frame for determining success or failure at six months. Pond questioned whether the program had done anyone any good outside of those who had served on the EJEC. He felt that listening to people's suggestions and ideas was valuable only in that people come to think they are being heard. Coy thought this itself was very positive outcome, and Seldon noted that "what is perceived is frequently more important than what is."

Legitimizing First-Order Change

The second joint EJEC-JQWLAC meeting continued the trend toward first-order rather than second-order change in Reginal. There was little or no discussion about new forms of corporate governance or about the human problems in the plant. Reasons for the animosity that surfaced during the survey feedback sessions were never identified. Rather, projects identified by supervisors, stewards, and most importantly, plant management were taken as the EJEC's own. Touchette, frustrated at this development and at Matson's refusal to deal with the issue of breaks, stopped coming to EJEC meetings even though she was one of the two chairpersons. She did not even attend the joint EJEC-JQWLAC meeting.

In Touchette's absence, the second joint EJEC-JQWLAC meeting took on the self-congratulatory tone, which had been written into participants' scripts. In the process, JQWLAC members, Deigh, and the other participants legitimized the trends that had characterized the program during the preceeding months. They had numerous projects and proposals to show for their efforts. Rather than challenge participants to negotiate a new consensus, however, Deigh allowed them to use their projects to justify and thereby maintain the perspectives they had when they started the program (Figures 3-1, 4-1). Deigh had orchestrated acceptance of the program at Reginal in a way that had failed to confront any group's perspective (Chapter 3). He orchestrated the presentations for this meeting in a similar way: that is, primarily as a series of success stories and recommendations for further development along lines already begun. The problems the EJEC had encountered with Matson were not addressed.

When dissent surfaced, it was quickly covered over. Seldon quickly responded to Premater's statement that employees on second and third shifts felt left out by congratulating the EJEC for their efficient reporting. When Nancy Daly noted that some employees were not being properly trained, George Newman asked Deigh to give his opinon of the Reginal project, and Deigh quickly complied. Newman also claimed that Touchette was very enthusiastic about the EJEC, a dubious claim at best. In the end, the role of the EJEC in the plant was inadvertently summarized by Josephson's answer to Atteberry's question about the EJEC's development of a new line-by-line project. As we noted earlier, Josephson turned to the plant manager and said, "Mr. Matson?"

10

Absorption

After the joint EJEC-JQWLAC meeting, Tim Deigh called for the EJEC to generate planning reports on several items. These included designing survey feedback sessions for the Time 2 questionnaires; planning a second off-site meeting between supervision, stewards, and EJEC members; involving Tom Gib in training programs and Martha Linz (an FWIU staff member) in communication projects; and diffusing the line 7 concept to the other lines in the plant.

Deigh's apparent enthusiasm contrasted with that of the EJEC members, particularly after they reviewed the results of the second plantwide survey. Despite some bright spots, these results were quite discouraging. As presented in Figure 10-1, slightly more than 40 percent of the union respondents agreed that "the employees' joint enrichment committee is doing a good job." This was up somewhat from the 35 percent in the first survey. However, management respondents were less positive than before. In the first survey, approximately 44 percent had reported that the EJEC was doing a good job. In the second, only 29 percent agreed with this assessment.

Over half of the union members and over 60 percent of the management respondents surveyed at Time 1 agreed that "the employees' joint enrichment committee represents my interests." The figures for the second survey were 38 percent and 26 percent respectively. Both union and management respondents believed they had less say in EJEC decisions at Time 2

Figure 10-1 Evaluation of the EJEC: Time 1 and Time 2 Comparisons

Time 1 Time 2

Percent agreeing with the statement:

The Employees' Joint Enrichment Committee is doing a good job.

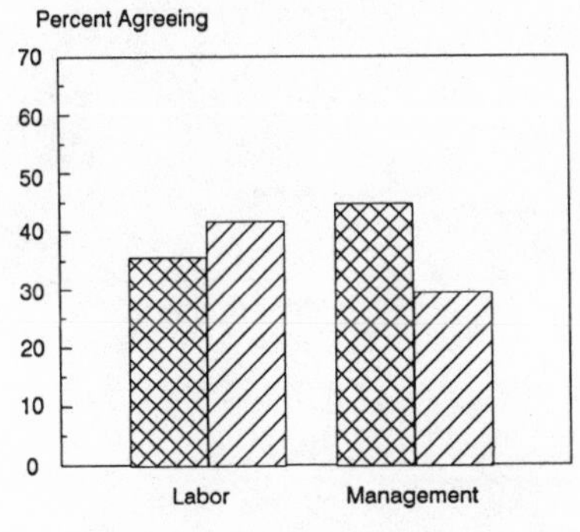

The Employees' Joint Enrichment Committee represents my interests.

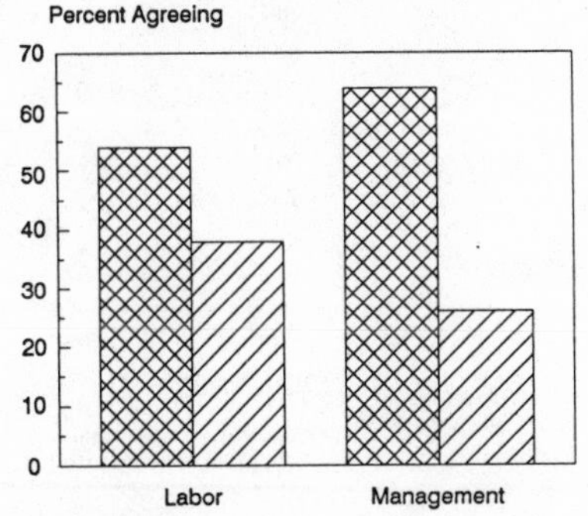

Percent agreeing with the statement:

I have a say in the decisions the Employees' Joint Enrichment Committee makes.

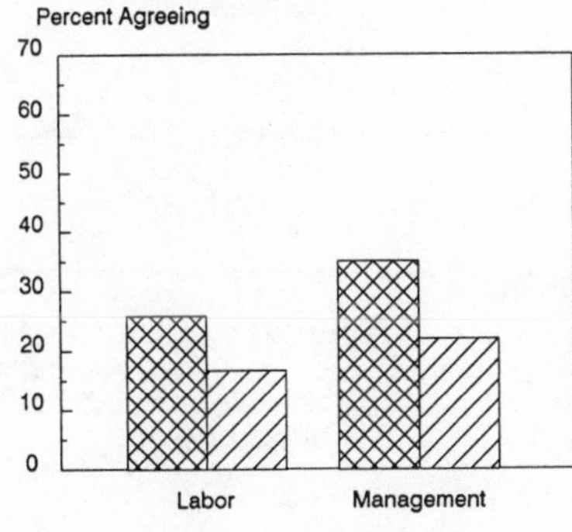

The Employees' Joint Enrichment Committee is needed here.

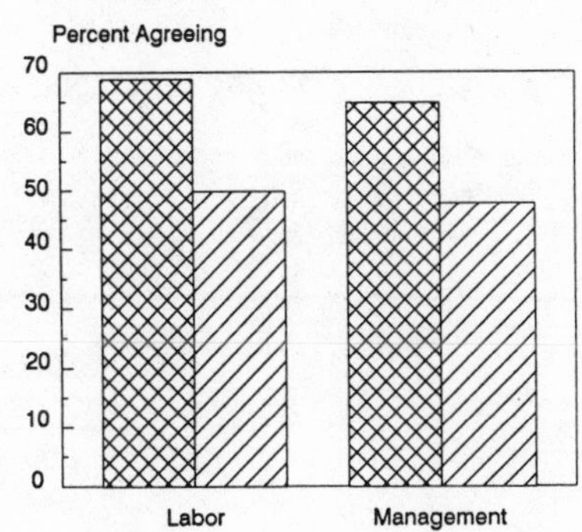

than at Time 1. Finally, although a majority of respondents in the first survey thought that the EJEC was needed, fewer than half thought so at Time 2.

EJEC members were discouraged that few of those responding to the survey seemed to have benefited from the various QWL projects. As shown in Figure 10-2, a significant percent

Figure 10-2 QWL Projects and Employee Responses: Labor-Management Comparisons

Responses to the question:
How much has this project increased the quality of your life at work?

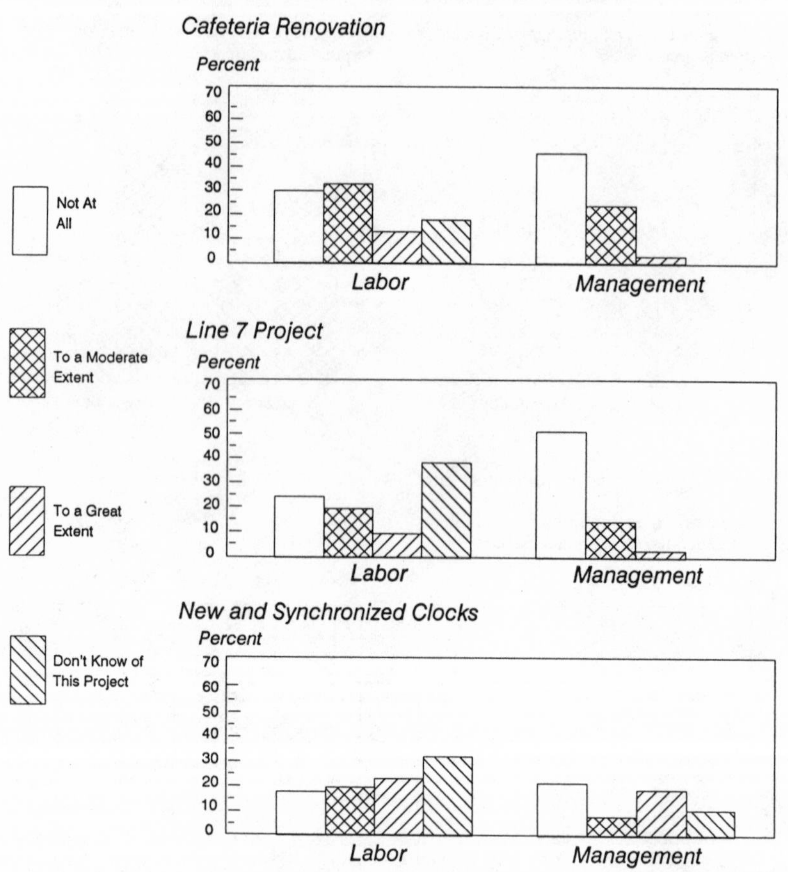

was not even aware of such projects as the cafeteria renovation, the line 7 project, new synchronized clocks, and the new departmental notebooks. Many who were aware of these activities reported that the activities had not increased the quality of their life at work. Although a significant number of respon-

Figure 10-2 (continued)

Responses to the question:
How much has this project increased the quality of your life at work?

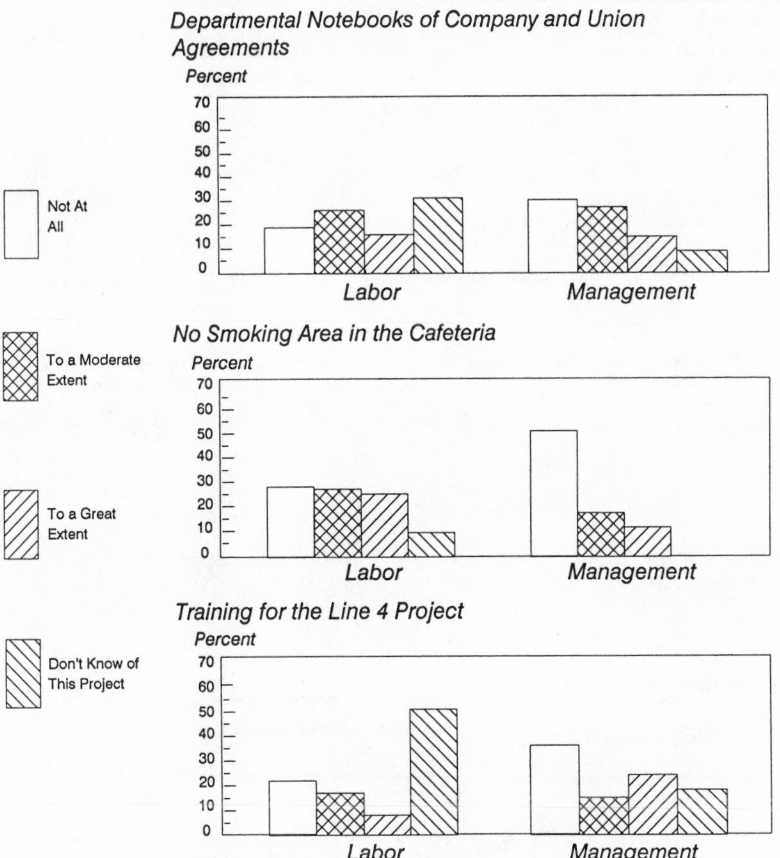

dents reported that the new clocks and the departmental notebooks had increased the quality of their work life, the EJEC viewed these as exceptions.

The data also indicated there had been little change in the percentage agreeing to several statements that had been discussed in the survey feedback sessions the year before (Figures

Figure 10-3 Employee Responses to Selected Items: Time 1 and Time 2 Comparisons

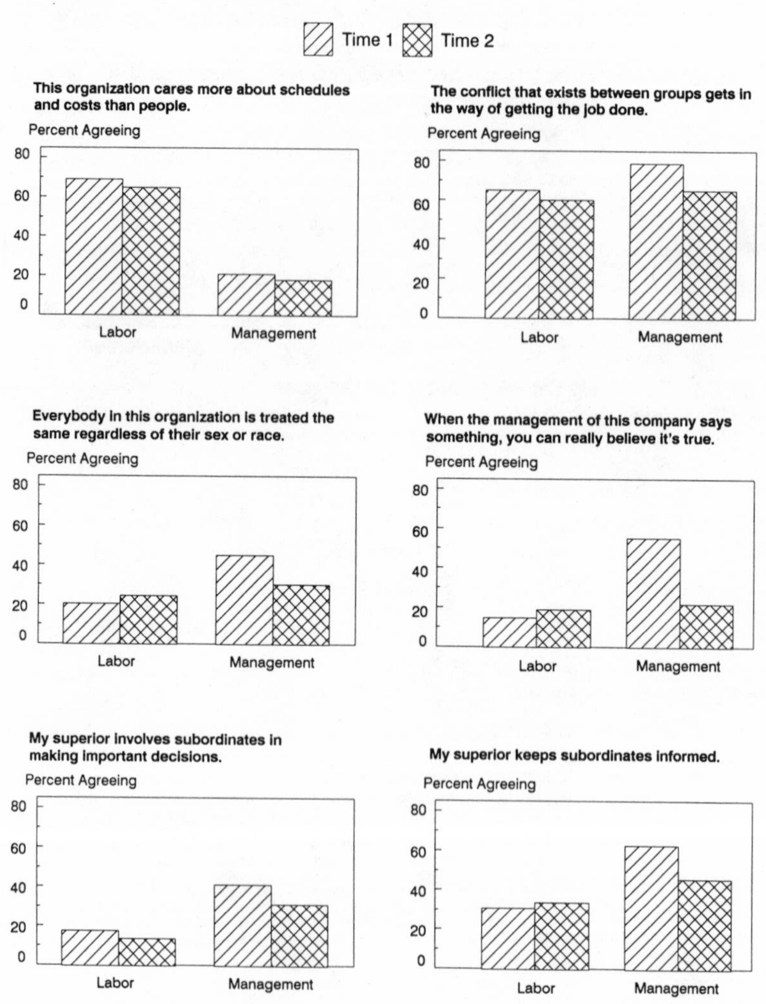

8-4 and 8-5). As noted in Figure 10-3, the percent agreeing that "this organization cares more about schedules and costs than people" had declined, but only slightly. Likewise, a slightly smaller percent agreed that "the conflict that exists between

groups gets in the way of getting the job done." Among union employees, there was a bit more agreement that "everybody in this organization is treated the same regardless of their sex or race." However, the percent of management respondents agreeing with this statement declined from about 45 percent to around 30 percent.

Union employees also were slightly more inclined to agree that "when the management of this company says something, you can really believe it's true." Managers, however, were less inclined to agree with this than they had been previously. During the first survey, approximately 55 percent of the managers agreed. During the second survey, only 22 percent of the managers did so. For both union and management, there was a slight decline in the percent agreeing that "my superior involves subordinates in making important decisions." The percent of union employees agreeing that "my superior keeps subordinates informed" increased slightly; however, the percent of managers agreeing with this declined from just over 60 percent to 45 percent. Overall, there were mixed results for union employees but consistent negative results for managers.

There were many possible reasons for these results. The committee had requested data from all personnel, rather than just those who had filled out Time 1 questionnaires. However, because the plant had experienced considerable increase in demand for its product, many additional employees had been hired. Consequently, a good number of the respondents to the second survey had not been working at FoodCom at the time of the first survey. Increased production demands themselves could have been responsible for some of the differences in results. The EJEC members, however, did not attribute the results to such factors. Meeting on June 29, they had a variety of other explanations. Some thought that the EJEC had done little good for employees, but had put more pressure on them. Others said that the EJEC wasn't doing enough to find out what the employees really wanted. There were other explanations and responses. A sampling, taken as the EJEC was reviewing the survey results, is presented in Exhibit 10-1.

EXHIBIT 10-1 Sample of EJEC Members' Reactions to Employee Responses Reported in the Second Plantwide Survey

Chuck Josephson:	What can you do to please people? Already people are complaining about the crowding in the new cafeteria. Also, we've rebuilt line 4 platforms four times.
Susan Sheffer:	EJEC members aren't talking to outsiders like we used to. . . . We're fallin' down on the job.
Chuck Josephson:	You can mention EJEC and they put you down.
Susan Sheffer:	Right!
Bobby Clayton:	I was gonna say the same thing. I try to explain. . . . One guy says the company wants to take money out of his check. You get put down every time you open your mouth.
Susan Sheffer:	Eighty percent of the people reject any kind of change.
Joel Barrett:	[We] haven't sold it to the people.
Nancy Daly:	They've been askin' for a stair on number 1. They need things they can see. The packaging department [subcommittee] chair [Johnny Pepin] has changed things and nothin' has happened.
Chuck Josephson:	This is the first I've heard about it.
Judy Martin:	Where are stairs needed?
Nancy Daly:	Number 99 line.
Judy Martin:	People feel a guard on the parking lot is more important.
Chuck Josephson:	That project is underway.
Judy Martin:	The lot sticker number fades.
Chuck Josephson:	That's not the sticker EJEC recommended. Some people took it on their own to do this.
Judy Martin:	EJEC gets blamed.
Joel Barrett:	Get a fast fry service.
Nancy Daly:	First shift is OK. . . . Second shift is terrible. When you order a hamburger, you don't know what color it is [going to be].
Judy Martin:	They was pre-fryin' and puttin' it in water . . . to give faster service. Have 'em come back at two or three [o'clock] with fresh food.

Chuck Josephson: Turn these problems over to the cafeteria subcommittee.

Judy Martin: People don't see any action.

Chuck Josephson: Have a survey.

Joan Franks: When we had the first survey, people on EJEC were talkin' to other people. This time we weren't.

Jose Martinez: Communication. People don't know enough about EJEC.

Nancy Daly: You always passin' out surveys and not doin' anything.

Chuck Josephson: Requisitions take time.

Louis Young: Very little time has been spent on these projects. We won't make faster progress until we get more time.

Chuck Josephson: We only work on projects once per month [in subcommittee meetings].

Louis Young: Until we complete a major project, nothin'll change.

Scott Lowery: JQWLAC didn't want to hear nothin' bad.

Nancy Daly: Not one major thing's been done in the packin' department. Clocks still off time.

Scott Lowery: The satellite lounge (for the packing department) was rejected by the committee. But JQWLAC didn't ask about that.

Vince Keeley: The assembly shop is OK, 'cause of the air conditioner.

Nancy Daly: We don't have anything.

Jose Martinez: People also are not aware these are EJEC projects.

Joe Gromanger: On the cafeteria project [survey], seventy-three people said they didn't know about the project.

Louis Young: Didn't know it was an EJEC project.

Joe Gromanger: People blamed the absence of knives and forks on the EJEC.

Judy Martin: We bring up different things, but nothin's ever pinpointed. Put a place on the bulletin board: EJEC Projects Completed. People can see what EJEC have accomplished.

Chuck Josephson: Will people pay any more attention than they are now?

Louis Young:	Three to four weeks ago the communication [sub]committee met with Matson. We're talkin' about an intercom. Why can't we report on the EJEC this way?
Susan Sheffer:	Here we go again, talkin' about two to three different things. When we leave today, we'll not have done nothin'.
Bobby Clayton:	We get off on tangents.
Nancy Daly:	We never get back to these things.
Judy Martin:	What exactly has the EJEC accomplished? Maybe if you put a poster out, people will notice.
Chuck Josephson:	I'm going to cut off discussion about the cafeteria. . . .

Modeling the Decline of Support for the EJEC in Reginal

Early proponents of the QWL program for FoodCom appeared to subscribe to a relatively undifferentiated model of how the program would work (Figures 2-2 and 3-1). This model was based on the assumption that management and union participants had shared interests and would be able to identify projects that would advance these interests (Cammann et al. 1984, ch. 1).

A version of this model is presented in Figure 10-4. It specifies that QWL projects would be found that were cost-justifiable, compatible with current management structures and procedures, directed toward increasing line employees' satisfaction with extrinsic aspects of their work, and consistent with union structures and procedures. This model, particularly the emphasis on extrinsic satisfaction, was not entirely consistent with the original design of the QWL programs (cf., Drexler and Lawler 1977; Nadler 1978). However, from the beginning of the project, employees in Reginal responded to the QWL program in terms of extrinsic factors.

Based on their belief in shared interests, the QWL change agents at Reginal initially assumed that activities and projects could be identified and undertaken by joint labor-management committees and that these projects would benefit members of all critical constituencies, including multiple unions. These

Figure 10-4 Initial Implicit Model of the QWL Process in Reginal

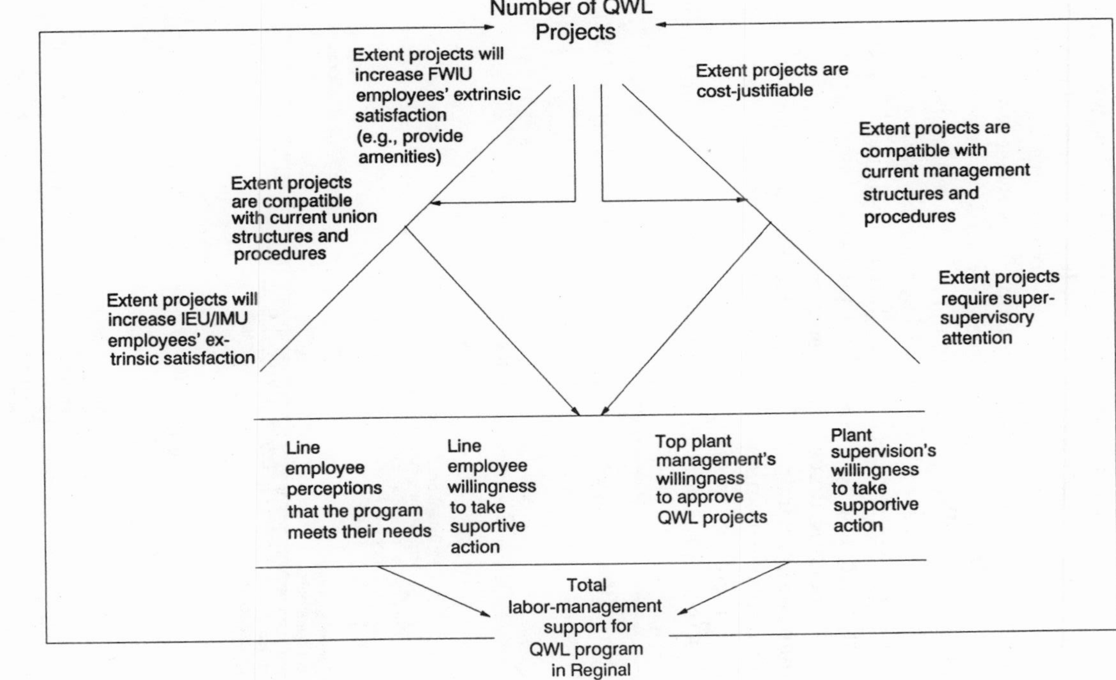

projects and activities would not require disproportionate effort on the part of supervision.

Finally, the initial model at Reginal assumed that adequate resources and slack would be available. This was not the case. The strict accounting control system specified standards for the number of labor hours allowed to produce a specified amount of product. The loss of time from employees who participated in EJEC activities therefore threatened to affect operating efficiency. Moreover, QWL projects that required additional labor hours—such as installing new clocks, changing shower heads, adding new lighting fixtures, and so forth—could add to costs in ways that could not be retrieved by receiving budgetary variances for EJEC meeting times. The ever-present accounting control system, therefore, restrained QWL projects because they caused short-term increases in costs, even though they might have led to long-term increases in efficiency.

A second model of the QWL process in Reginal is presented

Figure 10-5 Approximation of an Actual Model of QWL Program Processes

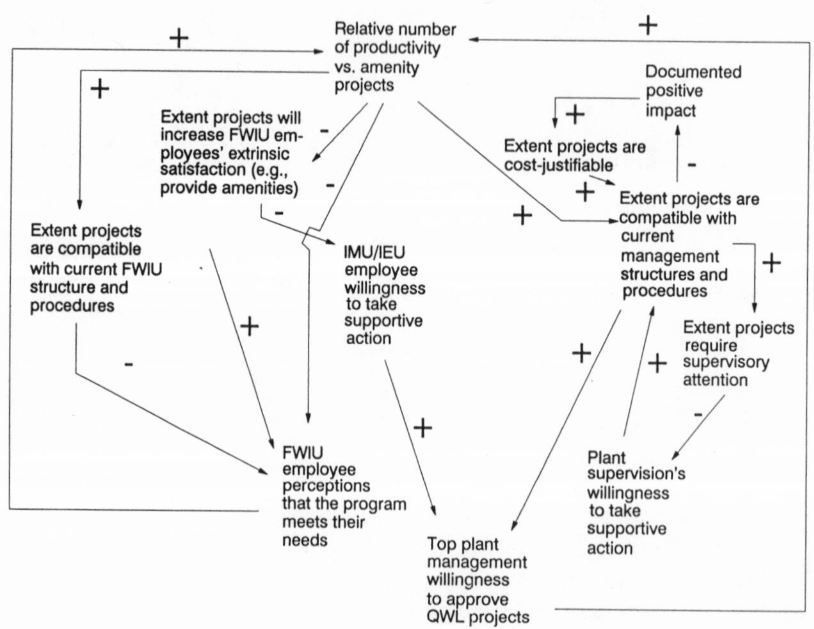

in Figure 10-5. Though it lacks detail, this model is a more accurate approximation of what eventually evolved in Reginal. It differs from Figure 10-4 in several respects. First, it acknowledges that there were different types of projects in Reginal and that different projects had differential appeal to different constituencies (cf., Figure 4-1). For example, managers tended to favor projects directed toward improving productivity, but line employees saw the QWL program as an opportunity to secure amenities. At any given time, the mix of QWL projects would reflect the program's emphasis on productivity versus the acquisition of amenities.

Figure 10-5 suggests additional conflicts embedded in the program in Reginal. The model differentiates among projects on the basis of their cost-justifiability and their compatibility with current management structures and procedures. Productivity projects were most compatible with current management structures and procedures. The more compatible the projects were with established practices, however, the less apparently cost-justifiable they tended to be. For example, assigning a line coordinator to the line 7 project was resisted because it would increase either the number of labor hours or the burden on the remaining supervisors. Unless the evaluation criteria or the assessment system changed, therefore—and this would represent a substantial departure from established practice—even relatively small changes would result in negative assessments, at least in the short run. In general, therefore, the projects most compatible with established management practice were the most vulnerable to negative assessments made using the criterion of short-term costs. Every project suggested involved short-term costs that exceeded short-term benefits.

The model in Figure 10-5 also differentiates among four considerations that affected labor-management support for the QWL program in Reginal: requirements for supervisory attention, top plant management's need to approve projects, line employees' perceptions that the projects were meeting their needs, and IMU/IEU employees' willingness to take supportive action. Contrary to the initial assumption of labor-management shared interests in Figure 10-4, the model treats these four considerations as separate, although interdependent. Each of these considerations involved contradictions that led to declining support for the program. For example, the more a project was compatible with current management structures and procedures, the more it required supervisory attention. However, this requirement increased plant supervisors' administrative burden, which decreased their willingness to support the project.

Plant management approved projects to the extent they were compatible with established practice. EJEC projects therefore became increasingly dominated by productivity projects that were not easily distinguishable from those that would, or should, have been undertaken by management in any case without the extra stimulus or support of the QWL program. The more this happened, the less likely the projects were to challenge the short-term orientation of the accounting control system and offer alternatives to supervisory authority. Consequently, the program received declining support from those alerted to declining performance by the accounting control system and from those who found themselves responsible for administering QWL projects.

The movement away from amenity projects to projects that were indistinguishable from those falling under the exclusive purview of management had another adverse consequence. Increasingly, FWIU employees thought that the program was not meeting their needs or representing their interests. Many also resented the EJEC's increasing involvment with essentially managerial functions. A declining percentage, therefore, believed that the EJEC was needed in Reginal.

The more EJEC members thought that QWL projects were not responsive to the interests of the rank-and-file, the more they pushed for projects that would improve employee satisfaction with extrinsic aspects of work. Touchette's attempt to extend break times for packing department employees is an example. Had she succeeded, packing department employees might have thought the QWL program was addressing their needs. However, because break time was a contractual issue, dealing with it through the QWL program was vigorously resisted by union officials, particularly Premater and the union stewards. Addressing the problem of differential break time between FWIU and IMU employees, moreover, was seen by several stewards as violating the traditional grievance procedure.

Additionally, had Touchette succeeded in extending break time for packing department employees, it is unlikely that IMU or IEU workers would have remained silent. The history of the relationship between the IMU and the FWIU was filled with concerns about the relative benefits received by both groups. Had FWIU employees—particularly the women in the packing department—received greater benefits, the IMU local would almost surely have pressed for a compensatory increase for themselves in order to restore the traditional relationship between the parties.

Given the dynamics underlying events in Reginal (as specified in Figure 10-5), support for the QWL program was bound to erode. Unless the interests of the contending parties could be reconciled or their underlying perspectives significantly altered, the program seemed doomed.

Proposals for reconciling divergent interests required significant changes in established management and union practices. They were rejected (as would be consistent with the model in Figure 10-5). Gain sharing, for example, was rejected by management and by union members of JQWLAC.

There were few attempts to generate alternative perspectives. Line employees continued to focus on amenities and blame management. Management continued to seek productivity gains based primarily on instrumental relationships with employees who were given little responsibility. As turnover occurred among the EJEC members, the familiar perspectives were called up by the new participants and became an institutionalized part of the QWL program in Reginal (cf., Levitt and March 1988).

PATTERNS OF OPERATING EFFICIENCY IN REGINAL

Management frequently cited efficiency concerns as reasons for curtailing EJEC activities, sometimes attributing efficiency declines to the QWL program itself. Advocates of the QWL program insisted that their efforts would lead to increased productivity in the long run. It is therefore important to attempt to document patterns of operating efficiency in Reginal during the program.

The accounting control system generated statistics reflecting pounds produced and discarded per labor hour, downtime due to a variety of factors, and what was called "yield" (the number of pounds of product produced per hundred pounds of flour). Statistics, particularly pounds produced and discarded per labor hour, were aggregated from dozens of products. These products varied considerably in weight per package, standard yield, and in the standard number of labor hours required for their production and packaging. To avoid the problems associated with aggregating across a variety of products, the assessors decided to focus on the patterns of efficiency of single products.

There were different mixes of products produced each week. Two products, however, were produced almost every week. One was produced exclusively on line 7, the line subject to the first line-by-line intervention. The other was produced primarily on line 3. However, the line 3 production process was sufficiently similar to that used on line 7 to allow some of the line 3 product to be produced on line 7. Line 3 production therefore might provide comparisons that could assist in teasing out any impact of the line-by-line project.

Data on pounds produced and discarded, the number of labor hours allocated to each product, downtime due to production problems, and yield were gathered on both of these products between January 1, 1977, and March 26, 1979. The data included separate numbers for labor hours allocated in the baking and packing departments. Because these were very highly correlated and produced precisely the same results, only labor hours for the packing department are considered here. Unfortunately, data for a three-month period starting on January 1, 1978 were destroyed before they could be logged by the assessors. The rest of the data are available for inspection below.

Beginning in late December 1977 and continuing throughout the winter of 1978, the plant experienced a substantial increase in the demand for many of its products. Consequently, additional employees were hired, and lines were run on more shifts than previously. The number of shift ovens (number of shifts × number of ovens × number of days in the week) running each week is presented in Figure 10-6. This graph vividly depicts the increase in plant activity that occurred after December 1977 (week 52).

Neither product selected for detailed assessment experienced greater demand. The number of line 7 units scheduled for production each week is presented in Figure 10-7. The number of line 3 units scheduled for production each week is presented in Figure 10-8. Line 3 production appears to peak in advance of January 1978 (week 53). By March, it was back down within a more normal range. After that, demand appears to have fallen off, before peaking again around December 1978 (week 87).

Because there were so many EJEC projects and other events, it is not possible to correlate specific projects with particular variances in efficiency. It is possible, however, to document patterns in efficiency over time and to note any correspondence between these patterns and management perceptions concerning levels of operating efficiency in the plant. Of particular concern is the relationship between the increased demand for the plant's product and efficiency on lines 7 and 3. If efficiency in producing these two products declined during the period of increased demand,

Figure 10-6 Number of Shift Ovens

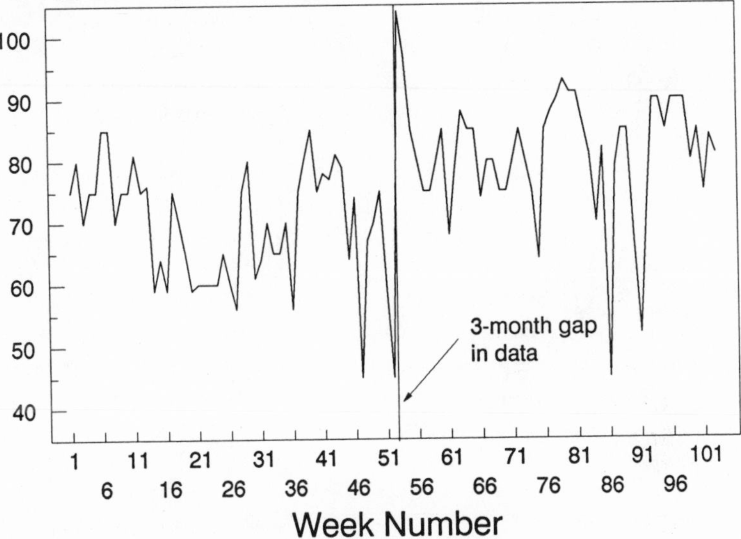

* Number of ovens multiplied by the number of shifts multiplied by the number of working days in the week

Figure 10-7 Number of Units Planned for Production: Line 7

Number of Units

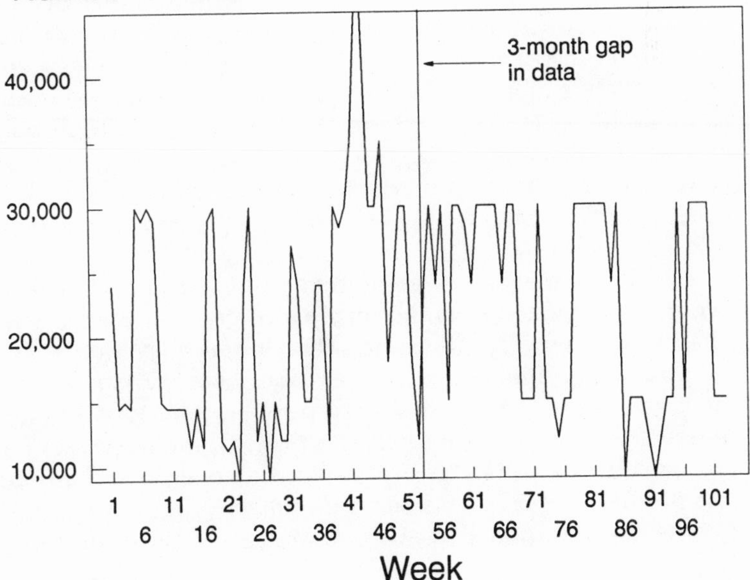

Figure 10-8 Number of Units Planned for Production: Line 3

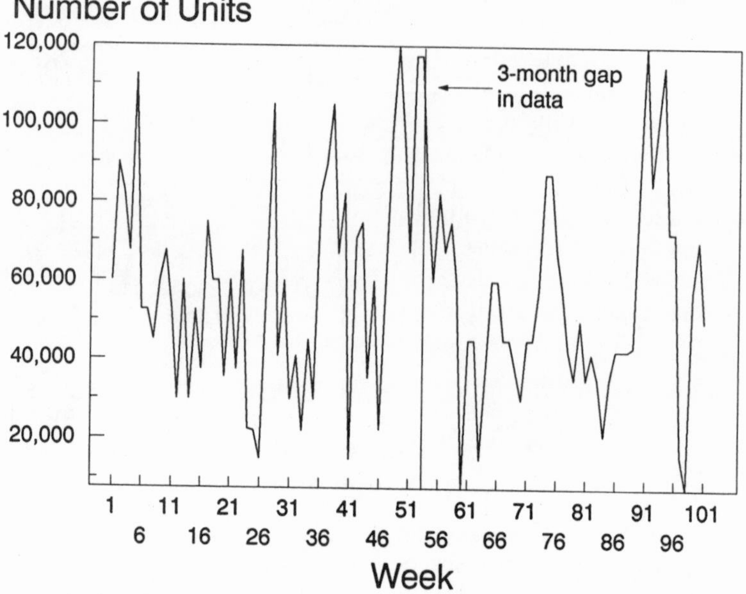

one might argue that the decline was due to increasing work load rather than the QWL program. Pounds produced and discarded, production downtime, and yield on lines 3 and 7 may have been a function of increasing pressure attributable to increasing demand for the plant's other products. Maintenance activities on lines 3 or 7, for example, might have been postponed in order to respond to other requirements. Hiring relatively untrained employees might have adversely affected productivity on lines 3 or 7 regardless of whether the demand for the two products produced on these lines had increased.

To address this issue, we present a number of figures, each of which includes adjusted and unadjusted graphs. In each case the first unadjusted graph illustrates the efficiency level on a particular measure (pounds discarded per labor hour, production downtime, yield, and pounds produced per labor hour) for a particular product over time. The second, adjusted graph corresponds to the same efficiency levels on this product over time adjusted for the number of shift ovens and the number of units scheduled for production. The adjusted measure of pounds per labor hour produced controls for the number of shift ovens, the number of units scheduled for production, pounds per labor hour discarded, production downtime, and yield. Controlling for the other three measures of efficiency as well as the two exogenous factors (shift ovens and product units scheduled) in the case of pounds produced per labor hour is justified, because discarded product, downtime, and yield (which to some extent was a function of humidity, among other things) were each determinants of bottom-line efficiency: pounds produced per labor hour expended. By looking at each of the determinants of bottom-line efficiency (pounds discarded per labor hour, production downtime, and yield) and pounds produced per labor hour *net of the primary determinants*, it may be possible to make more discriminating inferences from the data.*

Efficiency for the Product Produced on Line 7

To assist the reader in correlating events with plots of the efficiency data, we list the week numbers, dates, and significant milestones or events of the program. This information for weeks for which line 7 data were available is presented in Exhibit 10-2. The number of pounds discarded per labor hour in the packing department for the product produced on line 7 is presented in Figure 10-9. The unadjusted data suggest an upward trend. Peaks in pounds discarded per labor hour appear between weeks 41 and 55. The highest discard rate is logged for the first period following the

* Considerable effort was made to model the relationships among the respective time-series using transfer function time-series analysis (cf., Box and Jenkins, 1976; Liu and Hudak 1985). Using this approach, it is notoriously difficult to filter the dependent series sufficiently to eliminate autocorrelation. In addition, this approach was complicated by the necessity of conducting separate analyses on the various series before and after the three-month gap in the data. Between two to five transfer functions had to be considered simultaneously. However, since autocorrelation appears to bias estimates of the variances around parameters rather than the parameters themselves (McCain and McCleary, 1979, p. 234), it was possible to conduct standard regressions on each series and to plot the residuals. Due to the presence of autocorrelation, it is not possible to make inferences from significance tests of the coefficients for each of the independent variables. However, the estimates of the residuals are based upon the estimates of the coefficients rather than the variances around these coefficients and, therefore, ought to be unbiased by autocorrelation. While not an ideal procedure, this approach was considered acceptable for the purpose of the above analysis.

three-month gap in data, suggesting that pounds discarded might have been high during the high-volume winter period. Essentially the same pattern appears in the adjusted data. During the QWL program, the number of pounds of the line 7 product discarded per labor hour appears to have increased, net of variations in product or plant-level demand. As indicated in Exhibit 10-2, Matson complained of declining efficiency during October 1977. The first

EXHIBIT 10-2 Week Numbers, Dates, and Milestones: Line 7

Week	Date	Milestone	Week	Date	Milestone
1	1/3/77		41	10/10/77	Matson claims efficiency is down 20%.
2	1/10/77	First EJEC meeting occurs.	42	10/17/77	Product is lost on line 6.
3	1/17/77	Gromanger begins work in Reginal.	43	10/24/77	The first supervisors-stewards off-site meeting occurs.
4	1/24/77		44	10/31/77	
5	1/31/77		45	11/7/77	
6	2/7/77		46	11/14/77	
7	2/14/77	Assessors conduct open-ended interviews.	47	11/21/77	
8	2/21/77		48	11/28/77	
9	2/28/77	Deigh writes letter to Struthers attacking "efficiency-at-any-cost" mentality.	49	12/5/77	JQWLAC is told efficiency in Reginal is declining. New EJEC members are elected. Line 7 project starts. The new management training program is announced. COD reduces involvement in Reginal. Touchette fights for more break time. Cafeteria renovation begins.
10	3/7/77		50	12/12/77	
11	3/14/77	A nonsmoking area is created in the cafeteria.	51	12/19/77	
12	3/21/77		52	12/26/77	3-month data gap
13	3/28/77		53	4/3/78	
14	4/4/77		54	4/10/78	Premater and Coy visit Reginal.
15	4/11/77		55	4/17/78	Training committee submits recommendations.
16	4/18/77		56	4/24/78	
17	4/25/77		57	5/1/78	
18	5/2/77		58	5/8/78	Line-by-line project starts on line 7, second shift.
19	5/9/77	Training begins for line 4 conversion.	59	5/15/78	
20	5/16/77	The first plantwide survey is administered.	60	5/22/78	Communication committee submits recommendations.
21	5/23/77	The national QWL conference is held in Washington D.C.	61	5/29/78	Departmental record books become available.
22	5/30/77		62	6/5/78	Underweight packages are reported.
23	6/6/77	Uniform samples arrive in Reginal.	63	6/12/78	
24	6/13/77		64	6/19/78	Second joint JQWLAC-EJEC meeting
25	6/20/77	The cafeteria/restroom committee meets with Matson.	65	6/26/78	
26	6/27/77	The clocks are synchronized.	66	7/3/78	
27	7/4/77	Plant efficiency is seen as declining. The cafeteria/restroom committee meets with Matson. The parking lot committee meets with Matson. Sholl recommends a politial strategy to the EJEC.	67	7/10/78	
28	7/11/77		68	7/17/78	
29	7/18/77	The first joint JQWLAC-EJEC meeting occurs.	69	7/24/78	
30	7/25/77		70	7/31/78	
31	8/1/77	The plant fails a health inspection.	71	8/7/78	
32	8/8/77		72	8/14/78	
33	8/15/77		73	8/21/78	Second supervisors-stewards off-site meeting occurs.
34	8/22/77		74	8/28/78	
35	8/29/77		75	9/4/78	Matson reports breakdown on line 3.
36	9/5/77		76	9/11/78	
37	9/12/77		77	9/18/78	
38	9/19/77		78	9/25/78	
39	9/26/77	Survey feedback sessions begin.	79	10/2/78	
40	10/3/77		80	10/9/78	

Figure 10-9 Pounds Discarded per Labor Hour: Packing Department, Line 7

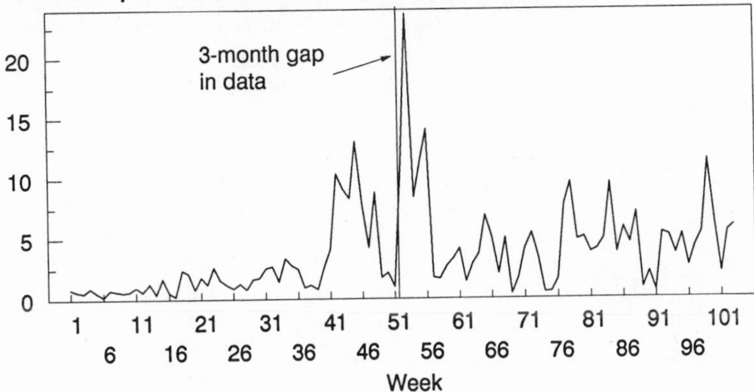

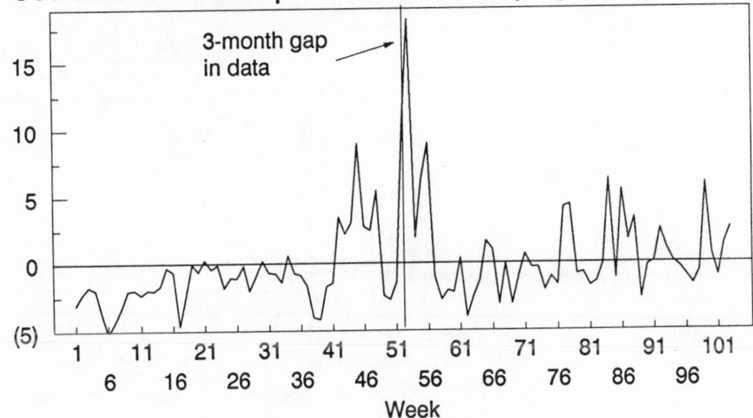

* Adjustments for run size and number of shift ovens

significant peak in pounds discarded started just after the first survey feedback sessions were initiated.

Unadjusted and adjusted production downtime for line 7, illustrated in Figure 10-10, appears to have been relatively stable over the course of the QWL program. If any pattern is visible, it appears that downtime after the three-month gap in data may have been lower than downtime before this period. Three of the peaks in

Figure 10-10 Production Downtime: Packing Department, Line 7

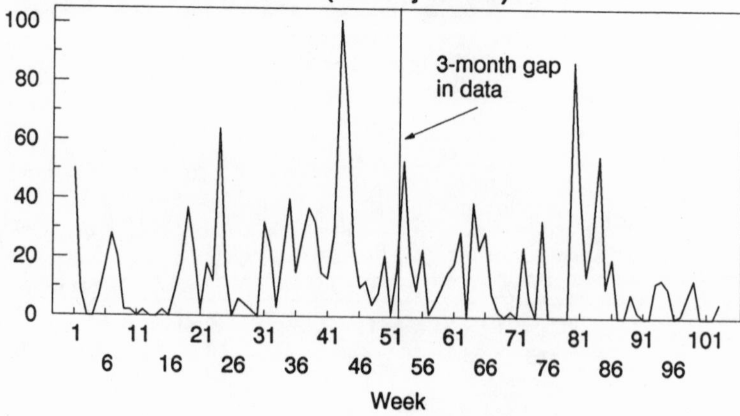

Production Downtime (Adjusted) *

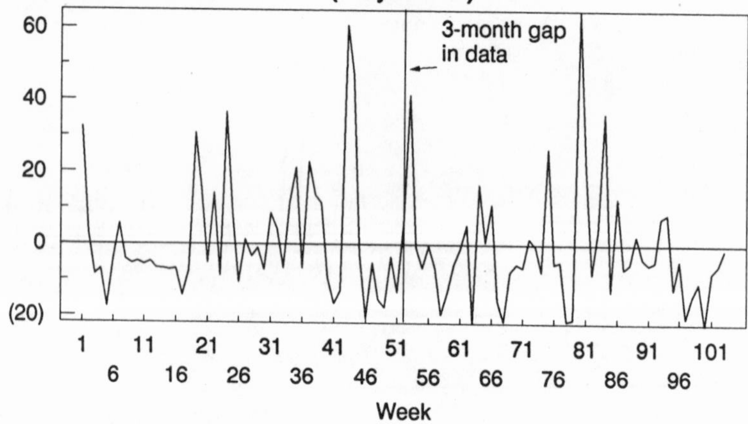

* Adjustments for run size and number of shift ovens

downtime for line 7 occurred during the period we have discussed to this point. The first, coming around weeks 19 through 25, covers the period during which training for line 4 conversion began and the first plantwide survey was administered. The second covers weeks 42 through 45, when the first survey feedback meetings were held. This is also the period of highest demand for the prod-

Figure 10-11 Yield: *Packing Department, Line 7

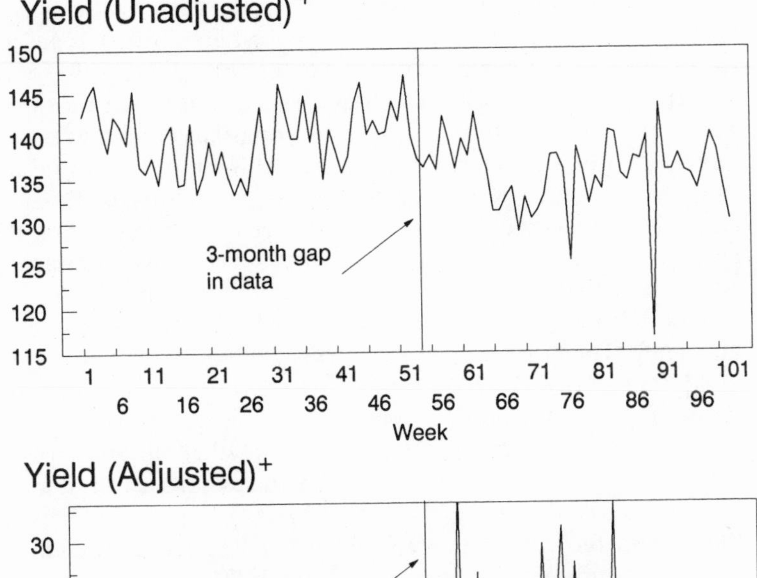

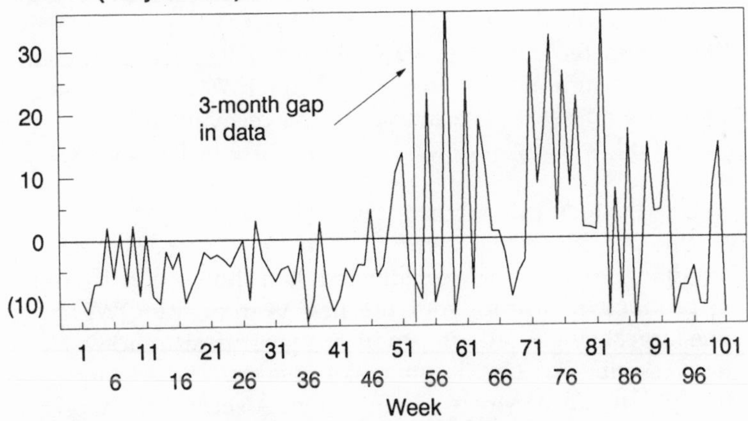

* Pounds of product produced per hundred pounds of flour
+ Adjustments for run size and number of shift ovens

uct produced on line 7 (cf., Figure 10-7). However, as noted above, the adjusted data controls for the number of units planned for production. It appears that production downtime peaked during weeks 42 through 45 *net of the impact of increased production demands*. The third peak covers the period immediately following the winter during which production demands on the plant increased substantially.

Adjusted yield for the line 7 product, reported in Figure 10-11, appears to have decreased and then increased during the first fifty-two weeks. It appears to have decreased substantially between week 53 and approximately week 65, whereupon it rose again to around mean levels. With the exception of week 91, which occurred after the period discussed so far, there are no obvious peaks or troughs in these data, suggesting that yield might be relatively immune to short-term shocks. This figure might be more sensitive to longer-term factors such as the nature of the wheat crop. The lowest yields during the first year of the program, however, occurred soon after the plantwide survey was administered. After that, there was a drop in yield at approximately week 41, a period subsequently identified by management as one of low efficiency. The line-by-line project was well underway by week 53. Yield between weeks 53 and 64 was well within acceptable range. It only fell after the second joint JQWLAC-EJEC meeting.

Adjusted yield figures present a somewhat different picture. Adjusted yield before week 51 is on the whole lower than it is after week 51. Moreover, the dip and recovery period observed in the unadjusted data after week 51 does not appear in the adjusted data. A trough around weeks 65 through 70 is in evidence; however, the adjusted data show a rapid recovery to above average yields followed by another period of more or less average performance.

Unadjusted and adjusted pounds produced per labor hour in the packing department for the line 7 product are presented in Figure 10-12. The unadjusted data show a consistent decline in productivity throughout the first year of the QWL program. The largest single drop in productivity occurs around week 19, the time training for line 4 conversion begins, and continues as the first plantwide survey is administered. A second fairly precipitous decline occurs after week 41, the same time as the single largest product demand. A third decline occurs around week 71; however, this decline does not coincide with any significant QWL program activity.

The unadjusted data during the second year suggest that the overall declining trend appears to have been reversed, with productivity rising to nearly preprogram levels. The adjusted data tell a somewhat different story. Drops in productivity are still in evidence between weeks 18 and 22 and around week 71. However, the decline around week 41 is gone, suggesting that production requirements (discarded product, downtime, and yield) were

Figure 10-12 Pounds Produced per Labor Hour: Packing Department, Line 7

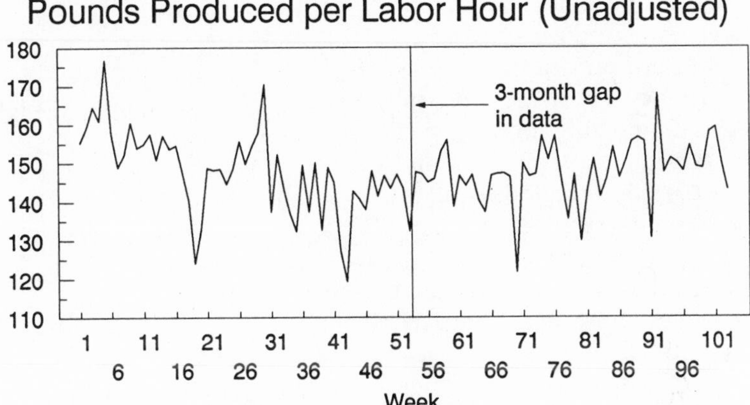

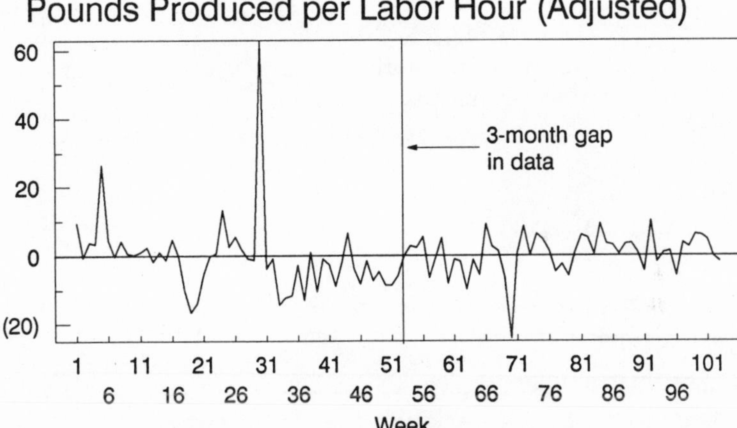

* Adjustments for run size, number of shift ovens, pounds discarded per labor hour, production downtime, and yield

responsible for the problem. In addition, the increase in productivity during the last fifty-two weeks is much less pronounced. It appears that much, if not all, of this increase was due to production demand, discarded product, downtime, yield, or a combination of these factors. The adjusted data further suggest that productivity declined from approximately week 32 to 52 and increased during the period of missing data. With the exception of the decline around week 71, productivity varied very little from the overall average during the second year of assessment.

In summary, the evidence suggests that efficiency for the line 7 product declined during the QWL program. Specifically, the number of pounds discarded per labor hour in the packing department appears to have increased. In addition, some variances in efficiency occurred concurrently with significant QWL program events, notably around weeks 19 and 41 through 50, when training for line 4 conversion and the first plantwide survey occurred, respectively. Pounds discarded per labor hour increased over the course of the QWL program. There were noticeable spikes in production downtime around the times of the training for line 4 conversion and the first survey feedback sessions.

Pounds produced per labor hour appear to have declined during the training for line 4 conversion. A precipitous decline in pounds produced per labor hour during the first survey feedback sessions appears to have been a function of other factors. Increases in pounds discarded, however, does not seem to be explained by demand factors. Co-occurrence of variation in pounds discarded, production downtime, and pounds produced also cannot be explained by production factors. We therefore cannot dismiss attributions made by plant management that some QWL projects, notably training for line 4 conversion and the plant-wide survey and feedback activities, adversely affected plant productivity and efficiency, at least in the case of the product produced on line 7.

Efficiency for the Product Produced on Line 3

The log of events by date for the line 3 data is presented in Exhibit 10-3. The numbers and dates are somewhat different than those reported for the line 7 product because neither product was scheduled for every week for which data were gathered. If no production was scheduled for a particular product one week, this week was not included in the data set.

As noted above (Figure 10-8), the number of units of the line 3 product scheduled for production did not appear to vary significantly across the period studied. The data presented in Figure 10-8, however, suggest that production for this product may have been lower during the middle of the second fifty-two weeks than during the first set of observations.

The number of pounds discarded per labor hour for the product produced on line 3 is presented in Figure 10-13. Here it can be

EXHIBIT 10-3 Week Numbers, Dates, and Milestones: Line 3

Week	Date	Milestone	Week	Date	Milestone
1	1/3/77		41	10/17/77	Matson claims efficiency is down 20%.
2	1/10/77	The first EJEC meeting occurs.	42	10/24/77	Product is lost on line 6. The first supervisors-stewards off-site meeting occurs.
3	1/17/77	Gromanger begins work in Reginal.	43	10/31/77	
4	1/24/77		44	11/7/77	
5	1/31/77		45	11/14/77	
6	2/7/77		46	11/21/77	
7	2/14/77	Assessors conduct open-ended interviews.	47	11/28/77	
8	2/21/77		48	12/5/77	
9	2/28/77	Deigh writes letter to Struthers attacking "efficiency-at-any-cost" mentality.	49	12/12/77	JQWLAC is told efficiency in Reginal is declining. New EJEC members are elected. Line 7 project starts. The new management training program is announced. COD reduces involvement in Reginal. Touchette fights for more break time. Cafeteria renovation begins.
10	3/7/77		50	12/19/77	
11	3/14/77	A nonsmoking area is created in the cafeteria.	51	12/26/77	3-month data gap
12	3/21/77		52	4/3/78	
13	3/28/77		53	4/10/78	
14	4/4/77		54	4/17/78	
15	4/11/77		55	4/24/78	Premater and Coy visit Reginal.
16	4/18/77		56	5/1/78	Training committee submits recommendations.
17	4/25/77		57	5/8/78	
18	5/2/77		58	5/15/78	Line-by-line project starts on line 7, second shift.
19	5/9/77	Training begins for line 4 conversion.	59	5/22/78	Communication committee submits recommendations.
20	5/16/77	The first plantwide survey is administered.	60	5/29/78	
21	5/23/77	The national QWL conference is held in Washington D.C.	61	6/5/78	Departmental record books become available.
22	5/30/77	Uniform samples arrive in Reginal.	62	6/12/78	Underweight packages are reported. The second joint JQWLAC-EJEC meeting occurs.
23	6/13/89		63	6/26/78	
24	6/20/77	The cafeteria/restroom committee meets with Matson.	64	7/3/78	
25	6/27/77	The clocks are synchronized.	65	7/10/78	
26	7/4/77	Plant efficiency is seen as declining. The cafeteria/restroom committee meets with Matson. The parking lot committee meets with Matson. Sholl recommends political strategy to EJEC.	66	7/17/78	
27	7/11/77		67	7/24/78	
28	7/18/77		68	7/31/78	
29	7/25/77	The first joint JQWLAC-EJEC meeting occurs.	69	8/7/78	
30	8/1/77	The plant fails a health inspection.	70	8/14/78	
31	8/8/77		71	8/21/78	The second supervisors-stewards off-site meeting occurs.
32	8/15/77		72	8/28/78	
33	8/22/77		73	9/4/78	Matson reports breakdown on line 3.
34	8/29/77		74	9/11/78	
35	9/5/77		75	9/18/78	
36	9/12/77		76	9/25/78	
37	9/19/77		77	10/2/78	
38	9/26/77	Survey feedback sessions begin.	78	10/9/78	
39	10/3/77		79	10/16/78	
40	10/10/77		80	10/23/78	

seen that the rate at which line 3 product was discarded as refuse declined at the time assessors were conducting open-ended interviews during the early weeks of the QWL program. Discarded product remained very low during the subsequent weeks for both unadjusted and adjusted data. It then increased starting around week 26, when EJEC members were planning the first joint EJEC-JQWLAC meeting. Discard levels were relatively high

Figure 10-13 Pounds Discarded per Labor Hour: Packing Department, Line 3

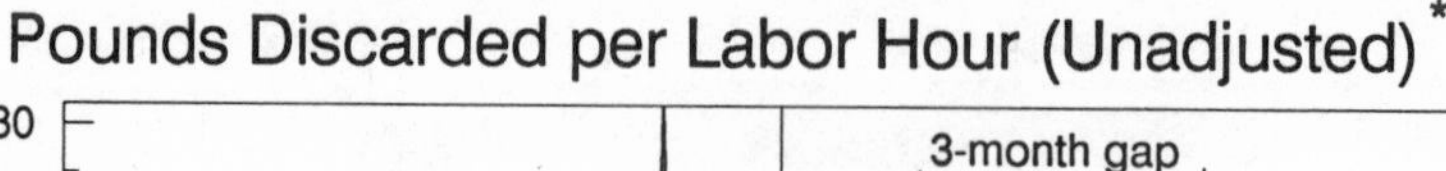

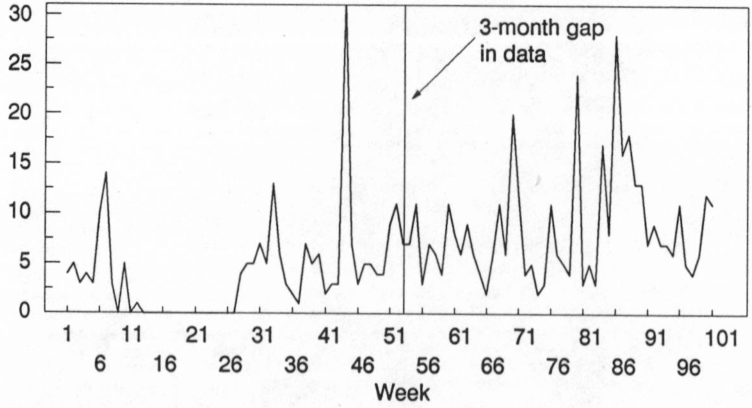

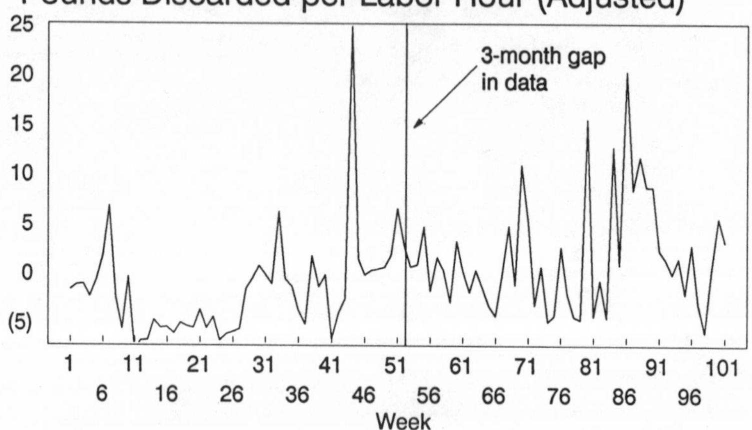

* Adjustments for run size and number of shift ovens

when the meeting was held and peaked around week 32. The highest discard level occurred around week 43, just after the first supervisors-stewards meeting. Another peak in the discard rate occurred just before week 71, when the second supervisors-stewards meeting was held. Starting around week 85, discard rate rose again and remained above average for several weeks. This pattern, coupled with the unusually low discard rate recorded for weeks 11 through 26, indicates a generally more efficient operation before the three-month gap in the data than afterwards.

Figure 10-14 presents the amount of downtime attributable to production problems for the product produced on line 3. Production downtime was a relatively infrequent occurrence before week 46. Subsequently, however, there were many instances of significant downtime attributable to production problems.

Figure 10-14 Production Downtime: Packing Department, Line 3

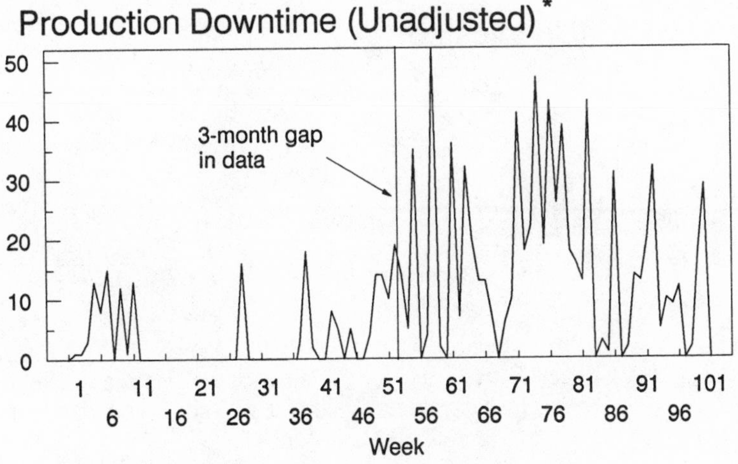

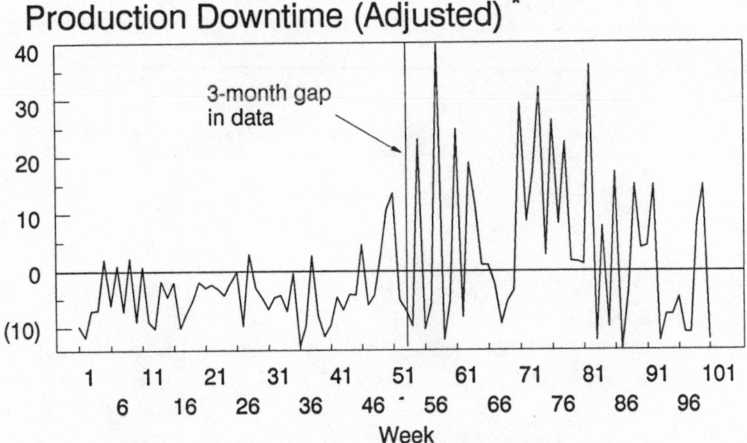

* Adjustments for run size and number of shift ovens

Peaks occurred around weeks 48, 53, 56, 60, 62, 70, 73, 75, 77, and 80. There were so many peaks that one could pick any number of QWL activities that would correlate with a marked increase in production-related downtime. Perhaps the only safe inference to be made, therefore, is that downtime increased over the period of the observations. Because adjusted downtime data show a similar pattern, the increase in downtime does not appear to be attributable to the increase in plant-level demand.

Figure 10-15 Yield: *Packing Department, Line 3

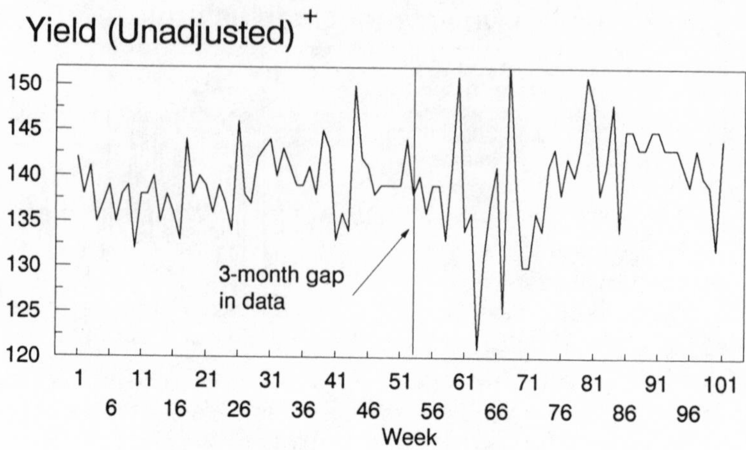

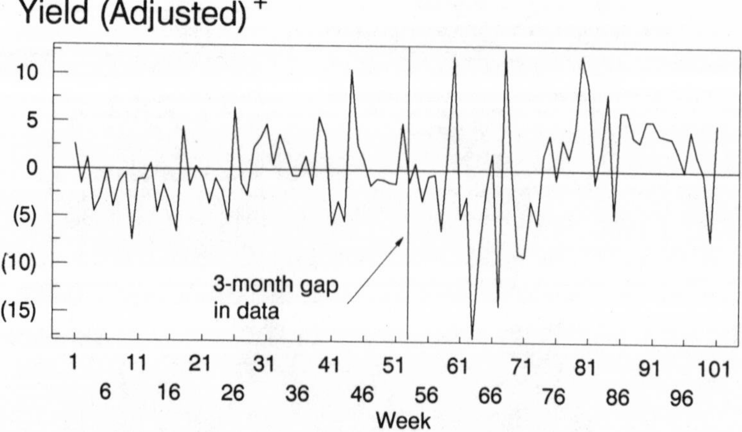

* Pounds of product produced per hundred pounds of flour
+ Adjustments for run size and number of shift ovens

Variability in yield appeared to increase after December 1977. This pattern was also evident for yield for the product produced on line 7 (Figure 10-11). As seen in Figure 10-15, significant peaks and troughs are much more frequent after the three-month gap in data than before. Mean levels are not obviously different, however. In addition, neither peaks nor troughs have any obvious relationship to distinctive QWL-related events. Confirming the qualitative data, the lowest yield for line 3 occurred just after week 61, when significant numbers of below-weight packages were reported.

The number of pounds produced per labor hour for the line 3 product is reported in Figure 10-16. The unadjusted data suggest that, over the period of observation, productivity increased somewhat until about week 22, then declined until about week 61, at which point it rebounded. The adjusted data indicate a similar pattern; however, with the unexplained peak between weeks 85 and 88, productivity does not appear to have rebounded much from its lows. Only one of the low points corresponds to an entry in Exhibit 10-3, the increase in underweight packages reported by plant management.

The line 3 data suggest that efficiency and productivity decreased over the period of the observations. Pounds discarded per labor hour increased, production downtime increased, variability in yield increased, and pounds produced per labor hour appear to have decreased. In addition, peaks in pounds discarded per labor hour in the packing department occurred more or less simultaneously with the first joint EJEC-JQWLAC meeting, the first supervisors-stewards meeting, and the second supervisors-stewards meeting. Moreover, these patterns do not seem attributable to increasing demand for the plant's product.

In summary, analyses of the plant's efficiency data do not refute the plant manager's frequent contention that efficiency was declining during the QWL program. This decline, coupled with the critical role played by the accounting control system in assessing short-term costs and benefits of plant activities, crippled the QWL program's ability to make significant changes. Declining efficiency ratings—whether or not the decline was caused by the QWL program—put so much stress on the system that all resources were directed toward short-term efficiency concerns. As will be seen below, resource problems even plagued the line-by-line project. Unless QWL projects could demonstrably improve short-term efficiency and effectiveness and be compatible with established man-

Figure 10-16 Pounds Produced per Labor Hour: Packing Department, Line 3

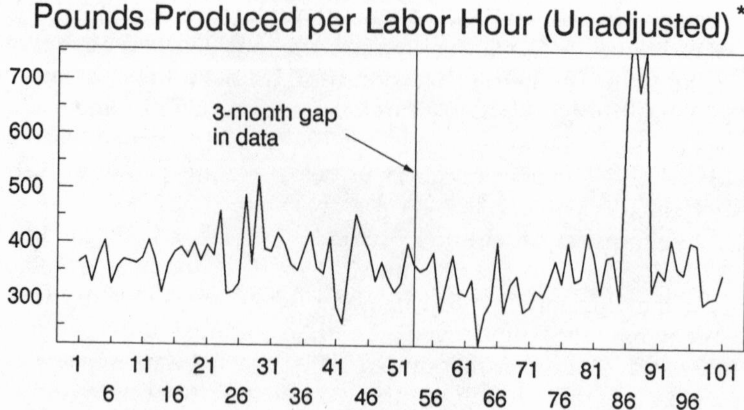

Pounds Produced per Labor Hour (Adjusted)*

300
200
100
0
(100)
3-month gap
in data
1 6 11 16 21 26 31 36 41 46 51 56 61 66 71 76 81 86 91 96 101
Week

* Adjustments for number of shift ovens, run size, pounds discarded per labor hour, production downtime, and yield

agement structures and procedures, therefore, they were unlikely to receive plant management approval (Figure 10-5). Gain sharing might have reconciled the interests of line employees to management's concern with productivity; however, it was not compatible with established procedures. Establishing truly autonomous work groups in which line employees were given new authority and responsibility might have helped supervisors support EJEC initiatives, but it too was a radical departure from established procedures. So long as QWL managers did not confront the underlying differences in perspectives among participants and forcefully present the QWL alternative in a way that could lead over time to a new, shared perspective, there seemed no alternative to failure. The system outlined in Figure 10-5 simply was not capable of resolving its own internal dilemmas.

Production Pressures, Turnover and Absenteeism on the EJEC

On June 22, the EJEC interviewed the two top candidates for the assistant coordinator's job, Alfred Thayer and Margaret Tippett. Joe Gromanger had prepared a list of assistant coordinator functions to help direct the inquiry. EJEC members took this information and the knowledge that Deigh preferred Alfred Thayer into account in their deliberations. After discussion and several votes, they elected Tippett the new assistant coordinator.

Tippett agreed to begin working on July 10. Joe Gromanger agreed to work with her during the rest of the summer, and together they set about fulfilling the assistant coordinator functions.

Before Tippett could begin work, Ben Ashley resigned as line coordinator for the first shift line 7 project in order to spend more time dealing with production problems. He was replaced by Susan Sheffer. In addition, Patricia Roper was promoted out of the packing department and therefore could no longer serve on the EJEC. It became difficult to find replacements for Roper. Most of the viable candidates were responding to production pressures. In addition, headquarters reported an increase in consumer complaints and scheduled a quality control audit in the plant. Some of the problem, it seemed, was due to increases in "foreign substances" in the product. Moreover, the division had apparently miscalculated its budget. The only way to operate within what was likely to be a more stringent budget was to increase productivity and restrict waste. Greater emphasis therefore was placed on maintaining standard line speeds. Matson cautioned, "If this is not accomplished, we will have to ask the baking division from world headquarters to come in and help solve the problem." Even the performance of line 7 had been disappointing. He detected, he said,"a resistance to productivity increase in the plant." When the July productivity figures were calculated, it appeared the plant was operating at only 90 percent efficiency. In a staff meeting on August 2, Matson suggested that this meant that supervision didn't care. He asked his senior supervisors whether they wanted to be treated as clock workers. In addition, he admonished his supervisors to set objectives, get line people involved, communicate with them, and educate them. The EJEC met the day after this staff meeting. Members passed a motion recommending efficiency meetings for employees on a line-by-line basis. They believed these meetings would "educate [employees] on how efficiency is dropping and ask for their help." Meanwhile, because of production pressures, several members of the EJEC training and communications subcommittees had stopped attending meetings. These committees were reconstituted with new members.

Because there were so many other activities, the standing departmental and project-oriented committees had been having trouble meeting. The EJEC decided to have committee meetings every other week and to devote the first hour to departmental subcommittees and the second to the special project subcommittees (cafeteria, social, etc.).

Touchette had taken an extended sick leave. In response to her absence and continuing production pressures, Deigh recommended that the EJEC be reorganized. A working committee composed of the old executive committee plus two regular members of the EJEC was established to oversee subcommittee activities on a weekly basis. Meetings of the full EJEC would be scheduled once a month. The two regular EJEC members serving on the working committee would rotate monthly.

The first working committee meeting was called to order September 14. Since the working committee concept was new, the first order of business was to ask the bylaws subcommittee to incorporate this and other changes into the bylaws. The members then decided to schedule a time for reviewing the current EJEC project list in order to establish priorities. Margaret Tippett was given the responsibility of providing liaison between the working committee and the chairpersons of each EJEC subcommittee. Finally, the working committee took it upon themselves to schedule subcommittee meetings.

EJEC Projects and Committee Activities

The Line-by-Line Project

The line-by-line project was moving with a momentum all its own. Meetings held on June 20 and 27 documented considerable activity on both shifts. The first shift was working on old problems, such as ordering a fan to overcome circulation problems encountered when the windows were welded shut. Members also began working on newer concerns, such as a heater for the spray machine reservoir. Second shift employees on line 7 also continued working on both old and new problems. General productivity problems, however, as indicated in Ashley's resignation and the line's poor efficiency rate in July, began to erode progress on this project.

The lead article in the July issue of the company newspaper was titled: "Experimental Line 7 Project Extended to Second Shift." It emphasized that "the line coordination concept expansion to second shift represents the second phase of the [plant's] quality of work life efforts."

First shift line 7 participants met with their new coordinator, Susan Sheffer, on July 11. They reviewed progress on old projects and initiated new ones. Second shift line 7 personnel, under line coordinator Irene Jones, also met. They considered thirty-six proposals, all of which dealt with production-related problems.

In mid-July, Jones took a vacation leave. She was not replaced during her vacation. Her fellow supervisors felt they could not afford to lose another of their number during a time of declining efficiency.

Matson was doing what he could to counter declining efficiency on the line. Members of the EJEC training subcommittee had complained that training line coordinators was hampered by the absence of procedural manuals. Without waiting to go through departmental superintendents, Matson ordered employees to write these manuals. He assigned members of management to write specific sections. The EJEC also got involved. They commissioned a special task force composed of people from the line 7 project to help participants from the different shifts share experiences and learn from each other. Just as the task force was getting started and as the procedure manuals were, presumably, being written, Susan Sheffer injured her back and had to take a sick leave. She was not replaced. The first week in August, therefore, found the line-by-line projects on both shifts without line leaders. Sheffer's injury proved serious. By the end of August she had not returned, and the EJEC began calling for a replacement.

Feeding Back Data from the Second Plantwide Survey

On July 20, the EJEC executive committee met to consider the planning reports they had prepared at Deigh's urging after the second joint EJEC-JQWLAC meeting. One of these reports concerned feeding back the Time 2 survey data. The report recalled supervisors' negative responses to the first survey feedback sessions and recommended that the second stewards-supervisors meeting be held before survey feedback sessions for line employees. EJEC members hoped that if supervisors and stewards viewed and discussed the data first, they would be less defensive during the feedback sessions and more receptive to proposals for a change. They tentatively scheduled the second off-site meeting for August 26. They asked management and the union to notify employees and encourage them to attend and to participate in the discussions and problem-solving sessions.

The planning report also recommended that feedback sessions for line employees be held September 13 and 14 and that makeup sessions be made available for employees who were absent or on vacation. Discussions would be led by EJEC discussion leaders, and each leader would be given two hours of training.

The report recommended that an additional thirty minutes be made available at the end of the regular survey feedback sessions. This time would be used to "inform the employees of the progress made in the quality of work life program" and "receive ideas for project areas and listen for areas which the employees would prefer us to avoid." EJEC members selected specific questions for review. Tippett and Gromanger agreed to compile a list of these questions for use in the feedback sessions, and the executive committee agreed to oversee the sessions as the "survey subcommittee."

The survey subcommittee's planning report was formally accepted by the full EJEC on August 17. Subcommittee members had selected twenty core questions and thirty optional discussion questions for use in the survey feedback. They had also drafted an agenda for the second supervisors-stewards meeting.

The meeting was to be run by Chuck Josephson. Like the others, it was scripted closely. Bobby Clayton and Joel Barrett were to review EJEC activities and update those present on the status of EJEC projects. Josephson was then to say; "We recognize the job we have to do. The errors made by a lot of people—not just the EJEC—are difficult ones to correct. We want this meeting to be the beginning of what we hope will be closer cooperation between EJEC, the union, and management to resolve problems we have in common." He was then to outline three goals the EJEC had for the meeting. First, supervisors and stewards would be introduced to the survey data before any of their subordinates. Second, they would give advice on how best to conduct the feedback to clock employees, and third, they would be asked to assess the performance of the EJEC to date and make recommendations for improvement.

After Josephson's introduction, participants were to break into small groups. First, they would review the results of the twenty questions selected by the EJEC executive committee. Then they would critique the proposed presentation of the feedback, suggest improvements, and summarize the results of their discussions for presentation to the larger group.

After a coffee break, participants were to gather again in small groups and select twenty items from the supplemental list selected by the EJEC executive committee. They were also to recommend the best methods for resolving issues raised in the feedback sessions. Then they were to focus again on the EJEC and how it could be improved and, again, report back to all participants.

As the meeting time approached on August 26, it became increasingly clear that relatively few people planned to attend. Although Newman, Matson, DeLeo, Griffith, and Keeley were present, several important figures—notably, Charlton, Pepin, and Dalton—were not. In all, only twenty-eight employees, including EJEC members, attended the meeting.

Those who did attend were led through the prepared program. By noon, they had developed recommendations for structuring the feedback sessions. Teams composed of department superintendents, supervisors, stewards, and EJEC representatives were to be established. They would meet to discuss the feedback presentation. The teams would then conduct the feedback sessions and meet together to discuss and summarize the results. Matson expressed a great deal of disappointment about the poor turnout for the off-site meeting. However, he became even more upset about scheduling meetings for the feedback teams. He said he couldn't allow so much time to be taken for EJEC-related activities. There were too many production problems in the plant.

Tim Deigh held two separate meetings with supervisors and stewards who had not attended the second off-site meeting. He reviewed the previous year's feedback sessions and the two off-site meetings. With Tippett's help, he also reviewed the plans for the upcoming feedback sessions and asked for comments. There were many, frequently negative. Several people were unable to understand, given all the production problems the plant was having, why management was willing to allow lines to be shut down for feedback meetings. One of the stewards said that, given current plant conditions, there should be a plantwide vote to decide whether or not to keep the quality of work life program.

With so little support for survey feedback sessions, EJEC members decided to postpone them. Instead, they decided to have Tippett prepare a brief summary of the results. This summary would be handed out to employees, along with a survey asking them whether or not they wanted to discuss the survey results in special feedback meetings. The summary and survey were sent out to employees on October 12. A copy of the review is available as Exhibit 10-4. At the end of the review employees were given the option of selecting a preferred form of survey feedback (for example, the same type of sessions as the previous year, voluntary sessions, or no feedback sessions at all).

EXHIBIT 10-4 Survey II Feedback Report

In the feedback sessions last year, the categories of communications and training came out as areas in need of improvement. The survey results this year again pointed to this need. Based on these two facts, plus the outcome of the off-site supervisory steward meetings this year, five areas were chosen to discuss in the feedback. These are: communications, training, job satisfaction, the EJEC, and the line 7 coordination project. Twenty questions, chosen from this year's survey to illustrate these areas, are listed below, along with a brief review of the results of these questions.

1. COMMUNICATIONS/INVOLVEMENT

5. My superior keeps subordinates informed.
6. When the management of this company says something, you can really believe it's true.
9. Communication between shifts is adequate.
12. It is necessary for groups to work together to get the job done.
13. The conflict that exists between groups gets in the way of getting the job done.

These questions show that communication has not improved enough over the past year. The response to question 5 did not show much change, indicating that 34 percent of all employees believe that superiors keep their subordinates informed. Although for union employees this is a little more true than last year (up to 34 from 32 percent), management employees feel it is less true (down from 62 to 46 percent). Credibility of management also declined for total management (56 to 22 percent) but increased slightly for total union (15 to 19 percent). Communication between shifts is thought to be better by union employees than last year (28 to 30 percent), but management employees believe it is worse (22 to 16 percent). About 95 percent of all employees still feel that groups have to work together to get the job done, although fewer people (62 compared to 69 percent) believe that conflict is getting in the way of this. Overall, there seems to be some improvement, but these results indicate we all need to work harder.

2. TRAINING

3. A lot of people can be affected by how well I do my job.
4. I have enough training to do my job well.
11. On my job, most of my tasks are clearly defined.
20. Management training by corporate headquarters (Tom Gib).

The results of these questions are about the same as last year. Many people are aware (71 percent of all employees) that how well they do their job affects other people, but only 61 percent feel they have enough training to do their job well. Also, only about 63 percent feel that the tasks on the job are clearly defined. This would indicate that most employees feel they need more information about what their job entails and especially need more training on how to do that job. On the question dealing with management training by corporate headquarters, 72.7 percent of all employees felt it had increased their efficiency.

3. JOB SATISFACTION

1. All in all, I am satisfied with my job.
2. What happens to this organization is really important to me.
10. The work I do on my job is meaningful to me.
14. This organization cares more about schedules and costs than people.
18. Cafeteria renovation.

None of these questions showed a large change over last year. However, not as many people this year feel the organization cares more about schedules and costs than people, and most employees (84 percent) care what happens to the organization. Satisfaction with the job declined somewhat for total management (72 to 66 percent) but increased slightly for total union (72 to 75 percent), while belief that the work is meaningful is a little lower for all employees (77 to 72 percent) than last year. About 46 percent of all employees believe the cafeteria renovation has increased the quality of their life at work.

4. EMPLOYEES' JOINT ENRICHMENT COMMITTEE

16. The Employees' joint enrichment committee is needed here.
17. The Employees' joint enrichment committee is doing a good job.

These two questions indicate that about 50 percent of all employees feel the EJEC is needed here and 42 percent (up from 35 percent last year) feel EJEC is doing a good job. However, 10.4 percent of the employees say they don't know whether EJEC is doing a good job or not, which would imply a definite need for better communication of EJEC activities to all employees.

5. LINE 7 COORDINATION PROJECT

19. Changed work organization of line 7.

This question shows that 33 percent of all employees believe this project has increased the quality of their life at work, and 27 percent say it has increased their efficiency. Since this project was limited to only line 7 at that time, this is a fairly high percentage. We have asked for, and will soon be receiving, additional information comparing Time 1 and Time 2 results by department for those people who took the questionnaire both times. Although we have some of this data now, we can give you a more complete picture when we receive the additional packet.

The working committee reviewed the results of this survey on October 30. Fifty employees had returned the questionnaire, and most of them wanted feedback sessions as had originally been planned. The working committee decided to go ahead with feedback sessions.

The full EJEC met on November 2. Members quickly agreed with the working committee's recommendations to initiate survey feedback sessions. These would be voluntary. Employees would have to sign up to attend, and only those signing up would be given time off to go to them. On December 12, the EJEC decided to send out a survey feedback sign-up sheet with the January 11 paychecks. Employees signing and returning this survey would be scheduled for feedback sessions. However, the EJEC made no effort to enlist Matson's support in this endeavor, and he continued in his opposition to taking supervisory time for this purpose.

Activities of the Training and Communications Committees

Training

Following the second joint EJEC-JQWLAC meeting, the EJEC members wrote a planning report recommending that Tom Gib become a more integral part of the EJEC training activities in Reginal. Results of the second plantwide survey had indicated that Gib's training activities were very popular among supervisory staff. More than 80 percent of the supervisors in the packing department, 60 percent of the supervisors in the baking department, and 75 percent in environmental services agreed this training had increased the quality of their work life. The majority in each department also agreed that the training had increased efficiency.

The report also called for world headquarters' assistance in developing (1) a more efficient method for collecting effectiveness data, (2) a training program for line coordinators, (3) an orientation program for employees, (4) a training procedure that would clarify the lines of authority in Reginal, (5) a training program for improving employees' interpersonal relations and communications skills, and (6) a line coordinator manual for training purposes. In its July 20 meeting, the EJEC accepted the report.

However, with the exception of some activity directed toward writing a procedures manual for line 7 personnel, little action was taken on the training committee recommendations.

In mid-September, the training committee met again and identified jobs in the baking and packing departments they felt required immediate attention by trainers.

Committee members thought that little action would be taken in response to their requests unless the requests could be cost-justified. They decided to gather data that would show how downtime attributable to errors arising from training had led to considerable dollar losses for the company. They also identified components of an effective training package, such as checklists of troubleshooting procedures. Committee members also believed that adequate training would require more formal job descriptions than currently existed. However, finding the resources needed to generate these descriptions could be difficult.

Finally, committee members agreed to contact qualified operators who might be involved in the training program during its early stages. They would ask these individuals to begin attending subcommittee meetings. By the end of November, however, they had few concrete accomplishments.

Communication

The communications subcommittee developed a planning report recommending that Martha Linz, an FWIU communications specialist, be given authority to visit the plant to work with the communications subcommittee in program development. At its meeting on July 20, the EJEC accepted this planning report.

Tim Deigh met with the communications subcommittee on September 28. Members reviewed the concerns they had reported to the EJEC and articulated their solutions. They identified two general topics: solving problems with the departmental notebooks and finding ways to contribute to plant efficiency.

The departmental notebooks were not being kept up-to-date. Subcommittee members recommended that Newman and Charlton go through the notebooks and update them. Moreover, employees were not sufficiently informed of the nature and purpose of the notebooks. Barrett and Martinez agreed to draft a statement of intent for insertion at the front of the notebooks.

The subcommittee then turned its attention to problems of efficiency. Members noted that few employees knew what the various effectiveness measures were and how they were determined. They agreed that a program should be devised that would educate employees regarding the efficiency measures and provide them with ongoing feedback on their performance.

Subcommittee members gave a good deal of thought and discussion to the specifics of such a program. They eventually recommended that a fifteen to twenty minute videotape presentation be produced that would detail the available efficiency measures. This tape would be played and discussed during group meetings of employees who worked on the same line, even though they were assigned to different departments. The subcommittee also recommended that efficiency data be prepared on a line-by-line basis and fed back to employees weekly. Finally, committee members identified top corporate management and international union officials who would be effective communicators through the proposed videotape.

Other EJEC Activities

The Cafeteria

After several delays, a cafeteria investigation committee established in mid-July submitted its report to the EJEC. The report included observations taken from July 14 to August 3. The committee members concluded that cafeteria service still was not adequate. On only one day was everything in proper working order. Some days the soft drinks, sandwiches, and pastry machines were out, either on second or third shifts. Other days the ice cream or milk machine was out. Sometimes coffee was unavailable. After receiving the report, EJEC members turned their attention to other matters. They did little else in response to these problems.

Cafeteria renovation continued. It soon became apparent

that the plans called for more than renovating the cafeteria. A new conference room replaced the room next to the cafeteria in which product samples had been displayed. The supervisory staff meeting room and plant manager's office were also being renovated.

Packaging Department Subcommittee Activities

The departmental subcommittees were convened on August 10. At that time, the packaging department subcommittee reported that two of the lines needed stools with back supports and that fans were required to increase air circulation. Some employees had returned from vacation to find their uniforms had been taken, and some were not getting their proper allotment of uniforms. Members also complained about management decisions on shift rotation and the implementation of the new overtime procedure. The subcommittee, however, did not address these issues.

The Baking Department Subcommittee

On August 10, the baking department subcommittee recommended the installation of hoods and exhaust fans over the discharge end of the assembly conveyors. Members also wanted a wall across the assembly area at the feed end of the ovens. No formal requests were made to redress these problems, however, and the baking department subcommittee made no further recommendations.

The Warehouse and Environmental Services Subcommittee

On August 10, the warehouse subcommittee reported that the new forklift had arrived and that the heating problem had been solved. It suggested getting a new paper cutter, because parts for the old one were unavailable. Subcommittee members made several other recommendations as well.

The environmental services subcommittee reported that parts had been ordered to repair the lawn sprinkler system and a new way of locating the shutoff valves had been devised. Its members had gotten management approval for a new water fountain and had selected a location for it. Sifters had been repaired to stop flour leakage, but there were still leaks in the north surge hopper housing. No new program was initiated to deal with this problem, but management had been alerted. After these reports, the warehouse and environmental services subcommittees became inactive.

The Bylaws Subcommittee

As noted earlier, the EJEC working committee was established to direct QWL program activities. A working committee had not been authorized in the bylaws, so it became necessary to rewrite the bylaws to incorporate this concept. Other structural and procedural changes had been made as well, and these too needed to be incorporated into the bylaws. Accordingly, the bylaws subcommittee was convened. With staff help, its members drafted new bylaws. These were accepted by the EJEC on October 10.

Established Patterns of Behavior Continue While Support for the QWL Program Erodes

Despite what seemed to some to be a breakthrough during the first joint EJEC-JQWLAC meeting, the schematic foundations underlying labor-management relationships in Reginal had remained intact. Top management continued to look for short-term increases in efficiency (Figure 3-1, column 1). Local management sought to respond to efficiency demands while simultaneously providing amenities for plant employees (Figure 4-1, model 2). The decision process outlined in Figure 5-1 was the result of this attempt to balance competing forces. However, during the next year cost-justification became an even more critical choice criterion, and staff resources for cost-justifying proposals and implementing them were effectively reduced to zero. The result, consistent with Figure 5-1, was increasing frustration that manifested itself in increased absenteeism in EJEC meetings and in increased turnover of key EJEC members.

By the second joint EJEC-JQWLAC meeting, top management support was also waning. Considerable resources had been expended to respond to EJEC proposals. A new cafeteria was being constructed, renovation of the parking lot was underway, new clocks had been installed, and a variety of other amenities had been provided. These activities had been carried out without an obvious positive result.

In the absence of a higher-level appeal, the patterns described in Figure 10-5 continued. Short of a major initiative spearheaded by the consultants, it seemed inevitable that projects would become increasingly managerial. Fewer proposals would focus on gaining amenities, while more projects would be directed toward improving day-to-day operations. However, even these projects became a liability. They were costly in the short term and received little supervisory support. Even the line 7 project seemed to be costing more than it was worth.

EJEC activities were blamed for declining efficiency. Employee satisfaction had not improved, as indicated by the second survey. In the face of these pressures, participants were changing their actions (Figure 1-1). The actions they were changing, however, were the activities introduced by the QWL program. They were returning to well-known and well-worn alternatives for increasing productivity.

EJEC subcommittees were having difficulty meeting. When they did meet, they were plagued by absenteeism. The training and communications subcommittees had to be reconstituted. Several of the most influential EJEC members left to concentrate on production problems. The second supervisors-stewards meeting was poorly attended.

The EJEC itself was restructured. The new working committee, however, was unable to accomplish much. It could not get management approval for a new round of survey feedback sessions, and it did not follow up on subcommittee recommendations. Instead, the working committee concentrated on sending out a survey feedback report, on documenting project work, and on redrafting the bylaws. There was little substantive the committee could accomplish. The resources and staff support simply were not sufficient to get the job done.

Deigh might still have launched a new initiative. Following the prescriptions outlined in Figure 8-1, he might have tried to highlight information that disconfirmed established perspectives and to present the QWL alternative vigorously. He might have insisted that JQWLAC members, EJEC members, supervision, and members of the local unions confront each other for the sake of the whole. However, Deigh acted as if the QWL program were on-track. Perhaps it was, with respect to comparative progress (or lack of progress) at other sites. Personnel in Reginal, however, viewed the program as being in severe jeopardy.

The EJEC Is Absorbed by Management

Two separate undercurrents were beginning to threaten the very existence of the QWL program. First, several union stewards and members who had voiced their opposition to the program began circulating a petition calling for it to be terminated. The EJEC reacted quickly and tried to involve these individuals more directly in EJEC activities. For example, two of the stewards were appointed to positions on the training and communications subcommittees. Nevertheless, the petition was circulated, and over 300 employees signed it. George Newman said he would divert the petition. However, its advocates sent the results directly to Donald Premater at the union's international headquarters.

The second undercurrent involved the company. Dalmar Pond had been skeptical of the program since its inception. He had been ordered to participate by Frank Struthers, but Struthers had been promoted and no longer had responsibility for manufacturing operations.

Pond, Coy, and other FoodCom executives had frequently expressed frustration at the administration of the project by the American Center for the Quality of Work Life (ACQWL). They believed the ACQWL had given the program undue publicity and had acted unilaterally without consulting them. Consequently, regardless of what happened in Reginal, they wanted to sever their relationship with the ACQWL. They asked Tim Deigh to work on the project on an independent basis, but Deigh declined.

Although EJEC members were aware of the petition to terminate the program, they did not know that the petition had been sent directly to international headquarters. Nor were they aware of the tension between FoodCom's world headquarters and the ACQWL. However, they did seek to counter criticisms raised by FWIU stewards. Meeting on December 4, the working committee urged stewards and others to attend EJEC meetings and told them that an effort would be made to allow them to do this on company time.

On December 7, the working committee met with several stewards and conveyed their message that EJEC was not going to assume anyone's role or get involved in contractual matters. They told the stewards that EJEC members believed they had not done an adequate job keeping stewards informed and involved, but that they now were making a real effort to assist them in ways they would find helpful.

The whole EJEC met on December 12 and discussed ways to inform employees better about the quality of work program. Two members agreed to narrate a four-minute tape describing EJEC activities. This tape was to be played during lunch breaks on each shift. Some EJEC members restated their willingness to describe EJEC activities at union meetings. Others accepted responsibility for communicating the same information to supervision during weekly staff meetings. Finally, to increase the visibility of EJEC projects, they suggested that decals or some other clear identifying marker be placed on each EJEC project. By marking the projects, employees would be able to see how much benefit they were actually getting from EJEC efforts.

While the EJEC was seeking to increase its local base of support, Tim Deigh was trying to soften the impact of the employee petition and to deal with the strained relationships between FoodCom management and the ACQWL. Deigh believed that top union management, especially Emil Hendy, who had replaced Edward Scigliano when the latter had been promoted to union president, wanted to mute the impact of the petition. He believed union officers were responding to the petition only because their rules required them to take such petitions very seriously. Deigh had also contacted William Coy. He believed that Coy would be willing to help postpone a decision on the proposal to separate the QWL program in Reginal from the ACQWL.

The JQWLAC met on December 14. Coy began the meeting by delineating his concern about the quality of work program in Reginal. "The time of decision is at hand," he said, declaring further that he was "disturbed." There clearly was progress, but there were so many projects and the speed of the projects was slow, especially on the line 7 project. Recent proposals in the areas of communications and training were constructive: however, people in the plant were creating pressure. "It's coming off the floor," he said. "There are a lot of dissenters. . . . Some are more verbal than others. . . . We have problems here."

Donald Premater responded:

> William has minimized the problems. I'm discouraged by the whole program. . . . I was down [to Reginal] a couple of months ago. Dissention. I don't think the program is working. We've got a petition from over 300 people for discontinuation. They say the program has done nothing useful. People say now that people are going to the program rather than to the grievance committee. There's a conflict with the union activities. There's no betterment of any work-related quality of work. Line 7 is slow and is the least troublesome. They should go to a line where the girls go home crying. . . . Lots of people feel nothing is being done. Some things, like shower heads, we've discussed these in contract negotiations. Stewards feel they're being left in the background, allocating overtime to people, etc. The program has hurt us and should be discontinued. The union has been reduced to practically a nothing organization in that plant. . . . We're wasting time, manpower and everything else.

John Papp said that the local committee should be allowed to proceed without JQWLAC interference. To facilitate this, he recommended that the candidates for the election coming up in January for a union position on the EJEC be restricted to union stewards. Premater retorted that it was the local union people who were trying to end the program.

Margaret Tippett interjected at this point that the stewards were becoming increasingly involved in EJEC activities. She reviewed several of the innovations designed to increase employee knowledge and appreciation of EJEC projects and concluded that EJEC projects were tending less and less to be of the shower-head and scooter variety. They were increasingly geared toward training, communications, and plant efficiency. There was, she said, even progress toward getting maintenance personnel involved.

Deigh said that Coy and Premater were both correct in their divergent assessments of EJEC. There was enough blame to go around, Deigh said, and he was due some himself. However, people had begun to get together to "clean up their own act." The petition had succeeded in getting only 300 signatures, despite weeks of campaigning. In addition, two of the stewards responsible for passing the petition had been brought on board and were now contributing members of the EJEC committees. A third had agreed to produce an EJEC tape that would be played during employee lunch periods.

Deigh felt that the stewards had a legitimate complaint at the time the petition was circulated and that the EJEC was not quick enough in responding. However, progress had been made, and their grievances had been met. Attitudes were beginning to change. Horace Seldon asked Tippett whether, should a vote be taken in the plant that day, the program would be voted out. Tippett believed it would not and that many employees were in fact afraid the program might be terminated. The discussion continued as follows:

Donald Premater: I wasn't proposing we should stop the program. I proposed this decision should be made by those in Reginal.

John Papp: People have identified with the company more as a result of the program. Are they now also more identified with the union?

Tim Deigh: I can't say. It's not identifying more with the company, it's identifying with their trade and their group. . . .

Dalmar Pond: We're not satisfied with the project either. . . . We went in with the premise that satisfying people's demands would result in better organization. I felt EJEC was a cumbersome method, but we felt that we might not see everything, so we let the program go without union or management guidance. From a management view, we didn't think the openness was useful, but we said: "Let it evolve." Why don't they have day care, etc.? We look at two operations—one at 98 percent and one at 90 percent. So we go to local management and say "What's wrong?" We've taken a problem-solving, not-blaming approach. There's no one there with a whip. We've told the local management the readings aren't good. We've spent a lot of money, over $300,000, there, and I can't show any tangible benefit now. . . . We want to run the program ourselves with the union and get the results better. . . . We have some recommendations we'll make later in the meeting.

Donald Premater: I know what I wanted from the program. Better work environment and happier people equals reduced absenteeism. Better for management and the union. I haven't seen that.

Tim Deigh: Look at the data from line 7 [comparisons between response of line 7 employees and the other respondents provided to JQWLAC and EJEC by the assessor]. The Time 2 data are clear. On Tuesday, internal management said absenteeism was down, amount of product rejected down, and efficiency slightly up. I agree with you, Don. Line 7, both parties are winning. EJEC recommends expanding line 7 to the rest of the plant.

Dalmar Pond: We don't see better lows in '78 than in '77 . . .. We spent so much time with EJEC trying to make them managers. Has this helped? Have we reached the 800 people?

Miles Farr: I support some of your statements, Don, 100 percent. Whether people are appointed or elected, it requires leadership from both union and management . . . I get the same theme: This was the EJEC's program. We kept hands off. Now they're confronting management problems we've tried to deal with for thirty years. It's hard to keep 600 people advised. If you took a vote from the natural leadership—union and management—I'd despair of the result.

Tim Deigh: I hear you saying to leave the future of the project in the hands of local people, right?

Dalmar Pond: That's what I'm saying.

Emil Hendy: In the beginning, we started a program that didn't have perfect communication, and [there were] some misperceptions about what we were trying to do. But in the last few weeks, there seems to have been somewhat of a turnaround . . . The petition says the company is violating the contract and threatening the stewards with threats and intimidation. We have to find out what the 311 people are saying. Are these management who are violating the contract under the guise of this program?

Donald Premater: No . . . We have good relations with the company here. That's not the problem.

Emil Hendy: I'm smart enough to see that there are individuals who have not been helping . . . even hurting. Now you say some of these people are changing their minds. Do we still have people who are trying to discourage the program? Has there been an attempt to resolve these problems—the gripes of these people?

Tim Deigh: No, not from the international union that I know of. People have gone down to find out how things were going, not to try to help out. It's been fact-finding mostly.

Emil Hendy: This is my own personal opinion. Maybe we don't have control over the Reginal committee by letting them do their own thing. We say we aren't going to be the ones to kill it. We ought to say, maybe, whether we want the program, and if we do, make sure it works. To me, the program is satisfactory and there are things we can do with it.

Dalmar Pond: In the beginning, we had some problems of seeing whether management was on board. We had problems with Roger Matson, because we hadn't straightened out our money commitment. Then manager and supervisor support was dubious. Now, I don't know whether Newman did anything with the stewards or not. If there are people actively deterring the program now, we don't know about it.

Tim Deigh: I'm not aware of an overt effort to kill the project from any quarter. Maybe, though, the JQWLAC has been too laissez-faire. The name for the group is "advisory," and maybe we ought to be giving more advice. In two years, we've had two joint meetings in Reginal. And two pairs of people visit. Perhaps you should consider greater involvement.

Emil Hendy: (to Donald Premater) Why haven't the things we wanted developed?

Donald Premater: I made suggestions, . . . but the company didn't seem to hear. The company said that Reginal has good absenteeism, but look at some of the lines. They would've established other programs . . . In Europe . . . people were cryin' cause they had to work with rejected product all around 'em . . .

Emil Hendy: (to Dalmar Pond) Why would you go to a line without problems?

Dalmar Pond: I assume it came out of the EJEC committee.

Tim Deigh: Let me give you some history. People thought they could debug on an easy line. The second line they did was on the same line second shift.

William Coy: We haven't shut this down on second shift. It's off and on. . . .

Tim Deigh: There are ways to move the concept more quickly. We could sit here and say if we had done this and that.

Miles Farr: And you'd get as many opinions as there are people here. We didn't have the expertise, so we were reluctant to give advice.

Dalmar Pond: The rejected product problem is due to . . . line [4] [being] done there. We're going down there after the first of the year with some technical people . . .

John Papp: I've gotten mixed reviews about line 7, from good to "all this is is setting up another supervisor."

Dalmar Pond: But we've taken these people into meetings and asked their opinions. It's more than just another supervisor.

Donald Premater: What kind of training are they talking about?

Dalmar Pond: We have cassettes to teach people how to operate the machines.

Tim Deigh: What's been proposed, Don, is that there's an EJEC training subcommittee. They propose to take one job in packaging and one job in assembly. Get good people to decide what kind of supervision is needed for those jobs. Even the maintenance department agrees to do this. They're asking for corporate resources to do this.

John Papp: So this isn't being imposed on them.

Donald Premater: What kind of training is going to be done?

Tim Deigh: That's what the subcommittee is going to do.

The discussion continued to focus on training. Premater criticized the company for having no training. Pond disagreed. Tippett explained in more detail what the training subcommittee's proposal was. Premater continued to criticize the company for the absence of training. Deigh tried to summarize his sense of the meeting up to this point: "I heard people say they aren't going to stop it, but they want to find ways to help it, is that right?" Hendy said he had heard no sufficient reason for stopping the program. John Papp suggested a plantwide vote prior to electing new EJEC members in January, but Hendy wanted to "talk about it among ourselves." He questioned why all the effort was being directed toward training, when the entire program might soon be terminated. Deigh believed that this was effort well spent, assuming the ultimate decision would be "go." William Coy said that everything at this point was "in limbo."

Emil Hendy: I'm concerned that 300 people asked this international union not to participate . . . . Let's not participate in an exercise in futility if the people don't want it.

Donald Premater: I'm gonna give this [petition] to Ed [Scigliano]. I'll recommend that they decide in a meeting of the local membership.

Emil Hendy: If I talked to people and they say give it more time, then maybe JQWLAC ought to get more involved. We have stayed out so far.

Dalmar Pond: It was like sending a kid to school. All they asked for was money.

Hendy and Deigh agreed that it would be usedful to discuss scenarios detailing alternative possibilities for the Reginal program. William Coy (at Dalmar Pond's urging) noted some of them.

> We have some recommendations. . . . We can terminate [or] . . .go to the American Center, like at the end of this year, and we would not have a need for Mr. Deigh on a regular basis. We may bring him in from time to time. Our recommendation is that Margaret would go onto our payroll. The union would also help [via Martha Linz].

Coy proposed that the EJEC be "streamlined" by making it smaller. Relationships between the ACQWL and the company would cease. This would hopefully not be destructive, he said, since "there's always JQWLAC to control." The company would provide additional support. Coy commented that "Tim has a grim face. Perhaps he disagrees." Hendy said he would have to discuss the proposal with Scigliano. Deigh suggested that the EJEC postpone its elections one month to give the JQWLAC time to make its decision. He urged members to make a date for a decision meeting.

Tippett, somewhat surprised, asked what she was supposed to tell the EJEC members.

Dalmar Pond: Tell 'em the whole status of the program is under review, that there was a petition signed by half the people.

Margaret Tippett: I don't want them to think that JQWLAC is against the program.

Tim Deigh: (to Tippett) I'd like to talk to you about that.

After the meeting, Deigh recommended to Tippett that she not tell EJEC members that the program was in jeopardy. Rather, Hendy would arrange for the local union to confront the problem and resolve it.

Deigh then reported to the ACQWL, describing the meeting and noting that the discussion had gone in a positive direction up to the point at which William Coy had presented the company's "recommendation." In Deigh's words,

> It was clear from the nonverbal communication that he [Coy] was doing this with a gun at his head! The recommendation was to terminate affiliation with the Center, effective the first of the year, to terminate any services on my part, to put Margaret Tippett on the FoodCom payroll, and to proceed with the project in this manner utilizing resources within FoodCom and the international union headquarters.

Deigh was convinced that Dalmar Pond was behind the proposed termination, but that Pond wanted the program to be stopped by the employees, not by management. He also believed that if an election were held, the employees would vote to continue the project. He was angry that Coy had not done what he had said he would do, namely present several alternative courses of action rather than the single recommendation to terminate relations with the ACQWL.

When Tippett returned from the JQWLAC meeting, she told EJEC members that the JQWLAC was positive about continuing the program, but she thought they had not been sufficiently supportive and helpful. She informed them that the union was also positive, but it had to do something in response to the petition. The EJEC then initiated a "floor hours" program in which labor-management teams walked through the plant and explained the quality of work program and described its accomplishments.

Donald Premater visited Reginal soon after the JQWLAC meeting. He took care to explain to Tippett that he himself didn't oppose the quality of work program, and he noted that the stewards who were the most negative toward the program now were more positive. Newman said that those who signed the petition didn't know what was going on and expressed disappointment that the international union felt it had to respond.

Marjorie Touchette, back on the job as well as on the EJEC, initially defended the EJEC in steward meetings. However, at an EJEC meeting, she proposed that the plant newspaper be labeled an EJEC project. Matson objected, saying that the newspaper was not an EJEC project. Touchette told Matson that he couldn't decide for the EJEC which projects to label and demanded that he either approve or disapprove of the proposal to label the newspaper. He shouted "Disapprove!" Bobby Clayton sought to soften the blow, saying, "Let's leave the door open," but Matson roared back, "I'm closing the door!" Touchette was livid, and her support for the EJEC collapsed. She again threatened to resign, but Joan Franks intervened and convinced her to stay, at least through the next EJEC elections. These were scheduled for February 8 and 9.

Donald Premater made a positive report to Hendy and Scigliano. They contacted William Coy, telling him that there was no need for the local union to vote on whether to terminate the QWL program. However, Coy pressed Tippett to accept a position on the company payroll. He assured her that she would still report to JQWLAC and would not be constrained by local or national management. Deigh, meanwhile, founded an independent consulting firm and moved out of the ACQWL.

EJEC elections were held as scheduled. Seven members were elected, of whom four were new to the EJEC. Joel Barrett (supervision) and Josh Atteberry (union) were elected cochairpersons. The social, training, and communications subcommittees were reconstituted, and Bobby Clayton and Chuck Josephson were retained as "EJEC advisory persons."

Tim Deigh and Tom Gib were present for the first full meeting of the new EJEC to help train the new committee in decision making and problem solving. Deigh broke the members into groups and conducted exercises that illustrated values of group decision making and cooperation. He then described steps in group problem solving, from problem identification through implementation and follow-up. The members posted the steps in the EJEC meeting room, so they would provide ready reference.

The March issue of "FoodCom News" was the first issue not to highlight any of the EJEC activities. There were two front-page items, one dealing with the annual meeting of plant supervision, and another concerning changes in the accounting system.

On March 5, Jim Kochems contacted the assessment coordinator to inform him that the company was going to terminate its relationship with the ACQWL. No decision had been made, however, concerning the assessment activities. Members of the assessment team believed that they had learned a great deal from the assessment effort. From a research point of view, their work had been successful. The assessment coordinator contacted Kochems and recommended a planned phaseout of the assessment activities.

EJEC activities continued. Tom Gib and Martha Linz began to put together a tape designed to inform employees about the free enterprise system, the nature and functioning of profit, the meaning of efficiency measures, and the way their jobs affected overall performance. Margaret Tippett drafted a document describing supervisor duties on the line-by-line projects. William Coy and John Papp visited the plant and encouraged Tippett and the others to vigorously address problems "as they come up." Coy was particularly interested in extending the line-by-line concept, and he encouraged Tom Gib to continue training line coordinators.

Greg Charlton took over Matson's duties as liaison between the working committee and plant management. Matson explained that production problems required him to stop sitting in on meetings. Tippett was put on the company payroll. Almost immediately, she sensed that supervisors began to treat her as if she were running the EJEC. Tippett began to plan the survey feedback sessions, to implement a suggestion to put speed bumps in the parking lot, and to put stop signs at several designated places in the lot. Charlton agreed to seek approval for these improvements and did so. However, Matson did not approve the proposal for the survey feedback sessions, despite the fact that many employees had opted for them via the sign-up sheet sent out with pay envelopes.

Charlton began to assign EJEC projects to department heads. Tippett believed that Charlton was "treating the EJEC as 'his group' " and herself as "a FoodCom employee." Supervisors and clock employees attending EJEC meetings were not being replaced. The new committee, with its inexperienced members and reconstituted committee structure, was meeting once every month and finding it difficult to conduct business. The problem was exacerbated by the 100 percent turnover on the executive committee. Tippett was discouraged and wondered how she could begin to train the new members without communicating her sense of discouragement. Josephson was helping in an advisory role, but Clayton was having difficulty getting permission to attend executive committee meetings.

The local union held an election. George Newman was defeated, and a new business agent took his place. The company immediately hired Newman and put him on special assignment in the Reginal plant. Seeing the program "backsliding," Tippett talked with Emil Hendy and John Papp. However, both Papp and Hendy expressed concern that the EJEC overlapped the union in several areas, including grievances.

Taking Control of a Voluntary Program

In Chapters 2 and 3 we raised questions about the means the JQWLAC took to achieve "participation" in and "voluntary" acceptance of the QWL program in Gorland and Reginal. In both cases it made several decisions for the potential participants even while the committee was in the midst of defining its role as solely advisory. In the Reginal plant the JQWLAC also orchestrated several events designed to ensure that the program would be accepted by participants who were understanding the program in almost contradictory terms.

We suggested in Chapter 3 that some of the dilemmas associated with the JQWLAC strategy for achieving program acceptance were to endure throughout the program. We have described these dilemmas in subsequent chapters. The focus of much of our discussion and analysis has been on the effects of the multiple perspectives that remained present during the course of the intervention.

A proposal to discontinue the program eventually caused a reenactment of the initial dilemma: Who should make the decision about removing the program? And how should this decision be made?

The original letter of agreement (Exhibit 2-2) specified that both the company and union could terminate participation with twenty-four hours notice. This would have been a very clear-cut decision about the program. However, the JQWLAC members did not make such a determination at their December meeting. Nor did they permit a plantwide vote on the program, even when that possibility arose.

Instead, the company, without opposition from the international union, orchestrated a set of events that completed the movement toward management control. The company put Tippett and Newman on the company payroll and terminated its relationship with the ACQWL. In the plant, the personnel manager started assigning EJEC projects to the department heads. Without any public decisions, the union-management joint quality of working life venture became a management program.

Deigh did not resist but turned his attention elsewhere. We have argued, however, that he implicitly encouraged the movement toward first-order change by using nonparticipatory processes to encourage participation. He was the primary architect of the process by which the QWL program was introduced into the Reginal plant. As noted earlier, this process was designed to have only two possible outcomes: acceptance of the program by employees or no decision at all. Problems with participants, for example with Newman and McCue, were resolved using linguistic or political tactics. They were not confronted openly.

Even as management began to absorb the QWL program, Deigh continued to avoid direct confrontation. He did not strongly advocate the QWL alternative to Pond's proposal. In association with Tippett, he decided to keep EJEC members unaware that Pond was trying to absorb the QWL program and to attempt to rescue the program by relying on union leadership at the national level. As in the case of not informing employees of problems with the first survey administration, Deigh did not want to demoralize QWL program supporters by letting them know that the program was encountering resistance. The QWL vision he was advocating, however, presumes that employees are responsible individuals fully capable of grappling with significant problems at work. By not inviting full participation, Deigh therefore was engaging in behaviors characteristic of the system he was trying to change. In the process, we have argued, he inadvertently reinforced a perspective he did not share and moved the QWL program in Reginal away from second-order and toward first-order change (Figure 8-1).

On March 20, the line 7 employees met to review their progress and initiate new projects. Although they had expressed the intention of coming, Matson, Charlton, and Keeley were not present when the meeting was called to order. Tippett went to get them from the cafeteria. Matson arrived and immediately began berating those present for not being out on the floor working. He blamed Tippett for taking them away from their jobs. The meeting did take place, however. The issues were important, and Matson kept those attending overtime to complete the discussions. Later Tippett talked with Matson to determine whether she had been laboring under false pretenses about the importance of the line-by-line project. Matson responded that he felt an obligation to support the employees' desires to be out on the floor rather than in meetings.

Training activities began. Trainers were identified and started training machine captains. On-the-job training took place, and audiovisual aids were developed. Tippett talked to Dennis Griffith, the packing department superintendent, and he agreed to find replacements for EJEC members while they were in meetings. Progress began to be made on extending the line-by-line concept to new lines. Tom Gib was scheduled to conduct orientation training for line coordinators during May. Extension of the concept to line 6 first shift was scheduled for June 1. A long-term schedule called for extending the concept to other shifts on line 6 and to first and second shifts on line 5 by December 1.

The assessors paid their last visit to the plant on April 19. The cafeteria renovation was complete, including renovation of the staff meeting room and Matson's office. There was an EJEC meeting that day, called to order by chairperson Josh Atteberry. Several members were absent and had not notified their alternates. Tippett left to scout up the missing members. Paul Morse moved that the rules be suspended for the day so business could be conducted without a quorum. Vince Keeley recommended that they consult the bylaws to determine whether motions could be passed with a vote of two-thirds of those attending, rather than two-thirds of the membership. The rules were consulted, and Atteberry recommended that they be changed to allow motions to pass when they received two-thirds positive responses of those present, rather than ten of sixteen votes. Meanwhile, Keeley left the meeting to help Tippett find missing participants.

Atteberry reported that survey feedback sessions had been tentatively scheduled for May 21, pending management approval. He asked for volunteers to conduct the session. No one responded. Atteberry smiled, and the other members present laughed. Keeley "volunteered" Paul Morse, Bobby Clayton, Joan Franks, Chuck Josephson, and Joel Barrett. The discussion then turned to specifying feedback procedures and to other matters that could be discussed without voting. Soon, however, Atteberry ran out of these kinds of agenda items and the meeting began to lose momentum. Morse began to doze.

Margaret Tippett recommended that members vote on issues, but that formal approval of decisions await the next EJEC meeting. Although they couldn't legally vote on this suggestion, they did accept it. Several items were then discussed under "old business." The line 7 group report was accepted. Members agreed to route subcommittee reports to department heads to get input before EJEC consideration. Vince Keeley reported on training committee activities. Morse complained that warehouse personnel were being bypassed by the new training program.

Several items were introduced under the heading of "new business": building speed bumps in the parking lot, putting shower curtains in the forepersons' dressing room, and other matters.

At this point, Vince Keeley abruptly changed the tenor of the meeting:

> I want to see this program survive. It will require more enthusiasm . . . I'm getting an overall [negative] feeling due to the lack of people here . . . You're the only EJEC there is. We made our mistakes. We came to some revelations. We beat some dead horses week after week. You've gotta feel that you're part of this program. We don't really need the program, because of the relatively good labor-management relations, but this program is needed more in other parts of FoodCom. Try to get together and realize the importance of this program . . . to FoodCom and to the union.

Bibliography

Alinsky, S. D. 1969. *Reveille for Radicals*. New York: Random House.

Allen, R. W., and L. W. Porter. 1983. *Organizational Influence Processes*. Glenview, IL: Scott, Foresman and Company.

Argyris, C. 1985. *Strategy, Change, and Defensive Routines*. Boston: Pitman.

Argyris, C. 1988. "Crafting a Theory of Practice." In *Paradox and Transformation: Toward a Theory of Change in Organization and Management*, edited by R. E. Quinn and K. S. Cameron, 255–278. Cambridge, MA: Ballinger.

Argyris, C., and D. Schön. 1978. *Organizational Learning*. Reading, MA: Addison-Wesley.

Bartunek, J. M. 1984. "Changing Interpretive Schemes and Organizational Restructuring: The Example of a Religious Order." *Administrative Science Quarterly* 29: 355-372.

Bartunek, J. M. 1988. "The Dynamics of Personal and Organizational Reframing." In *Paradox and Transformation: Toward a Theory of Change in Organization and Management*, edited by R. E. Quinn and K. S. Cameron, 137–162. Cambridge, MA: Ballinger.

Bartunek, J. M., and F. J. Franzak. 1988. "The Effects of Organizational Restructuring on Frames of Reference and Cooperation." *Journal of Management* 14: 579–592.

Bartunek, J. M., J. R. Gordon, and R. P. Weathersby. 1983. "Developing 'Complicated' Understanding in Administrators." *Academy of Management Review* 8: 273–284.

Bartunek, J. M., and M. K. Moch. 1987. "First-Order, Second-Order, and Third-Order Change and Organization Development Interventions: A Cognitive Approach." *Journal of Applied Behavioral Science* 23: 483–500.

Bartunek, J. M., and M. K. Moch. 1989. "Organizational Schemata Which Specify and Affect Intergroup Relationships Within Organizations." Paper presented at the Working Conference on Managerial Thought and Cognition, Washington D.C., August 9–12.

Bartunek, J. M., and R. D. Reid. 1988. "Expressions and Effects of Conflict During Second Order Change." Paper presented at the annual meeting of the Academy of Management, Anaheim, California, August 12–15.

Bartunek, J. M., and J. L. Ringuest. 1989. "Enacting New Perspectives through Work Activities during Organizational Transformation." *Journal of Management Studies*, 26: 541–560.

Bateson, G. 1972. *Steps to an Ecology of Mind*. New York: Ballantine.

Belgard, W. P., K. K. Fisher, and S. R. Rayner. 1987. "Vision, Opportunity, and Tenacity: Three Informal Processes That Influence Formal Transformation." In *Corporate Transformation*, edited by R. H. Kilmann and T. J. Covin, 131–151. San Francisco: Jossey-Bass.

Bernstein, P. 1985. *Family Ties, Corporate Bonds*. Garden City, NY: Doubleday.

Bernstein, W. M., and W. W. Burke. 1989. "Modeling Organizational Meaning Systems." In *Research in Organizational Change and Development*, edited by R. W. Woodman and W. A. Pasmore (3): 117–159. Greenwich, CT: JAI Press.

Blake, R. R., and J. S. Mouton. 1985. "How to Achieve Integration on the Human Side of the Merger." *Organizational Dynamics* 13, (3): 43–56.

Bougon, M., K. Weick, and D. Binkhorst. 1977. "Cognition in Organizations: An Analysis of the Utrecht Jazz Orchestra." *Administrative Science Quarterly* 22: 606–639.

Box, G. E. P., and G. M. Jenkins. 1976. *Time Series Analysis: Forecasting and Control*. San Francisco: Holden Day.

Brown, L. D., and J. G. Covey. 1987. "Development Organizations and Organization Development: Toward an Expanded Paradigm for Organization Development." In *Research in Organizational Change and Development*, edited by R. W. Woodman and W. A. Pasmore (1) 59–87. Greenwich, CT: JAI Press.

Bushe, G.R. 1988. "Developing Cooperative Labor-Management Relations in Unionized Factories: A Multiple Case Study of Quality Circles and Parallel Organizations within Joint Quality of Work Life Projects." *Journal of Applied Behavioral Science* 24: 129–150.

Cameron, K. S., and R. E. Quinn. 1988. "Organizational Paradox and Transformation." In *Paradox and Transformation: Toward a Theory of Change in Organization and Management*, edited by R. E. Quinn and K.S. Cameron, 1–18. Cambridge, MA: Ballinger.

Cammann, C., E. E. Lawler III, G. E. Ledford, and S. E. Seashore. 1984. *Management-Labor Cooperation in Quality of Worklife Experi-*

ments: Comparative Analysis of Eight Cases. Ann Arbor, MI: The University of Michigan.

Child, J., and C. Smith. 1987. "The Context and Process of Organizational Transformation." *Journal of Management Studies* 24: 565–593.

Cohen, M., J. March, and J. Olsen. "A Garbage Can Model of Organizational Choice." *Administrative Science Quarterly* 17: 1–25.

Cosier, R. A. 1981. "Dialectical Inquiry in Strategic Planning: A Case of Premature Acceptance?" *Academy of Management Review* 6: 643–648.

Crozier, M. 1964. *The Bureaucratic Phenomenon*. Chicago: University of Chicago Press.

Dandridge, T. C. 1983. "Symbols' Function and Use." In *Organizational Symbolism*, edited by L. R. Pondy, P. Frost, G. Morgan, and T. Dandridge, 69–79. Greenwich, CT: JAI Press.

de Mey, M. 1982. *The Cognitive Paradigm*. Dordrecht, The Netherlands: Reidel.

Drexler, J. A., and E. E. Lawler. 1977. "A Union Management Cooperative Project to Improve the Quality of Work Life." *Journal of Applied Behavioral Science* 13: 373–387.

Dunphy, D. C., and D. A. Stace. 1988. "Transformational and Coercive Strategies for Planned Organizational Change: Beyond the OD Model." *Organization Studies* 9: 317-334.

Dutton, J. E., and S. E. Jackson. 1987. "Categorizing Strategic Issues: Links to Organizational Action." *Academy of Management Review* 12: 76–90.

Edelman, M. J. 1964. *The Symbolic Uses of Politics*. Urbana, IL: University of Illinois Press.

Edelman, M. J. 1967. "Myths, Metaphors, and Political Conformity." *Psychiatry* 30: 217–228.

Elden, M. 1986. "Sociotechnical System Ideas as Public Policy in Norway: Empowering Participation Through Worker-Managed Change." *Journal of Applied Behavioral Science* 22: 239–255.

Feldman, S. P. 1986. "Management in Context: An Essay on the Relevance of Culture to the Understanding of Organizational Change." *Journal of Management Studies* 23: 587–607.

Ford, J. D., and R. H. Backoff. 1988. "Organizational Change In and Out of Dualities and Paradox." In *Paradox and Transformation: Toward a Theory of Change in Organization and Management*, edited by R. E. Quinn and K. S. Cameron, 81–121. Cambridge, MA: Ballinger.

Fredrickson, J. W. 1985. "Effects of Decision Motive and Organizational Performance Level on Strategic Decision Processes." *Academy of Management Journal* 28: 821–843.

French, W. L., and C. H. Bell, Jr. 1984. *Organization Development: Behavioral Science Interventions for Organization Improvement* (3rd ed.). Englewood Cliffs, NJ: Prentice Hall.

Frost, P. J., L. F. Moore, M. R. Louis, C. C. Lundberg, and J. Martin (eds.). 1985. *Organizational Culture*. Beverly Hills: Sage.

Gemmill, G., and C. Smith. 1985. "A Dissipative Structure Model of Organization Transformation." *Human Relations* 38: 751–766.

Gephart, R. P. 1978. "Status Degradation and Organizational Succession: An Ethnomethodological Approach." *Administrative Science Quarterly* 23: 553–581.

Gergen, K. J. 1982. *Toward Transformation in Social Knowledge*. New York: Springer-Verlag.

Giddens, A. 1979. *Central Problems in Social Theory*. Berkeley, CA: University of California Press.

Gioia, D. A., and C. C. Manz. 1985. "Linking Cognition and Behavior: A Script Processing Interpretation of Vicarious Learning." *Academy of Management Review* 10: 527–535.

Golembiewski, R. T., K. Billingsley, and S. Yeager. 1976. "Measuring Change and Persistence in Human Affairs: Types of Change Generated by OD Designs." *Journal of Applied Behavioral Science* 12: 133–157.

Goodenough, W. H. 1981. *Culture, Language, and Society*. Menlo Park, CA: Benjamin Cummings.

Gooding, R. 1989. "Structuring Strategic Problems: Antecedents and Consequences of Alternative Decision Frames." Unpublished Doctoral Dissertation, Michigan State University.

Goodman, P. 1979. *Assessing Organizational Change: The Rushton Quality of Work Experiment*. New York: Wiley.

Graham, J. W. 1986. "Principled Organizational Dissent: A Theoretical Essay." In *Research in Organizational Behavior*, edited by B. M. Staw and L. L. Cummings (8) 1–52. Greenwich, CT: JAI Press.

Gray, B., M. G. Bougon, and A. Donnellon. 1985. "Organizations as Constructions and Destructions of Meaning." *Journal of Management* 11: 83–95.

Greiner, L. E., and V. E. Schein. 1988. *Power and Organization Development*. Reading, MA: Addison-Wesley.

Hackman, J. R., and G. R. Oldham. 1980. *Work Redesign*. Reading, MA: Addison-Wesley.

Hanlon, M. D., D. A. Nadler, and D. Gladstein. 1985. *Attempting Work Reform: The Case of "Parkside" Hospital*. New York: Wiley.

Harrison, M. I. 1987. *Diagnosing Organizations: Methods, Models and Processes*. Newbury Park, CA: Sage Publications.

Hedberg, B. 1981. "How Organizations Learn and Unlearn." In *Handbook of Organization Design*, edited by P. C. Nystrom and W. H. Starbuck (1) 3–27. Oxford: Oxford University Press.

Hirschhorn, L., and T. Gilmore. 1980. "The Application of Family Therapy Concepts to Influencing Organizational Behavior." *Administrative Science Quarterly* 25: 18–37.

Hoffman, L. 1981. *Foundations of Family Therapy*. New York: Basic Books.

Huse, E. F., and T. G. Cummings. 1985. *Organization Development and Change* (3rd ed.). St. Paul, MN: West.

Jackson, S. E., and J. E. Dutton. 1988. "Discerning Threats and Opportunities." *Administrative Science Quarterly* 33: 370–387.

Johnson, D. W., and F. P. Johnson. 1975. *Joining Together: Group Theory and Group Skills*. Englewood Cliffs, NJ: Prentice Hall.

Kanter, R. M. 1983. *The Change Masters*. New York: Simon & Schuster.

Kegan, R. 1982. *The Evolving Self*. Cambridge, MA: Harvard University Press.

Kennedy, A. A., and T. E. Deal. 1982. *Corporate Cultures: The Rites and Rituals of Corporate Life*. Reading, MA: Addison-Wesley.

Kilmann, R. H., and T. J. Covin. 1988. *Corporate Transformation*. San Francisco: Jossey-Bass.

Kimberly, J. R., and R. E. Quinn. 1984. *Managing Organizational Transitions*. Homewood, IL: Irwin.

Kipnis, D., S. Schmidt, and I. Wilkinson. 1983. "Interorganizational Influence Tactics: Explorations in Getting One's Way." In *Organizational Influence Processes*, edited by R. W. Allen and L. W. Porter, 105–123. Glenview, IL: Scott, Foresman and Company.

Kotter, J. P. 1978. "Power, Success, and Organizational Effectiveness." *Organizational Dynamics* 6, Winter: 26–40.

Kotter, J. P. 1985. *Power and Influence*. New York: Free Press.

Krim, R. M., and M. B. Arthur. 1989. "Quality of Work Life in City Hall: Toward an Integration of Political and Organizational Realities." *Public Administration Quarterly* 13: 14–30.

Lakoff, G., and M. Johnson. 1980. *Metaphors We Live By*. Chicago: University of Chicago Press.

Lavoie, C., and S. Culbert. 1978. "Stages of Organization and Development." *Human Relations* 31: 417–438.

Lawler, E. E. III 1986. *High Involvement Management*. San Francisco: Jossey-Bass.

Lawler, E. E. III, and S. A. Mohrman. 1985. "Quality Circles After the Fad." *Harvard Business Review* 63(1): 64–71.

Levitt, B., and J. G. March. 1988. "Organizational Learning." *Annual Review of Sociology* 14: 319–340.

Liu, L-M and G. B. Hudak. 1985. *The SCA Statistical System Reference Manual*. DeKalb, IL: Scientific Computing Associates.

Louis, M. R. 1985. "An Investigator's Guide to Workplace Culture." In *Organizational Culture*, edited by P. J. Frost, L. F. Moore, M. R. Louis, C. C. Lundberg, and J. Martin, 73–93. Beverly Hills: Sage.

Love, H. M., A. L. Barrett, and L. M. Ozley. 1987. "The Transformation of National Steel Corporation." In *Corporate Transformation*, edited by R. H. Kilman and T. J. Covin, 397–434. San Francisco: Jossey-Bass.

March, J. G., and J. P. Olsen. 1976. *Ambiguity and Choice in Organizations*. Bergen, Norway: Universitetsforlaget.

Markus, H., and R. Zajonc. 1985. "The Cognitive Perspective in Social Psychology." In *The Handbook of Social Psychology*, edited by G. Lindzey and E. Aronson (1) 137–230. New York: Random House.

Martin, J. 1982. "Stories and Scripts in Organizational Settings." In *Cognitive Social Psychology*, edited by A. Hastorf and A. Isen, 255–305. New York: North Holland.

Martin, J., M. S. Feldman, M. J. Hatch, and S. Simkin. 1983. "The Uniqueness Paradox in Organizational Stories." *Administrative Science Quarterly* 28: 438-453.

Martin, J., and D. Meyerson. 1988. "Organizational cultures and the denial, channeling, and acknowledgment of ambiguity." In *Managing Ambiguity and Change*, edited by L. R. Pondy, R. J. Boland, and H. Thomas, 93–125. Chichester, England: Wiley.

Mason, R. O., and I. I. Mitroff. 1981. *Challenging Strategic Planning Assumptions*. New York: Wiley.

McCain, L. J., and R. McCleary. 1979. "The Statistical Analysis of the Simple Interruputed Time-Series Quasi-Experiment." In *Quasi-Experimentation: Design and Analysis Issues for Field Settings*, edited by T. D. Cook and D. T. Campbell. Boston: Houghton Mifflin.

Meek, C. B. 1983. "Labor-Management Cooperation and Economic Revitalization: The Story of the Growth and Development of the

Jamestown Area Labor-Management Committee." Unpublished Doctoral Dissertation, Cornell University.

Meek, C. B., R. Nelson, and W. F. Whyte. 1983a. "Cooperative Problem Solving in Jamestown." In *Worker Participation and Ownership,* edited by W. F. Whyte, T. H. Hammer, C. B. Meek, R. Nelson, and R. N. Stern, 6–32. Ithaca, NY: ILR Press.

Meek, C. B., R. Nelson, and W. F. Whyte. 1983b. "Lessons from the Jamestown Experience." In *Worker Participation and Ownership,* edited by W. F. Whyte, T. H. Hammer, C. B. Meek, R. Nelson, and R. N. Stern, 33–54. Ithaca, NY: ILR Press.

Meyerson, D., and J. Martin. 1987. "Cultural Change: An Integration of Three Different Views." *Journal of Management Studies* 24: 623–647.

Mills, T. 1975. "Human Resources—Why the New Concern?" *Harvard Business Review* 53(2): 120–134.

Mintzberg, H. 1979. *The Structuring of Organizations.* Englewood Cliffs, NJ: Prentice Hall.

Moch, M. K., and W. C. Fields. 1985. "Developing a Content Analysis of Language Use for Facilitating Understanding in Organizations." In *Perspectives in Organizational Sociology: Theory and Research,* edited by S. Mitchell and S. Bacharach (5) 81–126. Greenwich, CT: JAI Press.

Moch, M. K., and A. S. Huff. 1983. "Power Enactment Through Language and Ritual." *Journal of Business Research* 11: 293–316.

Mohrman, A. M., and E. E. Lawler III. 1985. "The Diffusion of QWL as a Paradigm Shift." In *The Planning of Change,* edited by W. G. Bennis, K. D. Benne, and R. Chin (4th ed.), 149–159. New York: Holt, Rhinehart, and Winston.

Morgan, G. 1984. "Opportunities Arising from Paradigm Diversity." *Administration and Society* 16: 306–327.

Nadler, D. A. 1977. *Feedback and Organization Development: Using Data-based Methods.* Reading, MA: Addison-Wesley.

Nadler, D. A. 1978. "Consulting with Labor and Management: Some Learnings from Quality-of-Work-Life Projects." In *The Cutting Edge: Current Theory and Practice in Organization Development,* edited by W. W. Burke, 262–277. La Jolla, CA: University Associates.

Nadler, D. A. 1979. "The Effects of Feedback on Task Group Behavior: A Review of the Experimental Research." *Organizational Behavior and Human Performance,* 23: 309–338.

Neilsen, E.H. 1984. *Becoming an OD Practitioner*. Englewood Cliffs, NJ: Prentice Hall.

Neisser, U. 1976. *Cognition and Reality*. San Francisco: Freeman.

Newell, A., and H. A. Simon. 1972. *Human Problem Solving*. Englewood Cliffs, NJ: Prentice Hall.

Nurick, A. 1985. *Participation in Organizational Change: The TVA Experiment*. New York: Praeger.

Nystrom, P. C., and W. H. Starbuck. 1984. "To Avoid Organizational Crises, Unlearn." *Organizational Dynamics*, 12 (4): 53–65.

Ortony, A. 1979. *Metaphor and Thought*. New York: Cambridge University Press.

Ouchi, W. G., and A. L. Wilkins. 1985. "Organization Culture." *Annual Review of Sociology* 11: 457–483.

Palazzoli, M. S., L. Anolli, P. Di Blasio, L. Giossi, I. Pisano, C. Ricci, M. Sacchi, and V. Ugazio. 1986. *The Hidden Games of Organizations*. New York: Pantheon.

Parkinson, C. N. 1974. *Big Business*. New York: Weidenfeld and Nicolson.

Pasmore, W. A., and F. Friedlander. 1982. "An Action Research Program for Increasing Employee Involvement in Problem Solving." *Administrative Science Quarterly* 27: 343–362.

Pava, C. 1986. "Redesigning Sociotechnical Systems Design." *Journal of Applied Behavioral Science* 22: 201–222.

Perkins, D. N., V. F. Nieva, and E. E. Lawler. 1983. *Managing Creation: The Challenge of Building a New Organization*. New York: Wiley.

Peters, M., and V. Robinson. 1984. "The Origins and Status of Action Research." *Journal of Applied Behavorial Science* 20: 113–124.

Pocock, J. G. 1973. "Verbalizing a Political Act: Toward a Politics of Free Speech." *Political Theory* 1: 27–45.

Pondy, L. R., P. J. Frost, G. Morgan, and T.C. Dandridge. 1983. *Organizational Symbolism*. Greenwich, CT: JAI Press.

Pondy, L. R., and A. S. Huff. 1985. "Achieving Routine in Organizational Change." *Journal of Management* 11: 103–116.

Porras, J. I., and S. J. Hoffer. 1986. "Common Behavior Changes in Successful Organization Development Efforts." *Journal of Applied Behavioral Science* 22: 477–494.

Quinn, R. E., and K. S. Cameron. 1988. *Paradox and Transformation: Toward a Theory of Change in Organization and Management*. Cambridge, MA: Ballinger.

Ramirez, I. L., and J. M. Bartunek. 1989. "The Multiple Realities and Experiences of Internal Organization Development Consultation in Health Care." *Journal of Organizational Change Management* 2: 40–57.

Ranson, S., B. Hinings, and R. Greenwood. 1980. "The Structuring of Organizational Structures." *Administrative Science Quarterly* 25: 1–17.

Ross, R. 1971. "OD for Whom?" *Journal of Applied Behavioral Science* 7: 580–585.

Rothenberg, A. 1979. *The Emerging Goddess*. Chicago: University of Chicago Press.

Schaubroeck, J., and S. G. Green. 1988. "Alpha, Beta, and Gamma Change as Outcomes for Organizational Entry Research." *Best Papers Proceedings of the Academy of Management*: 216–220.

Schweiger, D. M., W. R. Sandberg, and J. W. Ragan. 1986. "Group Approaches for Improving Strategic Decision Making: A Comparative Analysis of Dialectical Inquiry, Devil's Advocacy, and Consensus." *Academy of Management Journal* 29: 51–71.

Scott, R. W. 1987. "The Adolescence of Institutional Theory." *Administrative Science Quarterly* 32: 493–511.

Seashore, S., P. Mirvis, E. Lawler, and C. Cammann. 1983. *Assessing Organizational Change*. New York: Wiley.

Shani, A. B., and W. A. Pasmore. 1985. "Organization Inquiry: Towards a New Paradigm of the Action Research Process. In *Contemporary Organization Development*, edited by D. D. Warrick, 438–448. Glenview, IL: Scott, Foresman and Company.

Showers, C., and N. Cantor. 1985. "Social Cognition: A Look at Motivated Strategies." *Annual Review of Psychology* 36: 275–305.

Shrivastva, P., and S. Schneider. 1984. "Organizational Frames of Reference." *Human Relations* 37: 795–809.

Sims, H. P., and D. A. Gioia. 1986. *The Thinking Organization*. San Francisco: Jossey-Bass.

Siporin, M., and B. Gummer. 1988. "Lessons from Family Therapy: The Potential of Paradoxical Interventions in Organizations." In *Paradox and Transformation: Toward a Theory of Change in Organization and Management*, edited by R. E. Quinn and K. S. Cameron, 205–227. Cambridge, MA: Ballinger.

Smircich, L. 1983. "Organizations as Shared Meaning." In *Organizational Symbolism*, edited by L. R. Pondy, P. Frost, G. Morgan, and T. Dandridge, 55–65. Greenwich, CT: JAI Press.

Smith, K. K. 1982. *Groups in Conflict: Prisons in Disguise*. Dubuque, Iowa: Kendall/ Hunt.

Smith, K. K. 1984. "Rabbits, Lynxes, and Organizational Transitions." In *Managing Organizational Transitions,* edited by J. R. Kimberly and R. E. Quinn, 267–294. Homewood, IL: Irwin.

Smith, K. K., and D. N. Berg. 1987. *Paradoxes of Group Life*. San Francisco: Jossey-Bass.

Sommer, R. 1987. "An Experimental Investigation of the Action Research Approach." *Journal of Applied Behavioral Science* 23: 185–199.

Starbuck, W. H. 1982. "Congealing Oil: Inventing Ideologies to Justify Acting Ideologies Out." *Journal of Management Studies* 19: 3–27.

Starbuck, W. H. 1983. "Organizations as Action Generators." *American Sociological Review* 48: 91–102.

Staw, B. M. 1976. "Knee Deep in the Big Muddy: A Study of Escalating Commitment to a Chosen Course of Action." *Organizational Behavior and Human Performance* 16: 27–44.

Steel, R. P., and R. F. Lloyd. 1988. "Cognitive, Affective, and Behavioral Outcomes of Participation in Quality Circles: Conceptual and Empirical Findings." *Journal of Applied Behavioral Science* 24: 1–17.

Steier, F., and K. K. Smith. 1985. "Organizations and Second Order Cybernetics." *Journal of Strategic and Systemic Therapies* 4 (4): 53–65.

Strasser, S., and T. S. Bateman. 1983. Perception and motivation. In *Health Care Management,* edited by S. M. Shortell and A. D. Kaluzny, 77–127. New York: Wiley.

Takeuchi, J. 1985. "Motivation and Productivity." In *The Management Challenge: Japanese Views,* edited by L. C. Thurow, 18–30. Cambridge, MA: MIT Press.

Tannenbaum, R., and R. W. Hanna. 1985. "Holding On, Letting Go, and Moving On: Understanding a Neglected Perspective on Change." In *Human Systems Development,* edited by R. Tannenbaum, N. Margulies, and F. Massarik, 95–121. San Francisco: Jossey-Bass.

Taylor, S. E., and J. Crocker. 1981. "Schematic Basis of Social Information Processing." In *Social Cognition: The Ontario Symposium,* edited by E. T. Higgins, C. P. Herman, and M. P. Zanna (1) 89-134. Hillsdale, NJ: Erlbaum.

Tichy, N. 1974. "Agents of Planned Social Change: Congruence of Values, Cognitions, and Actions." *Administrative Science Quarterly* 19: 164–182.

Tichy, N. 1975. "How Different Types of Change Agents Diagnose Organizations." *Human Relations* 9: 771-779.

Tichy, N. M., and M. A. Devanna. 1986. *The Transformational Leader.* New York: Wiley.

Torbert, W. 1987. *Managing the Corporate Dream: Restructuring for Long-Term Success.* Homewood, IL: Dow Jones-Irwin.

Trist, E. 1981. "Micro-regions and QWL." *Proceedings of the International Conference on the Quality of Working Life.* Toronto, Ontario, Canada.

Trist, E. 1986. "Quality of Working Life and Community Development: Some Reflections on the Jamestown Experience." *Journal of Applied Behavioral Science* 22: 223–238.

Trist, E., and K. Bamforth. 1951. "Some Social and Psychological Consequences of the Longwall Method of Coal Getting." *Human Relations* 4: 3–38.

Trist, E., G. Susman, and G. Brown. 1977. "An Experiment in Autonomous Working in an American Underground Coal Mine." *Human Relations* 30: 201–236.

Tunstall, W. B. 1985. "Break-up of the Bell System: A Case Study in Cultural Transformation." In *Gaining Control of the Corporate Culture,* edited by R. H. Kilmann, M. J. Saxton, and R. Serpa, 44–65. San Francisco: Jossey-Bass.

Tushman, M. L., W. H. Newman, and E. Romanelli. 1986. "Convergence and Upheaval: Managing the Unsteady Pace of Organizational Evolution." *California Management Review* 29 (1): 29–44.

Tushman, M. L., and E. Romanelli. 1985. "Organizational Evolution: A Metamorphosis Model of Convergence and Reorientation." In *Research in Organizational Behavior,* edited by L. L. Cummings and B. M. Staw (7) 171–222. Greenwich, CT: JAI Press.

Vroom, V. H., and A. G. Jago. 1988. *Managing Participation in Organizations.* Englewood Cliffs, NJ: Prentice Hall.

Watzlawick, P., J. H. Weakland, and R. Fisch. 1974. *Change: Principles of Problem Formation and Problem Resolution.* New York: Norton.

Weick, K. 1976. "Educational Organizations as Loosely Coupled Systems." *Administrative Science Quarterly* 21: 1–19.

Weick, K. 1979. *The Social Psychology of Organizing.* Reading, MA: Addison-Wesley.

Weick, K., and M. Bougon. 1986. "Organizations as Cognitive Maps." In *The Thinking Organization,* edited by H. Sims and D. Gioia, 102–135. San Francisco: Jossey-Bass.

Woodruff, A. F., and T. Engle. 1985. "Strategic Therapy and Agency Development: Using Circular Thinking to Turn the Corner." *Journal of Strategic and Systemic Therapies* 4 (4): 25–29.

Whyte, W. F. 1948. *Human Relations in the Restaurant Industry*. New York: McGraw-Hill.

Work in America Institute. 1973. *Work in America*. Cambridge, MA: MIT Press.

Zucker, L. G. 1983. "Organizations as Institutions." In *Research in the Sociology of Organizations*, edited by S. B. Bacharach (2): 1–47. Greenwich, CT: JAI Press.

Name Index

Subject Index

About the Authors

Michael K. Moch is a professor of management at Michigan State University, where he has taught since 1984. He received his Ph.D. in industrial and labor relations from Cornell University in 1973. In addition to Michigan State University, Professor Moch has taught at the University of Michigan, the University of Illinois, and the University of Texas at Dallas. His current research focuses upon the cognitive and information processing aspects of strategic choice behavior in organizations. He has published in *Administrative Science Quarterly, American Sociological Review*, the *Journal of Applied Psychology, Organizational Behavior and Human Decision Processes*, and several other journals. He has served on the editorial boards of *Administrative Science Quarterly* and the *American Sociological Review*. He currently serves on the editorial board of the *Journal of Applied Behavioral Science*.

Jean M. Bartunek is a professor of organizational studies at Boston College, where she has taught since 1977. She received a Ph.D. in social and organizational psychology from the University of Illinois at Chicago and has served as a visiting assistant professor in organizational behavior at the University of Illinois at Urbana-Champaign. Her current research focuses on the intersection of conflict and organizational change. She is a member of the editorial boards of the *Academy of Management Journal, Administrative Science Quarterly*, and the *Journal of Applied Behavioral Science* and is the 1990 Chairperson of the Organization Development Division of the Academy of Management.